HULBERT'S HISTORY OF KOREA

Volume II

HULBERT'S
history
of korea

Edited by
Clarence Norwood Weems

*Professor and Director of Social Sciences,
Mansfield State College*

*Professorial Lecturer in Intercultural Relations,
The George Washington University*

Volume II

HILLARY HOUSE PUBLISHERS LTD.
New York - 1962

HULBERT'S
HISTORY OF KOREA
was first published in
Seoul, Korea in 1905

© Copyright 1962
by
HILLARY HOUSE PUBLISHERS LTD.

Library of Congress Catalogue Card Number 62-9992

Printed in the United States of America

COMPOSITE TABLE OF CONTENTS

Headings with page numbers marked "ED" refer to new material written by the editor. All other captions refer to material found in Hulbert's original volumes, but they have been composed in brief form by the editor to avoid a repetition of Hulbert's extensive notes at the beginning of each of his chapters. The McCune-Reischauer System is followed in romanizations in this table.

VOLUME I

ILLUSTRATION
EDITOR'S CHART: MAJOR PRIMARY SOURCES FOR KOREAN HISTORY
at end of Volume I

THE HISTORY OF KOREA

VOLUME II

Chapter I.

China's reply to the Japanese....the Chinese army....the Chinese commander interviews the King ...march on P'yŭng-yang....Chinese treachery....the new year ...Chinese help not all a blessing....P'yŭng-yang invested....the Chinese force an entrance....Japanese driven to bay....how they escape....they retreat....they mass at Seoul ...Chinese stop at Song-do....Koreans bridge the Im-jin ....Chinese retire to P'yŭng-yang....Korean victory in the north .. great victory at Hăng-ju ...the Japanese sue for peace .. conference on the Han ...Japanese evacuate Seoul ...the terrible condition of the city ...Chinese enter Seoul....they prevent pursuit ..Japanese desecrate a royal tomb ...Chinese accused of bad faith ...Japanese line of camps....Chinese reinforced ...the great battle of Chin-ju ...a loyal dancing-girl....admiral Yi still active ... Chinese troops retire.

We must now return to the north and witness the final struggle which was to begin the Japanese retreat from the whole north. It was not till long after the fifty days had expired that Gen. Sim Yu-gyŭng returned from Nanking. The Japanese had sent time and again, asking why he did not make his appearance, but now on the sixth day of the twelfth moon he entered the city of P'yung-yang, making no excuses for his tardiness but delivering his message as follows: "I have seen the Emperor and he says that if you wish to become vassals of China you must first give up all the territory taken from Korea. You must also give up the two princes whom you have captured. If you do not see fit to comply with these demands the Emperor will send a million men and destroy you." He then gave to each of the Japanese leaders an ornament for the hat, from the Emperor. This was a trick to

discover how large the Japanese force might be. It was determined that there must be about 20,000 Japanese troops in
the city. What reply the Japanese gave to the Emperor's
demands is not told, but that it was a negative one seems sure
from what followed.

The Chinese army of counter-invasion lay just beyond
the Ya-lu River. It was an enormous host and, as armies went
in those days, it was a thoroughly efficient one. In connection with this army was an official who held the rank of
"Military Adviser," by the name of Song Eung-ch'ang. The
office carried no active power in the field but it seems to have
been a sort of check upon the commander-in-chief, for the
duties of the office were to keep the Emperor informed of
what was going on at the seat of war. The actual General-
in-chief was Yi Yŭ-song. Under him were three generals, of
the right, left and center respectively. The General of the
Left was Yang Wŭn and under him were Generals Wang Yŭ-
jung. Yi Yŭ-mä, Yi Yo-o, Yang So, Sa Ta su, Son Su-ryŭm,
Yi Ryŭng and Kal Pong-ha. The General of the Center was Yi
Yŭ-bäk and under him were Generals Im Cha-yang, Yi Pang-
jin, Ko Ch'ak, Chŏn Sŭ-jong, Ch'ŭk Keum, Chu Hong-mo,
Pang Si-whi, Ko Seung and Wang Mun. The General of
the Right was Chang Se-jak and under him were Generals
Cho Seung-hun, O Yu-ch'ung, Wang P'il-jŭk, Cho Chi-mok,
Chang Eung-ch'ung, Nak Sang-ji, Chin Pang-ch'ŭl, Kok Su
and Yang Sim. The rear guard was under the command of
Gen. Pang Si-ch'an and the engineering corps was commanded by Generals Yu Whang-sang and Wŭn Whang. The
main army was composed of 43,000 troops, while in the rear
was a reserve force of 8,000. This army crossed the Ya-lu
on the twenty-fifth of the twelfth moon, the dead of winter.
It is said that when on the march this army stretched along
the road a thousand li (three hundred miles and more) and
that the sound of their drums was continuous along the whole
line.

General-in-chief Yi Yŭ-song, dressed in crimson robes
and riding in a crimson chair, arrived in Eui-ju and immediately sought an interview with the king. The latter said, "I
have governed this country badly. The Emperor has been
put to a great deal of trouble on my account and all these

good men have come a long, cold road to fight for us. Though
I lay open my vitals with a sword I cannot repay you all for
this kindness." Gen. Yi smiled and said, "The Emperor's
might reaches to the heavens. For the sake of Your Majesty's
happiness we have been sent, and all your enemies will soon
be put to flight." To this the king rejoined, "Our nation's
life hangs by a thread, and the result lies with you." Gen.
Yi raised his two hands in salute and answered, "I am come
at the Emperor's orders and life or death are all one to me.
When I started out my father said to me, 'Fight valiantly
for Korea and return victorious,' and so how can I do less
than my best ?" The Koreans say that this man's father was
a native of Eun-san in the province of P'yŭng-an, Korea, but
that for some offence he had fled to China and together with
many of his relatives was enjoying high position under the
Emperor.

Gen. Yi started for P'yŭng-yang with his whole army,
80,000 bags of rice and 20,000 pounds of powder. His troops
were not provided with muskets but they had small cannon.
The Japanese on the other hand had muskets but no cannon.
Upon the arrival of the Chinese at An-ju they were met by
the Prime Minister, Yu Sŭng-nyŭng, who laid before Gen. Yi a
map showing the roads leading to P yŭng-yang. Gen. Yi took
red ink and indicated on the map the various routes by which
he intended to lead his forces to that city. Calling Gen. Sa
Tă-su he sent him forward to deceive the Japanese by saying
that a few Chinese had come to effect a peaceful solution of
the difficulty. The Japanese were pleased at this and sent
twenty of their people to meet, as they supposed, Sim Yu-
gyŭng at Su-an. Gen. Sa feasted them there but meanwhile
had the place surrounded and in the midst of the banquet the
Japanese were treacherously assaulted and cut down, only
three escaping. From these the Japanese learned of the hostile intentions of the Chinese and were greatly disturbed, but
being forewarned they put themselves in readiness for an
assault.

And so the old year died—the terrible Im-jin year which
witnessed the indescribable horrors of the ruthless invasion
which swept it from end to end ; which saw, too, the gradual
awakening of the dormant military spirit of the people, until

at its close the wave of invasion had not only broken and spent
itself but had left the remnant of the invaders cut off from
their home land by one of the greatest naval geniuses of his
own or any other age, surrounded on all sides and hemmed in
by forces which though perhaps unable to cope with them in
the open field in a pitched battle could yet harrass and cut
them off on every side.   It must be clearly borne in mind that
the Chinese did not raise a hand to help Korea until the invasion virtually collapsed.   The Koreans without the aid of
China could probably have starved the Japanese out of P'yŭng-
yang and driven them southward, cutting them off on the left
and right till they would have been glad to take ship for home.
In a sense the Chinese counter-invasion was an extremely unfortunate thing for Korea, for the dormant energies of the people were just rousing themselves to action.   Armies were being levied, every day saw the Japanese forces melting away
and there was a magnificent opportunity for Korea to turn
upon her devastators and drive them headlong into the sea.
It would have given a tremendous impulse to patriotism and
national self-respect, and it might have been a stepping-stone
to a strong national life ; but the coming of the Chinese soldiery immediately threw everything into Chinese hands and
they reaped all the benefits of the situation.   Even the Koreans themselves did not realize how they were playing into
the hands of China.   The Japanese in P'yŭng-yang were
weary and sick, and at heart glad of any excuse for retreating
if it could be done without too great a loss of dignity.   It was
at just this moment that the Koreans put the game, already
won, into the hands of China to reap all the credit and all the
prizes of success.   The Koreans leaned back upon China and
relapsed into their old self-complacent "fool's paradise."

    With the beginning of the new year Gen. Yi moved
southward toward P'yŭng-yang as far as Suk-ch'ŭn where he
intended to halt for the night, as the winter days were short,
but hearing of the massacre at Sun-an and wishing to give as
little time for preparation as possible, pushed on by night, and
in the morning planted his banners before the ancient city of
P'yŭng-yang.   The city was forthwith surrounded.   The
Japanese could be seen covering the slope of the hill within
the wall with their blue and white flags, and soon they open-

ed fire on the besiegers. At the same moment they rushed to the walls and manned them. The Chinese Generals of the Left, Center and Right were stationed with their respective forces before the three gates Ch'il-sŭng, Ham-gu and Po-t'ong. The General-in-chief Yi, with a banner in one hand and a drum-stick in the other, rode swiftly from one division to another encouraging the men. His forces could hardly be held in check, they were so eager, in spite of their long, cold night march, to rush at the wall and scale it. They were not long kept from their desire, for at eight o'clock word was given for the whole assaulting force to advance to the wall. The cannon thundered, the fire-arrows flashed throught the air, the very ground fairly trembled with the noise of battle and the tramp of eager feet. One of the fire-arrows alighted in the quarters of the Japanese general-in-chief and it was soon in flames, which rapidly spread to all the surrounding buildings. The Japanese guarded the walls with the greatest gallantry, and with spear and arrow, hot water and stones they made it quite impossible for the Chinese to effect an entrance. The wall bristled with weapons, so that in the words of a native chronicler it was "a hedge-hog's back." So it happened that the Chinese forces fell back from the fierce defense of the Japanese. Many of them contemplated a general retreat and started to leave the field, but Gen. Yi, who was always found where most needed, saw the defection of his men and, pursuing them, struck off the heads of a few as an example to the rest. Then he turned and cried, "Fifty ounces of silver to the first man to set foot upon the battlements of P'yŭng-yang." This was doubtless a more powerful appeal than he could have made had he called upon their patriotism or love of glory. Immediately the tide of battle turned. A Chinese captain, Nak Sang-ji, a man well along in years and whose proportions were so ample that the Korean chronicler says of him that he weighed a thousand pounds, led on a company of men and by a mighty effort succeeded in reaching the top of the wall. He held his ground there while others could scale the wall at his back, and so an entrance was effected. The Japanese began to desert the wall, and soon the Chinese entered by the Po-t'ong and Ch'il-sŭng gates, while Korean allies entered by the Ham-gu Gate. By this time the Japanese had entirely

left the wall and had massed themselves as best they could
in various parts of the city, determined to make a desperate
stand. The Chinese infantry and cavalry both swarmed in
on every side and all Japanese stragglers were cut off, while
the fight throughout the city became general. Before the
Japanese could firmly establish themselves upon the hill and
in other defensible parts of the town they lost two captains,
2,285 men, and 45,002 weapons of various kinds, besides
1,051 Koreans whom they had held as captives.

Many of the Japanese had taken refuge in various government buildings which they had barricaded as best they
could. The Chinese went to work systematically to burn
these down, and in the few hours remaining before the fall
of night nearly half of the entire Japanese force succumbed to the weapons of Chinese. One instance will suffice to il-
lustrate the method of procedure. Many of the Japanese had
taken refuge in a large building on the wall, well up on
the side of the mountain and looking directly down upon
the waters of the river.. Gen. Yi had it surrounded with
piles of wood, the timbers of houses and hewn logs, and these
were set on fire. The entrapped Japanese then had the
choice of roasting to death or leaping down upon the ice of
the river. Hundreds chose the latter alternative, but the ice
was not strong enough to stand the tremendous strain and
they were all engulfed in the river and carried under the ice
below. As for those that remained, it is said that the smell
of burning flesh could be discerned a quarter of a mile away.

Gen. Konishi had taken refuge with a large body of troops
in a building called the Yŭn-gwang-jŭng, very near the Ta-
dong Gate which opens directly upon the water front. Night
had fallen and the fight had lulled for a time. What took
place at this time may be open to some doubt. The Korean
account says that the Chinese commander sent a message to
Konishi demanding the surrender of his whole force and that
Konishi replied, "Our remaining force is small and we wish
to evacuate the city and retreat if we may be allowed to leave
quietly." It is affirmed that Gen. Yi consented to this and
left the Ta-dong Gate unguarded, and in the dead of night
the Japanese troops passed swiftly out and crossed the river.
On the face of it this statement is hardly credible, but judging

from future events the Koreans believe that Gen. Yi received
a large bribe from the Japanese as the price of this act of
leniency. It is true that future events justified the Koreans
in suspecting some such thing, but as the Japanese were immediately beside the Ta-dong Gate and, under cover of night,
might easily have forced their way out, especially as the Chinese
were exhausted by their long forced march and the fight
about the city, we may well believe that the Japanese did not
need to appeal either to the pity or the avarice of the Chinese
in order to effect their escape. It may be, too, that Gen. Yi
did not wish to be hampered with so many prisoners of war
and was rather glad than otherwise to let them get away. Of
course the Koreans who had suffered so terribly at the hands
of the Japanese would have been glad to see every one of them
massacred, and their anger at seeing them escape may have
led them to impute wrong motives to Gen. Yi. Subsequent
events, however, gave some color to these suspicions, as
we shall see.

This retreat from P'yŭng-yang in the dead of winter was
like Napoleon's retreat from Moscow, on a small scale. The
Japanese were without provisions or proper clothing. Many
of them threw aside their arms and luggage and, turning from
the main road, begged their way from house to house. When
at last they reached the city of Seoul and found food and safety they were in a savage humor. Most of the Koreans who
had fled from the capital had now returned, and on them these
half-famished and wholly disappointed Japanese wreaked their
vengeance. They seized hundreds of the unoffending people
and put them to the sword. Scores of them were taken outside the South Gate and slaughtered like oxen.

Gen. Kato, who had led an expedition eastwards into
Ham-gyŭng Province, hearing of the evacuation of P'yŭng-
yang, immediately put his troops in motion and hastened down
to Seoul, burning and ravaging as he came. And in a short
time all the remnants of the Japanese army were congregated
in the capital.

The Japanese retreat from P'yŭng-yang was not without
its casualties. A Korean general, Ko On-băk, met a body of
the Japanese, probably a part of the retreating army, at P'a-
ju, seventy *li* out of Seoul, and punished them severely, taking

as it is said, seventy heads ; not a great achievement when we remember that the Japanese were practically unarmed.

But by this time the Chinese Gen. Yi was on his way south from P'yŭng-yang, rather tardily as the Koreans thought, but hearing of this engagement of Gen. Ko, he quickened his pace. Coming to He-on Pass, some seventy *li* out from Seoul, his horse slipped, throwing him heavily on his face. He was severely though not dangerously hurt. At that moment a company of Japanese was sighted on the mountain side and Gen. Yi ordered instant pursuit. The Japanese, probably a foraging party from Seoul, closed with them and as the Chinese were on a marshy piece of land, where they sank to their knees in the mud, and had no other weapons with them but their swords, the Japanese inflicted severe punishment on them, killing eighty of their number. Gen. Yi was so weak from loss of blood that he did not dare to prolong the fight. So he called a retreat and the next day went into camp at Tong-p'a, a hundred *li* from Seoul. From that point he immediately despatched a letter to the Emperor saying : "There are 20,000 Japanese firmly intrenched in Seoul and with my present force I dare not attack them. I am also ill and cannot fight. I would be glad if you would send someone to relieve me of the command." Then he retreated fifty *li* further, to Song-do, in spite of the earnest entreaties of the Koreans. The Korean General Yi Pin said, "You came to render aid to our country. Why is it that you now retreat?" whereupon one of the general's staff promptly kicked him out of the house.

Gen. Yi ordered Gen. Sa Tă-su to go and guard the ferry at the Im-jin river which was now partly frozen but impassable for boats and ordered the Koreans to go to work building a bridge for the transport of the Chinese army. Here was a piece of work that might have daunted a better engineer than the average Korean general. But the way the Koreans went about it and the brilliant success they achieved show what the Korean was capable of when really in earnest. And it shows as well how thoroughly they were determined to see chastisement inflicted upon the Japanese. A swift broad river partly frozen, no possibility of driving piles nor of erecting any supports from the bed of the river itself. It must be a suspension bridge or none at all. On either side of the river heavy timbers were planted firmly in the ground some twenty feet apart. Behind these horizontally were laid heavy logs. Then between these supports on either bank were stretched fifteen heavy strands of the tough fibrous vine called *chik* by the Koreans. It is the *pueraria thunbergiana*. Of course these sagged in mid-stream so that they swept the water, To remedy this, stout levers were inserted between the strands and twisted until the cables swung clear of the water by many feet. The foundation having thus been laid, willow branches were spread thickly upon the cables and finally a heavy layer of earth was added and the whole was packed down tight by the treading of many feet. And so was completed the first suspension bridge which history records. We see that during this war the Koreans had originated three important things, namely the iron-clad, the mortar and bomb, and now the suspension bridge. And on this bridge the whole Chinese army crossed in safety.

But Gen. Yi was tired of the war and was extremely anxious to get back to China. So when he heard that Nato was crossing the peninsula he said, "He may come to P'yŭng-yang and in that case I must hasten back to that place and hold it against him." So he started back toward that city, leaving Gen Wang P'il-jŭk in charge of the forces that were advancing on Seoul.

At this point mention must be made of the victories of Gen. Chŏng Mun-bu in Ham-gyŭng Province. In three successive fights he had defeated a large, though not the main, body of Japanese and seems to have entirely cut it off from forming a junction with Gen. Kato as he retreated toward Seoul with his dwindling though still formidable army. After the departure of the Japanese, Gen. Chŏng went to the far north, even to the far Tu-man River and inflicted severe punishment on all those who had aided the Japanese or had sided with them in the betrayal of the two princes. This done, he pacified the disturbed province as much as he could and then disbanded the militia and sent them to their homes.

Kwŭn Ryŭl, the governor of Chŭl-la, of whom we have heard before, took 4000 men and marched on Seoul, not by the main road but by way of Yang-ch'ŭn. Crossing the Han.

at that point he went into camp at Hăng-ju and surrounded
it with a paling of heavy logs. The Japanese in Seoul ridi-
culed it but sent a strong body of troops to attack it. A long
fierce fight ensued and the result was doubtful. At last the
Japanese succeeded in setting fire to the wooden paling and
had it not been for the most strenuous efforts on the part
of the Koreans they would have been burned out. But they
succeeded in quenching the flames. When their arrows were
gone their outlook was again apparently hopeless, but in the
very nick of time Admiral Yi Pin of Chŭl-la Province came
up the river by boat with 20,000 arrows and as the camp was
immediately on the river bank the Koreans were saved, and
soon the Japanese were driven back. Kyŭn Ryŭl took the
bodies of the Japanese who had fallen, cut them in pieces and
impaled the fragments on the top of the stockade. The next
day the Chinese general Sa Tă-su arrived and, seeing these
trophies of victory, praised Gen. Kwŭn highly and sent him
to P'a-ju to guard against any possible northward movement
of the Japanese. At the same time small companies were
sent in all directions to cut off foraging expeditions of the
enemy. In this way the Japanese in Seoul were cut off from
all supply of fuel. The Japanese general who had suffered
defeat at Hăng-ju thirsted for revenge, and he led many a
fierce sally from Seoul, but always with great loss.

In the third month confidence was so far restored in the
north that the king began to think of returning toward the
capital. The first stage of this journey was as far as Yong-
yu. At this same time the Japanese sent a letter to the Korean general Yu Sŭng-nyong saying that they wished to conclude a treaty of peace. Gen. Yu as in duty bound sent this
message on to the Chinese Gen. Yi in P'yŭng-yang. He in
turn despatched Sim Yu-gyŭng, who had before acted as an
emissary of peace between the Japanese and the Emperor, to
take charge of the negotiations and with instructions more
or less definite. When this commissioner arrived in the
vicinity of Seoul a meeting took place between him and the
two Japanese leaders, Konishi and Kato, in mid-stream off
the village of Yong-san. Gen Sim opened the conference
by saying, ''If you had listened to my advice in P'yŭng yang
you would have saved yourselves all this trouble. The Chinese,

40,000 strong, are all about you. They have gone south to
fortify the Cho-ryŭng Pass and thus cut off your retreat.
The Han River is guarded so thoroughly that you cannot
cross ; Gen. Yi Yŭ-song is returning from the north with
300,000 fresh troops (an unblushing lie) and I am prepared to
offer you the only possible way of escape. You must give up
the two princes ; you must leave the capital and move south
to the coast of Kyŭng-sang Province. Then and not till then
will we conclude peace and the Emperor will recogniz: your
king as his vassal.'' The vanquished invaders saw that
there was nothing to do but comply, and so in the name of
the thirty-seven Japanese generals they engaged to evacuate
Seoul on the nineteenth day of the fourth moon. It was
further agreed that they should leave untouched 20,000 bags
of rice which were stored in the government granaries. The
two princes were to accompany the Japanese as far as Fusan
and were to be handed over to the Korean authorities there.

In accordance with their promise, the Japanese evacuated
the city on the very day appointed, and Gen. Yi Yŭ-song,
who seems to have recovered his health rapidly after he found
that the Japanese did not mean fight, entered the city the
following day. The condition in which he found things is
almost indescribable. The Ancestral Temple and three palaces
had been burned. Only the Nam-pyŭl-gung, which the invaders had used as headquarters, was standing. The country
all about was lying fallow and a great famine stared the Koreans in the face. A thousand bags of rice were hastily
brought and made up into soup or gruel, mixed with pine
leaves, and a few of the starving thousands were fed. As
Gen. Sa Tă-su was passing along the street he saw a young
child trying to suck milk from the breast of its dead mother.
The sight aroused his compassion and he carried the child to
his quarters and ordered it to be cared for. Rice was so
scarce that a whole piece of cotton cloth could be purchased
with about three quarts of it. A horse cost but three pecks
of rice. Famishing men fought and killed each other, the
victors eating the vanquished, sucking the marrow from the
bones and then dying themselves of surfeit. It is even 'said
that when a drunken Chinese soldier vomited, half starved
men would crawl to the place and fight over the possession of

this horrible substitute for food. This state of things naturally brought on an epidemic of the native fever, a species of typhus, and the dead bodies of its victims lay all along the road, the head of one being pillowed on the breast of another. The dead bodies in and immediately around Seoul were gathered and piled in a heap outside the Water Mouth Gate and it is affirmed that the pile was ten feet higher than the wall.

It was on the twentieth of the fourth moon that Gen. Yi entered Seoul. He took up his quarters in the Nam-pyŭl-gung. He seemed to be in no haste to pursue the Japanese, so Gen. Yu Sŭng-nyong hinted that as the Japanese were in full flight it might be well to hurry after them and cut them down as occasion offered. The Chinese general had no intention of leaving his comfortable quarters that soon, but he gave consent to the project of pursuit and detailed 10,000 men under the lead of Gen Yi Yŭ-bǎk. A day or so later this doughty warrior returned saying that he had a pain in the leg. So ended the first attempt at pursuit. Then the Korean Gen. Kwŭn Ryŭl came in from P'a-ju and urged that there be immediate pursuit, but for some unexplained reason the Chinese commander forbade it, and the native accounts even add that he sent secretly and had the boats on the Han destroyed so as to render pursuit of the Japanese impossible.

After crossing the Han River, the retreating Japanese seem to have been in very ill humor, for they did not confine their exhibitions of temper to the living alone but even attacked the dead. They dug open the royal tomb at Chung-neung a short distance the other side of the river. Digging fifteen measures deep they found some rags and a few bones. These they scattered about on the ground. They then filled in the hole with rubble. Another royal tomb was opened and the casket and remains were burned.

In the beginning of the fifth moon a letter arrived from the Military Commissioner, Song Eung-ch'ang, in P'yŭng-yang, ordering a general pursuit of the Japanese. The Koreans believe this to have been a mere blind, for the Japanese had twenty days the start of them and pursuit was of course out of the question. At this point again the Koreans make a serious charge against the Chinese, asserting that the Japanese, before leaving Seoul, sent large sums of money toward P'yŭng yang for Gen. Yi Yŭ-song and Song Eung-ch'ang, and that by this means they secured immunity from pursuit. The delay was a cause of great wonderment to the Koreans and it is not unlikely that this theory of a bribe explained for them most fully the actions of the Chinese. And it must be confessed that there is little in the temperament or antecedents of the Chinese on which to base a refutation of the charge. An instance is cited to bring home the charge. A Korean who had come upon a Japanese straggler and killed him was severely beaten by order of the Chinese general in charge.

Finally, when all too late, Gen. Yi made a pretense of pursuit, but after crossing Cho-ryŭng Pass and still finding himself no nearer the enemy than before, he turned back and resumed his comfortable quarters in Seoul. If he thought the Japanese would hasten to take boat and return to their native land, he was much mistaken. It may be that they wished to do so, but the terrible punishment that Admiral Yi Sun-sin had inflicted upon the army of reinforcement made them wary of approaching the coast, and so the Japanese forces in the south found themselves practically entrapped. Had the Korean land forces been led at this time by a man of the skill and bravery of old admiral Yi the country would have been spared long years of war.

The Japanese in their flight south were brought face to face with this stern fact, and like the soldiers that they were they set themselves to solve the problem. They wanted to be near the sea, perhaps with a view to taking advantage of any opportunity that might present itself of slipping across to Japan, and yet they were so numerous that, living as they must on forage, it would be impossible for them all to encamp at the same place. So they adopted the plan of fortifying a long strip of the southern coast, reaching from the harbor of So-sang in the district of Ul-san in Kyŭng-sang Province to Sun-ch'ŭn in Ch'ŭl-la Province, a distance of over two hundred and seventy miles. There were in all between twenty and thirty camps. Being thus about ten miles apart they had room for forage and still were near enough each other to render assistance in case the Koreans or their allies the Chinese should besiege them at any point. These fortified camps were all of the same general kind, overlooking the sea from a bluff and on the land side surrounded by a moat and earthworks. These preparations were made with the utmost care, for there was no hope of immediate succor and the Japanese foresaw stirring times.

In course of time the Chinese court was informed of these events and the success of their generals in the north seems to have given them some enthusiasm for prosecuting the war; so additional troops were sent to the front under the command of Generals Yu Chung and Hŭ Kuk-ch'ŭng. These troops numbered 5,000 and were from southern China. Among them there are said to have been many "ocean imps," or savages from the southern islands. These men could enter the water, it is said, and scuttle the enemy's ships from beneath. We are told that there were also in this army some men of immense stature who came in carts rather than on foot. These forces went into camp at Sŭng-ju in Kyŭng-sang Province. At this place there was also a large Korean army under Generals Kim Ch'ŭn-il, Kim Sang-gŏn, Ch'oé Kyŭng-whé, Ko Chong-hu, Yang San-do and Yi Chong-in. Under them were large numbers of militia and raw recruits, and this accounts in part for the speedy fall of the town and the terrible slaughter that ensued. The Japanese laid siege to the place and after nine days, during which time the Japanese made a hundred separate assaults, the latter were reinforced and the defenders, exhausted by the long struggle, were finally driven from the wall and the Japanese effected an entrance. But even after they got in, the Koreans fought desperately and sold their lives as dearly as possible. Of this most sanguinary battle only one incident is preserved in the Korean accounts. When the Japanese entered the city and had advanced to a point on the wall which overlooks the waters of the Nam-gang (river), a desperate encounter took place, in the midst of which the Korean general, Yi Chong-in, seized two of the Japanese about the waist and, dragging them to the brink of the precipice, threw himself and them into the water below. Korean accounts say that in this battle the almost incredible number of 70,000 Koreans were killed and that an equal number of the Japanese perished. This latter must be an exaggeration, for the loss of that number must have swept well-nigh the entire Japanese army from the country. We must remember that the Japanese army had received practically no reinforcements from the time it first landed on Korean soil, and it is safe to say that what with the losses by sickness and accident, together with the thousands who had fallen at the hands of the Koreans and Chinese, the original force must have dwindled to 150,000 or less ; in which case the loss of 70,000 men must have put them *hors de combat* at once. This battle is called the greatest in the whole war, by the Koreans, though it is not considered the most important.

An interesting story is told of a dancing-girl of this town. When the Japanese took possession of the place she was appropriated by one of the Japanese generals. One day while they were feasting in a summer-house on the wall overlooking the river, she began to weep. He asked her the reason and she replied, "You have come here and driven away our people and our king. I do not know whether my sovereign is living, and yet I sit here and feast. I can hardly claim to be better than the beasts, to sit here and make merry. I must put an end to my life." Thereupon she threw her arms about her paramour and flung herself and him over the edge, thus ending her weary life and helping to avenge her native land at the same time. For this reason she was canonized at a later date and her spirit was worshiped at this place each year by royal edict.

All this time the great Admiral Yi was in camp at Hansan Island off the coast of Kyŭng-sang Province. His force was not large, but during his enforced idleness he prepared for future work. He set all his men to work making salt by evaporating sea water, and by this means he got together a great store of provisions. Needing barracks for the soldiers, he offered to the carpenters and workmen about a bag of salt for a day's work. His energy and patriotism were so contagious that many worked for nothing, and the barracks were soon built. At this point the king conferred upon him the admiralty of the three provinces of Ch'ung-ch'ŭng, Chŭl-la and Kyŭng-sang.

In the ninth moon the Commissioner Song Eung-ch'ang and Gen Yi Yŭ-song collected their forces and started back for China. They evidently considered the back bone of the invasion broken, and so it was ; but like most spinal diseases it was destined to linger on for years before it came to an end. When these generals set out on their homeward way they left 10,000 Chinese soldiers in the hands of the Korean gererals Yu Chŭng and O Yu-ch'ang to act as a bodyguard for the king. In spite of their suspicions of the corruptibility of Gen. Yi Yŭ-song, the Koreans speak in high terms of him. They describe him as a young man of thirty, of handsome person, broad mind and possessed of great skill in the art of war. When he was on the eve of returning to China he bared his head and showed the Koreans that his hair was already turning gray. He told them it was because he had worked so hard for them, which piece of bathos seems to have impressed them deeply.

Chapter I-A.*

The King re-enters Seoul....temporary palace....a royal lament ...a profligate prince....imperial rebuke...."The Flying General" ... uneasiness in Seoul....revenue reform ...reforms in the army ... King refuses to make peace with the Japanese....the Chinese retire ....plot against Konishi....Japanese envoy in Nanking....robbers put down....a good man ruined....Japanese trickery   a patient envoy....he absconds....his flight'covered by his second....home-sick Japanese ...Konishi sarcastic....Chinese envoy in Japan.... Korean envoy....Japanese army leaves Korea....prince refuses the crown....rebellion....death of a loyal general....envoys ill-treated in Japan....return....a new invasion determined upon ... comparison of Japan and Korea ...Japanese scheme to get Admiral Yi into trouble....Admiral Yi degraded ...second invasion ... Cho-ryŭng pass fortified .. Chinese give aid....Admiral Yi's successor a failure....great naval victory for the Japanese.

It was on the fourth day of the tenth moon of the year 1593 that the king reentered the gates of Seoul after his long hard exile in the north. But he found the city almost a desert. The palaces were burnt and the ancestral temple was level with the ground. Under the circumstances he decided to stop for some time in that part of the city which is called

* Inadvertently marked "XI" in original text.—Editor

Chong-dong, the present foreign quarter, near the West Gate. Here there had been the grave of one of the wives of the founder of the dynasty, but her body had long ago been disinterred and removed to a place outside the Northeast Gate. So the king took up his quarters at the Myŭng-ye-gung. It is the exact spot where the King of Korea lives today. A considerable tract of land about it was surrounded by a stake fence with a gate at the east and at the west. This royal residence was named the Si-ŏ-sa or "Temporary Residence." Here the king lived thirteen years while the palace now known as "The Old Palace" was being built. The king was desirous of rebuilding on the spot where his palace had stood before, the Kyŏng-bok-kung, but he was told by the geomancers that that would be an unpropitious site. In order to build the new palace a tax of half a piece of cotton cloth was levied upon each man throughout the country. In some cases rice was accepted as a substitute.

After the king had entered the city, one of his first acts was to go to the site of the ancient Confucian Temple and, standing on the melancholy spot, utter the following lament: "The spirit of Confucius permeates space as water permeates the soil beneath our feet. If my faithfulness is great enough, let the spirit of Confucius rest down upon this spot." He noticed that none of the people were in mourning and so ordered that all those who had lost parents in the war should assume the mourner's garb.

At this time a strong faction arose whose wish was to see the king lay aside his royal prerogative in favor of his son. This prince was a son by a concubine, for the queen had no children. He was an ambitious but profligate fellow and had in his heart no loyalty for his father. Some of the courtiers went so far as to memorialize the King to the effect that it might add to the contentment of the people if the king should put the reins of government into the hands of his son. He hesitated to do this, for he knew the young man and how unfit he was to rule. At the suggestion of Song Eung-ch'ang, the emperor sent to the king appointing the Crown Prince to the governorship of the southern provinces in conjunction with the Chinese general, Yu Chung. The prince was delighted at this and hastened to his post at Chŭn-ju. He practically took the whole jurisdiction of the south out of the hands of the king and even held the competitive examinations for literary degrees, which was an exclusively royal prerogative.

Another of the Chinese generals accused the king before the emperor of effeminacy and love of luxury and suggested that one of the best of the Korean generals be elevated to the throne in his place, but Gen. Suk Sŭng, who was very loyal to Korea, induced the emperor merely to send a letter upbraiding the king for his love of luxury and claiming that this was the cause of Japanese successes in the peninsula. The letter ended with an exhortation to arouse himself, work up a competent army, and complete the work of driving out the Japanese. The envoy bearing this missive was met at P'a-ju by Gen. Yu Sŭng-nyong and an escort. The Chinaman told him that his arrival in Seoul would be the signal for some very important disclosures. General Yu and Gen. Chŭk conferred together about this matter and decided that the king must in any event be prevented from abdicating, for their official heads depended upon his retention of the reins of power. They also persuaded the envoy to their view, so that when the king read the letter and declared his intention to abdicate, the envoy objected that this could not be done until he had sent a letter to the emperor and obtained his consent.

Meanwhile there was going on in the south a sort of geurilla warfare against the Japanese. It was led principally by Kim Tŭk-nyŭng, a self-made man who had the confidence of the prince. This man had put his whole fortune into the cause and had himself fitted out 5,000 men. His method was to pass from place to place with great rapidity and strike the enemy when they were least expecting attack. In this way he earned from the Japanese the name "The Flying General." He is said to have been uniformly successful.

Of another ilk were Song U-jin, Yi Neung-su and Hyŭn Mong. These gathered about them bands of desperate men and went about the country looting and burning. In Seoul there was consternation. At any moment one of these bands might enter the city and work their will. The Crown Prince, a cause of great uneasiness, was still at Chŭn-ju and for aught anyone knew he might be plotting the overthrow of the government. In fact this impression was so strong that the highwaymen dared to write to him complaining of the king and asserting that they were going to make a clean sweep. The implication was plain, that they intended to put the prince upon the throne. The solicitude of the people in Seoul took form in the rumor that Yi Tă-hyŭng himself, the Minister of War, was in league with the rebels. For forty successive days this injured minister went and knelt at the palace gate and begged that the king would have him executed, as he could not endure the charge of unfaithfulness.

It was customary for the emperor to nominate an heir apparent for the Korean throne, but at the beginning of this war it had seemed necessary to appoint one immediately and so the king had informally promised the prince that he should be king. The latter now demanded that this be confirmed by the emperor and a messenger was sent to the Chinese court for that purpose ; but as the emperor had no son himself except by a concubine and was loath to put him on the throne of China, so he was unwilling to see this prince put on the throne of Korea. The result was that he sent back a prompt refusal, which for the time dashed the hopes of the ambitious prince.

It appears that the rebuke which the emperor administered to the king was in some senses deserved. The king after all his wearisome exile in the north, probably paid more attention to the pleasures of peace that was for his own good or the good of the country. If so the rebuke had its effect, for the king immediately roused himself and set to work reorganizing the finances of the country and putting the army on a better working basis. Hitherto the revenue had all been collected in rice but now he allowed the revenue to be collected in any kind of produce, and the collection of it was farmed out to various individuals, a practice which at the time may have had its good points but which at the same time had within itself very bad possibilities. The reorganization of the army was a matter of great importance and the king set himself to it with a will. Heretofore each general had had his own following and there was no central power nor seat of authority. Each body of troops followed the caprice of its leader with no reference to any general plan. Before the

Chinese general Yi Yŭ-song left he put into the hands of the
king a book treating of the art of war, a work written by
Ch'ŭk Kye-gwang. This book the king put into use and appointed Cho Kyŭng and Yu Sŭng-nyong to have charge of
the whole matter of military reorganization. In order to put
the new plan into operation a large number of poor and destitute soldiers were gathered. They had to pass a physical
test which consisted in lifting a rice bag full of earth, and of
leaping over a wall as high as their heads. In ten days two
thousand men were found who endured the test. The drill
consisted of three parts, (1) firing with guns, (2) shooting
with bow and arrow, (3) using the battle axe. In time these
men became the royal guard and escort. The number gradually increased to 10,000, 2,000 being attached to each of the
government departments. The whole force was divided into
two parts and while one part was drilling in the city the
other was set to work farming in the suburbs. In this way
they raised the food necessary for the sustenance of the whole
force. The plan was extended to the country, and teachers
were sent to practice the country soldiers. It became a
species of militia. From this time the quality and discipline
of the Korean army improved in a marked degree.

It appears that the Koreans were not the only ones who
suspected Gen. Yi Yŭ-song of showing favors to the Japanese,
for the emperor took notice of it and deprived him of his
high rank. He was supplanted by Gen. Ko Yang-gyŭm.
This new appointee advanced toward the border of Korea as
far as Liao-tung and from that point sent a letter to the king
saying that the Chinese had already lost enough men and
treasure in the war and that the king had better hasten to make
friends with the Japanese and induce them to come and do
obeisance to the emperor. It appears plain that this man
wanted peace to be patched up before he should be called
upon to do active work in the field. When the king saw this
letter he said, "When the Crown Prince becomes king he
can do as he pleases but as for me I will never make peace or
friendship with the Japanese." But Yu Sŭng-nyong urged
the helplessness of Korea alone and the need of securing
China's help at all hazards. Sŭng Hou urged the fact that
the new Chinese general had a large force in hand and he

must be conciliated at any cost. So the king reluctantly sent
an envoy to China asking that overtures of peace be made
with the Japanese. Even while this envoy was on the way,
the emperor, apparently thinking the war at an end, sent
an order commanding the immediate return of Gen. Yu Chung,
with all his forces, from the province of Kyŭng-sang. The
Crown Prince sent begging him not to go. The people all
about the country were in distress about it. He was believed
to be the only hope against the Japanese. The command of
the emperor however was law and the general was forced to
obey. Taking his army, together with the wives and children of those who had been married to Korean women. he
went back to Liao-tung. It is said that ever 10,000 of the
Chinese took back their Korean wives to China, but six years
later they all returned to their native land.

Kato was desirous of meeting and having a talk with the
Korean general Kim Eung-sŭ, the general of Kyŭng-sang
Province. To this end he sent a Japanese named Yo-si-ra to
arrange a meeting, and in course of time they met at the town
of Ham-an and had a conference. Kato opened the conference as follows: "If Korea will help us to become the vassals
of China we will remove all our troops from Korea immediately and we will also consider it a great favor." But Gen. Kim,
who knew of the enmity which existed between Kato and
Konishi, waved the main question by asking, "Why is it that
you and Konishi cannot agree? It is plain that so long as he
is here such a plan as you recommend cannot be carried out."
Kato answered, "I have long wished to make an end of him,
but can never get a chance. If in some way we could work
up a charge against him and circulate it among the troops we
might be able to get all the army removed to Japan." As to
the further deliberations of these two men we are not informed, but we judge from this passing glimpse that Konishi the
younger man was so firmly intrenched in the affection of his
troops that Kato despaired of making head against him until
that affection was in some way alienated. In this Kato ac-
knowledges his virtual defeat at the hands of his youthful
rival.

The emperor was not as anxious as his generals to make
peace with the Japanese, and when he heard that his new ap-

pointee to the peninsula was in favor of a treaty with the invaders he promptly ordered his retirement, and Gen. Son
Kwang was sent to take his place. Hardly had this happened
when the envoy Ho Ok, from the Korean court, arrived,
asking that a treaty be made with the Japanese. When his
message was delivered all the court was in favor of the plan ;
but the Prime Minister said that as they had been deceived
once by the Japanese general So Cŭ-bi, who had accompanied
Gen. Sim Yu gyŭng from Pyŭng-yang on a similar errand
before, it would be well to test them with three propositions.
"(1) We will give the king of Japan the royal investiture. (2)
Every Japanese soldier must leave Korea. (3) The Japanese
must promise never to disturb Korea again." This plan pleased the emperor and Gen. So Sŭ-bi was sent for, that he
might appear before the emperor and accept these conditions.
On arriving at Peking the Japanese readily acceded to the
terms and exclaimed, "We will gladly agree to this and will
swear by heaven to abide by the terms." Thereupon Sim Yu-
gyŭng, who had always had a strange leaning toward the Japanese, now exclaimed, "Japan now evidently desires to become China's vassal. An envoy must be sent to invest Hideyoshi with the royal insignia, and all this trouble will end."
But Hŭ Hong-gang had a truer estimate of the visitor and
remarked, "The Japanese are a subtle people, and all this
talk of becoming vassals of China is mere pretense. There
is no use in sending an envoy to Japan." Gen. Sŭk Sŭng
said, "This man seems to be honest in what he says. Gen.
Sim Yu-gyŭng should accompany So Sŭ-bi back to Korea and
there confer with the Japanese leaders and then arrangements
can be made for investing the king of Japan." The emperor
so ordered and at the same time appointed Yi Chong-sŭng as
envoy extraordinary to Japan to perform the ceremony of investiture. Yang Pang-hyŭng was appointed his second.
These events all occurred in the latter part of the year 1593.

As the new year opened the political sky was dark enough.
Not only were the Japanese intrenched in the south but predatory bands infested the country and the government troops
had all they could do to hold them in check, let alone any
offensive operations against the Japanese. However, after a
hard chase a large band of the miscreants were brought to bay

at Hoe-mun Mountain and cut to pieces. At this time also the king sent again to Nanking asking that his successor be nominated, but again he was refused.

The career of Gen. Kim Tŭk-nyŭng whom, as we have seen, the Japanese had dubbed "The Flying General," affords us another example of the fatal weakness of Korea, in the envy excited against any really successful man ; for even while Gen. Kim was successfully combatting the Japanese in his own way, his very successes aroused the spleen of Gen. Yun Keun-su who accused him to the king of having killed plenty of Koreans, but never a Japanese. On the strength of this groundless charge, and without questioning its truth, the king brought Gen. Kim to Seoul and imprisoned him a year. And so a man of highest loyalty, of such unselfish patriotism as to devote the whole of his private fortune to the fitting out of soldiers to fight his country's foes, was dragged away from a successful field of work to languish in prison, simply because a less successful man begrudged him his fame.

And now began an amusing comedy between the Chinese, who took the Japanese seriously, and the latter who were merely playing off the Chinese in order to save time.

In the fourth moon of 1395 the embassy from China to Japan arrived in Seoul, and immediately Gen. Sim Yu-gyŭng posted southward to see Kato and tell him that the Chinese embassy had already come and that he must hasten to get all the Japanese troops out of the country before the embassy should arrive at Fusan.[1] To all this the wily Kato answered gravely, "You had better stay here a few weeks while I take a run over to Japan and ask Hideyoshi about it, and if he gives the order to take the troops back, it can be done immediately." When he came back, instead of answering the main question he said that it would be well for a Korean to accompany the envoy to Japan. Meanwhile the Chinese envoy Yi Chong-sŭng, in Seoul, sent messenger after messenger urging the speedy removal of the Japanese troops from the peninsula ; but Kato kept putting it off on one ground or another, and made no move to go. When, however, this part of the comedy had proceeded to such a point that the Japanese began to fear the Chinese would see that it was indeed a comedy, Kato took a few regiments of men from Ung-ch'ŭn and Kŭ-je and made

preparations as if to depart, meanwhile sending Gen. Sim to
Seoul to say that he was waiting for the envoy and his suite
to come south and accompany the departing army to Japan.
Five months had already elapsed since the envoy had arrived
in Seoul, and he therefore determined to accept this invitation.   Moving southward, he came to Nam-wŭn in Chŭl-la
Province where he stopped, fearing to go directly into the
Japanese camp.   While there he gained the soubriquet of
"frog-eater," for he was so fond of the flesh of that reptile
that he compelled the people to hunt for and procure it
for him.

    Gen. Son Kwang, from his comfortable quarters in Liao-
tung, sent him a letter charging him with cowardice and
ordering him to proceed at once on his way.   Under this
stimulus he proceeded to Fusan ; but Kato would not come
to see him, saying, "I must receive instructions from Japan before I can take you across the straits, so I will cross
once more and find out the will of my royal master in regard
to the matter."   After an absence of two months he came
back and opened another act of the comedy by asserting that
he must first take Gen. Sim across to Japan and arrange the
ceremony of investiture, and that the envoy proper might follow when all was ready.   By this time, what with the fear of
the Japanese and bewilderment at the intricacy of Japanese
diplomacy the poor envoy was well-nigh distraught.   When
therefore, with the beginning of the new year 1596 a Chinaman named So Hak-myŭng came from Japan and informed
him that Hideyoshi had not the remotest idea of becoming a
vassal of China and that if the Chinese envoy should cross to
Japan he would never come back again, it capped the climax,
and that very night the wretched envoy, taking only one servant and a few clothes tied up in a cloth, made his escape
from the Japanese camp and fled away northward.   He
traveled by night and hid by day, until at last he arrived
at Seoul.   And so the curtain drops on another act of the
comedy.

    When the Japanese found out that the envoy had made
his escape they were in a quandary, fearing lest they might
be punished for letting him go and so spoiling the fun.   They
therefore gave chase, but not being able to overtake the light-

footed envoy, they contented themselves with surrounding the house of the vice-envoy Yang Pang-hyŭng. The latter knew of his chief's flight, but to draw away suspicion from himself he pretended to sleep late that morning and claimed to know nothing about the matter. When at last he was told of it by the Japanese general Kuroda, he said quietly, "Well, he was a young man and a little nervous. He should have gone to Japan long ago instead of waiting around here. It will be of no use for you to chase him." He then deliberately arose, went to the room lately occupied by his chief, took possession of the Emperor's letter and returned to his own apartments. By his coolness and presence of mind he allayed the excitement of the Japanese and perhaps saved his own life.

The Japanese soldiers who had been detailed to return to Japan were of course delighted to go back to their homes and were eager to set sail from Fusan. They had their baggage all on board and were hoping to start at any moment. But when they heard of the flight of the Chinese envoy they knew there would be a long delay and they were sorely disappointed ; so much so in fact that many of them wept aloud. It is probable that every Japanese soldier in the peninsula would have been glad of an opportunity to return to Japan. Only the severe discipline of the Japanese army and the lack of boats prevented them from deserting in large numbers ; at least we may gather as much from the frequent references to the home-sickness of the Japanese soldiers.

Yang Pang-hyŭng called the weeping soldiers before him and said, "We have waited here so long that my chief got tired and went back. But I remain and the imperial missive is with me. He has fled only to Nam-wŭn and if you send there you will doubtless find him." This led them to believe that their fond hope of returning home would soon be gratified.

All this time the young Konishi, the rival of Kato, sat disdainfully silent watching the empty game which his unpopular rival was playing with the Chinese. When he heard of the flight of the envoy he laughed and said, "I knew he was no genuine envoy from the Emperor, for if he had been he would not have dared to show his heels like this." This remark was intended to imply that while Kato had been trying to hoodwink the Chinese, they, on the other hand, had hoodwinked him.

Yang Pang-hyŭng lost no time in informing the Emperor of the perfidy of his chief, and the Emperor immediately ordered the recalcitrant official to be caught and imprisoned. He raised Yang Pang-hyŭng to the position of Chief of the Embassy and appointed Sim Yu-gyŭng as his second. We will remember that Sim Yu-gyŭng had already gone to Japan with Kato, bearing the imperial gifts, which consisted of a royal robe with the embroidered design of a dragon, a jade belt, royal head-gear, a map of China, a book on war and various other kinds of treasures. He there married the daughter of a Japanese named Arima, and is said by the Koreans to have become a thorough Japanese. This may have been part of the game he was playing, and we may see the fruits of it later.

Kato was determined that a Korean envoy should accompany the Chinese one to Japan and to this end he told one of the Korean officials, "If a Korean envoy does not accompany the Chinese embassy to Japan the peace will be only between Japan and China, and Korea will have no part in it. This will lead to grave troubles." Gen. Sim also sent his nephew back from Japan to ask that a Korean envoy accompany the Chinese embassy. So the king appointed two men, Whang Sin and Pak Hong-jang to this work, conferring upon them the title of T'ŏng-sin-sa or "Faithful Messenger."

In the fifth moon of this year 1596 Gen. Konishi massed his troops in forty-six regiments on the southern coast and, leaving only four regiments to guard Fusan, set sail for Japan. With him went all the envoys, both Chinese and Korean.

Now that lasting peace seemed to be assured, the king no longer hesitated to hand over the reins of power to the Crown Prince. He accordingly sent the royal insignia south to him, and so doffed the responsibilities as well as the prerogatives of royalty. But, strange to say, the prince strenuously refused to accept them, insisting that he had no desire to take the scepter from his father's hand. Seven times he sent to his father protesting his unwillingness to have the honor thrust upon him. But the king would not listen. It was only after the courtiers had assembled before the palace for twenty days in succession and besought him to retain the scepter that they finally prevailed and he consented to continue in the exercise of the royal prerogative.

Yi Mong-hak, an unprincipled ruffian, ignorant but ambitious, had joined the forces of Gen. Han Hyŭn and had fought during the war. Now he started out on an independent line. Gathering a force of over ten thousand men he attacked and took Hong-san in Ch'ung-ch'ŭng Province, and he followed it up by taking Im-ch'ŭn, Ch'ung-yang, Chŏng-san and Hong-ju. Yi Mong-hak had been deceiving his followers by saying that Gen. Kim Tŭk-nyang was interested in this scheme. But now they found that this same Gen. Kim was arrayed against them and they saw they had been duped. That night every man deserted the adventurer and the next day he fell into the hands of the loyal troops and his head was forwarded to Seoul. This shows the extremely unsettled state of the country, and how any unprincipled man with money and effrontery could offer serious opposition to the government.

Here again we find a striking example of that petty jealousy whioh deprived Korea of most of her capable men. This Gen Kim Tŭk-nyŭng was a celebrated man. He was known throughout the Korean army for his strength and prowess. It is said of him that single-handed he would attack a tiger and pin it to the ground with a spear. They also say that he rode into battle with an iron mace of a hundred pounds weight in each hand and he gave the Japanese so many hard knocks that they gave him the name, "The General from under the Rock." The ministers at Seoul were suspicious of his rising fame and went their ways to have him dragged down. They charged him with having been in league with Yi Mong-hak and won the king over. He was arrested and brought to Seoul, where after a most disgraceful trial he was put to death. The Japanese had such a high opinion of this man's parts that Konishi sent and had a portrait made of him. When he saw the picture he exclaimed, "This man is indeed a General." When his death was announced, the Japanese held a great feast in honor of the event. This was just on the eve of their departure for home.

As we have seen, it was in the summer of 1596 that the Chinese and Korean envoys crossed to Japan with the returning army of invasion. When they were brought into the presence of Hideyoshi he treated them with scant courtesy. When asked why he did not bow before the imperial missive he replied that he had a sore leg and could not. He treated the Korean envoy much worse than the Chinese, and said to him, "I sent back the two princes as I agreed, but your king never so much as thanked me. He has now sent as envoy a man of inferior rank on purpose to insult me. I believe the original Chinese envoy ran away at the instigation of your king. I will treat the Chinese envoy civilly, but as for you I shall send another army and be avenged on you." After this there was but one thing to do. Both the envoys packed up their effects and started back home. When the Chinese envoy arrived at Nanking bringing insult instead of submission from Japan the Emperor was in a terrible rage and charged Sim Yu-gyŭng with having betrayed his country. The chief envoy was executed and the official who had advised the sending of an embassy was thrown into prison and starved to death, but Sim Yu-gyŭng in some way escaped with his head.

Chapter II.

A new invasion determined upon....comparison of Japan and Korea ....Japanese scheme to get Admiral Yi into danger . Admiral Yi degraded .. second invasion ...Choryŭng Pass fortified... Chinese give aid....Admiral Yi's successor a failure....great naval victory for the Japanese .. Admiral Yi reinstated .. siege and fall of Nam-wŭn....Korean naval victories....Admiral Yi's policy .. Japanese advance checked....rejoicing in Seoul ...siege of Ul-san....siege raised ..Roman Catholic missionaries .. the Japanese army ... the "ear and nose mound" ...number of Chinese ...a Japanese settlement....Chinese admirals....Admiral Yi's diplomacy.... Gen. Yang Ho recalled ...the King accused ...the defense.

We have now reached the halfway point between the two invasions, or rather between the two parts of the double invasion. Hideyoshi was still furious over the failure of his great plan of invading China, and he must needs find some way to

vent his spleen. He determined upon a second invasion of
Korea, not this time with a view to the invasion of China
but with the more modest desire to punish Korea, though
what Korea had done to deserve punishment it would be hard
to say. To be sure she had proved an obstacle to his vault-
ing ambition, for had Hideyoshi's original army sailed straight
for China instead of landing at Fusan, it probably would have
overthrown the Chinese capital. [2] We must notice the changed conditions which existed between the two countries. Korea
had now experienced the worst possible at the hands of the
Japanese and knew what to expect. Their soldiers had felt
the prick of Japanese swords and had in turn tasted the de-
lights of victory. That terrible glamor which surrounded the
dreaded islanders upon their first appearance had worn off and
some sort of equality had been effected between them. The
Koreans had meanwhile become possessed of firearms and
were measurably skilled in their use. They had learned never
to trust themselves to open battle when geurilla warfare was
feasible. They had demonstrated their great superiority on
the sea in the person of the Admiral Yi. When therefore we
remember that the Japanese had to leave their base of supplies
and live on what they could forage in the peninsula, it appears that in spite of their prowess they had not much advantage over the Koreans. But before making this second descent upon the shores of Korea it was necessary for the Japanese to get the redoubtable Admiral Yi Sun-sin out of the way.
No fleet from Japan would risk an encounter with him in his
"Tortoise Boat." The Japanese had seen how the mutual
jealousies of the Koreans worked in their favor and they determined to use this in getting Admiral Yi removed. So one
day a Japanese named Yo-si-ra made his appearance at the
camp of Gen. Kim Eung-sŭ, saying that he was tired of
being a Japanese and that he wanted to become a Korean.
He dressed in Korean clothes and kept going back and forth
between the Japanese and Koreans, giving the latter what
seemed to be much valuable information. He seemed to be
devoted to the Korean interests. One day he came in a state
of great excitement and said that the Japanese General Kato
was coming to Korea with a great fleet and that, as he was to
pass a certain island off the coast, Admiral Yi ought to be sent

to lie in wait there and drive the invading fleet back or to sink it. So Gen. Kim wrote to the king about it and asked for orders. The king, trusting in the prowess of Admiral Yi, gave his consent ; but when that officer received these orders he promptly replied that it was a trick to entrap him and thus clear a way for a descent upon the mainland of Korea. He therefore declined to run the risk, especially as the place mentioned was studded with sunken rocks and was specially dangerous for navigation. But the Japanese Yo-si-ra kept urging Gen. Kim to see to it that the plan was carried out and at last the General wrote to the king saying that Admiral Yi declined to go. As may be supposed Admiral Yi had enemies at court who could not let such an opportunity pass of getting him into trouble. Consequently the iniquitous decree went forth that Admiral Yi be seized and brought to Seoul and that Wŭn Kyun be put in his place. The king intended to put Admiral Yi to death, but one of the officials urged his former services in palliation of his present offense and so the punishment was commuted to loss of position alone. So it was that Admiral Yi, the best soldier that Korea contained and to whom the king owed his crown twice over, was degraded to the ranks and became a common soldier. But most remarkable of all, he made no complaint, but went quietly about his work as if nothing had happened.

In the first moon of the year 1597 the Japanese fleet set sail from Japan. This army was led by Kato and Konishi although the nominal commander in chief was a lad of seventeen named Hideyaki. It is said that it took a thousand boats to bring the army across the straits. Had Admiral Yi Sunsin been at his old post this fleet would never have touched keel on the Korean coast but as it was there was no difficulty, and the entire army landed safely at So-sang Harbor and immediately threw up fortifications and went into camp.

The first thought of the Koreans was to fortify Choryŭng Pass the one break in the mountain chain which the Japanese must pass if they wished to march on Seoul. Gen. Kwŭn Ryŭl with 23,000 men and other generals with troops hastily gathered from various districts hastened to that important pass and put the fortifications in good order, and the king forthwith sent Kwŭn Hyŭp as envoy to Nanking to implore the intervention of China. And now we see the evil results of Hideyoshi's ill-treatment of the Chinese and Korean envoys in Japan : for instead of making the Koreans send time and again asking for help the Emperor was eager to send troops into the peninsula to avenge himself upon the Japanese. The Chinese army was put in charge of three men : Gen. Yang Ho with rank of Military Commissioner, Gen. Hyöng Kă as general-in chief and Admiral Ma Gwi as commander of all the naval forces. Under these were Gen. erals Yang Wŭn, O Yu-ch'ung, U Păk-yŏng, Chin U-ch'ung, So Eung-gung, Chin Hyo and Tong Han-yu. Gen. Yang Ho came no further than P'yŭng-yang, his duties not requir- ing his presence on the field of battle. Admiral Ma Kwi and all the others came on to Seoul. From that point they branched out in several directions, one going to Nam-wŭn in Chŭl-la province, another to Song-ju in Kyŭng-sang Pro- vince, another to Chŭn-ju, Chŭl-la Province, and another to Ch'ung ju in Ch'ung-ch'ŭng Province.

Admiral Wŭn Kyun, who had supplanted Yi Sun-sin, went to Han-san where Admiral Yi had worked so diligently to build barracks with the proceeds of salt manufacture. His first work was to overthrow all the rules and regulations which his predecessor had so wisely promulgated. He then drove away all who had been at all intimate with the former admiral, who was now a common soldier under Kwŭn Ryul. He then built a paling about the council-hall that Yi Sun-sin had built and there he housed his harem and spent his time in revelry and feasting. He would frequently have innocent men called up and severely punished for mere amusement. And thus he soon alienated the good will of all the troops stationed there.

But Kato, the astute Japanese general, through his tool Yo-si-ra, kept at Gen. iKm, urging him to have a fleet sent to intercept a fleet of Japanese boats. He named a day on which the Korean fleet would be sure to intercept a fleet of the enemy. At last the order was given for Admiral Wŭn Kyun to carry out this manoeuvre and though he had no stomach for the enterprise he could not well demur, for this was the very thing that had cost Admiral Yi his position. So he got his boats together and sailed out to Chŭl-yŭng

Island off Fusan. [3] But a strong breeze sprang up and the sea was rather rough and in the darkness of night the Korean fleet became scattered. The next day the larger part of them rendez-voused at Ka-dok Island where they unexpectedly met the Japanese fleet and were vigorously attacked. Almost immediately all Admiral Wŭn's forces deserted him and his only recourse was flight. Beaching his boat on Ch'il-ch'ŭn Island he landed and drew about him what remnants of his force he could find. When Gen. Kwŭn Ryul heard of this he sent a stern order demanding that the admiral come out and fight. That valliant man first filled hemself with wine then sallied forth only to be deserted again by his men. So the doughty admiral again ran his boat aground and took to his heels. He was so fat however that he could not run far, so he sat down under a tree to get his breath. There the Japanese overtook him and carried away his head in triumph. The second in command, Yi Yŭ-geui, fled by boat after burning all the barracks and provisions that were stored at Han-san.

When these events became known the whole country was in consternation. Yi Hang-bok, the king's trusted councillor, said, "Yi Sun-sin must be reinstated in his former position." It was a case of dire necessity and so the king sent and conferred upon that faithful man his former office. The trusty Yi set out on foot and rested not day nor night until he reached his former position, Han-san. On all sides he met the scattered and flying remnants of his former force. He rallied them about him, promising that the Japanese should still be held in check.

But before Admirai Yi arrived on the scene of action a tremendous force of Japanese both military and naval had landed on the southern coast. Their objective point was Nam-wŭn, where the Chinese general Yang Wŭn had pitched his camp. Upon the approach of the Japanese the latter burned all the houses outside the wall to prevent their offering cover to an attacking force; but the Japanese soon built a rough fence or palisade about the town, from behind which they picked off the Chinese soldiers on the wall, at leisure. The Chinese attempted to make a sortie but in their eagerness to get out of the gate they became jammed in it and were mown down by the long swords of the besiegers. Unfor-

tunately for the Chinese and Koreans the following night was
full moon and the Japanese cut down every man that attempted to escape. To the line of stakes which they had
planted about the town the Japanese fastened swords, and
when the people from the town tried to make good their
escape they found themselves impaled upon these weapons.
The Chinese commander, 'Yang Wŭn, rode at this barrier and
his horse was so impaled, but he succeeded in getting over
and making good his escape. The Japanese attacked the wall
in its weakest point and forced an entrance. The massacre
within the town beggars description. The Korean generals
Chŏng Keui-wŭn, Yi Pong-nam, O Eung-jung, Kim Kyŏng-
no, Sin Ho, Im Hyŭn, Yi Tŭk-whe and Yi Wŭn-ch'un were
all killed, which indicates how sanguinary must have been
the fight.

Immediately all northern Chŭl-la was in confusion and
the troops everywhere began to fall back toward the north.
In Seoul itself there was consternation. The king called his
officials about him and asked what should be done. They all
urged that the king stay in the capital. The queen and the
crown prince however were sent to Su-an in Ham-gyŭng
Province and the king prepared to move whenever it should
seem necessary.

But by this time Admiral Yi was again on the stage of
action and as alert as ever. He had as yet only ten boats
under him, but he had no lack of men, for the people all along
the coast, when they heard of his reinstatement, flocked to
him. He drew up his little fleet of ten boats in the shadow
of a mountain on Chin-do (island) and sent out reconnoitering boats which returned just at night saying that the Japanese were approaching. As the moon dropped behind the
mountain it left the Korean fleet in complete darkness and
soon the Japanese boats came sailing along in single file.
Admiral Yi deployed his boats in a long line and suddenly
they all raised a loud shout and fired point blank at the un-
suspecting Japanese. The latter thought they had run into a
powerful fleet and soon scattered in all directions. The next
day there was more serious work, however, for a fleet of
several hundred boats appeared. The Koreans were in some
trepidation, but the fearless admiral made straight for the

enemy and though soon surrounded he succeeded in sinking thirty of the enemy's boats. The rest evidently recognized the master hand of Admiral Yi and turned and fled. He gave chase, and before the battle ended the Japanese commander Ma-da-si was killed. Returning from this remarkable fight Admiral Yi proceeded to Han-san and set to work rebuilding the barracks and making salt. It is said that in two months time he stored away 20,000 bags of rice. His former captains and soldiers came back to him in "clouds." He also found another source of revenue. The wealthy men all through the south desired to get away from the disturbed districts and so loaded their effects upon boats and sailed away. Admiral Yi however stood in the way and made them pay a toll of from one to three bags of rice for each boat. From this source alone he collected above a thousand bags of rice. He used this revenue in the purchase of copper for the casting of cannon, and for the building of boats. Thousands of people who feared to live on the mainland came and built huts about his camp, until the island actually became too small to hold more.

After the fall of Nam-wŭn the Japanese, flushed with victory, started northward toward Seoul, thinking without doubt that they would have as easy a victory as before. Yang Ho, hearing of the defeat of the Chinese came post haste from P'yŭng-yang and severely upbraided the generals and charged them with lack of bravery. Without an hour's delay it was arranged that Generals Ha Sang, U Pak-yung, Yang Teung and P'a Sa should take a strong body of troops and move southward to Ch'ung-chŭng Province and intercept the Japanese. This was done and the army ambushed at Keum-o-p'yŭng in the district of Chik-san. Soon the Japanese came streaming along, neglecting all precautions, for they had no idea of meeting an enemy. When therefore the ambuscade opened fire on them it took but a few moments to throw them into utter confusion. In the rout which ensued an enormous number of the Japanese were killed. On the following day the Japanese, who had mended their broken ranks as best they could, came on to the attack, but their losses had been so great that in spite of wonders of bravery which they showed they were again crushed. The remnant

of their force fled southward to Mok-ch'un and Ch'ung-ju.
This was one of the three great battles of the war and in importance it was exceeded by none; for, though the forces
engaged were not so numerous nor the number of slain so
great, it broke once for all the self-confidence of the Japanese,
and they never again had the hardihood to attempt the approach to Seoul. By this battle the war was definitely confined
to the southern provinces. The Commissioner Yang Ho suggested to the king that he go out and survey the battle field,
and so the royal cavalcade rode out the South Gate. One of
the Chinese generals suspected that the king was something
of a coward and so, to test him, he gave the horse the king
was riding a sharp cut with a whip. The horse leaped into
the air with terror but the king held his seat and showed no
sign of fear. The Chinese were pleased at this and their respect for the king was visibly increased.

Seoul gave itself up to universal holiday in honor of the
victory, for it was still fresh in the minds of many how Seoul
had fared before at the hands of the invaders.

In the tenth moon Gen. Konishi built a strong fort on a
bluff overlooking the sea at Ul-san in Kyŭng-sang Province.
He named it To-san. The Chinese Yang Ho determined to
cut the war short by attacking and taking this position and
by so doing he expected to cut off the right arm of the invading army. Collecting all the forces that were within reach,
he started south to attack Ul-san. The army consisted of
40,000 men and it went in three divisions. The left or eastern division being led by Gen. Yi Pang-ch'ŭn, the middle
division by Gen. Ko Ch'ak and the western division by Gen.
P ăng U-dŭk. Gen. Ma Kwi was sent on ahead and acted as
avant-coureur. Stopping a few miles from the Japanese position he ordered Gen. P'a Sa to go and make a preliminary attack upon the fort to discover something as to the lay of the
land, and if possible to discover the number and equipment of
the enemy. The attack was made with fire-arrows. Almost
immediately the Japanese made a sortie, but were driven back
with a loss of four hundred and sixty men. Shortly after
this the three grand army corps arrived. The Japanese were
arranged in three divisions. In the middle was the fort proper. On the north was a fortified camp called the Pan-gu-jun

and off the south was another called the P'a-wha-gang. It
was the first business of the Chinese and Korean allies to
drive these outer divisions into the central fort. To this end
the left division of the army attacked the Pan-gu-jun and the
right division the T'a-wha-gang.   Gen. Yang Ho put on his
armor and went into the thick of the fight and urged on his
men.   The air was filled with the noise of drums, musketry-
fire and shouts of the combatants, and a cloud of arrows
concealed the heavens.   Some of the Japanese huts were on
fire and great clouds of smoke and flame rolled heavenward.
Slowly the Japanese were forced back and finally they all entered the gates of the main fort of To-san.   This fort was set
on a rugged hill where it was difficult for an attacking force
to manoeuvre, but there was little water in the fort and the
Japanese were forced to come out secretly at night and draw
water from a well near by.   Being aware of this, Gen. Kim
Eung-sü, a Korean, placed an ambush about the well and
caught upwards of a hundred of the enemy.   They were badly emaciated and said that surrender was a matter of only a
few days.   It came on to rain, and this was followed by
severe cold, as it was now the beginning of winter.   Many of
the besieging army had their hands and feet frozen.   One
of Gen. Konishi's lieutenants wrote repeatedly to the Korean
general Song Yun-mun asking for terms of peace. Gen.
Yang Ho answered, "Konishi must come out and surrender
and he will be treated well."   By this time the Japanese were
well-nigh exhausted.   They had neither food nor water, and
every day they died in such numbers that it is said they had
"a mountain of dead."   Many a time Gen. Konishi meditated
suicide but each time was restrained by one means or another.
As a last resort the Japanese threw gold and silver over the
wall to bribe the soldiers without and keep them from making
an attack.

But the tables were about to be turned.   All the other
Japanese forces in the south had become aware of the desperate straits to which their comrades were reduced at To-san.
And so now at the last moment a large fleet appeared and the
hard won victory was snatched from between the teeth of the
Chinese and Korean allies.   The exposure had greatly weakened the besieging force.   Their provisions were almost ex-

hausted and they had used up all their arrows. They were
far stronger that the beleagured Japanese but were not fit to
cope with the fresh army which was burning with zeal to
avenge their starving compatriots. So it was that Gen. Yang
Ho was compelled to raise the siege and fall back toward
Seoul. During this siege the Chinese loss was fourteen
hundred, though many thousands were wounded.

From this time date the first efforts of the Roman Catholic Church to enter Korea. Japan had already many thousands
of converts to Romanism and Hideyoshi was determined to
leave no means untried to eradicate the foreign cult. To this
end he sent many of the Catholic converts to Korea. But the
most distinguished of them all was the young and vigorous
Gen. Konishi who had received baptism at the hands of the
Catholics and had received the name of Augustine Ariman-
dano. It may have been because of Hideyoshi's desire to get
the Catholics out of the country that Gen. Konishi was appointed to the post in Korea. Kato was as pronounced a Buddhist as Konishi was a Christian and this of course intensified
the hatred and rivalry between them. Gen. Konishi was desirous of having Catholic teachers come over to the peninsula
and attend to the spiritual needs of the Christians in the army;
and to this end the Vice-provincial of the Jesuits in Japan appointed Padre Gregoris de Cespedes to this arduous and important post. With him went a Japanese priest. The two
first went to Tsushima and finding no means of getting to the
peninsula remained there over the winter and carried on a
successful mission work. The next spring they made their
way to Korea and finally reached Gen. Konishi's headquarters at a place that the Japanese call Comangai, which was
without doubt the fort of Ul-san. Here they worked a year
but finally, through the machinations of Gen. Kato, who worked upon the prejudices of Hideyoshi, both the foreign and native priests were sent back to Japan, and this had no little to
to with the return of Gen. Konishi, who went to clear himself before his master.

To anticipate a little, we might here say that many Koreans who were carried captive to Japan from time to time
during this war, became Christians at Nagasaki and though
slaves were so firm in their belief as to be willing to suffer

martyrdom during the terrible persecutions which raged in Japan between 1610 and 1630, but with the departure of Cespides from Korea the distinctive work in Korea was abandoned.

Let us pause a moment here to compare the two contending armies. In this second invasion the total number of Japanese that reached Korean soil was 105,400, or about half as many as formed the first army of invasion. They were led by twenty-seven generals, prominent among whom were Kato and Konishi. As a mark of his spiteful spirit, Hideyoshi ordered that in this second invasion the noses and ears of all Koreans killed or captured should be cut off and sent to Japan. And so from time to time these half-savage soldiers sent loads of Korean noses and ears, pickled in salt, and they were buried in the monastery of Ta-bul-sa in the city of Kyoto, there to remain to all ages a disgusting memento of the most unprovoked and wanton cruelty that ever disgraced the annals of a great people. Many of the Koreans who lost their noses or ears at that time survived many years, and it cannot be wondered at that the Koreans have never since cared to accept favors at the hands of their island neighbors.

The total number of Chinese was 210,000. With them came 2,000 000 ounces of silver to pay for their sustenance. From Shantung were sent by boat 200,000 bags of rice. There were also sent for the relief of the army 5,832,000 ounces of silver. And for the relief of the Korean famine sufferers an additional 3,000,000 ounces were sent. When we consider the vast number of men and the millions of wealth that China poured into Korea at this time it may well be believed, as the Koreans affirm, that China, by so doing, impoverished herself so that she became an easier prey to the Manchus who, a few years later, wrested the scepter from her.

Large numbers of Japanese who had been in the country for years and were tired of the war deserted from the ranks, married Korean women and settled down to farming in various places in the south. At Mi-ryang in the Province of Kyŭng-sang there was a whole settlement of them. It was called the Hang-wă or "Settlement of the Surrendered Japanese." Some of them were also to be found in Ham-gyŭng and P'yŭng-an Provinces. These had been left behind and

abandoned by their fellows for one cause or another when the
Japanese retired from the north. They were all destined to be
destroyed a quarter of a century later during the rebellion of
Yi Kwal.

About this time there arose in the Chinese court a determined enemy of Gen. Yang Ho named Chung Eung-t'ă who
accused Gen. Yang to the Emperor in twenty-five specifications, five of which implicated the king of Korea and which
at a later date caused a deal of trouble.

We now enter upon a new phase of the war, the closing
epoch. In the first moon of the following year, 1598, the
Emperor sent two admirals to Korea, the one being Tong Il-
wun and the other Chil Lin. The former was to have charge
of the naval operations off the coast of Chŭl-la and the other
of those off Kyŭng-sang Province. Chil Lin, under the title
of Great Admiral came up the Han River with 500 boats as
far as Tong-jak, the first village above Yong-san. The king
and the court went down and reviewed this fleet and saw it
start off to join Admiral Yi Sun-sin in the south. This admiral, Chil Lin, was a good soldier but inordinately vain.
He would take no one's advice, and it looked as if stormy times
were in store for the plain, blunt Admiral Yi. The king told
Admiral Chil Lin that he was not sure about Admiral Yi, and
this of course had its influence with the Chinese admiral.
Admiral Yi was then at Ko-geum Island off Chŭl-la Province.
When he heard that Admiral Chil Lin was coming he showed
by his first act that he was as good a diplomat as soldier. He
may or may not have known what sort of man the Chinese
admiral was but he knew that in any case it would not do to
antagonize him, and he acted accordingly. He collected
a great store of fish and game and wine and went out to meet
the approaching fleet. Returning with the Chinese admiral he
spread a great feast and the whole company got splendidly
drunk and vowed that Admiral Yi was a royal good fellow.
Admiral Chil Lin himself joined in the praise. Soon after
this Admiral Yi had the good luck to take two score of Japanese heads, but instead of claiming the honor himself he
handed them over to the Chinese admiral to forward as his
own trophies. This finished Admiral Yi's conquest of Admiral Chil Lin's good graces. From this time on it was Gen.

Yi who suggested and planned and it was Admiral Chil Lin who assented and reaped the praise. This course of conduct was a master-piece of genius on the part of Admiral Yi, for by so doing he accomplished at least three important things. In the first place he kept himself in his position, which he would have lost had he antagonized the Chinaman. In the second place he saved himself to his country at a time when she could not have spared him. He was willing to forego the praise and let others reap the commendation if only he might ward off the enemies of his country. In the third place he made the Chinese seem successful and so encouraged them and got out of them for Korea all that was to be hoped. He was willing to seem to be toadying to Admiral Chil Lin when in reality that gentleman was, to use a pregnant Korean phrase, "in his sleeve." Being always near the Chinese admiral he could always see to it that no great blunders were made. At first the Chinese soldiery committed great excesses among the people of the country, stealing their valuables and otherwise injuring them. Admiral Yi quietly asked that the discipline of the army be put in his hands and from that day on the smallest irregularity was severely punished and the most perfect order prevailed. This did not escape the eye of Admiral Chil Lin, and he wrote to the king that Admiral Yi was a remarkable man and that the world did not contain another soldier like him. One day as they sat in a summer-house overlooking the sea a fleet of Japanese boats appeared in the distance. Admiral Chil Lin was much excited and a little nervous but Admiral Yi laughed and said, "Sit here and watch me give those fellows a whipping." He got out his boats and in an hour he had forty of the enemy's boats on fire and the rest fled. Admiral Chil Lin could not praise him enough after this and declared that the universe did not contain another man who could perform the feats that Admiral Yi apparently found easy.

In the seventh moon of this year the enemies of Gen. Yang Ho in Nanking were successful and he was called from Korea, much to the regret of the king who vainly sent an envoy to the Chinese court specially to plead that the decree be not carried out. Gen. Yang had been the best of all the generals that China had sent and his departure was a great loss to

Korea. When he went, the king and a large number of the
people accompanied him beyond the Peking Pass, and a stone
tablet was raised there in his honour. All of this of course
made Gen. Yang's enemies hate the king as well, and so that
official named Chung Eung-t'a fabricated some astonishing
stories about him. He claimed that while he had been in
Korea he had found a manuscript which proved that the king
had received investiture from Japan. He also charged the
Koreans with showing disloyalty to China by prefixing the
word *tä* (great) to the posthumous titles of their kings. He
also claimed that the first coming of the Japanese was with a
secret understanding with the king of Korea that they would
attack Liao-tung together. To these he added many minor
charges. The Emperor apparently believed these things and
immediately despatched an envoy, So Kwal-lan, to investigate
the matter and report. When the king was informed of these
charges he was dumbfounded. All his scrupulous care of the
interests of his Chinese suzerain and the extremes of hardship
which he and his people had endured, rather than grant the
Japanese a free passage through Korea to strike China—all
this was thrown back upon him and his devotion was counted
treachery. He left his palace and took up his abode in a straw
hut for one whole month as penance for having been even
suspected of such baseness. The whole country was stirred
to its depths by these unnatural and evidently baseless charges.
The king immediately sent his most trusted councillors Yi
Hang-bok and Yi Chung-gwi to Nanking with the following
memorable reply to the charges which had been preferred :

"These charges which have been made against me are
very grave and if they are true I deserve death. In order to
answer them I must repeat them, even though it defile my
mouth. In the first place the origin of the Japanese is far in
the eastern sea. The way thither by boat is exceeding far.
They are such barbarians that heaven has separated them far
from other men. They have always been bad neighbors, for
they live by piracy ; they come like a flash and are gone as
suddenly. Since the time of the fall of the Koryŭ dynasty
great uneasiness has prevailed in Japan. Law has been in
abeyance and bands of freebooters have been allowed to de-
vastate our southern shores until nothing but weeds and

briers grow there. The founder of our present dynasty drove them out for a time but they grew bold again and continued their depredations. The natives of Tsushima liked to come and trade with us and we permitted it at their request; then Japanese from the more distant islands came in flocks like birds. Our people never liked them, but we permitted the trade, as it was mutually profitable. We gave them rice to eat and treated them kindly. We built a house in Seoul for the reception of their envoys. In the days of king Se-jong they asked us to send an envoy to Japan and we did so, primarily to spy out the land and discover whether the country was rich or poor, strong or weak. The envoy obtained the information and we immediately reported the matter to China. We could not well refuse to send an envoy to Japan, but it does not argue relations of friendship, much less of intimacy. In the days of the Emperor Chong-t'ong the Japanese started to ravage a cerain part of the Chinese coast and took Quelpart on the way, but we attacked and drove them out and sent their leader alive to China to be dealt with. Also in the time of King Chung-jong the Japanese attacked the China coast at Yong P'a-bu. They killed the Chinese general and then made off, but we caught them and sent them to the Chinese authorities. Since that time we have twice prevented Japanese attacks on the China coast. Not once nor twice have we received high commendation from the Chinese Emperor for our firm loyalty. We have always used our wits and our strength in the interests of China. This was the duty of a vassal and this we have done. We let the Japanese live in the three harbors of Ch'e-p'o, Pu-san-p'o and Yŭm-p'o but we prescribed limits of five or ten /i beyond which they could not go. On the whole then is seems plain that the charge that we called in the Japanese and asked them for troops must be a pure fabrication. Again the book which Chung Eung-t'a claims to have found is an actual book and is named the Hadong Keui-ryak. It was written by Sin Suk-ju the envoy to Japan, on his return from that country, and it deals with the laws and manners of the Japanese. It contains a map of Japan, a genealogy and also the rules of etiquette to be observed toward the Japanese envoy. This book our accuser seized upon as a sure sign of our leaning toward Japan, and he twist-

ed its meaning to correspond to his theory. The Japanese
have a different name for the year from that which we use,
and the writer of this book put the Chinese name beneath
the Japanese name as a sort of commentary, so that the reader
could understand what year was referred to. In a Japanese
book one must put the Japanese name of the year and if he
wants to make plain the meaning he must put the Chinese
name underneath or in the margin. As to the charge that we
gave too high a title to our deceased kings we can only say
that we live beyond the sea and are ignorant and secluded.
From the days of Sil-la until now we have been accustomed
to name our dead kings in this way. The founder of the
dynasty was scrupulously careful not to overstep the recognized limits of his authority as a vassal of China and we never
for a moment have forgotten the gap which separates a vassal
king from his suzerain. The custom of giving these posthumous titles dates from the days of Sil-la, so how could we be
expected to know that it was wrong, especially as it has never
been called in question before? If we are blamed for ignorance and boorishness we cry guilty, but if for lack of loyalty,
we humbly deny it. We have our calendar, our official dress
and writing all from China. This alone should speak for our
loyalty. The year before the beginning of the present war
Hideyoshi murdered his master and usurped his throne. Burning with a desire to spring at the throat of China he sent us
letters inviting us to join in an invasion of that country. We
sent his letter back with contumely. In all this we advanced
solely the interests of China. This is as clear as day. When
the invading army came it seemed as if all Japan had alighted
upon our shores. They covered our whole eight provinces
and ravaged them. They seized our three capitals and desecrated two royal tombs. They burned our ancestral temple
and other sacred places and then swept northward to P'yŭng
Yang. We were unable to hold them in check or save our
capital from their hands. We were driven to the verge of
desperation and were about to cross into the parent land to
die. Is it conceivable that if we had the least friendship for
Hideyoshi we would have suffered all this at his hands? If
we look at nature do we find any analogy for such a thing?
If this charge is true why did our forces join with yours in

striking the invaders and why have we been hanging on their
flanks and harassing them for years?   Let the Emperor know
that there is a reason why we have suffered this slander at
the mouth of Chung Eung-t'a.   It is because we took Gen.
Yang Ho's part when Chung-Eung-t'a desired his recall from
Korea in disgrace.   Gen. Yang Ho was with us a long time
and he was a true friend of Korea.   We all had the utmost
confidence in him and it was a great pity that so good a man
should have met the reward he did.   It is a cause of poignant
grief to us.   We are a small people and our destruction is a
matter of small consequence, but for a general of China to be
treated in this manner is a serious matter.   We are an outside
people and we have never had the pleasure of visiting the
Emperor's court, and so there is no one to plead our cause
for us, but the Emperor will be able to judge our case without further plea.   Chung Eung-t'a has called me a traitor,
and I would rather die than live with such a charge upon me,
even though it be untrue.   Let the Emperor take this letter
and sit in judgment on the case and if it appears that I am
guilty let my head pay the penalty, but if not then let the
Emperor acquit me before the world and I shall again be able
to endure the light of day.''

This letter is clear, logical and to the point, and it
breathes a spirit of self-respect which does credit to the king.
It shows not a servile dependence but a true self-respecting
loyalty, and in the firm denial of the charges and the final
demand for condemnation or public acquital there is the ring
of genuine manhood which would do honor to any man in
any age.

When the Emperor read this letter his judicial mind found
in it the ring of conscious rectitude and like the man he was
he instantly acknowleged his error.   He ordered the letter to
be printed by the thousands and tens of thousands and scattered broadcast over his empire, for he apparently felt it a personal honor to have so true and genuine a man for a vassal.
He answered the letter in the following terms:

"I believed the words of slander spoken by that small
man Chung Eung-t'a, and doubted in my mind as to the loyalty of the king of Korea.   I cannot now be oblivious to the
unmerited sufferings of Gen. Yang Ho.   Chung Eung-t'a is

a radically bad man.   I was on the brink of a disastrous mistake.   I will now deprive him of rank and make him one of
the common herd.   Let him appear before me at once."

When Chung Eung-t'a arrived in Naking he was cut in
two at the waist.

Chapter   III.

Japanese mix with Koreans   ..Chinese and Korean advance ...Japan-
    ese victory ...attempts at bribery ...Admiral Yi Sun sin's last fight
    ....a young Korean captive ...Hideyoshi poisoned....his character
    ....Japanese recalled ...a Korean teacher in Japan ...a memorial
    temple ...party changes ...Japanese envoy .. posthumous honors
    ...factional strife ...revenue ...envoy to Japan ...a welcome
    heir....negotiations with Japan ...a dark outlook ...Chinese com-
    missioner duped....treaty with Japan ...reign of terror ...the
    young prince murdered.

By this time the Japanese were becoming mixed with the
Korean people among whom and near whom their camps were
placed.   They were probably good customers and the people
doubtless felt that it was not their business to fight them ; so
all up and down the coast for a distance of three hundred
miles the Japanese lived in their "holes" as the Koreans called them, and in many cases they took wives from among the
women of the country and devoted themselves to farming, except at such times as the Korean or Chinese forces came into
their vicinity.   There were three Japanese military centers.
One was at Ul-san on the eastern coast, held by Konishi.   In
the west was Sun-ch'un in Chŭl-la Province where Kato had
his headquarters, while half way between these two in the
town of Sa-ch'un on the Si-jin River a third station was held
by, Gen. Sok Mang-ja.   These three stations kept up regular
communication with each other, and in case of need rendered
each other assistance.

We now enter the last campaign of this eventful war.
We are not informed as to the numbers of the Japanese at this
time but it probably fell short of 100,000 men.   The Chinese
had assembled again in force at Seoul and in the ninth moon

of 1598 a grand move was made against the invaders. The
Chinese forces were led by Generals Hyöng Kă and Man Se-
dŭk. The whole army was divided into four grand army
corps. Gen. Ma Kwi led the eastern division southward to
attack Ul-san. Under him were eleven other generals and
24,000 men.

The central division, of 13,000 men, was led by Gen.
Tong Il-wŭn under whom were eight other generals. The
western division was led by Gen. Yu Chung and six other generals with a force of 13,000 men. The admiral of this campaign was Chil Lin who was already in the south with eight
other commanders handling 13,200 men. It is said that the
entire expedition numbered 142,700 men, but the above items
sum up to less than half that and we must conclude that there
were something less than 100,000 men in all.

On the last day of the ninth moon, already well on toward winter, the three divisions deployed before the walls of
Ul-san. Kato had not been idle all this time ; after the terrible scenes of the last siege he had made the best of preparations. He had accumulated an abundance of food, increased
the garrison, strengthened the defenses, and he could laugh
at any force that should try to sit out the winter before him.
The Chinese soon discovered this and turned aside to work
that promised better success. Gen. Tong Il-wŭn took a
powerful force and advanced on Sa-chŭn, the central station
of the Japanese. It is probable that the garrison here was
smaller than those under either Kato or Konishi, for when
its commander saw the force that was brought to bear upon
him he hastily evacuated the place and crossed over to the
island of Pom-neut and fortified it. Gen. Tong was over-
confident and pressed after him. The Japanese craftily drew
him on and on until his force was immediately under the wall,
when a mine was exploded which, though it killed but a few
hundred men, threw the whole attacking body into such confusion that the Japanese rushed out and found them an easy
prey. The Chinese lay in heaps where they had been cut
down. Gen. Tong barely escaped with his life and fled to
Sam-gă, being chased as far as the Nam-gang (river) where
the Japanese contented themselves with making way with
12,000 bags of rice belonging to the Chinese commissariat.

Gen. Yu Chung was commissioned to take a strong body
of men and attack the fortress at Sun-ch'ŭn in Chŭl-la Province.   Arriving at the neighboring village of Wă-gyo he
determined to overcome the old veteran Kato by treachery.
He sent to that general a proposition to make peace.   Kato
was now an old man and the war in Korea was bringing him
neither fame nor advancement, so he was ready to give up
the contest, now that it had been demonstrated that the Japanese arms could not penetrate the north.   He gladly assented and sent Gen. Yu a present of two handsome swords
It was agreed that they should meet at a certain point, ac-.
companied by only 3000 men each ; but Gen. Yu secretly
placed an ambush in such wise that when the Japanese force
should come out it could be cut off from return to the fort.
A whistle was to be sounded as a signal when the Japanese
came out.   But Kato was too old a bird to be caught by such
a child's trick.   He had seen two or three of the Chinese
lurking about in the vicinity of the gate and so delayed his
coming out.   By mistake the signal was given and the Chinese ambuscade rushed out only to become an object of ridicule
to the Japanese.   But even as it was some eighty or ninety
Japanese stragglers were cut off and taken by the Chinese.
Gen. Yu then surrounded the stronghold and at the same
time sent an urgent letter to Admiral Chil Lin to come that
very night and join in an attack on the Japanese.   The
admiral obeyed the summons and hurried up with his fleet.
Not knowing about the tides and supposing that the shouts
that he heard were the shouts of battle, he sailed straight up
under the walls of the fortress.   But he found that there was
no fight on for Gen. Yu had failed to connect, and the ebbing
tide left the astonished Admiral high and dry on the mud
flats under the very noses of the enemy.   In the morning the
Japanese trooped out and burned forty-eight of the stranded
ships and killed most of the men.   Admiral Chil escaped in
the early morning by boat and hurried to the camp of his
tardy compatriot, Gen. Yu.   In a rage he tore down with his
own hands that general's flag and rent it in pieces, meanwhile
heaping upon him every species of abuse for having gotten
him into such a plight.   Gen. Yu was exceedingly ashamed
and his face, they say, was "the color of dirt."   He beat upon

his breast and acknowledged that he deserved death. So Chil Lin went back to his decimated camp to nurse his wrath.

But Gen. Yu knew that Kato really desired to put an end to the war, and so he sent another messenger saying, "This time I really mean peace. If you will take all your forces and depart I will give you a clear path to escape. Our army numbers 140,000 men and you cannot hope to face that number." To this proposition Kato assented and began immediately to embark his soldiers to send them back to Japan. But as it happened they had to pass the position of Admiral Chil Lin who naturally sallied out and gave fight, sinking or burning a dozen or more of Kato's boats. The rest put back in haste to the starting place and Kato blamed Gen. Yu for having deceived him; but the latter claimed that he had merely forgotten to inform Admiral Chil Lin of the agreement and that he would do so. At the same time he advised Kato to send Admiral Chil a slight testimonial of regard, which he did in the shape of a hundred ounces of silver and forty-five swords. So Admiral Chil acquiesced. Again the Japanese fleet set out and succeeded in getting by Admiral Chil Lin's place ; but they had not reckoned upon Admiral Yi Sun-sin and his faithful warriors. Kato was again obliged to turn back and go to work to bribe that doughty leader. He sent him guns and swords in large numbers but the old gentleman remarked that as for weapons he was already pretty well supplied, and sent them back. He was then approached with an offer of 1,000 ounces of silver if he would wink at Kato's passage. This he likewise refused.

The Japanese were all embarked and it was determined to try and slip by the terrible Admiral in the gray of morning ; but he was well aware of the intentions of the enemy, and before break of day he massed all the ships at his command and came down upon the Japanese fleet as it lay at anchor before the fortress of Sun-ch'ŭn. As he approached he is said to have uttered the following prayer to his gods : "To-day I am to die. Give me but one more victory over these Japanese and I shall die content." He well knew that he had enemies at court who would eventually secure his downfall and so he determined to make an end in one last desperate struggle. The fight was short and fierce and when the morning breeze swept the smoke of battle away it disclosed fifty of the Japanese boats in flames and the water filled with struggling forms. The old veteran had taken upwards of two thousand heads in that brief time. But Gen. Kato had slipped away in a small boat and made his escape. The work however was only begun. The sea was covered with boats frantically endeavoring to escape from the dreaded arm of the merciless Admiral Yi. The good work went on and every hour added to the score that Admiral Yi had sworn to made before the night should fall. Notice reached him that a fresh Japanese fleet had come and was attacking Admiral Chil Lin's fleet. Hurrying thither he found that it was indeed true. He now changed his tactics and without coming to a hand to hand fight he circled round and round the Japanese fleet driving them closer and closer together. When all was ready he began playing upon them with a new machine of his own manufacture called the pun-t'ong or "spraying tube." What this was we can not exactly discover, but in a short time it sufficed to set the Japanese fleet on fire. A wind sprang up and fanned the flame and ere long the Japanese fleet was one mass of fire. Hundreds of boats were consumed with all their occupants. After seeing this well under way Admiral Yi turned his attention to the fugitive craft that were striving to make their escape. Standing in the prow of his boat in an exposed position he urged on the chase. While he stood in the midst of one of the grandest victories of the war, he was pierced by a bullet. They caught him as he fell, and his last words were, "Do not let the rest know that I am dead, for it will spoil the fight." Then he expired—the man who may well be called the NELSON of Korea.

Yi Wan, the nephew of the fallen Admiral, still urged on the battle; but the work was almost done. The fugitive boats became fewer and fewer. Admiral Chil Lin happened to come near the boat of the dead admiral and noticing that the sailors in it were quarrelling over some Japanese heads he exclaimed, "The Admiral must be dead." He entered the boat and found it even so. Throwing himself three times at full length on the deck he uttered this lament: "I thought that he would save me and still live, but here he lies dead and there is no soldier now left in Korea."

We have now come to the end of actual hostilities in the peninsula but we must cross to Japan and inquire into the immediate causes which led to the final recall of all the Japanese troops. The Korean account of these events is very remarkable and faith is to be put in it only in-so-far as it is not directly antagonized by the Japanese account. For events that transpired in Korea the Korean account must be taken as the standard, but for events that transpired in Japan the Japanese account must of course be accepted as the more trustworthy. The Korean account is as follows.

When the Japanese first invaded Korea, in the year 1592, it so happened that a young Korean boy named Yang Pu-ha, a native of Tong-nă, became attached to the Japanese army as a slave, and was eventually taken to Tsushima. From there he made his way to the mainland of Japan and at last reached the court of Hideyoshi. That observant man spied him out and said, "Korean and Japanese boys resemble each other strongly. Take this boy and teach him Japanese, and if he does not learn well cut off his head." With this incentive it would be strange if a less intelligent boy than Yang Pu-ha would not learn rapidly. In the space of three months he could converse creditably in Japanese, and Hideyoshi as reward made him one of his body-servants. For some years the boy performed the duties of this position, until at last the Chinaman Sim Yu-gyŭng arrived. That official was kept practically in confinement at the court of Hideyoshi. One day the Korean servant asked his master to be allowed to see Sim Yu-gyŭng. Permission was granted and the young man found the Chinese envoy in great perplexity, in fact in tears. This excited the pity of the young man and he secured the release of the Chinaman, who from that time was often called into the presence of Hideyoshi, with whom he soon became on familiar terms. One day as he sat with the great Taiko he took out a pill and swallowed it. He did the same on several days in succession until at last the curiosity of Hideyoshi was excited and he asked what it was. The Chinaman answered that it was an antidote to indigestion and that by eating it the strength and vigor of the body was preserved intact. Hideyoshi took one in his hand and eyed it suspiciously. On one side of the pill was written the Chinese character *so* meaning "hot." The Japanese deliberately took a knife and cut the pill in two and handing half to Sim said, "You eat half and I will eat half." Its immediate effects were stimulating and pleasant but in the end it proved a deadly poision for it slowly dried up the blood. Each day Sim shared one with his captor but upon retiring to his room swallowed a potion which entirely neutralized the effect of the poison. Before long Hideyoshi's hands began to grow hard and dry and one day when he happened to cut his hand he was astonished to find that no blood followed. He called for a moxa and applied it to his hand and yet no blood came. Then he laughed aloud and cried, "I am a dead man. When I cease to breathe take out·my bowels and sew my body up again with horsehair ; and then preserve my body in wine and do not let the outsiders know that I am dead." He wanted to have the fact concealed for he feared it would have a dispiriting effect upon the troops in Korea. Shortly after this he died and his orders were minutely carried out. For two months no one outside the palace knew of his decease, but at last the stench became so great that they confessed that the great Hideyoshi had passed away. Such is the Korean story.

The Koreans sum up his character as follows: He was a crafty and cunning man, and by his talk, now sharp, now suave, now sarcastic, now bullying, he managed to sway the minds of all who came near him. He managed all his generals like puppets. He liked to take boys and girls under his patronage and see them grow up together and marry them to each other and thus have them completely under his control. His two most powerful generals were Whi Wŭn and Ka Kang. They hated him and would have been glad of an opportunity to overthrow him, but it was out of the question. He knew them well, and for fear they might combine against him he made one of them governor of the east and the other of the west and ordered them to keep watch of each other. By thus pitting them against each other he made himself safe. He loved intrigue and diplomacy and had a most restless temperament. He was ever on the lookout for some kind of excitement. Gen. Ka Kang was with him when he died, and, fearing lest rebellion should break out, he filled the body with salt and so preserved it. He made a wooden form which would hold the body stiff in a sitting position and placing it in a place where the light was not very bright with the eyes wide open, the people saw him sitting there day after day and supposed of course he was alive. It was in the eighth moon when the odor was so strong that the truth could no longer be concealed. Thereupon Gen. Ka Kang took the son of Hideyoshi and made him Shogun. He then threw into prison the wives and children of Generals Kato and Konishi and sent a messenger ordering them to collect all their troops and return immediately to Japan. The order was obeyed willingly and all that was left of the Japanese army of invasion set sail from Fusan, and the great invasion was a thing of the past. 4

The Korean annalists say that when the invasion began the Japanese arms were far superior to those of Korea ; also that the Japanese displayed tiger skins, pheasant feathers, gilded masks and plumes ; all which glitter and show terrified the Koreans. Thus at first the Japanese had an easy victory, but toward the last it was not so. The Koreans had improved their arms and had learned not to fear the grand rush of the Japanese in their hideous masks which made them look more like demons than men.

At the time of the second invasion a Korean named Kang Han was caught and sent to Japan and, being unable to escape, he set to work learning Japanese. He became a teacher of Chinese and had a large following of students who treated him very well and supported him in comfortable style. At the end of the war they clubbed together and bought a boat into which they put this man with all his goods and sent him back to Korea. On his return he wrote a book entitled Kang yang-rok or "Relation of Adventures among Sheep," a sarcastic pleasantry.

The Chinese arms in Korea did not move till the following spring, and then the king sent to the Emperor asking that Generals Man Se-dok, Ta Cham and Yi Sung-hun be allowed to remain in Korea for a time until things should become thoroughly settled.

In the early centuries of the Christian era there was a celebrated Chinese general named Kwan U. He was of gigantic size and had a fiery red face, rode a powerful red horse, could walk a thousand li a day (!) and carried a sword that weighed 800 pounds (!!). It is said that while the Japanese were occupying Seoul the spirit of this great man appeared repeatedly near the South and East Gates and struck terror to the hearts of the Japanese. Now, as the Chinese generals were about to leave for China, Admiral Chil Lin built a shrine to this same Kwan U outside the South Gate. In the thirty-third year of King Sun-jo, namely 1600 A. D., the Emperor sent four million cash to build a temple to this Kwan U and the present temple outside the South Gate was erected. The Emperor at the same time ordered another to be built by the Koreans outside the East Gate, and it was done. The two temples are exactly alike. When the king asked the Emperor to name the temple he said "Call it the Hyöng-nyung-so dok-kwan-gong" which means "The great and bright appearance of the spirit of Kwan." The king also built shrines to him in Song-ju and An-dong of Kyŭng-sang Province, and at Nam-wŭn in Chŭl-la Province.

We have already seen that factious fights had been a great cause of weakness all through the years of the invasion, and from this time on party strife was destined to grow more and more fierce and determined until it brought the country to the very verge of anarchy a century later. We must note here briefly the changes which had taken place in the parties. We will remember that at first there were two parties, the Tong-in and the Sŭ-in. During the war the court favorite was Yu Sŭng-nyŭng who gave office to so many men from Kyŭng-sang Province that the name of Nam-in or "South Men" sprang up and a party by that name quickly became organized, but their opponents in order to preserve the political equilibrium instantly seized upon the name Puk-in or "North Men." At the close of the war the leader of the opposition, namely of the Puk-in, memorialized the king against Yu Sŭng-nyŭng the favorite, charging him with having desired to make peace with the Japanese, contrary to the honor of the country. The king listened to this and banished Yu, but his supporters turned the tables by a counter-memorial in which the charges were more than answered and Yu was restored to all his honors. With the rise of the Nam-in and Puk-in parties the old party lines of the Tong-in and Sŭ-in had not been broken up or lost. During the latter years of the invasion the Nam-in party lost its powerful grip and the Puk-in were often in power, but from the end of the invasion until far into the following reign the Tong-in held the power, and after that for a period of fifty years the Sŭ-in had control of affairs. It may be asked what principles underlay these parties, what settled policies they had that differentiated them either in domestic or foreign matters. We answer that the various parties had but one plank in their platforms, one settled plan of action, and that was to get the ear of the king and seize upon the office-making power and put in every position one's own partisans. It was the spoils system sublimated, for there was absolutely no admixture of any other element.

Now that the war was over the Japanese on Tsushima desired to open again commercial relations with Korea, which had always been mutually profitable; and so in the following year, 1601, an envoy, Kuroda, came from that island bringing with him three hundred men and women who had been carried away captive during the war. This envoy asked that there might be reciprocity of trade. The king referred the matter to Nanking and the reply seems to have been in the affirmative, for we find that soon after this an envoy was sent over to Tsushima with credentials; but after all the Japanese petition was not at this time granted. At the same time the Emperor gave orders for the return to China of all the remaining troops, but at the earnest request of the king 8000 men were left to help guard the southern provinces. Posthumous honors were heaped upon Admiral Yi Sun-sin who had been the very salvation of Korea, but who had sought death in battle, knowing that if he lived his detractors would drag him down. Yi Hang-bok and eighty-five others received high commendation and additional honors also. The year ended with the unsuccessful attempt of an insurrectionary party in the south which was nipped in the bud, the ringleader being forwarded to seoul to be beheaded.

An unscrupulous man named Yu Yong-gyŭng was the court favorite at this time and upon him devolved the task of appointing and dismissing officials; consequently he was the recipient of countless presents, and on one occasion two men

to whom he had sold the same office met at his gate and quarrelled over the matter, to the scandal of the court. The state of
affairs at the capital was anything but satisfactory, the reason
being that the strife of parties rendered honesty and fairness
impossible. It was a constant fight to gain the king's ear
and, having gained it, to turn out all enemies and put in personal adherents. About this time a remeasurement of all the
arable land of the country was ordered and it was discovered
that the total revenue of the country was 1,515,500 *kyul* of rice,
each *kyul* being about 120 pecks of rice, or over two hundred
pounds. It also included 300,000 bags of other grains.

In they year 1605 the Japanese again asked that a
treaty be made and that Korea send an envoy to the Japanese
court. The king complied and sent the same monk, Yu
Chung, ordering him to look carefully into the matter of the
military strength of the Island Empire and the distance by
boat. He returned the following year bringing with him,
it is said, three thousand Koreans who had been taken to
Japan from time to time during the invasion. The Korean
accounts tell us nothing of the booty that the Japanese carried
away to Japan during the war, nor of the transportation of
Korean artisans and their employment in Japan in teaching
the making of pottery and other works of use and art, but we
may well believe the Japanese reports, that assert that immense amounts of treasure were carried away and that the
making of the beautiful Satsuma ware was an outcome of the
teaching of Korean artisans.

This year was also signalized by a fierce conflict between
the savage tribe of Hol-cha-on, north of the Tu-man River,
and the government troops under Gen. Song U-gil. The latter
crossed the river by night and attacked the main settlement
of the tribe and utterly destroyed it, and effectually broke up
the tribe. Great quantities of goods which had been stolen
from the border settlements were also recovered.

We are now on the threshold of events which led up to a
very painful period in Korean history. It will be remembered
that the king had no heir by the queen and had therefore
nominated to the throne his heir by a concubine, the Prince
Kwang-hä. This was a man of violent temper, bad instincts,
corrupt, selfish, careless of the publc good. When therefore

the king, in the fortieth year of his reign, was presented with a son by his queen, his delight was as great as was the chagrin of the heir apparent. According to law it was impossible to set aside the man already nominated, but now that the king finally got the boy he had been looking for so long, his feelings got the better of his judgment and he was bent upon having the child receive all the honors due to the future wearer of the crown. So he sent out the order that officials should come to the palace and do obeisance as when an heir to the throne is born. This was the most impolitic thing he could have done, for it aroused all the hatred there was in the Prince Kwang-hă. who had for so many years looked upon his eventual occupancy of the throne as fully assured, and who saw in these demonstrations of affection on the part of the king a latent desire to change the decree which had already gone forth. If the king really desired to set aside that decree he should have sent to Nanking and had the Emperor do it, but it was not so to be, and the infant boy entered the world with one deadly enemy ranged against him, whose first act would be to put him out of the way. Nor was it the boy alone who gained the hatred of this prince. The queen herself became the object of his special hatred, and the official who sent forth the order that honor should be done to the infant.

The Japanese kept urging their point, that relations of mutual benefit be resumed, and kept protesting their good intentions toward Korea. The king had just received an envoy bringing gifts and a congratulatory letter from the king of the Liu Kiu Islands, in which grave doubts were cast upon the intentions of the Japanese, and an offer of assistance was made in case of another invasion. But the king seems not to have put faith in these doubts, and replied, to the reiterated request of the Japanese, that an envoy would be sent to Japan, when the men who desecrated the royal graves beyond the Han River should be sent to the Korean Capital for punishment. The Japanese went home, but returned late in the fall bringing two men bound, whom they delivered over as being the ones demanded. But these were mere boys who themselves urged the fact that they were still babes in arms when the deeds of which they were charged had been committed. The Prime Minister urged the king to send them back to Japan, but the favorite, Yu, persuaded the king to have them beheaded, after which Yö U-gil, Kyöng Sün and Chung Ho-gwan were sent as an embassy to Japan. Meanwhile Iyeyasu in Japan had deposed the son of Hideyoshi and usurped his place. So when the embassy arrived in Japan they were received with the utmost coldness, and the usurper said, "Who asked that envoys might be exchanged between Japan and Korea? But now that you are here we will receive you." The treatment that they received was bad almost beyond description. As a sample of the way the Japanese baited them it is related that the Japanese brought a dish filled with ordure sprinkled with something the color of gold-dust, and when the Koreans innocently put their hands in the dish, supposing that it was some form of food, the Japanese had a good laugh at their expense. The Koreans did not appreciate this sort of practical joke, and forthwith returned to Korea.

Late in the autumn the aged king was taken sick and all knew that the end was near. The conditions were not propitious. The young prince was only two years old and Prince Kwang-hä was fierce in his resentments and jealous of anyone who should attempt to block his path to the throne. The people were in a very uneasy frame of mind. The king had gone either too far or not far enough in the advocacy of the infant prince, and now he felt that he was leaving the child to the tender mercies of a relentless enemy. He therefore called in the Prime Minister and said, "Everything looks dark ahead and I am dying. I suppose the Prince Kwang-hä must become king?" But the Prime Minister dared not answer the question as the king wanted it answered, and hung back. By so doing he sealed his own fate. There were only two things for him to do, either to boldly advocate the claims of the child or else boldly advocate those of Prince Kwang-hä. By doing neither he made an enemy of the one and spoiled the chances of the other, and thus signed his own death warrant. As it happened, Prince Kwang-hä had an elder brother, but why he had not been nominated to the throne we are not told. This prince, named Im-hä, was now induced to make the attempt to wrest the reins of power from his brother so as to save the people from what they feared at the hands of Prince Kwang-ha, but the latter got wind of the plot and the elder prince was summarily banished, together with all his coadjutors.

So matters went on until one day in early spring of the following year, 1608, when a servant came from the king's private rooms saying that he was dying. All the officials assembled at the palace. It is said that Prince Kwang-hă had become impatient at the tenacity of life shown by the aged king and had assisted nature in taking him off, but this, we may surmise, is rather a general deduction from the character of the man than a proved charge, and this prince has so much else to answer for that we may well give him the benefit of the doubt and conclude that the king reached his end by nat- ural causes alone. The assembled noblemen sat in the room adjoining the one in which the king lay dying. Presently a eunuch brought out a note which read thus, "When I am dead let Prince Kwang-hă be kind to the infant boy." When the ministers had read it they sent it to the prince. Soon an- other note came from the sick room, "To the seven ministers of state ; I am dying. I have but one cause of anxiety ; the boy is young and I shall not be here to see him come to man- hood. Let him be tenderly cared for." This was the end. The king turned to the wall and expired.

Upon hearing the welcome news the Prince Kwang-hă hastened to assume the position he had coveted so long. His first act was to send the Prime Minister Yu Yŏng-gyŭng into banishment. Then he sent an embassy to China to announce his accession to the throne. The Emperor replied, "Why is not the elder son, Prince Im-hă, made king?" and sent a commission to inquire into the matter. Prince Im was brought from Kyo-dong Island to which place he had been banished. One of the creatures of the newly crowned king advised that the head only of Prince Im be brought, but the aged Yi Hang- bok opposed it so strongly that the king dare not follow his in- clination ; but when Prince Im was brought he was "made up" for the occasion. He was unkempt and filthy, his clothes were in rags and the very sight of him decided the unsuspicious commissioner and he ordered the wretched man to be sent back to his place of banishment at once. For fear of further complications and to satisfy his vengeful nature, the king sent a secret messenger to the prefect of Kyo-dong and had Prince Im poisoned in prison. He next proceeded to kill the banished Prime Minister, and then had his body brought to the center of the capital and cut in half lengthwise.

The Japanese had for several years been pressing for the resumption of the old-time relations, half diplomatic and half commercial, which had been carried on through the southern port of Fusan. Now in the first year of the reign of Kwang-hä, consent was gained and Yi Chi-wan for Korea and Gensho and Yoshinao for Japan met and worked out a plan for a treaty. The Japanese insisted that all three of the ports which had formerly been open should again be opened, but this was peremptorily refused and only Fusan was opened. The number of boats that could come annually was reduced to twenty. Great diplomatic agents from the Shogun were allowed to stay in Korea one hundred and ten days. The agents from any daimyo of Japan could stay eighty-five days and special agents could stay fifty-five days. The strictness with which the Koreans bound down the Japanese as to number of ships and men and length of stay, and the refusal to open three ports, show that Korea was doing this all more as a favor than by demand, and history shows that at any time she felt at liberty to withdraw support from them. The amount of rice and other food that Korea granted was hardly more than enough to support the embassy when it came.

It will be remembered that the king was the son of a concubine and not of the queen. He now went to work to depose the queen and set up his mother, though now dead, as real queen. He gave his mother the posthumous title of Kong-söng Wang-ho and sent the deposed queen into semi-banishment to the Myŭng-ye Palace in Chong-dong, where the king now resides. This act was looked upon as utterly unfilial and godless by the officials, and they almost unanimously censured his harsh treatment of this woman.

The next three years were spent in killing off all who had been specially favored under the last king, excepting the venerable Yi Hang-bok, who stood so high in the esteem of the people that even the wicked king did not dare to lay hands upon him. One method of getting rid of objectionable people was to promise release to some criminal if he would swear that he had heard the men conspiring against the king ; but the king's thirst for blood could not be quenched so long as the young prince was living. The latter was now six or seven years old. No one dared to make a move against him openly, but the officials knew that if they wanted to become favorites with the king it could be done only by suggesting some plan whereby the boy could be killed without bringing on a general insurrection. It was accomplished as follows. Pak Eung-su, a well-known resident of Yŭ-ju became a highwayman. He was captured and taken to Seoul for trial. After he had been condemned, Yi I-ch'ŭm the court favorite sent to him in prison and said, "You are to die to-morrow, but if you will declare that you and several other men have conspired to depose the king and place the young prince on the throne you will not only be released but rewarded as well." When therefore the king received the written confession of the wretch he feigned surprise but instantly caught and executed the principals named. His satellites also urged that he must kill the young prince and his mother, for they must surely be privy to the plot. And her father too must be beheaded. The king did not dare to go to these lengths all at once, but he began by beheading the queen's father, and banishing the boy to Kang-wha. When the men came to take him he hid beneath his mother's skirt but the brutal captors pushed her over and dragged the lad away. These acts enraged the people almost beyond endurance and memorials poured in upon the king from people who preferred death itself to permitting such acts to go unchallenged. The king however answered them one and all by killing the writers or stripping them of rank and banishing them.

As the boy had been separated from his mother and banished to Kang-wha, he could be dealt with at pleasure. His death would remain unknown for a time, and the matter would pass by unnoticed. So in the following year, at the instigation of Yi I-ch'ŭm, the magistrate of Kang wha put the boy in a small room, built a roaring fire under it and suffocated him, an extreme of barbarity which the world can hardly parallel. The news soon spread among the officials. Scores of memorials poured in upon the king who answered them as before by banishment and death.

Chapter IV.

The king insulted ...the "Mulberry Palace"....plot against the Queen
Dowager....her indictment ...she is degraded ...inception of the
Manchu power....China summons Korea to her aid....troops despatched....first battle with the Manchus ...Korean treachery ...
Koreans make friends with the Manchus....the Manchu court....a
Manchu letter to the king ...its answer....Manchu rejoinder....
message to Nanking....Chinese refugees....a Korean renegade
....the Queen intercedes for China ...Chinese victory....Manchu
cruelty....offices sold ...plot against the king ...king dethroned
..Queen Dowager reinstated ...reforms ...a thorough cleaning
out.

With the opening of the year 1615 the king further revealed his hatred of the deposed and degraded queen by
publishing broadcast the statement that she had gone to the
grave of his mother and there, by practicing sorcery against
him, had tried to bring evil upon him. This also brought out
a loud protest from all honest men, and banishment followed.
Even the children on the street spoke insultingly of the tyrant
saying that he was afraid of the imps at the Myŭng-ye Palace,
but had let his mother stay there with them though he himself would not go near the place. The king feared everyone
that was honest and upright even though they had nothing
to say. His own cousin, Prince Neung-ch'ang, whose younger brother afterward became king, was a perfectly peaceable
and harmless man, but the king feared him and could not
rest satisfied until he had gotten his satellites to accuse him
of sedition and had suffocated him in a heated chamber on
Kyo-dong Island. About this time a monk, named Seung-ji;
gained the confidence of the superstitious king and induced
him to build the In-gyŭng Palace which is commonly known
among foreigners as the "Mulberry Palace." To do this,
thousands of the houses of the common people were razed and
heavy taxes were levied throughout the country; and yet
there was not enough money. So the king began to sell the
public offices. Some were paid for in gold, others in silver,
others in iron, and still others in wood, stone or salt. The

people derisively called it the *O-hăng*, referring to the "Five Rules of Conduct" of the Confucian Code. The boys also made up a popular song which ran as follows, "Did you give gold, or silver, or wood for yours?" and they put the officials to shame by shouting it at them as they passed along the street.

Yi I-ch'ŭm, the favorite, could not rest until he had carried out his master's wish and had invented some way to destroy the degraded Queen. Finding no other way to accomplish this, he at last descended to the following trick. He instructed a man named Hŭ Kyun to write a letter to the imprisoned queen purporting to be from some party in the country, proposing a scheme for deposing the king. This letter was thrown over the wall of the queen's enclosure and there found by the servants of the crafty plotter. The king was ready to believe anything against her and this letter fanned his hatred into flame. Yi I-ch'ŭm followed it up by joining with scores of others in memorials urging the king to put to death the hated Queen Dowager. The Prime Minister, Keui Cha-hŏn, stood in the way, however, and it became necessary to banish him to the far north. In the eleventh moon the king finally decided to drive the woman from Seoul, and made all the officials give their opinion about it in writing. Nine hundred and thirty officials and a hundred and seventy of the king's relatives advised to do so, but the aged Yi Hang-bok with eight others utterly refused their sanction of the iniquitous plan ; and so these nine men, the last of those upright men who had stood about the late king, were sent into banishment.

The year thus closed in gloom and the new one opened with a memorial from the Prime Minister Hau Hyo-san enumerating ten charges against the Queen Dowager; (1) that she had had the officials do obeisance to the young prince although the successor to the throne had already been appointed ; (2) when the king was dying she asked him to set aside Prince Kwang-hă in favor of the young prince ; (3) she prevented, as long as possible, the king from handing over the scepter to Prince Kwang-hă; (4) she wrote the letters purporting to be from the dying king asking that the young prince be carefully nurtured ; (5) she instigated her father to conspire against the king ; (6) she sacrificed in the palace and prayed

for the death of Prince Kwang-hǎ; (7) she prayed for the same
at the grave of his mother ; (8) she corresponded with outside
parties with a view to raising an insurrection; (9) she sent to
the Emperor asking to have Prince Kwang-hǎ set aside, (10)
she sent to Japan asking that an army be sent to overthrow
the government.

The king feigned to be very loath to believe all these
charges and to act upon them ; he called heaven to witness
that the very thought of it was terrible to him and averred
that he would rather be banished to some distant shore than
even to mention such a thing. But after a great deal of urging he was prevailed upon, and said he could no longer be
deaf to the entreaties of his subjects and the welfare of the
country. So he took away her title of Tǎ-bi and decreed that
she should be called Sǔ-gung "West Palace," and that she
should receive no part of the government revenue, that officials
should no more do homage to her, that her marriage certificate be burned and that all her wedding garments be taken
from her. He determined also that in the event of her death
no one should assume mourning, that her name should be in-
scribed in no ancestral temple, and that she should be shut
up in her own apartments and strictly guarded.

And now there appeared in the northwest a cloud which
was destined to overspread the whole of Korea, and China as
well. Norach'i was chief of the Manchu tribes. He was from
the wild tribe of Kön-ju which, as we have seen, was broken
up by a Korean military expedition. His grandfather's name
was Kyu-sang and his father's name was Hapsiri. These had
both been put to death by a Chinese general, A-t'ǎ, and to the
unquenchable hatred caused by this must be ascribed the terrible reprisals the young Norach'i made on China, where his
descendants occùpy the imperial throne to this day. At the
time of his father's death he had fled eastward beyond the
reach of China's arm but gradually gaining power he crept
slowly westward again until he had a footing on the great
Manchu plains. But he was not yet ready to carry out his
plans against China, and when the Mongol, Hapuigeukosip,
entered the great wall and overthrew the Chinese general Yu
Pu, Norach'i caught him and sent his head to Nanking. The
Emperor was pleased at this and gave him the rank of "Dra-

gon Tiger General." Having thus disarmed suspicion, the hardy northman began gathering and training troops until there stood about him 10,000 skillful archers. Some years before this he had killed his younger brother for fear of complications and now in the year of the events of which we are writing he had overcome the three great Chinese generals Yi Yong-bang, Chang Seung-yun and Yang Yö-gwi. The ruling dynasty of the Ming in China became well aware of the gravity of the situation and saw that it was necessary to square themselves for a desperate fight with the great Manchu leader The first act of the Emperor was to send a summons to the King of Korea ordering him to send generals and troops at once to join the Chinese forces against Norach'i. The king responded by sending a man to find out the exact state of affairs, whether China was weak or strong and whether it would pay to help her in the coming struggle. This was paying China back in kind for her delay in sending aid when the Japanese invaded the peninsula, but Korea was thoroughly loyal to the Ming power. She may be criticised in many ways but there was never shown a deeper loyalty or devotion than Korea showed the Mings during the years of struggle against the Manchus, a devotion that always worked against her own selfish interests.

The Chinese general Yang Ho sent back to the king and said, "When we ask for aid do you merely send a spy to find out how matters stand? This war is as much in your interests as ours, so you had best send an army at once to form a junction with us in Liao-tung." However little stomach the king had for the war this appeal was too strong to be set aside. Even this base king could not overlook the tremendous obligation under which Korea lay on account of aid rendered by China against the Japanese. He therefore appointed generals Kang Hong-rip and Kim Kyöng-sŭ as first and second in command and under them three other generals, Chŭng Ho-sŭ, Yi Chung-nam and Chŭng Eung-jŭng. These men were put in command of 20,000 troops drawn from the five provinces of P'yŭng-an, Ham-gyŭng, Kyŭng-keui, Ch'ung-ch'ŭng and Chulla, and they were ordered to the northern border. This was toward the close of the year, but before its end the Chinese sent a messenger to hurry forward the Korean troops, as it was intended to make a grand demonstration with the opening of the new year.

In the first month of 1619 the troops went forward to the seat of war. It was in the middle of winter and most of the soldiers were going from a comparatively warm climate into the rigors of a semi-arctic region. The Chinese Gen. Yang Ho was advancing upon the Manchu position by four different roads. The whole army rendezvoused at Sim-ha in Liao-tung not far from the Korean border town of Eui-ju. The combined forces were led by four generals, Yang Ho, Yu Chŭng, Kyo Il-geui and the Korean Kang Hong-rip. Meeting a small body of five hundred Manchu troops they drove them back into the hills with considerable slaughter, and fondly supposed that all the Manchus could be put to flight as easily. In this preliminary skirmish the Koreans took a leading part, and one general was killed and another was wounded in the hand. The next day the whole force advanced to a place called Pu-go. The right and left flanks of the army were composed of Chinese and the center was held by Gen. Kang Hong-rip with his Korean troops. Suddenly, almost without warning, ten thousand Manchu horsemen swept down upon the right flank. The impetuosity of the charge carried everything before it, and almost instantly the whole right wing was thrown into confusion and took to precipitate flight, in which both Gen. Yu Chŭng and Gen. Yang Ho were killed. Then the Manchu chief Kwi Yŭng-ga with 30,000 men came across the Ka-hap Pass and fell upon the left flank, and that too was routed in short order. The center under Gen. Kang had not yet been attacked and stood unmoved by, and not unlikely unconscious of, the terrible destruction being meted out to their allies to the right and left. Now, Gen. Kang had been instructed by the king to watch the turn of events and if the Chinese could not hold their own to go over to the Manchus and make friends with them. This indeed does not look much like loyalty to China, but it must be remembered that we are dealing now not with the Korean sentiment as a whole but with the wretch who occupied the throne at the moment, and who had no more real loyalty toward China than he had love for his own country.

Gen. Kang followed his instructions and sent to the Man-

chu leader and said, "We are not enemies. There is no cause
for hostilities between us. We have been forced into this unpleasant position against our wills. As the Chinese showed
us favors during the Japanese invasion we have had to make
some show of interest in order to reciprocate the favor, but as
things have turned out we should be glad to make friends
with you."

The Manchu chieftain was willing enough to come to this
agreement and so the whole Korean contingent went over *en
masse* to the Manchus. Gen. Yang was brought before Norach'i to make his obeisance. That powerful man was seated
upon a throne, clothed in yellow silk, and on either side were
many young women with jewelled pendants in their ears.
Gen. Kang was told to stand some distance away and bow,
but he said that in his own country his rank was sufficiently
high to warrant a nearer approach. So he was led nearer.
He then made only a slight genuflection. This did not please
the choleric Norach'i and the general was compelled to make
a proper obeisance. Gen. Kim Kyŏng-su likewise went through
this humiliating ceremony.

It appears that Gen. Kang had decided that it was to his
interests to join himself permanently to the Manchus, for
when soon after this Gen. Kim tried to despatch a letter to
the king, giving a carefully detailed account of the Manchus
and their strength, the letter was intercepted by Gen. Kang
who gave it to Norach'i and advised that Gen. Kim be killed.
This was immediately done.

Three months later the Manchu chief sent a letter to the
Korean king, couched in the following terms, "I have seven
causes for hating the Ming dynasty and it is impossible for
me to keep my hands off them. Now you and I are not
enemies. To be sure you have injured us more or less in the
past, but we will waive all that. It will be nceessary for
you however to break off all connection with China and stop
aiding her in any way." Gen. Kang also wrote at the same
time saying, "The Manchus are training all their youth to
war, and soon they will have the whole of Liao-tung."
When the king received these letters he referred them to the
governor of P'yŭng-an Province to answer. The answer ran
as follows, "For two hundred years both you and we have

been the subjects of the Ming power and now that trouble has arisen between you and the authorities at Nanking it will be bad for you and us as well. China is like a parent to us and how can we refuse to aid her? We cannot listen to your demand and abstain from helping her. If you will make peace with us and clearly define our boundaries and abstain from conquest, China will not be only glad but will reward us both with gifts." To this the Manchu replied, "If you think that China will give presents you have been grievously deceived by her. They are all liars and cheats and I hate them. Put away this idea and stand shoulder to shoulder with us. We must take an oath and sacrifice a white horse to heaven and a black bullock to the earth. After that I will send back all your generals and soldiers. Let there be no more weapons used between us, but only horse-whips." This latter refers to friendly intercourse by means of horses. Gen. Kang also wrote, "Norach'i has taken Puk-kwan and Gen. Kim T'ă-sŭk is dead. Păk Yang-go has surrendered. Norach'i has joined the Mongol forces to his own and is advancing on Yogwang. His two sons Mangoda and Hongtasi advise him to first seize Liao-tung. Every day there are long debates to discuss whether it were better to strike Liao-tung or Korea first. This is a secret but I am sure of what I say. They are making great numbers of ladders and I am sure they are intending to invade Korea first."

This letter troubled the King, for it interfered with his own personal comfort. So he sent a swift messenger to Nanking begging the Emperor to send a large force to "guard your eastern territory" which meant that the king wanted China to stand between him and this Manchurian scourge.

The relatives of Gen. Kang were kept informed by him of the state of affairs in the north, and they sent large sums of money to Norach'i to buy him off and prevent him from invading Korea; and it may be that it was this, at least in part, that delayed it for some time. The king's messengers found the road to Nanking blocked by the Manchus and so had to turn back. The king thereupon sent envoys one after another by boat, but as the Koreans were poor sailors, they failed to land at the right place and fell into the hands of the Manchus or were wrecked by storms.

The Manchus now, in 1621, held the whole of Liao-tung and the Chinese residents were fleeing in all directions. Thousands of them crossed into Korea and many crossed over to the islands of Ok-kang and In-san near the mouth of the Yalu River and there, huddled together in wretchedness and want, bewailed their pitiable condition.

The prefect of Eui-ju implored the king to forward troops to hold the Manchus in check and the Chinese Gen. Wang wrote the king demanding a contingent of Korean troops to oppose the wild horde that threatened the Ming power. But the king was utterly incompetent. and all Seoul was in a ferment. The king thought only of himself, and looked to it that a comfortable place was arranged for him on the island of Kang-wha, in case it should become necessary for him to leave Seoul. In the early summer a Korean named Yi Yŏng-bang, who had gone over to the Manchus body and soul, and had become son-in-law to Norach'i, took a body of Manchu cavalry, crossed over to the islands of Ok-kang and In-san and massacred all the Chinese refugees he could lay hands on. This again struck terror to the heart of the king, and it threw Seoul into a fever of excitement. The king collected nine thousand troops from the southern provinces and stationed them at Su-wŭn, but there was no one whom he could appoint general-in-chief ; so he had to recall from banishment Han Chun-gyŭm and confer this honor upon him. Han Myŭng-yŭn was made second in command. He was a man of low extraction but had acquired a certain amount of fame in the Japanese invasion.

In the following year, 1622, the Manchus entered China and were everywhere victorious. They wanted to make a treaty with Korea, but the king could decide neither one way nor the other. His envoys had not reached China and he had no word from the Emperor. The queen memorialized the king in the native script and said, "Those northern savages want to make peace with us, not because of any feeling of friendship for us but because they think they cannot handle China and Korea both at once. So they do this to keep us quiet until they finish with China. The king should make up his mind one way or the other and act. Think of what the Chinese did for us during the late invasion ! We were on the very

edge of destruction and they succored us. Both king and
people should be of one mind and hasten to send soldiers to
oppose this common enemy. Even if we do not succeed we
shall have clear consciences, for we shall know that we have
done what we could to aid China in the hour of her distress.''
In the third moon a letter arrived from the Manchu headquarters which read as follows, "You say that you are the child
and China is the parent. Well, I am now striking your parent,
but you seem not to be able to help her. There is no use in
trying to do so."   In answer to this grim pleasantry the
craven king sent an envoy with gifts to the Manchu camp,
but the gifts and envoy were both spurned with insults.

The Chinese general Mo Mun-nyŭng fled from Liao-tung
by boat and landed at Yong-ch'ŭn in Korea. Finding there
many Chinese fugitives, and among them not a few soldiers,
he organized a little army and marched against the Manchus.
In his first fight he was quite successful, coming from the
field with the head of the Manchu general, T'ung Yang-jŏng.
He then made his headquarters at Ch'ŭl-san. With the approach of winter the Manchus crossed the Ya-lu in force and
he was outnumbered and had to flee. He sent a letter to the
king saying, "I am now here in your territory with a small
force, let us unite and drive back this Munchu horde. But
nothing came of it.

The Manchus were exceedingly cruel toward their captives. Having collected a large number they made them sit
down in rows and then the Manchu braves went along the
line and shot arrows into their victims. If the wound was
not instantly mortal the victim was compelled to pluck out
the arrow with his own hands and give it back to his executioner.

Meanwhile Korea was going from bad to worse. For
many years all official positions had been sold to the highest
bidder. Governors and generals paid 30,000 cash, prefects
20,000 and clerks paid 3,000. No office could be procured
without an immediate cash payment. The price put upon the
office of Prime Minister was so great that for many years no
one could afford to take it, and so the place remained vacant,
perhaps to the benefit of the people. The king was ruled by
a favorite concubine and she made use of her power to enrich

her relatives and those attached to her. She and other concubines sent men to the country to peddle offices. Half the
money they kept themselves and the other half went to the
pockets of the concubines. Such was the desperate condition
of affairs when the year 1622 came in ; and we must now record the downfall of this wretched parody of a king.

A man by the name of Yi Kwi had desired for a long time
to find some way of ridding the land of the desperate tyrant,
and at last he found five men who were willing to engage with
him in the good cause. They were Sim Kyŏng-jin, Sim Keui-
wŭn, Kim Cha-jŭm, Ch'oe Myŭng-gil, Kim Nyu. After thinking the matter over and discussing it, they decided that if
their plan succeeded they would put on the throne the grandson of Sŭn-jo Tă-wang. Kim Nyu was made the leader in
this plot. Collecting money they fitted out a small but select
body of soldiers and put Gen. Yi Heung-ip at their head, and
the day for the event was set. But one of the men connected
with the plot turned traitor and told the king the whole plan.
The conspirators learned of it immediately and decided to carry out their program in spite of all. As it happened, the king
was in a drunken carouse at the time this interesting bit of
information was given him and he forgot all about it. That
very night the band of conspirators met at the appointed rendezvous beyond the Peking Pass. But there was trouble,
because some soldiers who were expected from Chang-dan had
not yet arrived ; so a swift messenger was sent to find them.
They were met twenty *li* out and hurried forward. Yi Kwal,
with several other generals, went to meet these troops beyond
the pass and lead them into the city. They found several
hundred soldiers ready for the enterprise ; but a man named
Chang Yu came in haste from the city and said, "The king has
been told. The government troops are coming out to seize
us." Yi Kwi seized Yi Kwal by the hand and said, "Kim Nyu
who was to lead us has not arrived and you must be our
leader." So he consented. He gave each soldier a piece of
paper to fasten to the back of his collar so that they would be
able to recognize each other and not be thrown into confusion. At the last moment Kim Nyu arrived and then there
was a quarrel between him and Yi Kwal as to the leadership ;
but as day was about to dawn they let Kim Nyu take charge.

Having heard that the government troops were coming out of the West Gate they hastened around the mountain and entered the Northwest Gate. When the government troops learned by the great noise and tumult in the city that they had been outwitted, they returned only to find the insurrectionary troops before the palace. They had cut their way through the gates with axes and were setting fire to everything inside. As they entered the king's apartments he slipped out the back door and scaling the back wall found refuge in a monk's room. From that place he made his way to the house of one An Kuk-sin where he secured a suit of mourner's clothes and then went to the house of a physician, Chöng Nam-su. This man however informed the new government as to his whereabouts and he was seized. This occurred in the year 1622.

Prince Neung-yang, the nephew of the deposed king, was elevated to the royal position and crowds of people came and bowed to him as he sat in state before the palace. His posthumous title is In-jo Tă-wang.

His first act was to send a chair to bring back the queen dowager from the Myŭng-ye Palace ; but she, thinking that it might perhaps be a trick on the part of the wicked king, refused to go. She said, "The king himself must come and take me out." So he came and showed her that the good news was indeed true. She sat on the throne just as she had done in the days of King Sŭn-jo, and when the new king came in he prostrated himself before her and wept ; but she said, "Do not weep ; this is a day of deliverance, and you should rather rejoice." Then they brought in the depraved and fallen creature who had tried to play at king but had made a lamentable failure. The queen dowager exclaimed, "This arch-traitor and bloody man has come, and he must be judged here and now or I cannot leave this place. For ten years I have been imprisoned here. Day before yesterday I dreamed that the aged king Sŭn-jo came and said, 'In a few days you will be delivered.' " The eunuchs brought the royal seals and the insignia of royalty and gave them to the newly appointed king. He banished the deposed king to Kang-wha and his son to Kyo-dong Island. He then gave posthumous honors to Princes Im-hă, Neung-chang, Yŭn-heung, Pu-wön and Yöng-ch'ang whom the tyrant had caused to be murdered. He also called the queen dowager's mother from exile on the island of Quelpart.

He found the government in a profoundly wretched condition and he forthwith began a systematic house-cleaning. He appointed new ministers to the six departments and a proclamation was sent to the eight provinces saying that every prefect who had bought his place should be driven from office and that all the land that had been stolen from the people should be returned to them ; also that every prefectural clerk should pay up the arrears of revenue which he had withheld from the government. He drew up a company of soldiers at Chong-no, the center of the city, and there executed the former favorite Yi I-ch'ŭm and seventeen other men who had aided and abetted the deposed king in his monstrosities. Sixty more were banished to distant places where they were confined in small enclosures surrounded with brier hedges, and their food was handed them through small holes in the hedges. Pang Yŭp, the governor of P'yŭng-an Province, and two others in the country, were executed by special messengers sent down to the country for the purpose. This Pang Yŭp was a most desperate villain. As he had something of a body-guard, resistance was anticipated, but the special messenger of death managed to draw off the guard on some pretext or other and then the work was done swiftly and surely. This governor was so detested by the people that they cut his body into small pieces and each man carried away a small piece "to remember him by."

The king made Yi Kwi General-in-chief, conferred upon his father the title of Prince Chong-wŭn and upon his mother that of Pu-pu-in and gave her a palace to live in where the government hospital now stands. He drove out from the palace all vile women, all musical instruments, and he burned at Chong-no the wooden semblance of a mountain which the former king had caused to be made and which was always carried in his procession. This "mountain" was covered with growing shrubs and flowering plants. He made Gen. Chang Man commander of all the provincial forces, with his headquaters at P'yŭng-yang. He beheaded the brother of the deposed queen and also the prefect who had suffocated the young prince at Kang-wha. Spies were sent throughout the country to ascertain the actual state of affairs.

This king was a deadly enemy of Buddhism, and he it was who ordered that no monk should set foot inside the gates of Seoul. The law was promulgated that whenever a common person entered the gates of Seoul he must dismount from his horse. Sacrifices were offered by the king in person at the tomb of Ki-ja and at the blood-marked stone at Song-do, the spot where Chöng Mong-ju had been murdered when the dynasty was founded. It was decreed that revenue should be collected to the extent of a tithe of the grain, which was much less than before, but was collected more regularly. We cannot but sympathize with the wife of the son of the deposed king, who had been banished to Kyo-dong Island. She followed him into exile and attempted to secure his escape by digging with her own tender hands a tunnel seventy feet long. She had no other implement than a piece of iron resembling a common fire-poker. At the very moment of his escape the plot was discovered and the poor wife hanged herself out of grief and disappointment. When the king heard of this he ordered that honorable burial be given her remains and he put the young man out of misery by administering poison. That same year the deposed queen died and the king gave her the burial honors of a princess. She had been a devoted Buddhist and had endowed many monasteries with wooden or clay images. But she was not happy as queen and prayed that when, according to the Buddhist doctrine, she should take on another life it might not be that of a queen.

Chapter V.

ju....the king retires to Kang-wha....Manchu conditions....panic
in Seoul....an interesting game of chess....Korean hostage and
tribute....oath at the altar....Koreans firm in their loyalty to
China....the Manchus praise them   Manchu cruelties .. the
Manchu garrisons....opposed by the Koreans ...sound argument
....Japanese assistance declined.

The story of Yi Kwal's rebellion shows how great a matter a little fire kindles. The king wished to honor in a special manner the men who had been instrumental in putting
him on the throne. Among them were two especially deserving men, Kim Nyu and Yi Kwal. Kim was from a higher
family than Yi but was less deserving of praise in this affair.
When all knelt before the king and Yi Kwal found that he
was given second place, he was enraged and refused to kneel,
but stood glaring about him. He was pacified, but was still
very sore at heart. He was given the position of governor
of P'yŭng-an where there was a considerable force of soldiers ;
among them three hundred Japanese, who had become naturalized and who where excellent swordsmen. With the
opening of the new year Gen. Yi Kwi, who knew the calibre
of Yi Kwal, obtained the post of military instructor at Song-
do. This he sought that he might have an opportunity to
stand between the king and any treachery that Yi Kwal
might attempt. A courtier, Mun Whe, told the king that Yi
Kwal was gathering an army with bad intent, and the king
hastily called a council. Kim Nyu did not believe it possible
that Yi Kwal should revolt, but Ch'oe Myŭng-gil insisted
that it was true, and in the high words that followed Kim
Nyu was charged with being privy to the plot. But the remark passed unnoticed. We shall see however that Kim
had little to do in putting down the insurrection. Perhaps
it was because of a lurking suspicion that he might be implicated. A large number of men known to be intimate with
the disaffected general were arrested and thrown into prison.
Two executioners were sent to kill Han Myŭng-yun who was
said to be in league with Yi Kwal, and to catch Yi Kwal's
son. Arriving in P'yŭng-yang the messengers went boldly
into the presence of Yi Kwal and announced their message.
As Yi was already on the point of marching on Seoul he
answered by taking off the heads of the messengers. Hastily

summoning all the neighboring prefects he addressed them as follows : "The king is surrounded by bad men and I propose to go up to Seoul and clean things out a little." Then putting in motion his 20,000 troops with the Japanese swordsmen at their head, he marched toward the capital. The whole country instantly burst into a flame of excitement. The king appointed Gen. Yi Wŭn-ik to lead an army in defense of the capital, and he put Yi Si-bal second in command. Yi Su-il became general of P'yŭng-an Province, and the combined forces marched northward to block the rebel's path. Gen. Wan P'ung-gun fortified Song-do in preparation for an attack. O Yong-su fortified the banks of the Im-jin River at the ferry. The eight provinces were all requisitioned for troops. Kang Kak was placed at Su-an with militia from Su-an and Sŏ-heung to check the advance of the enemy. Gen. Chŏng Ch'ung-sin who had been stationed at An-ju north of P'yŭng-yang, together with other leaders, moved southward on the rebellious city, to take Yi Kwal in the rear. Chang Man asked him what he thought were the chances of Yi Kwal's success, and he answered, "If Yi Kwal goes straight to Seoul and the king stays there till he arrives the result will be doubtful, but if he delays a while in Whang-hă Province, or if the king retreats southward and Yi Kwai delays in Seoul we will kill him like a dog."

Gen. Chang Man then called about him all the forces within reach, led by fifteen captains and prefects. When he saw how small his army was compared with that of Yi Kwal he despaired of doing anything, but some-one said, "Many of those under Yi Kwal are not faithful to him. Let us send and call out the loyal ones from among his army." So they sent a slave of Gen. Yi Yun-sŭ, who followed Yi Kwal, and told him to go and bring his master out of the rebel ranks. They offered him a hundred thousand cash but he refused it saying "I will go and save him from rebellion if I can, and if I succeed it will be time enough to reward me." The slave entered the rebel ranks and that night the sentries heard the voice of Gen. Yi Yun-sŭ calling aloud from outside the lines saying, "I am going over to the side of the king." Arriving at the camp of Chang Man, the penitent general burst into tears at the thought of how near he had come to being a trai-

tor. Yi Kwal sent eight assassins to kill Chang Man but they
were caught and brought before their intended victim, who,
instead of punishing them, gave them a good dinner and sent
them away. Yi Kwal himself was so fearful of assassination
that he not only slept in a different tent each night but moved
from one tent to another several times during a single night.

Gen. Chang Man started for Seoul, the advance guard
being led by Chöng-sin, the skirmish line by Pak Yöng-sŭ, the
right and left flanks by Yu Hyo-gŭl and Chang Tŭn, the sap-
pers by Ch'o'e Eung-il, while the commissariat was in charge
of An Mong-yun. The whole force consisted of 1800 men.
The first day was spent in getting the army across the Ta-
dong River. The next three days brought them to Whang-
ju, where they fell in with part of the rebel army. After a
brisk skirmish, two companies of cavalry were seen riding out
from the robel ranks as if to surrender, but when they had
come close to Gen. Chang Man's forces they made a sudden
charge which threw the loyal forces into confusion and soon
the entire army was routed. Turning from this complete
victory, Yi Kwal led his forces to Su-an. It was his intention
to approach Seoul by way of Sak-wŭn but as the government
had a strong force there he changed his plan and came by
Keui-rin which is an exceedingly rough road. Meanwhile.Gen.
Chang Man had collected the scattered remnants of his army
and followed as far Sö-heung where he was joined by Gen.
Yi Su-il and together they proceeded southward to P'yŭng-
san. There they were joined by 800 more troops. On the
sixth of the moon Yi Kwal arrived at the Cho-t'an ford and
found it guarded by a royal force under Yi Chung-ho and Yi
Tŭk-bu. Yi Kwal forced the passage and put the government
troops to flight, taking the heads of both the generals. A day
or so later, being met by more loyal troops, he sent them the
two heads as warning. They did not heed it and in the fight
that followed their leaders too lost their heads.

Meanwhile interesting events were happening in Seoul.
The king put to death forty-nine men who were suspected of
being privy to the plot, though many of them were doubtless
innocent. Yi Kwi begged him to spare some of them, but he
was obdurate. Gen. Yi Sö took 2,000 men and went to the
gate on the main road a few miles beyond Song-do and tried

to hold it against the insurgent army. Yi Kwal attacked at night and found little difficulty in breaking through the barrier. But instead of advancing on Song-do he made a circuit and thereby avoided both Song-do and the force which was set to guard the passage of the Im-jin River. He effected a crossing by a ford higher up that stream. Learning of this, Pak Hyo-rip who was holding the ferry hastened back to Seoul where he arrived at dusk and announced that the king had not a moment to lose but must take to flight that very night. Without an hour's delay the king mounted his steed and fled by way of the South Gate, leaving the city in a perfect frenzy of fear. He arrived at Han-gang in the dark and found that the ferrymen had taken all their boats to the other side for safety. They peremptorily refused to obey any summons, and at last U Sang-jung was obliged to throw off his clothes and swim the stream. He succeeded in getting six boats. It took all the rest of the night to get the royal cavalcade across the river. It was on the ninth of the moon when the king arrived at Sa-p'yŭng just beyond the river. He had nothing to eat till noon that day, when Sin Chun brought him a bowl of gruel and a few dried persimmons, Night found him at Su-wŭn completely tired out After a rest of a few days he passed on to Kong-ju the provincial capital and there he was made comfortable for the first time since his flight from the capital. The governors of Ch'ung ch'ŭng and Chŭl-la Provinces met him there. A strong guard was placed along the southern bank of the Keum River.

At noon of the day following the king's flight, thirty followers of Yi Kwal entered the city and announced that there was no need for fear, as a new king had arisen. The next day Yi Kwal entered the town. Many small officials and a great crowd of people went out to meet him and scattered red earth along the road in front of him, which is a special prerogative of royalty. Entering the city he pitched his camp where the Kyŏng-bok Palace now stands. Even the king's own uncle went over to Yi Kwal, perhaps through fear, or perhaps because the revolution was a success. This uncle was proclaimed king and posters were sent out to quiet the people. Thousands of adventurers and low fellows sought and obtained official appointments under the new regime.

But what had been going on in the north? Chang Man, arriving at P'a-ju, learned that the king had fled, and immediately called a council of war. It was decided that, as the people of Seoul were not largely in favor of Yi Kwal, it would be a good thing to make a demonstration at once lest the people should come to recognize the government. So one body of troops was sent to watch the road outside the East Gate and to cut off supplies. Another guarded the roads outside the South Gate. Gen. Chŏng Ch'ung-sin said that they must encamp on the hills immediately outside the West Gate and then Yi Kwal would be forced to fight. In order to do this Kim Yang-ŏn took cavalry and surprised the signal fire station beside the Peking Pass and so prevented any signal being given. That night Chang Man and all his forces came around the hills and stationed themselves behind the hill just back of Mo-wha-gwan. This movement was further favored by a strong east wind that carried the sound away so that all Seoul was ignorant of the extreme proximity of the enemy. At the same time Yi Whak with two hundred troops secreted himself outside the Northwest Gate, to enter the city when the insurgent troops should go out the West Gate to attack Chang Man's forces. The latter also sent thousands of slips of paper into the city and had them distributed among the people saying, "Tomorrow, anyone who refuses to stand by Yi Kwal and remains loyal to the king, let him present one of these slips and he small receive a reward."

In the morning Yi Kwal spied a small band of soldiers on the hill outside the gate, for most of the force was concealed behind it, in order to deceive the rebels. Some of Yi Kwal's followers said, "They are so few we had better go outside the Northwest Gate and so surround them; but the enemy seemed so insignificant that Yi Kwal marched straight at them. All Seoul was on the walls watching the fight with breathless interest. Han Myŭng-yŭn, Yi Kwal's right hand man, took the Japanese contingent and moved up the steep hillside, and Yi followed with the main body. The strong east wind that was blowing materially aided the attacking force, for it lent speed to their arrows and they had the wind at their backs instead of in their faces. The loyal forces were forced to give way a little and their leaders had to stike down some in order to prevent a general stampede. At this critical juncture the wind suddenly veered to the west and drove the sand and dust into the eyes of the attacking party. This was the turning point in the battle. Yi Kwal was forced to give ground. Han Myŭng-yŭn himself was wounded by an arrow. Gen. Chang Man fought fiercely for two hours, gaining ground all the time. At this time the standard-bearer of Yi Kwal turned and fled. The cry arose, "Yi Kwal is on the run," and in less that a minute the whole force was thrown into confusion and every man took to his heels, including Yi Kwal himself, who hastened back toward the West Gate. But the citizens on the wall had not been idle, and he found the gate locked and barred. Turning aside he hastened along under the wall till he reached the South Gate which he entered. Gen. Chang Man said, "Let us not chase him, for his men might turn on us and beat us after all. Let him go ; the people will bring his head in soon enough." So Yi Kwal with a small band of followers fled out the Water Mouth Gate, crossed the Han at Song-p'a, killed the prefect of Kwang-ju, scaled Yi-bu-ja Pass and fled away eastward. Gen. Chŏng Ch'ung-sin chased him as far as Kyŏng-an. By that time the traitor's band had dwindled to twenty-eight men. He fled by night as far as Muk-pangi in the prefecture of I-ch'ŭn and there two of his followers, seeing that the game had been played to a finish and hoping to save their own lives, went into his room by night and severed his head from the body. His son was treated in the same way, as were also Han Myŭng-yŭn and six others. They carried the heads to Kong-ju and laid them before the king. The king's uncle who had been set up as king fled to Kwang-ju, where he was caught and turned over to Gen. Chang Man, who imprisoned him and waited the orders of the king. But another man, Sim Keui-wŭn, said, "No, he is a traitor," and slew him with his own hand. When the king returned to Seoul this man Sim was imprisoned for a few days as nominal punishment for having killed a relative of the king.

On the twenty-second of the month the king returned to Seoul. Gen. Chang Man went to the river and escorted him in with a large retinue, but Gen. Chŏng Ch'ung-sin did not go and bow before the king, for he said, "I did not stop

the traitor, but let him drive the king from the capital." So
he went up to P'yŭng-yang without seeing the king. When
the latter heard of this he sent for him and gave him a present of gold and made him governor of P'yŭng-an. It is said
by some, in extenuation of Yi Kwal's conduct, that he understood that the king had driven the former king from the
throne and was a usurper. This must be false, for Yi Kwal
was one of the principal actors in those events and must have
known the truth about them. He was simply jealous and,
having a strong force, thought to avenge himself. However
that may be, the report was spread that it was patriotism that
prompted the revolt, and to dispel any such idea the king
made proclamation saying, "Kwang-hă, the former ruler, was
a wicked and undutiful man. He killed his father and elder
brother and imprisoned his mother. The country was on the
verge of destruction and so I could not but attempt to drive
him out. It was not because I wanted to usurp the royal
honors, but it was for the sake of the line. Yi Kwal's raid
was prompted by idle rumors gotten up by certain of Kwang-
hă's men, but let all the people know surely that I have done
this for the sole purpose of saving the kingdom."

In the ninth moon another revolt was attempted, with
the object of putting Prince In-sŭng, the king's younger
brother, on the throne. It was discovered in time and the
principal movers were killed and the prince was banished to
Kan-sŭng in Kang-wŭn Province.

On account of the frequent conflagrations in the city of
P'yŭng-yang, the governor petitioned the king to promulgate
a law requiring all houses in that town to be tiled instead of
thatched. The king not only complied but gave money for
the purchase of tiles. That law has not been abrogated to
this day.

The year 1625 opened with warlike preparations. Gen.
Yi Sö collected a band of strong, stalwart men, the pick of
the land, formed them into companies and regiments and drilled
them at the Hun-yŭn-wŭn, inside the East Gate, and also
at Mo-wha-kwan outside the West Gate. Near the close
of the year the king promulgated a most important law,
sweeping away the disabilities of sons by concubines and giving
them the right to become officials. One must know the prev-

alence of concubinage in Korea in order to understand how vitally this law must have affected the whole body of the people, of all ranks and classes. This was the more true from the fact that concubines are commonly taken because of the lack of an heir. Eligibility to office on the part of sons of of concubines worked therefore in two directions. It elevated the position of the concubine and at the same time made the position of the barren wife more endurable.

We have already given a sketch of the beginnings of the Manchu convulsion which was about to shake the whole of eastern Asia. During the interval occupied by the events narrated above, the Manchus were quietly preparing for the future. Gen. Kang Hong-rip, the Korean renegade, was still with them. Another Korean went over to the Manchus. It was Han Yun who fled to Kwi-sŭng in northern P'yŭng-an, from which place he crossed the Ya-lu and found Gen. Kang among the Manchus. To him he said, "My relatives have now all been destroyed by the king and I am an outcast. Let us get an army together and go and be avenged on the Koreans." Gen. Kang gave his hearty consent and together they sought the throne of the Manchu chief to lay their plan before him.

Sŏ U-sin, the Ming governor of Liao-tung, heard of this plan and despatched a messenger to the King of Korea setting him on his guard against these two men. The king did not believe that Gen. Kang was irrecoverably lost, for he appointed his son to go to the Manchus as envoy. Had this young man succeeded in reaching his destination he might have induced his father to remain faithful to Korea, but just beyond the border he encountered Manchu soldiers who did not understand him and would not let him pass. So he was compelled to return with his mission unaccomplished. It is probable that there would have been an invasion of Korea by the Manchus at that time had it not been for the arrival in Liao-tung of the great Chinese general Wŭn Sung-whan. He was so skillful in the handling of soldiers that superhuman powers were ascribed to him. The Manchus could make no headway against him, and it is said that Norach'i's chagrin at having failed to storm a town held by this famous general aggravated an illness caused by a carbuncle on his back and brought about his death. Upon his decease his second son Hongt'asi took the reins of government and carried to completion the ambitious plans made by his illustrious father.

It is apparent that the Korean court was well awake to the dangers confronting them, for we learn that in the seventh moon of this year 1626 the wall of Nam-han was completed. This is the great mountain fortress about twenty miles to the south-east of Seoul. It was formerly the site of one of the capitals of Păkje.

The year 1627 no sooner opened that the long dreaded event took place. On the fifth moon 30,000 Manchu soldiers crossed the Yalu River and a few days later stood before the city of Eui-ju. Approaching the gate a herald cried, "The second king of the great Golden Kingdom is now laying his heavy hand on Korea. If you do not come out and surrender we will raze your town to the level of the ground." Unfortunately for the good name of Korea the perfect was at that moment sleeping off the effects of a drunken debauch in the house of a dancing girl. He came forth and tried to get the garrison together, but it was too late, for already the traitor Han Yun had entered the town in Korean clothes and had thrown the gates open to the ruthless invaders. The prefect and his whole garrison were set up in line and shot down by the savage Manchus, after which they boiled the body of the prefect in a kettle and sacrificed to heaven with the flesh. They then sent a letter to the king couched in the following terms : "You have committed four crimes. (1) You did not send an envoy to commiserate with us on the death of the great Norach'i. (2) You have never thanked us for sparing your army when we beat you and the Chinese together. (3) You afforded asylum to our enemy, Mo Munnyŏng. (4) Your people have killed many of the residents of Liao-tung in cold blood. It is for these reasons that our wrath is kindled against you." And so the invading army moved southward, forcing the Koreans to cut their hair and compelling them to act as guides. But they did not come unopposed. They were met at Yong-ch'ŭn by its prefect at the head of 2,000 men, but a small official turned traitor and opened the gates to the Manchus. On the seventeenth they arrived at Kwak-san where they were told by the Korean garrison that death was preferable to surrender ; the Koreans found it so, for they were soon overpowered and massacred. Two prefects whose wives had been confiscated by the Mancus thought to save themselves and recover their wives by going over to the enemy but when they did so they found their wives still held as concubines while they themselves were compelled to hold the bridles of the men who brutally refused to give back the women.

Seoul was meanwhile going through one of those period-ical eruptions which she was destined to suffer for many years to come. Gen. Chang Man became general-in-chief, with Chŏng Ch'ung Sin as second. They immediately took all the available forces and marched northward. Gen. Sin was plac-ed at the Im-jin River to block the approach of the enemy Gen. Kim went south to collect troops in Ch'ung-ch'ŭng Province, and others went in other directions. A call was made to all the eight provinces for men. Gen. Yi Sö was put in command of Nam-han. The king recalled many men from banishment, probably with a view to bringing into har-mony all the different elements and securing unanimity among all classes.

On the twenty-first the Manchus arrived before An-ju. They cried, "Come out and surrender," and received the answer, "We are here to fight and not to surrender." The next day at dawn in a heavy fog they approached the wall. They had an enormous ladder mounted in some way on the backs of camels. This was placed against the wall and the enemy swarmed over, armed only with short swords and knives ; but these they used with such good effect that they soon gained a foothold. The commandant of the town. Nam Yi-heung, stood by the gate and shot many of the Manchus with his good bow and when his arrows were all gone he ordered bags of powder to be brought, and by exploding these he killed many of the enemy but was himself killed in the process.

P'yŭng-yang now being practically without defense, the prefect fled southward to the capital and told the king what had happened. The Crown Prince was immediately sent into the south for safety and the king himself with the ancestral tablets and with his court hastened to the island of Kang-wha, leaving the city of Seoul in a condition better imagined than described.

One of Gen. Kang's grievances against Korea was that he thought the king had killed his son, but when he learned that this was not only not true but that the king had sent that son as envoy, though unsuccessfully, to the Manchus, there was a strong revulsion of feeling in his mind and he expressed his sorrow at the invasion but said that it was now too late to stop it. He however advised the king to send gifts to the Manchu chief and sue for peace.

When the Manchus arrived at Whang-ju they sent a letter forward to the king on Kang-wha saying, "There are three conditions on which we will conclude a peace with you. (1) You must hand over to us the person of Mo Mun-nyŭng. (2) You must give us 10,000 soldiers to help invade China. (3) You must give up the two northern provinces of P'yŭng-an and Ham-gyŭng." On the ninth of the moon the envoy bearing this letter, accompanied by the Korean renegade Gen. Kang, took boat from Song-do for Kang-wha. The next day the king gave them audience and the envoy bowed before him, but the king did not bow in return. This made the envoy very angry, but the king said through an interpreter, "Tell him not to be angry, for I did not know the custom."

The king sent one Kang-In to Whang-ju ostensibly to sue for peace but in reality to find out what the Manchus were doing there. Not long after this the Manchu envoy returned to the same place but Gen. Kang remained on Kang-wha. When the enemy had advanced as far as P'yŭng-san, only a hundred *li* from Kang-wha, the whole court urged the king to make peace on any terms, as all the soldiers had run away and the enemy were so near. When Gen. Kim, who had been left to guard Seoul, learned of the proximity of the Manchus, he fired all the government treasure and provisions and made good his escape. This was the signal for a general exodus of the people who swarmed out of the city and scattered in all directions seeking safety among the mountains or in remote provinces.

Yun Hŭn had been imprisoned for having fled from P'yŭng-yang without so much as attempting its defense, and

many of the officials begged the king to pardon him ; but they
overdid it, and so many petitions came in that the king thought
he was dangerously popular and ordered his execution. When
the messenger of death reached the doomed man he found
him playing a game of chess. The man with whom he was
playing burst out crying, but he said, "What are you crying
about? I am the man who am going to die, not you. Let
us finish the game." So they finished the game, after which
Yun Hŭn quietly submitted to his fate. This is a sample of
sang froid which never fails to elicit the applause of the Korean.

On the twentieth the Manchu general Yu Hă left P'yŭng-
san and went to Kang-wha to have an audience with the king.
He advised the king to discard the Chinese calendar and use
the Manchu one instead and he also said said the king must
send his son to the north as hostage. The king answered
that his son was too young, but that he would send his younger brother. Accordingly he sent Wŭn Ch'ang-yŭng, not his
brother but a distant relative. At the same time he sent
30,000 pieces of cotton, 300 pieces of white linen, 100 tiger
skins and 100 leopard skins. Gen. Yu Hă was pleased at this
and said that he wished to have Korea at peace but that it
would first be absolutely necessary for the king to take a
solemn oath of fealty to the Manchus. And he said it must
be done immediately, before the Manchus should enter Seoul.

The next day a letter came from the Manchu Prince Yi
Wan urging that a treaty be made and the solemn oath be
sworn, and he added, "Either there must be such a treaty or
we must fight." He ordered that the king have an altar made
at once, on which to slay the animals and swear the oath.
The Koreans hung back and said, "Have we not sent gifts and
hostages to the north? Why then should we be compelled to
take this oath?" In a rage the Manchu messenger rode away
toward P'yŭng-san. This sudden departure was ominous and
it frightened the Koreans, so that they hastened to set about
building the altar. When, therefore, a few days later the
Manchu generals Kang Hong-rip and Yu Hă came with an
escort and demanded that a treaty should be ratified at once,
the Koreans hastened to comply. The king went with Gen.
Yu Hă to the altar and the king was ordered to plunge the
knife into the victims, a white horse and a black bullock which

signified the heavens and the earth respectively. At this the courtiers all exclaimed, "The king cannot do it. It must be done by deputy." The king replied. "It makes no difference now. We have eaten their insults and the people are all about to perish. I will do it." But still they opposed it so strongly that at last Yi Chŭng-gwi was appointed as substitute for the king.

It was on the third day of the third moon of 1627 when the ceremony was performed outside the West Gate of the fortress of Kang-wha. They killed the white horse and black bullock and sacrificed to heaven. The Manchu oath ran as follows: "The second king of the Manchus makes a treaty with the king of Korea. From this day we have but one mind and one thought. If Korea breaks this oath may heaven send a curse upon her. If the Manchus break it may they likewise be punished. The two kings will have an equal regard for truth and they will govern according to the principles of religion. May heaven help us and give us blessings." The Korean oath was as follows: "This day Korea takes oath and forms a treaty with the Keum (Kin) Kingdom. We too swear by this sacrifice that each shall dwell secure in the possession of his own lands. If either hates and injures the other may heaven send punishment upon the offending party. These two kings have minds regardful of truth. Each must be at peace with the other." The next day the three highest Korean officials went to the Manchu camp to settle the details of the treaty. They said, "As we have made a treaty with you, of course you will not let your troops advance on Seoul. It will be best for you to move backward at once. Now you are the 'elder brother' and we the 'younger brother,' so you will see the propriety of staying on the other side of the Yalu River. The Ming dynasty of China has been as a parent to us for two hundred years and our kings have always received investiture from the Emperor. We have made a treaty now with you, but that does not require us to cast off the suzerainty of China." This raised a storm about the Koreans' ears, and for days they disputed over the point with the Korean commission, but could not move them a hair's breadth from this position. At last in astonishment Gen. Yu Hă sat down, folded his hands and said "The Kingdom of Korea is like a small island or like a hair, and if we should but raise our foot it would be destroyed, and yet though destruction stares them in the face they will not forswear their fealty to China. This is greatness. Such righteousness and faithfulness are admirable. If the Manchu king consents, you shall do as you please in this respect." They sent to the Manchu Prince who was with the army at P'yŭng-san and he gave his consent. Gen. Yu Hǎ then put in the Manchu claim for yearly tribute. It was an enormous amount but the Koreans decided they would send at least a small part of what was demanded.

The Manchu army then moved northward beyong P'yŭng-yang to An-ju, being opposed there by Gen. Chŏng Ch'ung-sin they told him that they had made a treaty with Korea and were on their way back to Manchuria. He thought they were retreating and were trying to deceive him, so he said, "I have received no intimation of all this from headquarters, so you will have to wait here until I get word from the king."

The Manchu army on its way north through Whang-hǎ Province had stolen right and left, oxen, horses and women. They bored holes through the hands of children and fastened them together with cords and drove them north to make slaves of them. In the province of P'yŭng-an they did not commit these outrages, for there was a large sprinkling of Manchus among the people. When they left P'yŭng-yang they burned it to the ground. North of that place they put a garrison in every large town, namely An-ju, Chŏng-ju, Sŭn-ch'ŭn and Eui-ju. Strangely enough Koreans were put at the head of these garrisons. Of course these bodies of troops had to live off the people, and it seems that they did not scruple to plunder and confiscate in a wholesale manner. This is indicated by the fact that Chŏng Pang-su the prefect of Chŭn-san got out of patience and said it could no longer be borne. So gathering about him as many soldiers as possible, he began to make war on the Manchu garrisons wherever encountered. The Manchus were cut down by hundreds, as the country was being scoured by small bands of foragers who fell into this prefect's hands. Three of the Manchu captains joined their forces and tried to make headway against this Korean combination, but they were all killed and their forces cut to pieces. The king, when he heard of these actions, was loud

in praise of the Koreans who so successfully opposed the un-
lawful acts of the Manchu garrisons.

Not long after this a letter came from the Manchu headquarters saying, "Having made a treaty of peace with us, why
do you now set upon and kill our people?" To which the
Koreans boldly replied, "It was one of the conditions of that
treaty that all Manchus should move beyond the Yalu. If
they had done so, there would have been no trouble. But
many of your people stopped in P'yŭng-an Province and stole
our cattle and our women. The people could not endure it
and so revolted. But it was not at our instigation. It is
evident that the trouble began with you. It would be well if
you would send back the 2,000 people you have carried away
captive to Manchuria." The argument was conclusive, as
the Manchus acknowledged by sending back the captive Koreans. When the Japanese heard that the Koreans had been
successfully opposing the Manchus they sent a present of 300
muskets, 300 swords and 300 pounds of powder, but the Koreans wisely declined the gifts and sent them back to Japan.

Chapter VI.

The king returns to Seoul....military reforms....message from China
.... Manchu familiarities .... conspiracies frustrated .... Manchu
complaints .... pacified....Japanese offers....a naval station....
a lawless Chinaman....beheaded....factional fights....courier system   a disloyal Chinaman .. envoy to China meets Roman Catholics .... quarrel with the Manchus....tribute....Chinese ren-
egades....two great Manchu generals....a stirring memorial .... a
frightened envoy .... war inevitable .... omen .... Emperor con-
gratulates the king....divided counsels....fatal mistake....panic in
Seoul....the king takes refuge in Nam-han.

On the tenth of the fourth moon the king started back
towards Seoul, which he entered two days later. He was now
fully awake to the need of a well drilled army, and he set to
work in earnest drilling one. He stationed a general at
Kang-wha permanently and instituted the custom of requiring
military duty of every citizen under forty years of age and

over fifteen. Some were sent to Seoul to drill for three years. The first year was spent in learning the methods of guarding gates and walls, the second in musket practice, and the third in swordsmanship and archery. When they had been thorroughly drilled they were sent to the country to drill the militia. In this way an available force of 700,000 men is said to have been trained. If this is the estimate of the number of able-bodied men between fifteen and forty it gives a valuable clue to the entire population of the country at the time. At this time the custom was revived of having the men stand in squads of ten, five in front and five behind. When the front rank had discharged their pieces they fell back and the rear line stepped forward and discharged theirs, while the others reloaded. A Chinese envoy was sent from Nanking with a message to the king but refused to come further than Ka-do Island, from which place he forwarded his message, which ran, "How does it happen that you have made peace with the Manchus?" The king made reply, "The Manchus overwhelmed us with their vast numbers and it meant either a treaty or our extinction We had no time to send and explain matters to the Emperor." The Emperor sent a reply to this saying, "I have received your reply and I am truly sorry for you. You are in no wise to blame. Now hoard your wealth and by-and-bye you and I will rise and strike these Manchus to the earth."

It will be remembered that the king had sent one of his relatives as hostage to the Manchus, but now, according to the stipulations of the treaty, he came back, escorted by the Manchu general Yu Hă. The king sent high officials to meet them outside the South Gate, but this did not satisfy the Manchu, who was angry that the king did not come in person. So the king had to go out and meet them and give a feast to the returning party. When Gen. Yu Hă met the king he wanted to kiss him, saying that it was a custom by which he showed friendship and a demonstration that the oath still held firm between them ; but the king refused the osculatory salute and so the general compromised by patting him on the back.

Late in this year two dangerous conspiracies were made against the government. The first was by Yi In-jo a former official living in Kang-wŭn Province. He had a goodly following among the people and made bold to liberate all the criminals. After looting several towns he went into camp on a mountain top. The government troops, however, surrounded him and finally captured him and sent him up to the capital where he was beheaded together with his two sons. The other attempt was of a different nature. Yu Hyo-rip, an exile in Che-ch'ŭn, a relative of the deposed king's wife, decided to work up an insurrection. He sent his son up to Seoul in disguise to make arrangements with a disloyal eunuch. Soldiers also came disguised as merchants, but all armed to the teeth. The palace was to be seized on the fourth day of the new year. As fortune would have it, Hŭ Chŭk, a relative of one of the conspirators, learned of the plot in time, but only just in time, to inform the Prime Minister. So when the attack was made the whole party was seized and with them Yu Hyo-rip himself, who had come up to Seoul in woman's clothes and in a woman's chair. Being questioned about the affair he testified that he was not the prime mover in the matter but that he had been set on by the queen dowager, who wanted to put the king's uncle on the throne. That aged and respectable woman indignantly denied any knowledge of the plot and as proof of her innocence she urged that the said uncle be put to death. All united in this request and it was finally granted, though against the better instincts of the king who believed him innocent. We shall see later that the king was right.

The Manchus were still fretful. A letter came post haste from the north saying, "We have now sent back many captives and you agreed to pay for the rest, but when they got across the border and were lost to us we never saw the money. Not a year has passed since the treaty was ratified and yet you break it with impunity. When the Chinese acted thus we retaliated by seizing twenty-four of their districts. Now you must send those men straight back to us." Among all the courtiers there was but one dissenting voice, that of Chang Yu, who said, "The government is for the people and if it gives up any of the people thus, from that hour it ceases to be a government. Sooner should we let the Manchus destroy the government outright than comply with such a demand."

This carried the day, and an envoy was sent north bearing a present of a magnificent sword, 300 pounds of ginseng, seventy sable skins, but only five of the men demanded. The Manchus were highly pleased and forgave all that had been done to displease them. The Japanese hearing of this again sent an envoy saying, "Those Manchus are a bold lot. They have made a treaty with you but they do not treat you well. Just say the word and we will come and whip them for you." This frightened the king and he wanted to forward the message to the Manchus but Kim Sin-guk said, "If you do that you will get the Manchus and the Japanese to fighting each other on Korean soil and we will be the little fish between two whales." This argument carried the day.

In the year 1629 the king established a naval station on Kyo-dong Island and placed there an admiral to guard that island and Kang-wha from attack from the seaward side. This was with the expectation that the court might again find it necessary to seek asylum on the island of Kang-wha.

A Chinese general, Mo Mun-nyŭng, had been stationed by the Emperor on Ka-do Island near the mouth of the Yalu, to withstand the Manchus, but this man was not loyal to China, and had a leaning himself toward the Manchus. He could see that the Manchus were destined to become masters of the situation. He was very angry when Korea made a treaty with the Manchus for he feared that they would try to hurt his reputation with them. When the Manchus attacked the Chinese in the neighboring mainland of Liao-tung he never raised a hand in their defense, though it in said, perhaps wrongly, that he had an army of 300,000 (!) men. On the other hand he vented his spite against Korea by harrying her northern shores and killing many captives on their way home from the Manchu territory. The Emperor tried to call him to account for this but received no reply. Meanwhile this Gen. Mo Mun-nyŭng styled himself "Son of Heaven beyond the Sea." As he thus showed his hand, the question as to his disloyalty was settled, and Gen. Wŭn Sung-han came from China to call him to account, a thing he had not foreseen. When Gen. Wŭn approached and called on him to come and report to him, he dared not refuse, fearing that the troops uu-

der him would not be willing to attack their fellow-countrymen under Gen. Wŭn.   As may be surmised he lost his head
as soon as he arrived in the camp of the latter.

In spite of her military activity Korea was anything but
strong.   The two leading parties, the *Noron* and *Soron* were
quarrelling like cats and dogs together.   There was one constant succession of banishments and recalls, as one party or
another obtained temporary control of the government.   There
was no sort of harmony or unanimity in the discharge of the
public business and it had to look out for itself, while those
who should have been attending to it were wrangling.   There
was a high honorary title called Chŭl-lang, and the leading
men quarrelled so much over it that the king was at last compelled to abolish it altogether.   And yet in the midst of this
strife the king found opportunity to establish the Mu-hak, a
body of 200 men to act as swift couriers   It is said they could
cover 300 *li* a day, or 100 miles.

The Manchu Gen. Yu Hă, of whom we have spoken, was
originally a Chinaman living in Liao-tung, but had gone over
to the Manchus.   The Emperor was furious at this and offered
a reward of 1,000 ounces of silver and high position to anyone
who should apprehend him.   For a time he went under an
assumed name, but finally with his three brothers he came to
Gen. Mo Mun-nyŭng whom he knew to be secretly disloyal
to China.   When Gen. Mo had been executed Gen. Yu came
of course under the jurisdiction of Gen. Wŭn.   Shortly after
this Gen. Yu was killed in a battle but his three brothers decided to rise up against the loyal Chinaman.   In the midst of
the funeral obsequies of their brother they rose and killed Gen.
Chin who had been left in charge of the Chinese forces, and
they tried to kill the Koreans as well, but in this they were
unsuccessful and shortly afterward were driven out by the
Korean forces.   When the Emperor heard of this he was highly pleased and praised the Koreans.

The Manchus naturally considered this occupation of
Ka-do as a menace to them and they sent a force of 20,000 men
to attack the Chinese, at the same time demanding boats of
the Koreans whereby to transport their troops.   This was not
granted, but the Koreans in order to avoid the effects of a
too evident leaning towards the Chinese, gave the Manchus 200

bags of rice. But the Chinese did not wait for the Manchus to cross to the island. They crossed to the mainland and attacked the Manchus unexpectedly, killing 400 and putting the rest to flight.

During this year, 1631, an envoy to China, Chong Tu-wŭn, while in Nanking, fell in with an aged Roman Catholic priest named Jean Niouk, who engaged the attention of the envoy because of his venerable and almost saint-like appearance. This man was one of the companions of the celebrated P. Ricci. From him the envoy received some volumes on science, a pair of pistols, a telescope and some other articles. The mention of a cannon in the native records is probably a mistake of some copyist who wrote the word cannon in place of pistol.

The king was told by his officials that the Manchus were sure to invade Korea again before long and so the island of Kang-wha was well provisioned and arms were prepared. He was urged to form a junction with the Chinese on Ka-do Island and make an attack on the Manchus. The fortresses of Ch ŭl-san and Un-san in P'yŭng-an Province were built at this time and every effort was made to put the country in a state of defense against the northern hordes. A fortress was also built near Eui-ju, which was the equivalent of a declaration of war against the Manchus. The result was soon apparent. A Manchu envoy made his appearance bearing a missive which said, "Korea has seen fit to break her treaty with us and she is no longer to be called 'younger brother,' but a vassal state. She shall pay us annually a tribute of 10,000 ounces of gold, 10,000 ounces of silver, 10,000,000 pieces of linen." The king replied that he had no gold but that he would give some tiger skins. These the envoy scornfully refused and returned to the north. The king was somewhat disturbed by this and ordered an envoy to go to Manchuria with gifts, but they were all returned untouched. At this the king was furious and ordered an envoy to go and say that Korea would never again send tribute nor make peace with the Manchus. Kim Si-yang expostulated with the king and told him that such a message would be suicidal, but he was banished on the spot. It is probable the message never reached the Manchu camp, for we learn that with the opening of a new year the king had come to his senses and sent trib-

ute to the north to the extent of 800 pieces of silk, 800 pieces
of linen, 800 pieces of grass cloth, 800 pieces of cotton, 60
tiger skins, 300 sea-otter skins and 800 quires of heavy
paper.

The Korean territory became the asylum for several renegade Chinese generals who demanded sustenance, and what
between these and the Manchus it became well-nigh impossible to keep on good terms either with the Emperor or
with the Manchus. The latter were continually ravaging
the northern border and were apparently losing all their
former feeling of friendship. This cannot be wondered at,
for the king was openly siding with the Chinese.

In the spring of 1636 the king ordered a remeasurement
of all the arable land in the three southern provinces. It
seems that the people were thriving and the margin of cultivation was broadening so that a remeasurement became
necessary for a re-estimate of the revenue. At the same time
he despatched two envoys to the Manchu court at Mukden.
The Manchus had just begun to style their empire the Ch'ing
or "clear." And now for the first time we meet the names
of the two great Manchu generals who were destined to play
such a prominent part in the invasion of Korea. They were
called Yonggoldä and Mabudä. These two men came to the
Yalu River and received the king's missive addressed to the
son of the Ch'ing Emperor. The two envoys were brought
into the Manchu Emperor's presence, where they were ordered to bow, but refused. They were forced to a stooping position, but resisted, whereupon they were stripped, beaten and
driven away.

The Manchus were now fully determined to invade
Korea and bring her to her knees once more. In preparation for this the two generals above named were sent to Seoul
as envoys, but in reality to spy out the land and learn the
roads   The officials almost with one voice urged the king to
burn the letters brought by these envoys and to kill the men
themselves. To show the extent of the infatuation of the
Koreans it is necessary to subjoin a memorial which was presented the king at this time. It said "Since I was born I
have never heard of two emperors   How can these wild
savages claim imperial power? Once before a rebel (referring

to Kang Hong-rip) came with these robbers and the king was compelled to flee to Kang-wha. If at that time we had only cut off the traitor's head it would have been to our honor and it would have shone like the sun and moon. These Manchu robbers are wolves and tigers. How can we think of casting off our allegiance to China? All our troubles have arisen because we did not kill Gen. Kang. This news about the Manchus rends my heart, for, though we live in a distant corner of the world, we have manners. From King T'ă-jo's time till now we have been loyal to the Ming power. Now that the northern savages are growing strong and we, through fear, are compelled to follow them, we may for a time escape harm, but in the end the world will scorn us. It was a mistake for the government to give those envoys a polite reception, and now the officials sit still while the king is being insulted by outsiders. Our situation is not only dangerous, it is pitiable. Here we sit and do nothing to prevent the enemy entering our territory. I see what the Manchus want. They know we are weak, and they want to hold us in their hand and make a boast of us. If they want to play at empire why do they not do it among themselves and not come to us with it? They do it so as to be able to say that they have Korea in their train. Now let us be men and cut off these envoys' heads and put them in a box along with their insulting letter and send the whole back to their so-called emperor. If the king does not like my advice let him cut off my head and send it. I cannot live to see and hear the insults of these savages. The people of the nothern provinces grind their teeth at them and swear that they cannot live with them. Today must decide the continued existence or the destruction of this kingdom. The king should send out a proclamation far and wide for the people to flock to the support of the royal banners. Then would we all rejoice to die, if need be, for our country." This speech is probably an exact expression of the feeling of the vast majority of the officials and people at that time, but most of them had the good sense to keep still, for such talk was sure to bring swift retribution. It is evident the king thought so, for he answered this warm appeal by saying, "You have spoken very well but it is a little permature for us to go to cutting

off the heads of envoys from a neighboring power ; we will
consider the matter however.''

The Manchu envoys had with them some Mongol soldiers
to prove to the Koreans that the Mongols had actually surrendered to the Manchu power. The envoys asked that these
be treated well, but the king had them treated as slaves.
The object of the embassy was nominally to attend the funeral of the king's grandmother, but the king deceived them by
sending them to an enclosure in the place where a screen was
closely drawn around. The envoys supposed this was the
obsequies and began their genuflections, but a violent gust
of wind blew the screens over and they saw that they had
been duped. They immediately were seized with fear lest
they be foully dealt with and rushing out they mounted
their steeds and fled by way of the South Gate. The boys
pelted them with stones as they passed. The people knew
that this was a serious matter and messenger after messenger
was sent after the fleeing envoys pleading with them to come
back, but of course without avail.

The Prime Minister told the king that war was now inevitable and that it was necessary to call the people to arms
at once. The king consented and the proclamation went
forth saying. ''Ten years ago we made a treaty with these
Manchus, but their nature is so bad and they are so insulting
that we never before were so ashamed. From the king,
down to the lowest subject all must unite in wiping out this
disgrace They now claim to be an empire and that we are
their vassal. Such insolence cannot be borne. It may mean
the overthrow of our kingdom but we could do no less than
drive the envoys away. All the people saw them go. Of
course it means immediate war and all the people must now
come up to their responsibilities and swear to be avenged on
the Manchus even at the cost of life itself.''

The Manchu envoys delayed on Korean soil long enough
to secure a copy of the proclamation and, armed with this,
they crossed the border and made their way to the Manchu
headquarters.

In Seoul there were various counsels. One side argued that
the palace at Kang-wha should be burned so that the king's
mind might not turn toward that as an asylum. Others said

that the king should go to P'yung-yang and lead the army in person. We are told that there were many omens of impending danger at this time. They are of course fictitious, but they show the bent of the Korean mind. They say that at one place large stones moved from place to place of their own accord. In another place ducks fought on the water and killed each other. In another place a great flock of storks congregated in one place and made a "camp." Outside the South Gate there was a great fight among the frogs. In the south, toads came out and hopped about in mid-winter. A pond in the palace became red like blood. In summer the river rose so high that it lapped the foundations of the East Gate. At twenty-seven different places in Seoul the land rose and fell. Such are some of the popular supersititions.

The Chinese general in charge of troops on Ka-do Island sent word to the Emperor that Korea had broken with the Manchus, whereupon the Emperor sent a letter congratulating the king and praising his boldness. The Chinese envoy further said, "I came to bring the letter of praise from the Emperor but at the same time he recognises the great danger in which you are and he grants permission for you to conclude a peace with them if you so wish." But the king had decided on the arbitrament of war and this pointed hint was not taken.

The king had now collected an army in P'yŭng-yang and he gave each soldier a present of cotton cloth. The whole number of the army is not given, but we are told that there were 10,234 skillful archers and 700 musketeers. It seems that the review did not satisfy all, for one of the leading officials said, "If we take this final step and go to war we shall all perish, so it might be well to send an envoy and try to patch up matters with them." To this another replied hotly, "All the people are bent on war and are determined to rid themselves of these savages. You are a traitor to your country to talk of sending an envoy. You are insulting the king. You are over-riding the will of the great majority." But the other answered calmly, "We have no army that can stand before them an hour and some fine morning we shall all he found dead in bed. There is no place to take the ancestral tablets, so my advice is to send generals to P'yŭng-yang and have

soldiers well drilled, and at the same time send an envoy to
the Manchus to see how they talk.   It may be that things may
be so arranged that we can go along quietly as before.   At
any rate it will give us time to prepare.   If worse comes to
worst and we have to defend the Yalu we will do our best, but
it is evident that if they once cross we will necessarily become
supplicants."   This was too good logic to be withstood and
yet it was worse than nothing, for it was either just too strong
or just too weak, and it threw the whole court into a fatal un-
certainty.

In the tenth moon the Manchu general Mabudă, appeared on the west bank of the Yalu and sent word to the prefect
of Eui-ju saying. "On the twenty-sixth of the next moon our
armies are to move on Korea, but if within that time you send
an envoy we will desist, even though it be at the last moment."
Gen. Kim Nyu told the king this and urged that the envoy
be sent, but only an interpreter was sent with a letter to the
Manchu chief.   When the Manchus saw this man they said
"Go back and tell the king that if he does not send his son
and the Prime Minister and another high official to perform
the treaty ceremony before the twenty fifth of the next moon,
our armies will instantly be put in motion."   Yonggoldă
brought out the copy of the proclamation he had brought with
him from Korea and said, "Look at this.   It cannot be said
that it was we who broke the treaty first."   A letter was given
the messenger for the king in which was written, "They say
you are building many forts.   Is it to block my way to your
capital?   They say you are building a palace on Kang-wha to
find refuge in.   When I have taken your eight provinces will
Kang-wha be of any use to you?   Can your councillors overcome me with a writing-brush?"

When this ominous letter reached Seoul the king and the
highest of the officials wanted to make terms with the Manchus at once, but they were opposed stoutly by the whole mass
of the lesser officials.   At last however a man was dispatched
to convey the acceptance by Korea of the Manchu terms ; but
the fatal day had passed, and when the messenger met the
Manchus advancing upon Eui-ju, he was seized.   As war was
now beyond peradventure Generals Kim Nyu and Kim Cha-jŭm
advised that the prefectural towns along the route that the

Manchus would come be moved back from the main road. This was ordered and the prefectures of Eui-ju, P'yŭng-yang and Whang-ju were moved from ten to a hundred *li* back. All the towns along the way were deserted by their inhabitants.

Gen. Kim Cha-jŭm forced the people at the point of the sword to rebuild the fortress at Chŏng-tang Mountain, but he did not attempt to guard the Yalu, for he was possessed by the the infatuation that the Manchus would not come after all. There was a line of fire-signal mountains from Eui-ju all the way to Seoul but he ordered the fires to be lighted only as far as his quarters, in case of war, as it would cause great consternation in the capital. His criminal incredulity and carelessness were so great that when in the twelfth moon the double fires gleamed forth along the line from the north telling of the approach of an invading army, he still averred that it was nothing more nor less than the envoy heralding his return. He sent no messages nor warnings to Seoul. He sent à messenger north to discover where the Manchus were. This man came running back and announced that the north was full of them. Still the general would not believe it and wanted to kill the man for deceiving him. The report was however confirmed by so many eye-witnesses that he was at last compelled to believe it and sent word to Seoul that the Manchus had come. On the twelfth a letter from the prefect of Eui-ju announced in Seoul that the Manchus had crossed the river 140,000 strong. The next day a letter from the tardy Kim announced that the Manchus had already traversed the province of P'yŭng-an. This news was like a thunder-bolt from a clear sky to the people of the capital. They were thrown into a panic and are described as having resembled boiling water. The roads were choked with fugitives from the city. The king said, "Liberate all the captives and prisoners and grant an amnesty to all who have been banished." All prefects who had not gone to their posts were sent forthwith. The king desired to start at once for Kang-wha, and he appointed Kim Kyŭng-jeung to have military control there with Yi Min-gu as second. An aged Minister Yun Pang together with Kim Sang-yong took the ancestral tablets and went ahead to that island. Then followed the Queen and the Princes,

Finally the king appointed Sin Keui-wŭn to guard the capital.

On the fourteenth the Manchu army entered Whang-hă Province and almost immediately the news came that they had arrived at Chang-dan only 120 *li* from Seoul. There they caught the prefect, cut off his hair, dressed him in Manchu clothes and forced him to act as guide. At noon the next day the king and the Crown Prince passed out the South Gate on their way to Kang-wha, when suddenly messengers came hurrying up saying that the Manchu horsemen had already arrived at Yang-wha-jin on the river and that the road to Kang-wha was consequently blocked. The king and his immediate followers went up into the pavilion above the gate and conferred together. The native chronicler says that "their faces were white and their voices were like the croaking of country frogs." And well they might be. Chi Yŏ-hă said, "They have come down from the border in five days and must be very tired. I will take 500 men and go out and hold them in check until the king can get to Kang-wha." But Ch'oe Myŭng-gil said, "We must decide immediately, for the enemy is at our very doors. We cannot fight them, but I will go out the gate and parley with them and meantime the king can escape to Nam-han." To this the king eagerly assented and Ch'oe took ten cattle and ten tubs of wine and went out to meet the enemy. All the gates on the south side of Seoul were closed and the king aud his suite started for the East Gate. The crown prince's groom ran away and the prince was compelled to hold the bridle himself. The people crowded around the royal party so closely that it was almost impossible to move, but finally the gate was passed and the party hurried forward. At seven o'clock that night the royal cavalcade entered the welcome gate of Nam-han. So rapid had been the pace that only six men in the king's retinue remained until they arrived at their destination. The rest arrived some time before midnight. They all urged the king to start at day light and reach Kang-wha by a circuitous route. This was determined upon, but a storm of sleet and rain came on, which rendered the roads so slippery that the king was compelled to dismount and walk. It soon became evident that this would not do. The king was very cold and the progress was hopelessly slow. So they placed him in a litter hastily extemporised and brought him back to the fortress. It turned out that this was fortunate, for the Manchus had guarded every approach to Kang-wha so carefuly that the king never would have been able to get through. Gen. Ch'oe, who had gone to parley with the enemy, went beyond the Peking Pass and met Gen. Mabudä and said, "We made a treaty with you some time since, but now you come down upon us with this great array. How is this?" The Manchu answered, "It is not we who have broken the treaty but you, and we have come to learn from the king the reason of it." Gen. Ch'oe replied, "Well, you cannot see him. He has gone to the fortress of Nam-han."

Together they entered Seoul and there the Manchu general had Gen. Ch'oe send a letter to the king as follows, "The Manchu general has come to make a treaty with us, but he says we are all afraid of him and that even the king has fled. He says that if the king wants to make peace he must send his son and the prime minister together with the man who advised the king to break the treaty. They demand an immediate answer." That night no answer came and Mabudä charged Gen. Ch'oe with having deceived him and wanted to kill him on the spot, but the rest dissuaded him saying "Let us go to Nam-han ourselves." They made Gen. Ch'oe act as guide and soon they stood before that renowned fortress. Gen. Ch'oe went ahead and entered alone. The king seized his hand and said, "You are come to save us." But the general said "The Manchu general was exceedingly angry because you did not answer my letter last night, so he has now come with a third of his whole force. In order to pacify him we cannot but comply with his three conditions." The king replied, "You are deceived by him. Do you think he has come all this way to be satisfied so easily as that?"

Chapter VII.

Manchu camps....the garrison of Nam-han ...a trick ...divided counsels ...the king determines to fight it out ...Koreans eager to fight ....the garrison put on half rations....terrible cold ...message to the provinces ...successful sallies ...the king's kindness....the

Manchu fence ...the gift refused....help from the outside....un-
seccessful venture ...plenty and want . imperial edict .. the answer ...a night attack ...relief party defeated ...other attempts
to relieve the king ...a cowardly general ..a clever trick   Korean defeat....mutual recriminations ...a ghastly trick....desper-
ate straits ...correspondence....a starving garrison ...a heroic
answer ...king wants to surrender....Manchu demands....fight-
ing continued.

The Manchu army encamped along the southern side of
the city from Mo-wha-gwan to the South Gate and out side the
East Gate, and the air resounded with the sound of music and
drums.   At first the soldiers committed no excesses beyond
the theft of a few cattle and an occasional woman, but now
that it was learned that the king had run away to Nam-han
the license became unbounded and men and women were
killed in large numbers.   The royal treasure houses were
looted and nothing was too sacred to be dragged about the
streets.   That same night a band of the Manchus completely
encircled Nam-han, which must be well-nigh ten miles
around.

The king set a strong guard all about the wall, appointing Gen. Sin Kyŏng-jin to guard the East Gate, Gen. Ku
Kweng the South Gate, Gen. Yi Sŏ the North Gate and Gen.
Yi Si-bǎk the West Gate.   Generals Wŭn Tu-p'yo, Ku In-
hu, Han Whe-il and Pak Whan went all about the wall with
strong bodies of troops, to prevent the entrance of any scaling party.   The whole number of troops in the fortress was
about 12,000.   Gen. Nam An-gap held the important position
of Commissariat Chief.   The king's retinue and court consisted of 200 officials, 200 of his relatives, 100 clerks, and
300 servants of different degrees.   All these received their
salary in rice.   Officials of the first and second grades
were allowed to have three servants and two horses, those of
the third, fourth and fifth grades could have two servants and
one horse, while those below these could have but one servant
and one horse.   The commander-in-chief was Gen. Kim Nyu.
His advice to the king was to send the crown prince and the
prime minister at once and make the best terms possible.
It was decided to deceive the enemy if possible, so Neung
Pong-su, a distant relative of the king, assumed the name of
the king's younger brother and Sim Chip assumed the role of

crown prince.   Together they sallied out to try their hand on
the Manchus.   When they came before Mabudā, that hard-
headed warrior looked them over, turned them inside out
and sent them back to the king with the curt reply that, "As
you have been trying to play a trick on us we will now consent to treat with no one whatever except .he crown prince
himself.   If you will send him we will talk with you."   This
they demanded in spite of the statements of the messengers
that the crown prince was still in mourning for his mother.

When this ultimatum was delivered to the king there
was a division of opinion.   Gen. Kim Nyu and several others
averred that there was nothing to do but comply with the
demands   But the king said, "I will die first."   Kim Sang-
hön took the other side and said, "Whoever talks of surrendering so tamely is a traitor."   On the seventeenth the king
sent Hong Sö-bong to the Manchu camp and said, "I am willing to send my second or third son to you but they are all in
Kang-wha."   They answered as before, "We will see no one
but the crown prince."   When the crown prince expressed
his willingness to go, a courtier said, "We have a good strong
garrison and shall we tamely surrender and send our future
king into the clutches of these highwaymen?   If he goes I
shall strangle myself with my own bridle "   Another said,
"Let us fight them.   We are men, not straw manikins."   So
the king made up his mind that it would be war and not surrender and he so proclaimed, "We shall fight to the bitter
end.   Let no one expect or hope for peace."   He then despatched a letter to Kim Cha-jūm in P'yŭng-yang, saying "We
are hemmed in here and our forces are small and food scarce,
but we have determined to fight it out even though it ends
the dynasty.   So hasten and come to our aid with all the forces
at your command."   The next day the guard of the North
Gate made a successful sally, returning with six Manchu
heads.   This excited the soldiers almost to frenzy, and they
were eager to rush out and engage the besiegers.   Unfortunately all the rice that had been stored at the river for the
provisoning of Nam-han had been seized by the Manchus,
but the arms and ammunition were safe within the walls.
The king took advantage of the elation of the soldiers over
this successful sally to make them a little speech, in which he

remarked, "Shall we surrender or fight? It is for you to say." Sim Kwang-su answered grimly for them all and said "Show us the head of the man who advised to surrender " This referred to Gen. Ch'oe Myŭng-gil, but the rest did not dare to second the request. From that time the walls were guarded with renewed vigilance. Day after day the smoke of the Manchu camps went up to heaven round about the beleagured fortress. On the nineteenth the king sacrificed at the tomb of On-jo, the founder of the ancient kingdom of Păk-je, of which Nam-han was for many years the capital. On the same day Gen. Ku Kweng made a sally from the West Gate and took twenty Manchu heads. This again excited the garrison almost beyond control. The following day a renegade Korean who had gone over to the Manchus came near the gate and parleyed with the guard, urging that the king surrender and make peace ; but when the king heard of it he ordered that if the man came again he should not be met at the gate but that the guard should only talk down at him from the top of the wall.

The matter of provisions was one of prime importance, and the king called the chief of commissariat and asked him how many days' rations there were remaining in the storehouses. He replied that there were enough provisions to last sixty days, but that if great economy were exercised it might last seventy days. He said the horses could have but one measure of beans a day and the servants must get along as best they could, on barley and oats. Someone suggested that as there were a large number of people present who held no important position, the king ought not to feel obliged to support them, but the king vetoed this by saying, "They came here trusting in me and now shall I deprive them of food ? No, we will all eat or go hungry together." The weather was very cold and the men exposed upon the wall suffered severely. Their cheeks, being frost-bitten, cracked open in a very painful manner. In view of this the king ordered that night guards be dispensed with and that no old or feeble men should be put on picket duty in these exposed positions.

The king again sent out a letter to the governors of the different provinces saying, "We are here hemmed in ; our life hangs by a thread. Let all loyal men rally to our support, and march agaist the besieging force." To Kim Cha-jŭm he wrote, "For seven days we have now been immured and we have come to the brink of destruction. Come immediately to our aid."

On the twenty-first there were two simultaneous sallies, from the East and West Gates respectively, and each resulted in the securing of a few trophies. For the encouragement of the soldiers Kim Sin-guk suggested that a schedule of rates be issued offering prizes for Manchu heads. The king's intention not to surrender was still unshaken, for when a courtier memorialized him urging surrender he burned the document in anger. On the twenty-second a Manchu messenger rode up to the gate and asked if the king were ready to surrender yet. The answer came in the shape of fierce sallies on the South and East sides in which forty heads were taken and in which Gen. Yi Chi-wŭn, with an iron club, killed two mounted generals. The soldiers were so elated by these successes, which of course could make no difference in the strength of the besieging force, that on the following day they made simultaneous attacks on several sides, in each of which the Koreans had some advantage. The Koreans lost but twenty men while the Manchu loss was much greater. As the Manchus carried their dead from the field, however, the exact amount of their loss is not known. The king celebrated the victory by making a circuit of the wall. The next day was wet and foggy and the cold was even harder to endure than when the weather was clear. Both the king and the crown prince came out in the rain to encourage the soldiers and they and many of the officials gave mats and blankets and the mud-guards of their saddles to help the soldiers to keep dry. The inmates of Han-heung Monastery, inside the fortress, presented the king with forty quires of paper, and several bags of vegetables, but the king distributed them all among the soldiers. Other monks presented three large bowls of honey, for which the king thanked them and gave presents in return.

On the twenty-fifth the Manchus completed a wattle fence completely encircling the fortress. It was thirty miles long and twice the height of a man. Some idea can be formed of the numbers in the Manchu army when we know that this was completed in seven days Every eighty paces a bell was attached in such a way that if anyone attempted to break through, warning would be given to the sentinels.

There were those outside who sincerely desired to give succor to the king and the court. Gen. Kwŏn Chŏng-gil, of Wŭn-ju, gathered a small force and camped on Kŭm-dan mountain in plain sight of Nam-han, and the king was greatly encouraged, hoping that the Koreans were rallying to his support. When this loyal band attacked the Manchus they were immediately overwhelmed and cut to pieces.

The Manchus caught every Korean they could lay hands on. The more vigorous of these they forced into their ranks, the old men were made hewers of wood and drawers of water, the young women were made concubines and the older women were compelled to cook and wash.

On the twenty-eighth the king sent a present of a bullock and ten bottles of wine to the Manchu headquarters, but received the reply, "Heaven has given us all Korea and we have no need of these things. Take them back to your starving soldiers."

Chŏng Se-gyu, the governor of Ch'ung-ch'ŭng Province, was consumed with grief on hearing that the king was reduced to two side-dishes with his rice; so he gave a monk two pheasants and told him to effect an entrance in some way or other and give them to the king. The governor himself came with a handful of men to Ma-heui-ch'ŭn, only forty *li* from the beleaguered fortress, and there he was attacked in the rear by the enemy. His whole force was annihilated, though he himself escaped by leaping into a deep gorge, intending to commit suicide. But the fall was not fatal. Nam Yang, also, the prefect of Yun-gye, wanted to do what he could, and when he learned of the distress of the king, he arose even on his wedding night and started for the seat of war. His little force was surrounded and he was ordered to surrender, and then it was that he made that memorable reply, "You can conquer my neck but never my knees." His tongue was cut out and his body was dismembered.

Gen. Kim Nyu had the idea that the Manchu force was weakest on the south and that if a sudden, determined attack were made the line might be broken through. So on the twenty-ninth he called all the generals and gave his orders. They all disagreed with him and considered the project hope-less, but would not show insubordination. A considerable body, therefore, emerged from the South Gate, hastened down the valley against the surrounding line of beseigers. These men had no faith in the plan, however, and were prevented from turing back only by the sword of Gen. Kim Nyu which he used on a few as a warning to the rest. Gen. Sin said, "This is actual suicide. Let me take my company and go out here and show you at the cost of my life that this cannot be done." He pushed rapidly forward and was soon surrounded by the Manchus who had lain concealed in a bend of the hills, and he and his men were all cut down. When the ammuni-tion of his men was gone they clubbed their muskets and fought to the bitter end. Two hundred Koreans fell in this rash adventure and Gen. Kim returned crest-fallen and ashamed. Having no excuse, he tried to lay the blame on others, claiming that they did not support him properly. He also told the king that only forty men had been killed.

Sim Keui-wŭn who had been left as guardian of Seoul sent a letter to the king saying that he had made a fierce at-tack on the Manchus encamped at A-o-gă outside the West Gate, but the king afterwards learned that this was false, and that Sim had fled incontinently from before the face of the foe.

When the last day of the year 1636 arrived it found the relative position of the Koreans and Manchus as follows : The Manchu camps were filled with plunder and with women which the soldiers had captured ; but what of the children ? These the soldiery did not want, and so they were killed and their bodies thrown outside the camps. There they lay in piles and a pestilence was prevented only by the intense cold of winter. In Nam-han the greatest distress prevailed. The provisions had not held out as had been hoped. Food was all but exhausted and horses and cattle were dying of starvation. The king slept in his ordinary clothes, for he had given all his blankets to the soldiers. All he had to eat with his rice was the leg or wing of a chicken. On that last day of the year some magpies gathered and began building a nest in a tree near

the king's quarters.   This was hailed as a hopeful omen.   It
shows to what straits the garrison was reduced that it should
have pinned its faith to this childish superstition.   It was the
sole subject of conversation for some time, but it did the caged
Korean king no good.

The next day was new-years day of 1637 and the king
sent Kim Sin-guk and Yi Kyŭng-jik to the Manchu camp to
offer the compliments of the season.   They were there informed that the emperor's son had arrived and had inspected
the army and the forts.   Consequently on the following day
Hong Sŏ-bong, Kim Sin-guk and Yi Kyŭng-jik hastened to
his headquarters and were met, not by the emperor's son but
by a general who said, "You have called us slaves and thieves
but our course has been straight and consistent throughout."
He then laid before them an edict of the emperor written on
yellow paper, and whey were ordered to bow before it.   Its
contents were as follows :

"The great, the good, the wise, the kind Emperor to the
king of Korea.   As you preferred allegiance to the Ming Emperor rather than to us and, not content with throwing us
over, despised and insulted us, you now have an opportunity
to see the fruits of your choice.   Of a truth you acted wicked-
ly in breaking your oath, in throwing off the Manchu yoke
and in offering us armed opposition.   I heve now brought an
immense army and have surrounded your eight provinces.
How can you longer hope to render assistance to your "father,"
the Ming Emperor ?   The Mings are now hung up by the
heels, as it were."

On the next day the king sent his answer couched in the
following terms :   "The great, the glorious, the righteous
Emperor.   The little country has indeed sinned against the
great one and has drawn upon herself this trouble which lies
hard by the door of destruction.   We have long wanted to
write thus but we have been so surrounded and hemmed in
that it seemed well-nigh impossible to get a letter through
the lines ; but now that the Emperor's son himself has come,
we rejoice, and yet we tremble.   The Ming Emperor is no
longer our suzerain.   In this we have completely reformed.
The people on the border have acted badly in ill-treating the
Manchu envoys.   We are truly on the brink of destruction

and we confess all our sin.   It is for us to confess and for the Emperor to forgive.   From this day forth we wash from our mind all other thought of allegiance and enter upon a new line of conduct.   If the Emperor will not forgive, we can only bow the head and die.''

When this abject document was read before the court, before sending it, some thought it too humble, but the leaders said it was the only course left ; so it was forwarded to the Manchu camp.   Answer was returned that the Emperor's son had not yet arrived but that when he came he would re- ply.   Strange to say no truce was made and the Manchu sol- diers, fearing perhaps that a truce might rob them of the pleasure of scaling those walls that had defied them so long, approached the wall that very night and with scaling ladders a considerable number effected an entrance.   But they had underestimated the determination and courage of the defend- ers, and those who got in were quickly dispersed by Gen. Yi Si-băk.   Many Manchus fell in this desperate assault.   Almost at the same hour a similar attack was made on the south side but there also the Manchus were check-mated by the watchful guard.

And now a diversion occurred.   Generals Hŏ Wan and Min Yŏng from the provinces approached with a force of 40,- 000 men and seriously threatened the Manchu flank.   They were stationed on two opposite hills with a line of sharp- shooters between.   In the fight which ensued the Koreans held their ground gallantly and at first even made the invad- ers retreat ; but this exhausted their ammunition and when the enemy reformed his lines and came on again to the attack there was nothing to do but retreat.   The retreat became a rout and large numbers of Koreans were cut down, including Gen. Hŏ Wan.   The other part of the army under Gen. Min Yŏng held out a little longer but an unfortunate accident oc- curred which threw his troops into confusion.   A large quan- tity of powder which was being paid out to the soldiers sud- denly exploded killing a large number of men and depriving the rest of means for continuing the fight.   So they met the same fate as the others.   Those that the Manchus killed they stripped and burned but many fugitives likewise died of ex- posure and fatigue.

Gen. Sim Yun had been fortifying Cho-ryang (Pass) but when he heard of the rout of the 40,000 men he took fright and retreated precipitately, telling all he met that there was no use in attempting to do anything. Gen. Kim Chun-yong. however, had more perseverance and came and encamped twenty miles from Nam-han, occupying a position that was specially annoying to the enemy. A fight was the result, in which the Koreans were at first successful, but during the night the Manchus were reinforced and cannon were brought to bear upon the Koreans. All the next day the Koreans fought desperately. Night put an end to the battle and the Koreans finding that all their ammunition was gone, silently separated, burning all bridges as they went.

The admiral of Chŭl-la Province desired to render aid to the king and so getting together a little fleet of boats he came north to Kang-wha and joined the royal forces there. The governor of Kang-wŭn Province excused himself from taking active part in the relief of Nam-han on the score of scarcity of food. For this he was afterward banished.

Singular events were happening in the north where Gen. Yang Keun lay with a considerable force a short distance north of Seoul. He was however a coward and dared not move hand or foot. Two other generals felt that they might get into trouble if they did do not something, and they had the happy thought that they ought to report to their superior, Gen. Yang Keun, for they knew he would do no-thing, and thus they would be safe, for their responsibility would cease. So they went to him and urged him to advance against the Manchus. But he declined to do so, and even gave them a written statement to that effect. Armed with that they felt quite safe. So there they lay a month till they heard at last of the fall of Nam-han.

Of another stamp was Gen. Yu Rim. He was on the road between Seoul and P'yŭng-yang and, being attacked by the Manchus, he and his little band defended themselves with such good effect that the Manchu camp resounded all night with wailings for their dead. The Koreans, finding that their ammunition was almost exhausted, then planned an ingenious retreat. Loading their muskets they tied them to trees, attached fuses of different lengths and then silently retreated.   The guns kept going off all night and so the enemy knew nothing of the retreat until it was discovered in the morning.

Another effort that was made about this time was that of Generals Kim Cha-jŭm and Yôk-dal who had a following of some 7,000 men. Starting from the north they came down to the vicinity of Song-do.   Unfortunately they had no scouts out and suddenly falling in with a Manchu force in the narrow passage a few miles beyond Song-do, they were thrown into a panic and it is said that 5,000 men were killed, though it seems almost incredible that only 2,000 men survived out of 7,000. Gen. Kim escaped by scaling the steep mountain side but his second was caught and bound.   The two thousand survivors rallied and attacked the Manchus with such fury that they were forced back and the captured general was rescued.   Gen. Kim Cha-jŭm then made his way to where Gen. Yang Keun was idling away his time, and together they awaited the surrender of the king.   We may anticipate a few months and say that after peace was made these two generals were banished to distant places for their criminal cowardice.

Gen. Sin Kyöng-wan, stationed at Ong-jin in Whang-hă Province, was surrounded by the enemy, but the place was so difficult of approach, owing to the roughness of the ground, that they could not reduce it ; so, hoping to draw out the garrison they feigned retreat.   Gen. Sin was not to be caught thus, and sent out one of his lieutenants to reconnoitre. That man happened to be just recovering from a wound, and so he did not go far, but spent the night in a neighboring inn.   He came back in the morning and reported the enemy gone.   Gen. Sin then led out his troops to take them to the vicinity of Seoul ; but the Manchus, who were lying concealed in the vicinity, rushed out upon him and captured him. He was released only after peace had been declared.

At Nam-han a severe mental struggle was going on. They well knew that surrender and humiliation were inevitable but their pride revolted at the thought, and each tried to throw the blame on the other.   This may be illustrated by a single case which will show how mutual recriminations were being made in the very presence of the siege-weary

king. Yu Păk-jeung memorialized the king in these words :
"Gen. Kim Nyu who holds the rank of General-in-chief is a
man of no military skill, a man of jealous, vindictive temperament and his house is full of bribes. When the king
came to Nam-han it was almost without retinue, but he, for-
sooth, must bring sixty horsemen at his back. And the fe-
males of his household came in litters. He it was who urged
the king to give up the crown prince to the tender mercies
of the Manchu wolves. He it was who compassed the humiliation of the king by advising him to send that self-effacing
letter which, though so humble, was rejected. This is all the
work of Kim Nyu." Here as elsewhere we see that personal
spite has alway been the rock on which the interests of Korea
have been wrecked.

The emperor knew that he had the king secure, and he
determined to delay the ratification of a treaty until his captive was reduced to the last crust, in order to brand upon the
memory of all Koreans the indubitable fact of their vassalage
and to teach them a lesson that they should never forget.
And so the days slipped by.

On the sixth of the moon Korean messengers succeeded
in getting through the Manchu lines and brought the king
letters from his two sons on the island of Kang-wha, but the
Manchus were aware of this and redoubled their diligence in
guarding the approaches, and so the king was completely cut
off from the outside. A few days later a costly joke was
played by the Korean Gen. Kim On-yun. He led a small
party outside the West Gate and soon returned with two
heads. The king praised him and gave him presents of silk.
The heads were raised on pikes, but behold, no blood came
from them. A soldier in the ranks cried out, "Why is my
brother killed twice?" The truth is that the General had beheaded two corpses of Koreans whereby to obtain praise and
favor from the king. The king replaced the heads by those
of the general and his second.

On the twelfth the king's emissaries went into the Manchu camp bearing a letter from the king. They were told
that a great Manchu general was about to arrive and that
they must come again the next day. The people in Nam-han
were in desperate straits. All who had advocated continued

resistance now urged surrender, excepting Kim Sang-hön and Chöng On, who said, "Not till every soldier is dead, and all the common people as well, will it be time to think of giving in."

The next day the messengers presented themselves in the Manchu camp as ordered. The general who received them said, "You broke your former treaty with us. Are you prepared to keep it if we make another?" The messengers beat upon their breasts and cried, "It was our fault and not the fault of the king. We are willing to prove this with our lives." "But why do you not come out and fight?" "We are an insignificant power and how can we hope to cope with you?" was the humble reply. The Manchu then broke the seal of the king's letter and read, "When we signed the former treaty you were the elder brother and we the younger brother. When a younger brother does wrong it is for the order brother to correct him, but if it is done too severely a principle of righteousnessss is broken, and the Supreme Being will be offended. We are dwellers in a corner of the sea. We know nothing but books. We are no warriors. We are weak and must bow before superior force. So we accept the clemency of the Manchus, and we are now vassals and you are our suzerain. When the Japanese invaded our land and we were on the verge of destruction, China sent her hosts and saved us. Our gratitude to them lives in the very fiber of our bones. Even at the risk of incurring your anger we could not bear to cast them off. If now the Manchu power shows us kindness and goes back across the Yalu, our gratitude toward them will be the same. We have been a long time imprisoned here and we are tired and cramped. If you consent to overlook our faults we will engage to treat the Manchu power rightly. These sentiments are engraved on our very hearts and we surrender ouselves to the clemency of the Manchu emperor."

Food was now practically gone. The officials themselves were put on half rations and even the king's daily supply was diminished by one third. At the very most there was enough to last but twenty days more. At this time the Manchus burned the buildings in connection with the royal tombs outside the east Gate, and also those near Nam-han. The smoke of the burning went up to heaven. These acts of

vandalism must have been a bitter drop in the cup that was
being put to the king's lips. On the sixteenth Hong Sö-bong
again went to the Manchu camp and asked why no answer
was sent. The truth is that the Manchus had determined to
first send and reduce the Island of Kang-wha. They answered, "Gen. Kong Yu-dŭk has gone with 70,000 men to take
Kang-wha. We must wait till he returns." The next day
they sent the king an insulting letter saying, "Why do you
not come out and fight? We thought we would get at least
a little fight out of you. Have not your soldiers learned to
load and fire? China is your good friend ; why does she not
send and help you? Now you are starving and yet you have
the impudence to talk about righteousness. Heaven helps the
good and punishes the evil. Those who trust us we aid,
those who oppose we decapitate. As we have become your
enemies you see us here in force. If you will come back to
your allegiance we will treat you as a brother. If you wish
to live, come out and surrender ; if you will come out and
fight so much the better. Heaven will decide between us."
This received from the Koreans, starving though they were,
the following memorable reply, "We will die and rot here in
our fortress before we will surrender thus. Then there will
be no one to answer your insulting summons."

On the eighteenth a Manchu general came near the South
Gate and demanded that the king should come out and surrender or else come out and fight. The king thereupon sent
a letter to the Manchu headquarters saying that he wanted to
come out and surrender but that he did not dare to do so while
the Manchu soldiers were prowling about the wall. As the
king handed this letter to the messenger Kim Sang-hön snatched it from the messenger's hand and tore it in fragments
saying, "How can you bear to send such a letter. Heaven
will still favor us if we are patient, but if we send this we are
truly undone " Then followed a scene in which the courtiers
almost came to blows. Ch'oe Myŭng-gil took the fragments
of the letter and pasted them together and the next day in
company with another general took it to the Manchus. They
were met with the gruff reply, "We do not want your letters.
We want your king to come out and surrender." That night
the Manchus scaled the wall on the east side and a great panic

followed, but Gen. Yi Keui-ch'uk, with a body of picked men succeeded in driving back the enemy. On the twentieth an answer was received from the emperor who said, "The reason why we demand that you come out and surrender is that we may have a visible proof of your sincerity. If we depart now leaving you still king of Korea all will be well. Why should I deceive you since I am conquering the whole world besides? Need I use guile? I desire to punish only those who advised you to cleave to China and prove untrue to us. Before surrendering you must send those men bound to me. I shall kill them but the rest of you will be safe. One thing is certain. I will read no more of your letters." When the king saw this he cried, "I cannot send those men bound to him." In spite of the ominous closing words of the emperor's letter the king again wrote saying, "Korea to the worshipful, glorious, puissant, merciful emperor, greeting. We are narrow and provincial people and very deficient in manners but the contrast between our present mental attitude and that of a few months ago is surprising. Among our councillors some argued one way and some argued another but now starvation has brought us all to the same point and we know that we must become subjects of the Manchu power. But since the days of Silla there has never been seen such a thing as a king going out from his fortress to surrender. We cannot do it in that way. If you insist upon it you will soon have nothing left but a fortress full of dead. I have signified my willingness to surrender but if I should go out to you the people would never again recognize me as king and anarchy will result. I long ago banished the men who opposed the making of peace with the Manchus, so I cannot send them to you, but the emperor must now be gracious and forgive our mistake." When the Manchu general was about to send this scornfully back Yi Hong-ju told him that it was written by the officials and that nothing more was possible ; and that if anyone suggested to the king the advisability of coming out it would mean instant death. But the Manchu drove them away in a rage. One official named Chöng On violently opposed all these attempts at securing a cessation of hostilities and said it would be better to sit there and rot than to surrender. He urged that the fighting be continued.

Chapter VIII.

The refugees on Kang-wha .. crossing the ferry....the Princess blames
the commander....grain saved....cross-purposes ..Manchu rafts
..Manchus gain a footing on Kang-wha ...Gen. Kim's flight
Koreans massacred ...royal captives ...suicide ...ancestral tablets
dishonored ...list of the dead ...from Kang-wha to Nam-han ...
fierce attacks ...bombardment ...the king learns of the fall of
Kang-wha ...Manchu victims sent ...arrangements for the surrender....the Manchu conditions ...the king comes out of Nam-
han ...the ceremony ...disgraceful scramble ...the king enters
Seoul ...condition of the capital ..Manchu army retires ...a high-
priced captive....king and Crown Prince part ...rewards and punishments ...the island of Ko-do taken ...an unselfish act.

We must leave the king and his court, facing starvation
on the one hand and the deep humiliation of surrender on the
other, and see how it fared with the people on Kang-wha.
This island had earned the reputation of being impregnable,
because of the failure of the Mongols to take it when the king
of Koryo found refuge there.   Kim Kyŭng-jeung was the
commander of the garrison there and Im In-gu was second in
command. Chang Sin had charge of the naval defenses.
When the king sent the Crown Princess, the royal concubines, the second and third princes and the aged officials
and their wives to Kang-wha a few days before his flight to
Nam-han they were under the escort of Gen. Kim Kyŭng-
jeung, who was also taking his wife and mother to the same
place for safety.   It was a long cavalcade, stretching miles
along the road.   Arriving at the ferry which was to take the
party across the narrow channel to the island, Gen. Kim deliberately began by filling the boats with the members of his
own family and fifty horse-loads of furniture which they had
brought along, and the Princess and the other royal fugitives
had to wait.   For two whole days the Crown Princess was
obliged to stay on the farther side in imminent danger of seizure by the Manchus.   At last she summoned Gen. Kim and
said, "Are not these boats the property of the king? Why
then do you use them only for your relatives and friends while
we wait here in danger?"   As there was no possible excuse

for his conduct he was obliged to accede to the demand, but only just in time ; for, though there were thousands of people still waiting to cross, a foraging band of Manchus arrived on the scene and the terrified multitude rushed headlong into the water, "like leaves driven by the wind," and multitudes were drowned. Large store of government rice was lying at Kimp'o and Tong-jin, and as the Manchus had not as yet discovered it, Gen. Kim was able to get it across to the island ; but no one excepting the members of his own family and following were allowed to have any part of it. He had such faith in the impregnability of Kang-wha that he set no guards and spent his time in feasting and playing chess. Prince Pong-im suggested that it would be well to keep a good look-out, but the general replied sharply, "Who is in command of this place, you or I?" This Gen. Kim was the son of Gen. Kim Nyu who had charge of the defence of Nam-han and between them they managed things about as they pleased. There was a running fire of dispute between Gen. Kim and the other leaders on Kang-wha and anything but good order and concerted action prevailed among the forces set for the defence of the people there. The Manchus, although without boats, had no intention to leave the island untaken, and so they pulled down houses far and near and made rafts with the timbers.

As it was in the dead of winter there was much ice on either bank of the estuary, and as the tide rises some thirty feet there the crossing was a difficult feat, even though the actual distance was small. Soon the message came from the ferry guards that the Manchus had finished their rafts and would soon be attempting the passage. Gen. Kim called them fools for thinking the Manchus would dare to cross in the face of such obstacles, but when it was announced that they had actually embarked in their improvised craft he bestirred himself. He sent a force under Yun Sin-ji to guard the upper ferry, Yu Chŭng-nyang took charge of the middle ferry, Yu Sŭng-jeung guarded the lower ferry and Yi Hyŭng was on guard at Ma-ri-san, still lower down. Gen. Kim stationed himself at the middle ferry. There was a great lack of arms, but as there were plenty in the Kang-wha arsenal the soldiers demanded them ; but Gen. Kim refused. It was the intention of the Manchus to cross under fire of certain huge cannon which they had planted on the opposite bank. When the shot from these began kicking up the dust about Gen. Kim he found he was urgently needed elsewhere and was hardly restrained by the indignant outcry of his lieutenants. The Manchus were then seen boarding their strange craft and in the very fore front came a raft with seventeen men who held shields in one hand while they paddled with the other. Admiral Chang Sin was lower down with a fleet of boats and he made desperate efforts to come to the place where this crossing was taking place, but the tide which runs there like a mill-race was against him and he could make no headway at all. He simply stood in his boat and beat his breast with anger and chagrin. Kang Sin-sŭk was farther up the estuary with other boats and he hastened to come down ; but it was too late. The first raft full of Manchus had gained a foothold on the island. The Koreans found their powder wet and the arrows exhausted. As a consequence the whole force, numbering about two hundred men, turned and fled before seventeen Manchus. These men paced up and down the shore waiting for reinforcements, for which they had signalled. Gen. Kim had already fled in a small boat, which finally landed him far down the coast. Then the whole Manchu army made its way across, some on rafts and some in boats which were sent from the island. The Crown Princess wanted to make her escape with her little two year old boy, but the Manchu soldiers at the gate of the fortress would not let her come out. She then gave the boy to Kim In and he managed to get through the lines and escape to the main land with the child, which he took to Tang-jin in Ch'ung-ch'ŭng Province. The Princess attempted suicide with a knife but did not succeed. The Manchus called out to Minister Yun Pang and said, "We will occupy the right side of the fortress and you and the royal personages and other persons of high degree can occupy the other side." They then took all the common people outside the North Gate of the fortress and set them in long lines. These people were all wondering what was about to happen, when out came a standard bearer carrying a red flag and behind him came a soldier with a bared sword. Walking along the lines they cut down every one of these innocent, unoffend-

ing people. The Manchus issued passes to the Koreans in
the fortress and no one could go in or out without showing his
credentials.   All the people living in the vicinity who did not
run away were massacred.

Having thoroughly subdued the island, the next move of
the victors was to rejoin the main army encamped before
Nam-han.   As a preparatory measure they burned all the
government buildings on the island and put to death all the
people they could find, that had not already perished.   Then
taking the Crown Princess and her retinue, and all the officials, they crossed the ferry and marched toward Nam-han.
The Princess was treated with all deference, as befitted her
exalted station.   As the company was about to leave the
fortress of Kang-wha on their way to Nam-han, the aged
Minister Kim Sang-yong was so deeply moved that he determined to end his life.   He entered the pavilion above the
South Gate where he found a box containing powder.   Yun
Pang also accompanied him, saying that he too was weary of
life, but Minister Kim said to him, "You are in charge of the
ancestral tablets, you must not prove recreant to that sacred
trust."   So Yun Pang sadly went about that task.   Divesting
himself of his outer garments the Minister gave them to an
attendant and told him to bury them in place of his body.
Then lighting his pipe with flint and steel he thrust it into
the box of powder.   The explosion which followed blew the
whole gate to fragments and Minister Kim Sang-yong and
Kim Ik-kyŭm and Kwŭn Sun-jang and the minister's little
grandson, thirteen years old, were blown to atoms.   In order
to convey the ancestral tablets in safety to Nam-han, Yun
Pang put them in a bag, but the Manchus, who did not care
to be burdened with such impedimenta, threw the whole thing
into a ditch.   Yun recovered them and cleaned them off as well
as he could, and managed to carry them along.   Perhaps it
was only because the Manchus wished to show an indignity
toward these most sacred of all the royal treasures.   The
following are the names of the most noted men killed in the
taking of Kang-wha.   Sim Hyŭn, Yi Sang-gil, Yi Si-jik,
Song Si-hyŭng, Yun Chŭn, Chŏng Păk-hyŭng, Kim Su-nam,
Kang Wi-bing, Yi Ton-o, Yi Ka-sang.   and the following
ladies of rank were killed: The wives of Sim Pyŭn, Yun Sŭn-

gŏ, Yi Sang-gyu, Han O-sang, Kwŏn Sun-jang, Yi Ton-o, Hong Myŭng-il and the mother of Kim Kyŭng-jeung.   These people died, some by the sword, some by strangling and some by drowning.   There were darker crimes than murder too, for the Manchus did not hesitate to seize and insult many honorable women, and even to this day a slight taint clings to one family of the nobility because the wife and daughter-in-law were subjected to indignities than which death were preferable.   From among the women taken there, the daughter of Whe Wŭn, a relative of the king, became sixth wife to the Mamchu Emperor, but shortly afterward he gave her to one of his favorites as a present.   And so we leave this long line of captives wending their way eastward and find ourselves again within the grim walls of Nam-han.

The ravages of hunger were beginning to make the Manchu proposition seem more feasible.   The council came to the conclusion that the men whom the Manchus demanded must be bound and sent to their fate.   When the Crown Prince heard of this he said, "I have a son and several brothers and there is no reason why I should not go myself."   Then Chŏng On said "I am the one who have most strenuously opposed the Manchu claims.   Let me go."   Kim Sang-hŏn exclaimed, "Who opposed them more than I?   I am surely the one to send."   Yun Whang, Yun Chip and O Tal-ch'e all offered to go and immolate themselves on the altar of Manchu vengeance. While the council was going on many of the soldiers came down from the wall and looked in at the doors and shouted, "As the Manchus have demanded these men why do you not send them rather than let us come thus to skin and bone?" It was with difficulty that they were sent back to their places. It was remarked that the soldiers under Gen. Yi Si-bǎk did not participate in this unruly demonstration.   That night at nine o'clock a party of Manchus approached the West Gate and one of them actually scaled the wall before the guard was aware of it.   He was speedily driven back with a battle-club, and stones and other missiles were rained down upon the assaulting party.   Gen. Yi Si-bǎk was twice wounded but did not make it known until the skirmish was over.   At the same time an assault was successfully warded off on the eastern side by Gen. Sin Kyŭng-jin who, not content with simply driving off the attacking party, sallied out and killed their leader and many of his followers.

The Manchus next tried to reduce the fortress by bombardment, and it is said that the projectiles came over the wall with such force as to bury themselves twenty inches in the earth.

On the morning of the twenty-fifth the Manchus sounded a parley at the West Gate and three of the officials accompanied them to the camp of the enemy.   There they were told, "The Emperor is very angry because you do not surrender, and has ordered the destruction of the kingdom.   He is to leave tomorrow and then you will have no opportunity to surrender, though you should wish."   The bombardment was renewed and many breaches were made in the wall and many of the garrison were killed, but the survivors quickly piled bags of sand in the breaches and poured water over them. This instantly froze and made a good substitute for a wall. But the soldiers were discouraged and came to the king in crowds demanding that the men whom the Manchus had called for be sent.   It was evident that something must be done at once, and Hong Sŏ-bong undertook another visit to the enemy's camp, where he said, "Tomorrow the Crown Prince and the other men that you have demanded will come out to you."   But they answered, "We do no want to see the Crown Prince, but the king himself."   To emphasize this, letters were shown proving that Kang-wha had fallen into Manchu hands, and a letter was delivered to them from one of the captive princes to the king.   They were likewise told, "The Crown Prince and one of his brothers must go to Manchuria as hostages.   The king must understand that there is nothing to fear in coming out.   The kingdon will in that way be preserved."   So they took the prince's letter and wended their way back to the fortress.   When the letter was opened and read a great cry of sorrow arose from the whole court.   Some-one suggested that the Manchus were trying to deceive them, but the king answered, "No, this is my son's own hand," and he added, "As Kang-wha is taken of course the ancestral tablets have been destroyed.   There is then no longer any need to delay our surrender."   As a preliminary to that final act the king ordered that all documents in which the Manchus were spoken of slightingly be collected and burned.

The next day a letter from the king was taken to the
Manchu headquarters, wherein he said, "As the emperor is
about to return to the north, I must see him before he goes.
If not, harm will result.   If evil befalls me in this step it
were better that I take a sword and end my life here.   I pray
you make some way whereby I can surrender without endan-
gering my kingdom."   The messenger explained that the
king feared that the Manchu soldiers might fall upon him
when he came down from the fortress.   The Manchu general
answered, "Wait till you get orders from me; then come down."
Kim Sang-hön could not endure the thought of surrender and
so attempted to take his own life by hanging, but someone cut
him down.   Chöng On likewise after an apostrophe to his
"frosty sword" plunged in into his bowels, but the wound
did not prove fatal and the king had him well cared for.

On the next day, the twenty-eighth, two men who had
most strenuously opposed the Manchus, O Tal-ch'e and Yun
Chip, were made ready to send to the Manchu camp to meet
their fate.   Before setting out they were brought in before
the king who wept and said. "Is it possible that we have come
to this?   I am ashamed to look you in the face."   But they
answered cheerfully, "There is no cause for mourning on our
account.   It is our own fault."   The king then made them
sit while a eunuch brought wine and poured it out.   Thi
was the greatest honor the king could show them.   Then he
said, "I will see to it that your families are well cared for."
Then they set out to meet their fate.   The emperor was pleased at this sign of submission and gave Ch'oé Myŭng-gil a fur
robe and a cup of wine.   Calling the two men before him the
emperor asked them why they had always opposed the Manchu rule.   They answered that after so many centuries of
adherence to the Ming dynasty they found it impossible to
give it up or to advise to do so.   The emperor then ordered
them to be loosed but to be kept in the camp under strict
surveillance.

The next day Hong Sö-bong, Ch'oe Myŭng-gil and Kim
Sin-guk repaired to the Manchu camp and said they had come
to complete arrangements for the surrender.   They were told
that an altar had already been prepared at Song-p'a and that
the ceremony must take place on the morrow.   The Manchu

general said, "We have a special form of ceremony for surrender. First, the one who surrenders is placed in a coffin;
but as this is rather humiliating we will waive it this time and
begin with the second article." Ch'oe asked, "Shall the king
come out in his royal robes?" "By no means. He must come
out dressed in blue." This was because blue is the color corresponding to east, and was therefore appropriate for Korea,
which has always been called the "East Country." "Shall he
come out the South Gate?" was the next question asked.
"No, how can one who has done wrong come out the South
Gate? He must come by way of the West Gate. After the
surrender he will proceed to Seoul and he need fear no danger,
for we have recalled all our foraging parties and no one will
offer to molest him. We will send back all the Koreans that we
have taken to Manchuria and we will have a new royal seal
cut for the king." That night the Manchu general Yonggolda brought the king a letter from the emperor saying, "Are
you indeed afraid to obey the command to come out and surrender? You may rest assured of your safety, and not only so
but I will make it to your great advantage to come. I will
put you back on your throne, I will forgive the past, I will
make a firm and binding agreement with you as between vassal and suzerain. If you would have your son and your grandson reign after you, you must receive a new seal of office from
us. You must stop sending embassies to China and you must
discard the Chinese calendar and adopt ours. The Crown
Prince, the Prime Minister and the latter's son must go with
us as hostages. When you die I will send the Crown Prince
to rule in your stead. I am about to invade China and you
must give us boats and troops. I must first take the Island
of Ka-do and to this end you must furnish us fifty boats and
sailors to man them, and you must give us bows and arrows.
Before our troops leave this place you must feast them. Here-
after you must observe the birthdays of the Manchu empress
and Crown Prince. You must treat our envoys exactly as
you have been accustomed to treat Chinese envoys. I will
send back across the Yalu all our Korean captives but you must
pay for them. Your people must intermarry with ours. You
must release and return all Manchu captives that you hold in
your border fortresses along the Tu-man River. As for com-

merce with Japan you may do as you please. I make no law
about that. You must build no more fortresses. Now, behold, I lift you as it were from the very dead. I have recreat-
ed your Kingdom. Do not forget my great kindness and mercy.
Beware of harboring guile in your heart. Every year you
must send tribute; one hunderd ounces of gold, a thousand
ounces of silver, ten thousand bags of white rice, two thousand pieces of silk, three hundred pieces of white grass-cloth,
ten thousand pieces of colored cotton, four hundred pieces of
fine linen, one thousand pieces of coarse linen, one thousand
quires of fine paper, one thousand quires of common paper,
two hundred bows made of sea-cow's horns, twenty-six swords
the length of a man's stature, four fine window screens, forty
mats with red flowers, twenty common swords, two hundred
pounds of dye-wood, ten pecks of black pepper, one thousand
packages of tea, one hundred tiger skins, one hundred deer
skins, four hundred otter skins, two hundred squirrel skins.
You will commence sending this tribute three years from now.
As I have taken one of the king's relatives to wife I will remit
nine thousand of the bags of rice."

Such were the conditions on which the Manchus proposed
to give the kingdom of Korea a new lease of life. The demand for tribute was so enormous that the Koreans never seem
to have taken it seriously, and they never once attempted to
fulfill more than the merest fraction of the demand.

It was on the last day of the first moon of the year 1637
that at last, having exhausted all other means, having endured the rigors of a winter siege in a fortress but half prepared
for the emergency, having seen his faithful soldiers die about
him from hunger and exposure, the king was driven to surrender to the Manchu power. The day broke with a great
bank of fog enveloping everything. The West Gate of the
fortress swung open and the royal cavalcade appeared, bearing manifest signs of the long confinement. The king and
Crown Prince, according to the directions of the victors, were
clad in blue. Behind them came the hollow-cheeked, but loyal
soldiers who would have stayed and defended the walls to the
bitter end had the king but given the word. As the royal
party descended the winding road to the valley below, they
came upon long lines of heavy-armed Manchu cavalry drawn

up on either side of the road. The king was startled, and
anxiously asked what it meant, but was told that it was simply in honor of the coming of the king. Soon the party met
the two Manchu generals, Yonggolda and Mabuda. The king
dismounted and the proper salutations took place between
them. Then they sat down and went through a formal in-
terchange of civilities, seated so as to face east and west according to the proper rule of etiquette. When these formalities were completed, they escorted the king to the place where
anciently the town of Kwang-ju stood, at which point there
was a short pause. The king's immediate staff consisted of
three ministers of state, five officials of the second rank, five
of the rank of royal scribe and one or two others. Besides
these there were only the Crown Prince and his tutor. In front,
and at a condsiderable distance, was a raised platform covered
with a yellow silk awning, under which the emperor sat upon
a throne. In front were drawn up a company of trumpeters.
General Youggolda and the king dismounted and the former
led the king toward the imperial dais. Upon reaching the
eastern entrance to the imperial presence they bowed three
times and struck the hand on the back of the head. Then they
entered and bowed on a mat before the emperor. The king
was then told to ascend the platform. The emperor sat facing
the south and the king sat on his left facing the west. To the
left of the king and also facing the west sat the emperor's
three sons, and finally the king's sons who had been brought
up from Kang-wha. Below the platform sat the Korean officials and at a distance the common people. The emperor's
gilded throne sat on a dais raised nine inches above the platform, beneath a yellow silk umbrella and the "plume banner."
The emperor sat twirling an arrow in his hand. A cup of tea
was handed the king. Then the emperor said to the Korean
Prime Minister through an interpreter "Now we are inmates of
one house, let us try our skill at archery." The Minister answered, perhaps with a shade of irony, "We know letters, but
we are not skilled in archery." Food was brought in and
placed before the king, the same in quality and amount as that
placed before the emperor. Each drank three cups of wine and
then the food was carried away. This was simply a formality
intended to put the king at his ease. A servant then brought

in the emperor's dogs and with his own hand he cut meat and threw it into the air for the animals to catch. Descending from the platform the king had the pleasure of meeting the Crown Princess. Their brief conversation was interrupted by General Yonggolda who came up with a magnificent horse sumptuously caparisoned, and with a splendid sable robe. These he announced were a gift from the emperor, but at the same time he asked why the king had not brought the royal insignia that had been given by the Chinese emperor, that it might be destroyed. The answer was that it had been lost at the time of the making of the former treaty with the Manchus, but that it would be hunted up and handed over to the Manchu general. General Yonggolda also presented each of the ministers about the king with a sable robe. At five o'clock in the afternoon, as night was coming on, the emperor gave word that the king might proceed to Seoul. It will be remembered that the Crown Prince and Princess, together with Prince Pong-im, were to be taken away to Manchuria as hostages. Before starting for Seoul the king bade them adieu and then with a heavy heart turned toward his capital.

The retinue that followed the king was so numerous that when they came to the ferry at Song-p'a and found there were too few boats to convey them all, there was a disgraceful scramble for first place, and the king was hustled and dragged about in a most unbecoming manner. Finally the crossing was effected and as the cavalcade proceeded toward Seoul they saw the Manchu camps along the way crowded with Korean women, some of whom were wailing as if their hearts would break, while others were making merry over the prospect of being carried away to the north.

The Manchu soldiery had been ordered out of Seoul to make room for the king and so the royal party found the way blocked by an immense crowd of Manchu soldiers loaded down with booty and leading hundreds of captives. As the king passed by, these miserable beings cried out to him to save them, but their captors urged them on with word and lash. The crowd was so dense, and the out-going stream of men pressed so closely against those entering, that many in the king's retinue were taken for captives and were seized and carried away. Even some men of noble blood were thus, in the darkness and confusion, spirited away and never heard of again.

It was seven o'clock when the king entered the gate of Seoul. The city was almost deserted. Dead men lay in heaps along the streets. The houses on both sides of the street were in ashes. All the poultry and pigs were gone and only dogs remained, and these had been transformed into wolves and were gorging themselves on the dead bodies along the way. As the Ch'ang-gyöng Palace was nearest the East Gate the royal party went there to spend the night. All night long, in spite of the Emperor's orders, Manchu soldiers scoured the streets, burning and pillaging and working their terrible will for the last time on the deserted capital.

Two days later the Manchu army was to start on its long journey to the north and the king went three miles outside the East Gate to bid adieu to the emperor, for it was determined to pass around Seoul on the east and so strike northward. It took thirteen days for the whole army to get on the move. There were 120,000 men in all. Thirty thousand of these were Mongols and they took the road to the east through Ham-gyŭng Province and crossed the Tu-man River. There were 70,000 Manchus and 20,000 Chinese from Liao-tung. Generals Kong Yu-dŭk and Kyŏng Myŭng-jung with 20,000 men took boat at Yong-san and sailed north to stike Ka-do Island.

The day following that on which the king took leave of the Emperor, the generals Yonggolda and Mabuda came to the palace to confer with the king. The Minister Kim Nyu, as if to anticipate them, said "The relation between us now is that of son and father. We stand ready to fulfill our obligations on that basis even though you ask for soldiers to help on the invasion of China and the seizure of Nanking." Hong Sö-bong asked that in view of the scarcity of gold in Korea part of the tribute be remitted, but it was not granted. Kim Nyu's daughter had been carried away captive to Manchuria and he had plead with the two generals and the king himself had aided him but without avail. He now offered a thousand ounces of silver for her ransom. It was accepted but the result was disastrous to others for it set a precedent, and a like sum was asked for each of the high-born captives, with the result that few of them were ever ransomed.

The Emperor's ninth brother had charge of all the captives, and on the fifth day of the second moon the crown prince was allowed to go to the king to say farewell. He was accompanied by a guard of six Manchus who cut the interview very short and hurried him away to the camp outside the East Gate. On the seventh the king and his court went out to this camp to say good-bye, and the Manchus set out a fine banquet, at which some of the Koreans ate greedily while others would not touch a morsel. The next day the order was given to start on the long march into Manchuria. The royal hostages were accompanied by fifteen high officials. The king and his court accompanied the party twenty *li* out, as far as Chang-neung, where with many tears the final separation took place.

The work of reconstruction was now to be commenced, and of course the first work was to punish those who had proved unfaithful and to reward those who had proved loyal. First Gen. Kim Cha-jŭm, who had lain so long at Yang-geun and would not move to help the king, was banished and with him Sim Keui-wŭn, Sin Kyŏng-wan and the governor of Kang-wŭn Province who had hesitated to throw away their lives and those of their men in the perfectly hopeless task of breaking up the siege of Nam-han. Admiral Chang Sin, who had been prevented by the swift outflowing tide from opposing the crossing of the Manchus to Kang-wha was killed by strangulation outside the Little West Gate. Kim Chyŭng-jeung who had been in command of Kang-wha, and his lieutenant Yi Min-gu were both banished to distant points. The king gave a great feast at Mo-wha-gwan to those who had aided him while besieged, both nobleman and common soldier. The four most prominent generals each received the gift of a horse. All the courtiers were advanced one step in the ladder of officialdom. Other gifts and positions were distributed. Those who had deserted the royal party when on that hard ride to Nam-han were seized and imprisoned. Sim Chip, who had refused to lie about his companion who went to the Manchu camp to personate the king's brother, was banished to a distant point. Kim Sang-hŏn had fled to the country when the king came out of Nam-han to surrender. Being now included in those who received marks of royal favor, he wrote declaring that the could not receive them, for in the first place he had urged the king not to surrender and in the second place had run away and had also torn to pieces the letter written by the king. "But," he added "though weak and forced to surrender, the king must always keep these things in mind and seek for means to be avenged on the Manchus."

The king had sent Generals Yu Rim and Im Kyŏng-ŭp to aid in the taking of Ka-do Island in the north. In the third moon Gen. Mabuda took fifty boats and crossed over from the mainland to the west side of these islands, which the Chinese garrison had left unprotected. Landing his force he ascended at night a hill to the rear of the Chinese camp. With the morning dawn he made a sudden and fierce attack. Meanwhile the Korean general Im Kyŏng-ŭp had arrived with forty boats and had disembarked on the esatern shore. The Chinese, thrown into confusion, rushed down to the shore and tumbled into these forty boats that they found unguarded. But the crowd was so great that only a small fraction could be accommodated. As a consequence they swamped most of the boats and hundreds perished. The Chinese commander, seeing that all was lost, committed suicide. There were still great numbers of Chinese among the mountains fighting desperately. These were all cut down. It is said that in this short campaign between forty and fifty thousand Chinese were killed. During the unequal battle the Chinese kept calling out, "What cause for enmity is there between Korea and China?" This was of course addressed to the Koreans who fought with the Manchus. After the battle the Manchu general Kong Yu-dŭk gave generals Im and Yu a present of 250 Chinese captives, but the former said, "I do not care for these men. Exchange them for a like number of Korean captives who are going into Manchuria as slaves." This was done, and Gen. Im's name has come down to posterity fragrant with the odor of this unselfish deed.

Chapter IX.

It was during the year 1637 that the stone tablet was set
up beside the road to Nam-han, commemorating the Manchu
victory.   It had been sent thither by the Emperor, but was
not immediately set up.   A Manchu envoy came to superintend its erection.   It is said that there were two stones, one
of which was set up; the other, remaining on the bank of the
river, was finally washed into the stream.   The envoy announced that he had come to erect the monument at the point
where the surrender had taken place.   A solid foundation
was built, with an ascent of several steps.   The stone was
put in place and over it a pavilion was built to protect it from
the weather.   On one side the inscription was in Chinese and
on the other side in Manchu.   The inscription is as follows :

"The Emperor Ch'ung Tě' ôf the Great Ch'ing Empire,
in the twelfth year of his reign, learned that we had broken
our treaty with him and he was angry.   He gathered his forces
and entered our territory.   He marched through it, for there
was none to say him nay.   We a weak and insignificant king,
fled perforce to Nam-han.   Our fear was like that of one who
walks on ice in spring-time.   We sojourned there fifty days.
Our soldiers from the east and south fled before the Emperor's
troops.   Those of the north and west hid among their mountains and could lift neither hand not foot.   Famine stared us
in the face.   If the Emperor had stormed our fortress then

we would have been like the leaves in autumn, or like hair
in flames. But the Emperor did not wish to destroy us. He
said 'Come out and I will be your helper. If not I will destroy you.' Generaals Yonggoldä and Mabudä and other
great men were in constant communication with us. Our
councillors, civil and military, assembled, and we said
to them 'For ten years have we been at peace, and
now we have been blind and foolish to bring all this
upon ourselves. Our people have become like meat or
fish beneath the chopping-knife. We alone are to blame for
it all'. The Emperor was patient and did not destroy us utterly but told us to surrender. How could we refuse, for by
so doing we saved our people. All the courtiers were agreed.
With a score of horsemen we went forth from the fortress to
the Emperor's camp and there confessed our faults. He
treated us with kindness and by his goodness calmed our
agitated minds. When we beheld him our heart went out to
him. The Emperor's goodness extended even to our courtiers.
He then sent us back to the capital and recalled the Manchu
cavalry who were scouring the south. Our people, who had
been scattered like pheasants, now returned. All things became as they had been. Snow and frost were gone and spring
smiled forth again. After the drought showers fell. All that
had been destroyed revived again. Things that had been
broken grew together. Here beside the Han at San-jun-do
where the great Emperor rested, here is the altar and the
enclosure. Here we, a weak king, through our Minister of
Public Works, have made the altar higher and broader than
before and have placed this monument to keep alive in the
minds of generations yet unborn the memory of these events,
to show that the goodness of the Emperor is as high as heaven
itself. Not that we alone have seen it, for all Manchuria as
well was witness to it. Throughout the world that gracious
voice cannot be resisted. Though we write with characters
as broad as the very earth and as clear as the sun and moon
we could never describe his greatness and his glory. For such
cause is it written here. Frost and dew are both from heaven.
One kills the other vivifies. Thus it is that the Emperor
shows goodness in the midst of terror. The Emperor came
with over 100,000 soldiers. Many of them were like the

tiger and the dragon. Before them, brandishing their spears, went the savages from the far north and the distant west. Fearsome men! But the Emperor's gracious words came down in a letter in ten lines clear and beautiful, whereby our blind-ed minds were enlightened. The Emperor's words are lum-inous and precise, and we, a small king, confessed and sur-rendered; not so much because we feared his terror as be-cause we delighted in his graciousness. He treated us kind-ly, paying all attention to the ceremonies and the rites. Then we were glad and laughed, and every weapon sought its sheath. Then we donned the garment of peace. The people of Seoul, both men and women, burst into singing and said that the Emperor had given us back to our palace. The Emperor pitied the distress of the people and encouraged them to till the fields again. To the dead roots of the tree was brought back spring-time. This stone is lofty and it stands here at the head of the river to show forth the Emperor's goodness to the Sam-han."

Such was the statement that the Manchus put into the mouth of Korea and until recent years they have claimed Korea as their vassal state. The claim originally was per-fectly good. Never did a country make herself more abject in her acceptance of a vassal's position. And the only line of argument that can be used to prove that that condition did not hold till the treaty of Shimonoseki was signed in 1895. is in China's occasional disavowal of it, to shield herself from re-sponsibility for Korea's acts.

The Japanese had been keeping watch of events that were transpiring during these troublesome times, and at this junc-ture an envoy came from the island empire announcing, as between friends, the name of the new Japanese year. This letter was not received by the king, who asked what use it would be to him. The Japanese replied, "You have given up China and are now a masterless dog. Why is our name not good as any?" It shows how pride had been crushed out of the Koreans to find that Ch'oé Myŭng-gil himself said, "We have done wrong to surrender to the Manchus. Now let us make friendly advances toward Japan." From that time on it was customary to receive politely the annual message from Japan, but there seems to have been no more *rapport* between the two countries than this.

As the Manchu emperor passed north through P'yŭng-an province he gave orders to the prefect of Cheung-san to seize and deliver up to him the person of Hong Ik-han who had been especially virulent in his opposition to the Manchus. It was done, and the man was carried captive to the Manchu capital at Sim-yang (Mukden). There he was decently lodged in a house of detention called the Pyŭl-gwan, until a certain day when he was called before the emperor, who sat in state surrounded by soldiery. Being asked why he had opposed the Manchu influence he replied in writing, "All men within the four seas are brothers but there can be but one father. From the first the king of Korea acted uprightly and mannerly. In Korea we have censors who chide and correct him. Last year, being censor, I heard that you, who held to us the relation of elder brother, had styled yourself emperor and by so doing had ruptured the actual relations subsisting between us. From the earliest times we have owed allegience to China and how could we then advise the king to hold to a false relation? This is the reason I advised the king to stand out against you. This war and all its attendant miseries are my work alone and I would that you might decapitate me ten thousand times." The emperor, who seems to have cherished the idea that he had overawed the man, was thrown into a great rage by this brave avowal and instantly threw the man into a dismal dungeon where he doubtless starved to death, for nothing more is heard of him.

The two men who had been delivered up by the king in Nam-han were also carried north. They were also arraigned before the dreaded chieftain Yonggolda who attempted to flatter them into making a complete surrender to the Manchus and taking up their abode permanently in Manchuria; but they utterly refused and asked to be killed at once. The Manchu chief argued, urged and threatened, but the men were not to be moved. Being ordered to execution they looked the chieftain in the face and cursed him. Chöng No-gyŭng, an attendant of the Crown Prince, begged for their bodies that he might carry them back and bury them on Korean soil, but the favor was not granted.

That summer the people of Seoul and of the country immediately to the south, were thrown into a panic by the antics of what they call ch'ăk-ch'ăk, a species of imp or demon which appeared nightly in various places and terrified the people. The Koreans are peculiarly subject to such hallucinations. They said they were the spirits of those who had died at the hands of the Manchus and the popular fears were not alleviated until the king had ordered a monstrous sacrifice in their behalf at two places near Nam-han, called Ma-heui-ch'ŭn and Sang-nyŭng.

The king despatched an envoy to China in the ninth moon to inform the Chinese emperor that he had been forced to surrender, but he assured his former suzerain that the act was by no means voluntary. To this the emperor replied in a tone of commiseration, attaching no blame to the king's enforced allegiance to the Manchus. He himself was destined ere long to feel the full weight of the Manchu arm.

We have at this point an account of the first general use of tobacco in Korea. It is stated that tobacco was first brought to Japan by the Nam-man or "southern barbarians" and from there was brought to Korea, thirty years before the date of which we are now writing. It was first used by a man named Chang Yu who was closely connected with the royal family, being the father of a Crown Princess. It was called tam-p'agwe which is the Korean pronunciation of certain Chinese characters which were used to translate into Chinese the Japanese words for tobacco, which is ta-ba-ko. It is commonly supposed that the Japanese took their word from the occidentals, but we here have the word embedded in Korean history back in the very first years of the seventeenth century before it had even yet firmly established itself in European countries. It seems almost incredible that the spread of its use should have been so rapid as to have arrived in Korea within ten years of the beginning of its common use in Europe, but it may have been so. Portugese traders came in large numbers to Japan and the fragrant weed was probably brought by them. At the time of which we are writing, namely the end of the Manchu invasion, its use had become common. It was supposed to possess valuable peptic qualities and was recommended especially to those who ate much meat. The Manchus had become much addicted to the habit, but so many conflagrations were the result that the Manchu emperor attempted to intedict its use. It is needless to say that he failed. When first introduced, it cost ten thousand cash for half a pound but merchants obtained seed and it soon became common.

In accordance with the demands of the Manchus, the king sent 5,000 troops to accompany them in their invasion of China, but as they arrived a month later than the set time they were sent back home by the angry Manchus. Early in the following year, however, Generals Yi Wan and Im Kyöng-ŭp started with 5,000 troops and joined the Manchu army. The plan was to attack Teung-nă on the Shantung promontory; whether by land or sea is not clear, but probably by land. This being known to the Koreans, three boats were secretly despatched to the threatened place, giving warning of the attack, and stating that the Koreans joined in the attack with the Manchus because forced to do so. It was suggested that whenever feasibly the Chinese and Korean forces should use only blank charges against each other. This was gladly agreed to and in a battle at Puk-sin-gu, which followed, not one man was killed among the Chinese forces that were brought in contact with the Korean contingent, and the latter suffered as little. The Chinese general managed to get a letter to the Koreans saying "The emperor reminds you of the vital aid he gave Korea at the time of the Japanese invasion and he now offers the half of his kingdom to anyone who will seize and deliver to him the Manchu general in command." This reveals in a striking manner the desperate straits to which the Chinese had been brought by the Manchus. The Korean generals did not see their way to accede to this but they kept the Chinese informed of every movement of the Manchus; where they were weak and where they were strong, where they were likely to attack and where they might be successfully attacked. In this way the Manchus were continually thwarted and the Chinese encouraged.

It was proposed that there be a combined Manchu and Korean attack upon Kou-ju-wi near the point of the Shantung promontory, the Manchus to attack by land and the Koreans by sea; but the latter said they had no provisions and their boats were in very bad order. The Manchus replied "Then you had better go home," an injunction that they were by no means loath to obey.

Meanwhile the king had been doing what he could to mitigated the sufferings consequent upon the invasion. He ordered all the eight provinces to give rice to help the poor, the widows and the orphans, and to provide proper burial for those who had no near relatives who could afford the expense. He likewise gave strong encouragement to the Confucian School in the capital. He sent spies throughout the land to discover whether the prefects were attending to their duties well. Fearing that the guard along the Tu-man R ver might be suffering, he made them a grant of 4,000 pieces of cotton. He likewise gave money to repair the ancient altar on the top of Ma ri-san (Mountain) on the island of Kang-wha. This altar is said to have been used by the Tan-gun two thousand years before Christ, and may well be believed it to be the oldest monument in Korea.

This period of rest and recuperation was broken in upon by the appearance, on the northern border, of Manchu troops under Yonggoldä and Omokdo. Rumors had again reached Manchuria that certain Korean officials had been advising against the Manchu power. As a result of this, four prominent officials were sent captive to the north. Early the following year King Chilga, the emperor's brother, came to try these man, and held a proper court at which the Korean Crown Prince was present. Each of the accused men was brought in turn and questioned, and each had some plausible excuse to give. The result was sure from the beginning. They were all condemned and were thrown into a dungeon with a door in the top, a sort of Black Hole of Calcutta, where they all languished with cold, hunger and disease. They even excited the pity of their jailors, and when the Crown Prince plead for them before the emperor, they were ordered sent to Eui-ju, but heavily guarded.

In 1640 the Japanese who had settled at Fusan complained that the harbor was too small, for it did not include the whole bay, but only that part directly in front of the settlement, which was about half way between the present Japanese town and the Korean town of Pu·san. The harbor was called Tu-mo Harbor. Consent to the enlargement of the harbor was refused.

In 1641 Prince Kwang-hä, the deposed and banished

wretch, died on the island of Quelpart. So great is the respect for royalty in the abstract, in Korea, that the king fasted four days, had the body brought up to Yang-ju and buried it with royal honors. To the one surviving daughter the king gave a comfortable house and an annuity.

The next year a seditious movement was made by Ch'oé Hyo-il of P'yŭng-an Province, and two accomplices. They took boat for China, being provided with funds by the prefect of Eui-ju. Arriving at Teung-nä they joined the Chinese forces, received commissions in the Chinese army and despatched a letter to the prefect of Eui-ju asking him to gather a force and with them make a combined attack upon the Manchus. As fate would have it the Manchu Younggoldä was at Eui-ju when this letter arrived, and it fell into his hands. He immediately sent to the king demanding the seizure and execution of all the men implicated in the plot. In spite of the expostulations of the Prime Minister, who wished to see only the prime movers punished, eleven men in Eui-ju and elsewere were seized and met their fate before the palace gate in Seoul.

That Japan and Korea had not forgotten each other is evinced by the fact that the Japanese emperor sent to the king asking him to suggest a name for an ancestral temple that he was erecting. The king declined but allowed his uncle to do it. The name suggested was "The Illustrious Place at Il-gwang Mountain."

One more sacrifice was necessary before the last remnant of opposition to the Manchus should be extinguished. It was now six years since the surrender. Soon after that surrender the king had sent to China explaining that it was a hard fate and not his own inclination which had forced the surrender from him. Not knowing whether the letter had ever reached the Chinese capital he sent another letter two years later by a monk, Tok-po, who had come from China to ascertain whether Korea had really surrendered or not. Arriving at P'yŭng-yang he had been received by Gen. Im Kyŭng-ŭp who sent him on to Choé Myŭng-gil the Prime Minister. He was handsomely treated and was provided with a new vessel and a complete outfit of clothes and provisions for the return journey. He carried a letter from the king stating his ex-

cuses as above narrated. Four years passed and at last in the
year under review the emperor's answer was forwarded by
way of Chefoo. In it he exhonerates Korea from all blame
and mourns the fact that he cannot come to her aid as when
the Japanese invaded the peninsula. The bearer of this missive was feasted and treated with the most flattering atten-
tions by the governor of P'yŭng-an. This would have amounted to nothing had it not been known to Yi Kyu the prefect of
Sŭn-ch'ŭn who was carrying on trade with China by junk
across the Yellow Sea. He was seized by the Manchus and
carried north. Fearing the worst, he offered to tell his captors an important secret as the price of his life. He thereupon unfolded the whole transaction between Seoul and Nanking. The Manchus were furious and sent a demand to the
king for the persons of Choé Myŭng-gil, Im Kyŏng-úp, Yi
Kyŏng-yo and Yi Myŭng-han, all leading men. There was
nothing to do but comply, and as these men went the king
wept and gave Ch'oé Myŭng-gil 500 ounces of silver for traveling expenses. Arriving at Pong-whang Fortress beyond the
Yalu they were taken in hand by Generals Yonggoldã and
Mabudã. Ch'oé asserted strongly that he alone was to blame
for the whole transaction. When the emperor had looked
over the evidence he sent word that fines should be accepted
from the others, but that Ch'oé be sent in a cangue and hand-
cuffs to Puk-kwan goal. And there he leaves the stage of history, on which he had played no mean part. The traitor Yi
Kyu plumed himself on his newly acquired Manchu citizenship and presumed on his services to write the emperor a
memorial under twelve heads; but the emperor in fine contempt exclaimed that a man who was not true to his own king
must be a rascal at heart and ordered him bound and sent back
to Korea where we may well believe the axe did its work
without delay.

The next few years of the reign witnessed the return of
many captives taken by the Japanese during the years of the
invasion; they beheld the promulgation of the law that no one
could marry during the three years of mourning for a parent;
also a scourge of cholera so terrible as to cause the king to
send and sacrifice upon the eight high mountains of Korea.
A powerful conspiracy, led by the prime minister, Sim Keui-

wŭn, came near overthrowing the dynasty, but the alarm was given in the very nick of time and he and his fellow conspirators were seized and executed.

The twenty-first year of the reign, 1643, beheld the fall of the Ming dynasty in China. The pretext given by the Manchus for marching on Nanking was the revolt of Yi Cha-sung who burned Nanking and drove the emperor to suicide. Then, terrified at his own deed, he fled and the Manchus stepped in. When Nanking fell, a letter was despatched to Korea saving "I am the greatest of rulers. You have long been my vassal and I will now show you a favor by returning your hostage, the Crown Prince."

A word is necessary as to the fate of Im Kyŏng-ŭp, one of the men who had been sent to Manchuria with Ch'oé Myŭng-gil. He succeeded in making his escape before the party reached the Yalu and in the disguise of a monk made his way in a merchant boat to Teung-nä where he attached himself to Gen. Whang Chong-ye and made himself very useful. It is said that he made himself famous by capturing a notorious pirate. He sailed straight for the island on which the pirate had his headquarters and having gotten the pirate and his crew drunk with wine he bound and brought them safely to the Chinese camp. Later he fell into the hands of the Manchus through treachery but was so steadfast in his refusal to do obeisance to them that he excited their unbounded admiration, and they let him go back to Korea. This was an unfortunate move for him, for in the meantime Kim Cha-jŭm had been recalled from banishment and had become court favorite. As these men were deadly enemies the returning general was immediately seized and put to death. This same year saw the publication of the historical work named the Tong-sa Po-byŭn.

In the following year the Crown Prince and his brother returned from China but the Crown Prince soon after sickened and died. It had been customary heretofore for the king and queen to assume mourning for three years for a Crown Prince but now an innovation was made and thirteen months was the limit set. Of course the succession fell to the infant son of the dead prince, but the wife of prince Pong-im, the second son of the king, was extremely ambitious to become queen, and so she went about to gain the desired end. By every means in her power she brought pressure to bear upon the king to induce him to set aside the infant prince and nominate her husband as heir to the throne. She was partially successful and the following year the king called his courtiers together and consulted as to the advisability of the plan. He urged that the real heir was but a babe in arms and that he himself was old and about to go the way of all the earth. It was evident that he desired to put Prince Pong-im on the throne, and a very animated discussion followed. Most of the leading ministers and officials argued against the plan saying that it was contrary to the best traditions of the land and that the people all looked to the young prince as their future ruler. To all these arguments the king opposed counter arguments which revealed plainly that he had already made up his mind as to his course, and that he was merely seeking for confirmation of his views. Kim Nyu then said, "If the king has already made up his mind let him speak out and put an end to this useless discussion." The king then announced that Prince Pong-im was to be his successor.

About this time a dangerous rebellion broke out in Kong-ju the capital of Ch'ung-ch'ŭng Province, but by the prompt action of the troops from the South it was put down. This is worthy of mention only as it illustrates a curious custom in Korea. On account of this rebellion the name of Kong ju was for many years changed to Kong-san and the province of Ch'ung-ch'ŭng to that of Hong-ch'ŭng.

The Prince Pong-im, though now by royal edict in full view of the throne, feared that by some turn of fortune's wheel he might fall short of that goal and so he much desired to have the infant prince and his mother taken from his path. The aged king had entered upon a period of mental semi-decrepitude and was easily managed by the wife of Prince Pong-im. Six palace women were accused of poisoning the king's food and were summarily put to death. The king then summoned the courtiers and accused the wife of the deceased Crown Prince of having assumed the garments of royalty while in Manchuria, of having used disrespectful language to him on her return and of having instigated the palace women to poison him. He said she must be killed. All agreed that some positive proof of guilt must be produced but the king insisted upon her immediate execution which was accomplished by the use of poison. Her two brothers were likewise beaten to death. Three of the leading men who had advised against the nomination of Prince Pong-im were also banished.

The next year passed quietly, but the official corruption had become so prevalent and the people were ground down by the prefects to such an extent that the king made the law that each prefect must have three bondsmen who would be liable to punishment in case of his malfeasance.

The next year saw the introduction on the field of politics of a noted man, Song Si-ryul, who was destined to be a leading spirit for many a year. He was a celebrated scholar and the king induced him to come to Seoul only after repeated invitation.

The very last year of his life this king cherished a bitter enmity toward the Manchu power and in the twenty-seventh year of his reign, selecting generals and planning to equip an army, he hoped to throw off the hated yoke; but it was not to be, for in the early summer of 1649 the aged monarch breathed his last and the heir assumed the reins of power. He is known in history as Hyo-jŭng Ta-wang.

The accession of a new king was the signal for the combined attack of all the officials upon Kim Cha-jŭm who had been so long the practical autocrat. He was deposed, but the king would not have him executed, because of his former services. Song Si-ryul also took offense at the king because of a supposed slight and departed to the country in anger, after publishing three accusations against him.

The reign began with a storm. Kim Cha jŭm who had retired to the country in disgrace, took advantage of the fact that the Japanese had made a proposition to the prefect of Tong-nä to come over and join the Koreans in an invasion of China, and sent a detailed account of it to China, adding that the Korean government was preparing for war and had discarded the Manchu calendar. This news caused tremendous excitement in China and the veteran generals Yonggoldä and Mabudä were sent forward to the Yalu with a powerful force.

Six envoys were sent to Seoul one following the other at intervals of only two days.   These six arrived at Eui-ju, stopped there and sent forward letters demanding what it all meant.   Of course this was like thunder from a clear sky to the court at Seoul, and Minister Yi Kyŏng-sŭk rode in person to Eui-ju and met the envoys.   He invited them to Seoul and after a long discussion and a present of a thousand ounces of silver and the promise of a princess to go to China to wed one of the Manchu princes and the banishment of a few of the officials, it was found that no blame was attached to the king. Thus began an eventful reign of ten years.   The first years were signalized by severe famines in the north and the government had to bring large quantities of grain from the south to relieve the suffering.   Corruption had crept even into the system of examinations and it was found necessary to preserve the incognito of the candidates by having each one write his name on the margin of his examination paper and than have this portion of the paper cut off through the middle of a stamp so that at last when the papers were examined and the successful ones selected, the writers' names could not be known until they had been matched on, and found to fit.

An unsuccessful attempt at rebellion was made by the notorious Kim Cha-jŭm and Kim Sik, son-in-law to the late king.   They persuaded the latter's wife to place a fetich under the floor of the king's sleeping apartment.   This is supposed to bring about the speedy death of the person so cursed, but someone found it out and divulged the plan.   The three leaders were beheaded, the woman poisoned and her brothers banished.   Some wanted the king to move because the palace had been defiled by the fetich, which consisted of a dead rat with the king's name written on its belly, but it was voted down because it would tend to confirm the people in their belief in this foolish superstition.

This king inherited much of his father's hatred of the Manchu power and we find him building a palace at Kangwha and storing provisions there in case of a break in the peaceful relations then existing.   He instituted some useful reforms also, forbidding the cruel practice of beating criminals to death.   He likewise legislated in the interests of the people

when he forbade the exacting of rent for water drawn from
the government reservoirs for their rice fields.

Twenty-two years before this, Kim Hyŭk, one of the envoys
to China, had there met a Westerner who is known in Korean
history as Tang-yak-mäng. This was one of the Jesuit priests.
He came first to Canton as a missionary but his great
talents were recognized in Nanking and the emperor called
him to the capital and questioned him about his religion, and
employed him as court astronomer. There the Koreans saw
the calendar called Si-hön-yük. When the Ming dynasty fell
the Manchus urged the Westerner to remain and they allowed
him a regular salary. Kim Hyŭk brought back a book from
Peking which is probably a copy or abstract of the celebrated
book above mentioned. For these twenty-two years a scholar,
Kim Sang-bŭm, had been studying this book, and at last having
mastered its secrets, he came out with a calendar of his own.
It is stated that the Westerners Yi Ma-du and Sa Su-sin had
already been many years in China when Kim Hyŭk visited
Nanking. ('These are Ricci and Schaal).

It was discovered that the country people were evading
the revenue laws by cultivating the hill sides above the margin of cultivation set by law. Commissioners were sent out to
remeasure the taxable land and to set limits to hillside cultivation, for it was feared that the cultivation of the hillsides
would diminish the fuel supply too much. It was in this same
year that the ill-fated sailing vessel Sparwehr sailed from
Holland with Hendrik Hamel as super-cargo. There seem to
have been sixty-four men on board, and when she went to
pieces on the island of Quelpart only thirty-six of them reached shore in safety. They were taken to Seoul by the authorities and for fourteen years lived, now on the royal bounty, now
by the work of their own hands, and at times they were even
compelled to beg for food. At last however the remnant of
them made good their escape by night and finally reached
Nagasaki. Hamel afterwards wrote an account of his capitvity
in Korea.

In the year 1654 the hostility of the king toward his suzerain took more definite shape. He appointed Yi Wan, a brilliant young general, to have charge of all military matters,
and he sent military instructors all through the south where

the great mass of the population lived, to drill the people in the science of war. He likewise built fortresses at Sŭng-jin in Ham-gyŭng Province and at Yi-bam-keum-sŭng and at Kyŭk-p'o in the south. He appointed four generals to be stationed about Seoul to guard its approaches, and he collected great quantities of grain, much of which he massed at Wha-ryang near Chemulpo to be in readiness to ship to Tientsin when he should invade China. He provisioned Kang-wha thoroughly and built a monster store-house at Chang-san in Whang-hă Province, because of the difficulty experienced by the boats in rounding the exposed point of that province; he founded a school for the training of military officers and twenty of the best men were detailed for study there. Any sign of indolence insured a prompt dismissal.

This sovereign was an ardent advocate of dress reform. At first he made the soldiers wear shorter sleeves and skirts and for the sake of lightness they were often made of silk. From that he made a more general application of his ideas. He found the hats too broad of brim and the flowing sleeves very inconvenient in the breeze. These points were ordered to be changed and the palace hat as seen today was introduced. It was first invented by the celebrated Chŏng Mong-ju whose blood still marks the stone bridge at Song-do. It was he too that introduced the hyŭng-p'ă or embroidered storks to be worn on the breasts of civil officers, and the tigers to be worn by military officers.

Chapter   X.

trouble brewing....change of party....unutterable cruelty....the
queen deposed....concubine made queen....a great statesman dies
of poison.

In the tenth year of his reign, 1659, having exposed
himself to the sun and rain while sacrificing to heaven to secure the cessation of a great famine that was on the land, the
king was taken ill, an abcess broke out on his temple and
after a short illness he expired. In connection with his death
arose a contention that was destined to cause the death of many
men. The mother of the dead king was still living. She had
worn mourning for three years after the death of her elder son,
and now the question was whether she should assume it for an
equal length of time for this her second son. Song Si-ryŭl and
Song Chun-gil argued that one year only was sufficient. The
other side was taken by Yun Hyu and the debate was fierce and
long. The classics were ransacked for proof texts in support
of either contention. The Prime Minister decided in favor of
the shorter term and the Queen Mother wore mourning for
but a year. Song Si-ryŭl also laid up wrath against himself
by neglecting to have the king's body wrapped tightly in
bandages, until it had swollen so that it required two planks
joined together to form the bottom of his coffin. This was
considered a great misfortune and ere a year had passed Song
was obliged to retire precipitately to the country to avoid being mobbed for the offense.

The new king entered upon the duties of his exalted
position as a mere lad, in 1660. His posthumous title is
Hyon-jong Tă-wang. His first duty was to give his father
burial. The geomancers said he ought to be buried on a site
near the town of Su-wŭn, but the courtiers thought that was
too near the main road, so a place was selected outside the East
Gate. This first year was one of reform. The penalties for
murder were too small. If a high class man committed murder
he could get off with a hundred blows and ineligibility for
office for a short time, but now the king, with the advice of the
court, made all high class murderers permanently ineligible for
office. It must be borne in mind that the demarcation between the upper and lower classes was much more distinct in
those days than it is at present.

Looking carefully into the condition of things, the king

found many abuses that required correction. He ordered that
the army be better clothed; he examined into the cases of
many of the prisoners of state and liberated not a few; he remitted the tax on hemp and ginseng in Ham-gyŭng Province;
he remitted the tax on the gold mines at Tan-ch'ŭn which had
amounted to a thousand ounces a year; he lowered the land
tax in Ch'ung-ch'ŭng Province, These voluntary retrench-
ments called for economy at the capital and the king discontinued the royal stables, to meet the falling off in revenue.

A word is necessary here as to the complexion of the
political parties. The old Tong-in had gone to pieces and in
its place we find the Nam-in, the So-ron and the Sŭ-buk parties. We have in all then the

Nam-in	with	H ŭ M o k	as l e a d e r
So-ron	"	Yun Cheung	" "
No-ron	"	Song Si-ryŭl	" "
Sŭ-buk	"	Yu Yŏng-gyŭng	" "

Among these the names of the Nam-in and No-ron were
the most prominent and their leaders, Hŭ Mok and Song Si-
ryŭl were deadly enemies of each other. There was no inter-
marriage between these different parties. Each had its separate color. The Nam-in was red, the So-ron blue, the No-
ron white and the Sŭ-buk black. It was not the men but the
women who wore these distinctive colors and even to this day
it is common to see the party colors in the collars of women's
coats. The men were distinguished by the shape of the coat
collar. The No-rons and Nam-ins had a collar cut square at
the bottom; the So-rons had a bulging curve at the bottom and
the Sŭ-buk had a plain curve. These things sound childish
but in those days they meant life and death. The number of
men who have been sacrificed upon the altar of party strife
mounts up into the hundreds of thousands. The violent and
unreasonable strife between them prevented anything like
concerted action when the country was threatened from without.
They made it impossible for any man to be judged according
to his true merits. They effectually blocked the efforts put
forth by honest men to secure a clean and honest government.
There is nothing more despicable in political life than the
continued excitement of fierce passions when there is no principle at stake and when personal aggrandisement is the only
goal.

But at the time of which we write the No ron party, with Song Si-ryŭl at its head, was so overwhelmingly predominant that party strife was for a time almost held in abeyance. The remarkable character of this reign is largely due to his efforts. The reign from beginning to end was one grand march of progress, reform following reform with such rapidity that the reign fairly scintillates with them. To realise how great a part Song Si-ryŭl played in these movements it is necessary to know the enormous power wielded by a Prime Minister in Korea, especially when he enjoys the entire confidence of the king. His power to keep the king informed or misinformed makes him practically the ruler of the land. That Song Si-ryŭl was a real reformer is shown by the frequency with which; during many a decade after his death, statesmen would break out in panegyrics on his memory. It is shown also in the passionate hatred of political enemies who saw in him a successful rival. We have little evidence that this man ever lowered himself to the plane of common party politics. Let us then review the fifteen years of this reign and see the stamp of his great presonality upon it.

We have already mentioned some of the reforms inaugurated. First he gained a signal victory over his rival Hŏ Mok who tried to have him degraded because of his position in regard to the period of the queen's mourning. Song Si-ryŭl went over the whole ground again, cited history in support of his views and silenced by a simple and conclusive argument the captious criticism of his detractors, but he showed his greatness in not using his power to have his enemies killed, an act of generosity which later cost him his life. The following are some of the reforms instituted, and we give them here in full, for they afford a deep insight into the condition of the people.

It had been very common for men to leave their families and go off to some monastery and become monks. Now, the Buddhist monasteries are the poor-houses of Korea. Beggary is uncommon, but often, when a man has no visible means of support, he will shave his head, don the garb of a monk and spend part of the year at some monastery and the remainder in receiving donations from the people in the shape of rice or money. To do this they necessarily desert their families. To counteract this evil the king sent forth and edict that no more men with family ties should desert them in this way, and furthermore that all monks who had families living should doff their religious garb and come back to the world and support their families like honest men.

The *ajun* is a peculiar excrescence on the body politic of Korea.   He is the prefect's clerk, or factor, or agent, or pimp, or jack-of-all-trades.   He is in a large sense the incarnation of all his master's vices, to which he adds many of his own.   A royal edict was promulgated which brought a host of these men to justice and compelled them to disgorge much of their illgotten gains, which were given back, so far as possible, to the people from whom they had been extorted. In this case the reform was notable because of the limit which was put to it.   Ordinarily in Korea, when a man is caught and made a public example of in this way, the law extends the punishment to the near and remote relatives of the culprit, and many innocent men suffer with the guilty ; but in this case only actual offenders were punished.   It was strictly forbidden to call to account any man's relative because of his fault.

For many years all the salt factories and fisheries had been groaning under a heavy tax which went to support an almost unlimited number of the king's relatives ; but now these taxes were entirely remitted.   We are not told what the relatives did.   Let us hope they went to work.

It had become customary for the tax collectors to demand a poll tax not only from grown men, who alone were taxable according to law, but from children as well.   This abuse was likewise remedied.

The king gave up entirely the wild project of assaulting China, which had been a pet scheme of his father, and he likewise found no cause for supporting such a large millitary retinue about his person, and they were discharged.

There was a flourishing Buddhist convent just west of the Kyöng-bok Palace, in Cha-kol.   The king wished to do away with it, but some objected on the ground that it formed an asylum for aged palace women, and because there were many royal tablets stored there.   We may well imagine the consternation of these objectors when the king said concerning the tablets, "Well, dig a hole and bury the whole lot."

The useless custom of having masked dancers accompany the royal procession when returning from the ancestral temple was done away. The king put an end to the custom of taking girls by force and compelling them to become palace women. It must be only with the free consent of the girl's father. He consented to send men to various places where sulphur was mined to see that the people of the surrounding country were not ill-used. At the same time he ordered that no more sulphur should be dug at Tal-sŭng-wi-gung inside the South Gate. He ordered that the tombs of the king of Koryŭ should be kept in good repair. He quelled a great popular excitement in the south, which arose from the rumor that various Buddhas in the monasteries were sweating, by showing that it was caused by the frost bringing out the moisture which had been absorbed during the rainy season. The rumor was probably false, but how politic it was to take it for granted and turn it off by giving some natural cause rather than merely to deny the rumor. He added however the command that as these Buddhas had caused such a disturbance they must be burned.

At that time the province of Chŭl-la contained about 190,855 kyul of land, a kyul being supposed to produce forty bags of rice. The revenue was set at thirteen pecks of rice from each kyul. The revenue from 24,084 kyul was set aside for the support of the king's relatives, royal grave-keepers and for men whom the king particularly desired to honor because of distinguished services. The revenue from the remaining 169771 kyul, amounted to 147,134 bags of rice, 69,280 of which came up to the capital and 85,916 were stored for use by officials in the country. A certain amount of forest land was customarily set aside for fuel supply for the different palaces, but through maladministration these palaces each had much more forest land that it was entitled to, and as a consequence the people had to suffer. So the king ordered a redistribution of the forest lands and a correction of the fuel bill. He sent twenty bags of cotton seed into Ham-gyŭng Province, for he desired to see this useful plant grown in every one of the eight provinces. The island of Quelpart being still very wild and the people uncultivated, the king, for the first time in the history of the peninsula, made an attempt to civi-

lize them, by offering them government offices and by establishing schools for them. He also did the same for the river
towns along the Yalu. As the wild tribes of Sŏl-han and
Pyŭl-hă frequently came across the border and looted the
people's houses at and near Chang-jin, a general was sent to
take care of Korean interests. When 1403 scholars from the
country came to the capital and memorialized the king against
Song Si-ryŭl they were told that they were engaged in a mere
party strife and had not the interests of the country at heart,
and that if scholars meddled with the affairs of government
they would be severely handled. Along the Tuman River the
people were utterly ignorant, and scarcely knew whether there
was a king at all; so men were sent to found schools among
them and teach. Nepotism existed to such an extent, especially in connection with the government examinations,
that the king decided that no relative of any of the examiners
should be a candidate for honors. He established a criminal
court in Seoul and took all criminal cases out of the hands of
the prefects, as they often judged from prejudice rather than
from the facts. He lessened by half the tax that had been
levied for the making of arms. The government seized all
common prostitutes and made them government slaves. Being
a devout Confucianist the king commanded that the names of
Confucius' four disciples be never pronounced aloud. He
diminished the garrison of Su-wŭn from 6000 to 4000 on the
plea of economy. He gave presents of money to all unmarri-
ed women over thirty years of age, as some compensation for
what, in Korea, is considered the hardest of hard lots. He
was so affected by distress which he saw in the country during one of his frequent trips to the hot springs, that when he
returned to the capital he laid aside many of the luxuries both
of his wardrobe and his table. He made camps for the poor
who flocked to Seoul because of utter want in the east country. One was outside the Water Mouth Gate, and the other
at A-o-gă. He likewise furnished them food and medicine.
When a boatload of Chinese belonging to the Ming dynasty,
which had fled southward, was driven by a storm on Quelpart
the king promptly forwarded them to Peking rather than lay
himself open to any possible charge of bad faith toward the
Manchu power.

When some one tried to evade the payment of revenue by claiming that the boat that was bringing it was wrecked, he decided that if this happened again the owner should be decapitated. The king restored the copper types which had been destroyed at the time of the Japanese occupation of Seoul. He built a shrine to the unfortunate Tan-jŏng Tă-wang. He remeasured the lands in the southern provinces for a proper adjustment of revenue. He decreed that though a traitor's family must be punished with him, married daughters should be exempt from punishment. He acquiesced in the suggestion of the minister of war that the scaling of the city wall be made a capital offense, but when the courtiers represented that if such a small crime deserved death everybody would be a candidate for the executioner's sword, he recalled the edict.

One of this king's most interesting edicts was in connection with the census. Having ordered a numbering of the people, he found that objections were raised, because it would mean a more systematic and thorough collection of taxes. So he put forth the edict that whenever murder occurred, if the murdered man's name was not on the list of tax payers, the murderer would be immediately pardoned. Of course everybody hastened to get their names on the books and to let it be known.

He forbade marriage between people of the same family name. A commission was appointed to go and break off the point of dangerous rocks that obstructed the channels along the coast and among the islands. No governor was allowed to appoint any relative of his own to any position in the province. A man who came up from the south and charged Song Si-ryŭl with treason, but could give no evidence to substantiate the charge, was put to death.

It was customary to expose infants born of incest, and they were allowed to die in the streets. The king ordered that the government pay the expense of the rearing of such unfortunates. He gave decent burial to those who died in the mat sheds outside the wall, where contagious cases were carried and left to die. He named nine kinds of men who would make good prefects. (1) Men of good life and conduct. (2) Good scholars. (3) Skillful men and those who fostered trade. (4) Natural leaders. (5) Fearless men. (6) Students of human nature. (7) Men without an itching palm. (8) Men renowned for filial piety. (9) Good authors.

In the fifteenth year of his reign, 1674, he was taken ill. The death of his mother worked upon his spirits and aggravated his disease, and death ensued. He needs no encomiums except the bare list of the great things that were done during his reign. They will go down to posterity as his lasting monument. His genius coupled with that of his great adviser, Song Si-ryŭl, ranged through every phase of political and social life, revenue, finance, political economy, agriculture, mining, official rectitude, civil service, social ethics, sanitation, education, internal improvement, the army, popular superstition, slavery, penalties, foreign relations, border police, famine relief, consanguineous marriage, publication; these and many other important topics demanded and secured from him careful attention. He put down party strife with a heavy hand, and only once or twice during the whole period of his reign does it raise its malignant head

His son succeeded to the throne, known by his posthumous title Suk-jŏng Tă-wang. Party spirit had not been dead but only in abeyance during his father's strong reign. It now broke out again. Memorials poured in upon the young king urging the evil practices of Song Si-ryŭl, and the young king thought there must be some truth in them because of their very numbers. He became the center of a very storm of charge and counter-charge, of attack and defense. Being but fourteen years old and of a naturally vacillating temperament, he was first the tool of one party and then of another. His whole reign, which covered a period of forty-six years, was one maelstrom of party strife and was fruitful of more startling than useful events. His leading characteristic was capriciousness. Again and again he turned from one party to another, each turn being accompanied by numberless deaths. But we must not anticipate.

It will be noticed that when his reign began in 1675 the Nam-in party was in power with Hŭ Jŭk at its head. The strife over Song Si-ryŭl had resulted in his banishment to Wŭn-san. He was the Bismarck of Korea in that when his master died the aged councillor found in the son the same gratitude that the Iron Chancellor did.   It would be an endless as well as a fruitless task to describe the party fights that took place.   It will be enough to say that the reign was one long fight from beginning to end.   During the early part of the reign, in 1677, a complete census of the country was made. It was probably the conclusion of work begun by the former king.   It was found that in the whole country there were 1,234,512 houses, containing 4,703,505 people.

Some excitement was caused when it was found that Chinese histories were claiming that Prince Kwang-hä was a good man, and that In-jo Tä-wang had revolted against him. After a sharp party fight the king decided to send an envoy and request the emperor to have the mistake corrected.

In 1678 the Japanese again insisted that their quarters in Fusan be enlarged.   Consent was given to move the settlement seven *li* to the south, to the town of Cho-hyang. This is the present site of the town of Fusan.   From east to west its length was 372 *tsubo* and 4 feet.   From north to south it was 256 *tsubo*.   Two official reception halls were built, one called the East Hall and the other the West Hall.   The houses were all built by Japanese carpenters from Tsushima and the work covered a period of three years.   The Korean government gave 9000 bags of rice and 6000 ounces of silver to cover the expense, and undertook to keep the place in repair.   That this colony was kept up in good style is shown by the fact that Korea made repairs on these buildings in 1721, 1724, 1748, 1765, 1780, 1786, 1794, 1801, 1813, 1822, 1831, 1836, 1850, 1853, 1857, 1864.

The most trivial matters were made occasions for party fights.   A storm occurred on a day when the king was to go out, and the No-ron party claimed that it was a dispensation of providence to spoil a plot of the Nam-ins to revolt and seize the reins of power.   Whoever took a firm position on any point found later that it became the basis for an accusation and a cause for death.   So it was with the Prime Minister Hŭ Jŭk who advised the building of a fortress near Songdo.   This later caused his death.   The courtiers accused each other in the royal presence about the most trivial matters, such as quarrels between their concubines, the cutting of fuel timber, the profligacy of the Prime Minister's son, and such like, while great matters of state seem to have taken care of themselves.

And so we arrive at the year 1680. The Nam-in are still in full power and Hŭ Jŭk is still master of the situation. But see how small a thing accomplishes his downfall. The day arrived for ancestral worship in Hŭ Jŭk's house, but it was very rainy. The king thoughtfully ordered the eunuchs to get out the palace awning of oiled paper and carry it to the Minister's house and let him use it during the ceremony. The eunuch replied that Hŭ Jŭk had already taken it. Instantly the king's kindly feeling was changed to anger and hatred by the insolence of the Minister in thus appropriating the awning. He sent a messenger and discovered that a crowd of the adherents of the Nam-in party had congregated at Hŭ Jŭk's house. They were immediately denounced as traitors. The generals were called and the house was surrounded with troops. All the leading men in the Nam-in party were killed on the spot. The names of the killed are Hŭ Jŭk, Hŭ Kyŭn, Yu Hyŭk-yŭn, Yi Wŭn-jŭng, O Chŭng-ch'ang, Yi T'ă-sö, Chŏng Wŭn-no, Kang Man-ch'ŭl, Yi Wŭn-sŭng and Yun Hyu. The king's two cousins, Princes Pok-sun and Pak-pyŭn, and eight others were banished. The No-ron party were then called back to power. The king brought back from exile the great Song Si-ryŭl and also Kim Su-han, whom he made Prime Minister. In twenty-four hours a trusted minister and party were totally overthrown and every place was filled with a member of the opposition. The next few months were spent in hunting down the remaining leaders of the Nam-in party and securing their execution. Some were hung, some poisoned and some decapitated. One instance of this will suffice. Hŭ Să and Hŭ Yŭng, two influential men lived at Yong-san. There was no valid charge against them, so Kim Sŭk-ju told the king he would find one. To this end he sent one Kim Whan-go to Yong-san and gave him money to build a fine house adjoining that of the prospective victims. Before long he had them involved in treasonable plans and as soon as enough evidence was collected the two men were seized and put to death, and with them a large number of their immediate friends. Man-hunting was not so much a public necessity as a private pastime.

The newly installed general-in-chief found great abuses in the army and thousands of names on the rolls, of men long since dead. Taxes were being collected in an utterly lawless way. These abuses were done away and others probably as bad or worse took their places, for as power meant spoils the newly victorious party was not likely to forego any of its privileges. We are borne out in this supposition by the fact that about this time the king began the custom of making an annual visit to the temple of heaven to pray for good crops. This indicates that the people were being badly governed. He paid considerable attention to the navy and appointed An-ju, Suk-ch'ŭn, Sun-an, Yŏng-yu, Cheung-san, P'yŭng-yang, Yong-yang, Kang sö, Sam wha, Ham-jong and No-gang in P'yŭng-an Province and Chang-nyŭn, Eun-yul, P'ung-ch'ŭn, Hŭ-sa and An-ak in Whang-hă Province to be naval stations. It was only at this late date that the second king of the dynasty received the posthumous title of Chŏng-jong Tă-wang.

Attention was paid to the border forts along the Yalu, expenses were curtailed and garrisons were supported out of the land tax of the adjoining districts. It was a time of many severe calamities. A fire in P'yŭng-yang burned 344 houses and a flood in Ham-gyŭng Province destroyed 906 more with great loss of life. Song Si-ryŭl had not forgotten his old master, now some ten years dead, and he suggested to the king that Hyo-jong Tă-wang be honored with the Se-sil, that is, that his tablet be not removed from the ancestral temple after the fourth generation, as was customary, but should remain there permanently. It caused a great commotion, but the aged minister carried the day. It is true that few monarchs of the line better deserved that honor than did Hyo-jong Tă-wang.

The year 1684 beheld a sort of "reign of terror." It arose in the following manner. A messenger from the Japanese on Tsushima came post haste announcing that a large band of Chinese pirates was about to land on Korean soil. A panic followed in Seoul and thousands fled precipitately to the country. Bands of thieves took advantage of the confusion to commit many lawless acts. They formed a sort of secret society and their principles were anarchistic. They made it an object to raid houses where money was to be found. They seized ladies as they were passing along the streets in covered chairs, and violated them. They seized officials whom they hated, and put them to death. The government found one of their books and in it was written their oath of membership. Three cardinal principles were set forth ; (1) To kill as many noblemen as possible, (2) To violate as many women as possible, (3) To steal as much personal property as possible. Seven men who had carried away and ravished a widow of Kong-ju were caught and decapitated. One of them was her own cousin and he belonged to the so-called "knife gang." After a time the disturbance was suppressed.

One incident of a peculiarly Korean character deserves mention. Some money was stolen from the strong room of a fortress near Song-do. The store-house keeper was suspected but there was no evidence. So the commandant secretly questioned the keeper's little son and found that the suspicion was correct. The keeper was punished but the commandant was also cashiered from the fact that he had induced a boy to incriminate his own father.

The native records say that in the twelfth year of this sovereign, in 1686, Roman Catholicism entered Korea for the first time. Certain foreigners entered the country and preached the new doctrine. We are not told of what nationality these men were but it was long before any European attempted to enter Korea. We are told that the new doctrine spread rapidly and that some of the highest officials asked the king to send the foreigners out of the country. Whether this was done cannot now be learned. Nothing is said of this in the French work on the Roman Catholic Mission in Korea, and it is somewhat difficult to understand. It would hardly be found in the records, however, were there not some ground for the statement.

The following year beheld events that were to result in another violent revolution and in the driving from the seat of power the No-ron party and the reinstatement of the Nam-in. It all grew from the king's taking a concubine, Chang, who soon gained complete ascendency over him. A rumor arose that the queen was to be deposed and when Han Söng-u expostulated with the king, the latter flew into a passion and drove him away. The following year the concubine presented

the king with a son, the most unfortunate thing that could
have happened, for, the queen being as yet childless, it served
to put the king more entirely under the influence of the concubine. Trouble followed immediately. The king said "I am
now forty years old and have no son by the queen. The people are getting uneasy. As I have gotten a son by a concubine I intend to make him Crown Prince, and anyone may
object at his peril." In this way he threw as it were a torch
into a powder magazine. The No-ron party who were in
power, were in arms at once for they knew that the opposition
had been using the concubine to undermine their influence.
Memorials poured in from all sides reminding the king that he
was still young, that there was no need of haste in appointing
the queen a successor. These memorials the king answered
by banishing the senders. Even Song Si-ryŭl who had entered
a mild protest, was stripped of rank and sent outside the city.
The Nam-in party then stepped once more into power. From
the Prime Minister down all offices were again turned over to
them. Song Si-ryŭl was banished to Quelpart, but the Nam-
in were not content with that, and demanded his death. So
he was summoned back to Seoul. Posthumous honors were
given to many of the Nam-ins whom the king had ordered
killed at the house of Hŭ Jŭk.

Not long after this the king began to make preparations
to put away his queen. To this end he made the following
statement. "For a long time I have been aware of the queen's
jealous disposition and evil mind, and I have borne with it
patiently but now I can endure it no longer. Since I have
taken the concubine Chang it has been still more unendurable.
The queen and the concubine Kim have been putting their
heads together in an attempt to frighten me into putting away
Chang, but I saw through the plan. Now what shall we do?"
Time and again the officials came pleading for the queen, but
the king was utterly deaf to all they had to say. He piled
unjust accusations upon her without deigning to give a single
proof. Large numbers where banished and a few killed outright
because of their intercessions with the king. The most notorious case was that of Pak T'ă-bo whose name has passed into
a proverb. He with two others memorialized the king begging him to drive away the concubine and retain the queen.

The king's rage knew no bounds.   He came out and took his
seat in front of the In-jŭng Gate of the Chang-dŭk Palace and
had the man brought before him.   When asked why he had
written the memorial he answered, "Because of the treatment
the queen has received."   The king then ordered red hot
plates to be passed along his limbs.   Still he would not express sorrow.   Then bowls were broken into small pieces and
the fragments were piled up on the man s already burned
limbs, a plank was placed across them and men stood on either
end of it and jumped up and down.   The pieces of pottery
were of course ground into the man's legs.   As he still remained firm he was tied with a rope and hoisted to the top of
a high pole in a cruelly painful position.   As he still remained
unmoved he was banished to the south.   His aged father accompanied him as far as the river and there he died of his
wounds.   This, so far from stopping the flood of petitions,
only increased it, for immediately 16,000 men with Chŏng To-
gyŭng at their head sent in an appeal and likewise all the
country scholars and all the students of the Confucian school.
But every petition was returned by the passion-blinded king.

    In the fifth moon of the year, 1689, the king deposed the
queen, stripped her of all here titles, degraded her to the level
of the common people and sent her back to her father's house,
not by way of the great gate of the palace but by a side gate,
in a white sedan chair, the badge of a criminal.   Concubine
Chang was proclaimed queen and her father became a prince.
We will remember that the aged Song Si-ryŭl had been ordered back from Quelpart to meet his fate at the capital, but even
the popular sympathy which a public execution at Seoul would
have aroused was denied him, for the king sent a draught of
poison to be administered on the way, and so in an obscure
country village the grand old man drank the deadly potion
and passed away.   Some of his followers who afterwards memorialized the king in regard to him were killed or banished,
together with the deposed queen's relatives.   The following
year the son of the newly appointed queen was made Crown
Prince.

CHAPTER XI.

Heavy tax remitted .. a *tendens* novel....the wheel of fortune turns
. ..the queen restored....sorcery ...Puk-han built....mourning
....a weak king....a lucid interval....terrible reprisals....a desecrated tomb ...contact with the West ...king's suspicious death
...enemies killed ...party strife put down ...seals for Japanese
....prohibition of manufacture and sale of wine ...a powerful conspiracy .. preparations for defense ...Ch'ung-ju falls....rebellion
put down with a heavy hand ...honors distributed ...mining prohibited ...incipient rebellion ... reforms....reservoirs ...use of
wine interdicted ...bureau of agriculture ...important secret service
...dress reform ...cruel punishments stopped....a new war vessel
..honest measurement .. imperial tombs ...monument to the
dead political parties....musical instruments.

Each year a large Chinese embassy visited Seoul, and it
was customary to feed them from silver dishes, which were
given them as presents when they returned to their own land.
This expense was met by a tax on the people of Song-do.
While the king was making a small tour in the country he
arrived at Song-do and there he asked about this tax. The
people replied that they had to sell their very children to
meet it, for it amounted to 1,200 bags of rice, 900,000 cash,
3,000 bags of other grain, 3,000 pieces of cloth as well as
other things. The king listened to their petition and remitted
the tax.

Only five years elapse before we find the king making
another complete change in his household, by driving out the
new queen, who had been the concubine Chang, and reinstat-
ing the old queen in her rightful place again. These sudden
and complete changes of face in the king would have been
amusing had they not been accompanied by the shedding of
so much innocent blood. The king had tired of his new
queen. He seems to have been one of those men who require
a periodical outbreak of some kind, but who in the intervals
are perfectly quiet. The time had come for such an outbreak
and Kim Ch'un-t'ăk was the instrument by which it was
brought about. He had bought himself into the good graces
of the palace women, and as a first step toward the accomplishment of his plans he wrote a book in which was illustrated, in romance form, the evils of putting away the true wife

for a concubine. The copy of this book which was given to the king materially hastened the catastrophe. The Nam-in were in power but they looked with concern upon the king's growing antipathy toward them and they urged him to put the too bold novelist out of the way; but the leaders of the No-ron party, knowing that all depended on a quick, decisive blow, went in a body to the king at night and urged him to follow the evident bent of his inclinations. This he proceeded to do by banishing the brother of queen Chang, and with him the leaders of the Nam-in party. Then once more the No-ron stepped to the front and prepared to enjoy the good things. High posthumous honors were given to Song Si-ryŭl and to the deposed queen's father and to many others of the No-rons who had perished during the last outbreak. The king, to save his "face," called the deposed queen back little by little. He first put her in a little palace in An-dong; then he transferred her to the "Mulberry Palace," and finally brought her to the palace proper. The woman Chang was again reduced to her former place and a stringent law was made that henceforth no royal concubine should ever be raised to the position of queen. The martyr Pak T'ä-bo was given posthumously the title of Prime Minister. The reinstated party tried to induce the king to kill the concubine, but, as she was the mother of the heir apparent to the throne, he could not consent. A slave of this concubine's resorted to a clever trick in order to turn the tables on the No-ron party. Enticing to his house a slave of one of the leaders of the No-ron party, he got him intoxicated and then stole from him his name tag, a piece of wood which each person was supposed to carry and on which his name was written. This he took and dropped beside the grave of the father of the conbubine where it was discovered that a fetich had been buried. This was to show that a No-ron leader had resorted to the black art to win back his way to power. The king, however, looked into the matter, discovered the fraud and killed the prime mover in the plot, a Nam-in leader. Many others were also banished.

Four years passed without any events of importance, and then the queen became afflicted with boils and expired. The records tell us that that night the king dreamed that the dead queen came to him with her garments covered with blood. To his enquiries she made no answer except to point toward the apartments of the concubine Chang. The king arose and went in that direction, and his ears were greeted with the sound of laughter and merriment. Wetting his finger in his mouth he applied it to the paper window and soon made a peep-hole. There he beheld the concubine and a large company of sorceresses engaged in shooting arrows into an effigy of the queen and making merry over having done her to death by placing a fetich under her room. This was the signal for another of the king's periodical outbreaks. In spite of her being the mother of the Crown Prince, he poisoned her and killed all her sorceress companions. A host of the Nam-in party also met their death. The almost incredible number of 1,700 people are said to have met their death as a result of this disturbance. There must have been in connection with it a sort of "star chamber," or secret tribunal where many went in but none came out, for we are told that a few years later a secret prison in the palace was abolished.

The year 1711 was marked by the building of the great mountain fortress of Puk-han among the mountains immediately behind Seoul. There had been a fortress there in the ancient days of Păk-je. It is an almost ideal place for a place of retreat, being surrounded with very steep mountains.

When this king died in 1720 the custom was first inaugurated of having the whole people put on mourning clothes, and wearing them for three years in honor of the dead king.

The new king, known by his posthumous title of Kyöng-jong Tă-wang, was the son of the disgraced and executed concubine Chang. By this time the so-called Nam-in party had practically passed off the stage of history; its leading men had all been killed and it had left the field to its two great rivals the No-ron and So-ron, although as we have before said the No-ron was overwhelmingly predominant.

King Kyöng-jong was a man of feeble intellect and he took no interest in the affairs of government. He merely served as a center about which factional fights went on. It is said that his mother, the concubine Chang, when about to be led to execution, said to him, "If I am to die you must die with me," and at that she struck at him with an improvised weapon, a piece of wood. She succeeded only in wounding him, but it was in a portion of the body that rendered it impossible for him ever to have an heir. He swung like a pendulum back and forth between the Noron and Soron parties, agreeing with whichever happened for the moment to gain his ear. This caused the Noron party some uneasiness and they desired to see the reins of government in more responsible hands. They warmly favored the king's brother as a candidate for the throne. The king was always ailing, for he never thoroughly recovered from the wound which his mother had inflicted, and he was unable to perform the ancestral rites. He was also afflicted with sores on his head, so that for months at a time he was unable to wear the headband which is such a distinctive mark of the Korean. The Noron leaders induced someone to memorialize the king asking him to make his brother his heir. They all added their advice of the same tenor, and finally induced him to consult the Queen Mother about it. She entered heartily into the plan and the decree went forth that the king's brother was heir apparent. This was like a thunder-bolt among the Soron ranks. The whole transaction had been carefully concealed from them, and now a man who could not, under the circumstances, be other than a warm friend of the Noron party was heir to the throne, and every Soron was in danger. They stormed and protested and memorialized but to no avail. The appointment of an heir was like the laws of the Medes and Persians, unalterable. But the Noron people knew the weakness of the king and they feared what might take place in some unguarded hour when the enemy might get the king's ear, and so they played a bolder game still. They asked the king to resign in favor of the heir. He promised to do so, but the unguarded hour which the Norons feared came, and the promise was not kept. Not only so, but when it was whispered in the king's ear that the Norons were trying to usurp the power the worst fears of that party were realized. They were driven from power and the Sorons came up smiling. But the king who liked quiet and repose had one lucid interval when he said, "There is no love of country in all this; it is simple party prejudice and thirst for blood."

At the head of the triumphant party were Cho T'ă gu, Ch'oé Kyu-su and Ch'oé Sŭk-hang. They began the performance of their official duties by bribing the palace women and eunuchs to kill the heir to the throne. The plan was to shoot him "by mistake" while pretending to hunt for a white fox which they said was haunting the palace. The heir was informed however and took measures to insure his own safety. He asked to have two of the palace women killed and two of the eunnchs, but the king himself was in mortal fear of the Sorons, whom he had brought back to power, and he dared not do so. Thereupon the heir said "I will resign and go out from the palace and become one of the common people."

The Noron party were not idle. They knew that the Sorons would soon be hunting their heads, and so they attempted to take the offensive by assassinating the king; but, as usually happened, they were betrayed, and terrible reprisals followed. Twelve of the Noron leaders were beheaded and hundreds were beaten to death or banished. It is gravely stated that in this one connection eighteen hundred men lost their lives.

The close of the king's second year witnessed a severe famine on the island of Quelpart and the king sent thither 7,000 bags of grain and remitted the tax of horses, for which that island has been from time immemorial celebrated.

The desperate state of affairs at this juncture is well illustrated by two incidents. First, the king was so enamored of the Soron party that he took Mok Ho-ryong, their leader, outside the gate one night and sacrificed a white horse and, tasting its blood, swore that until time's end Mok Ho-ryong's descendants should hold high office under the government. Second, the Soron officials went to the shrine of the great Song Si-ryŭl and tearing the tablet from its place, dragged it through the filth of a dung-hill. Meanwhile we hear nothing about the people and the country. The government was not for them and they probably cared as little for it as it did for them.

But even these sanguinary scenes could not entirely stop the march of enlightenment, for we learn that at this very time foreign clocks, barometers and water-hose were being brought into Korea from Peking where they had been intro-

duced by foreigners.   This was done by the envoy Yi
I-myŭng who met missionaries in Peking.   He had a conversation with them on the subject of religion and professed to find
great similarity between Christian doctrines and those of the
Chinese classics.

The fourth year of this unfortunate king, 1624, opened
with a reform that augured well.⁵ It consisted in the destruction of all the convents outside the city gates, especially outside the West Gate which was at that time about half a mile
west of the present New Gate.   The reasons are not specifically given, but these convents had obviously become dangerous to the morals of the people, and hot-beds of sedition. But
the king was not permitted to continue his reforms, for he
died in the eighth moon, of poison, it is said, administered in
a shrimp salad.   It is further alleged that it was the work of
his brother, probably on the principle that he was the one to
gain most by the king's death.   But we may well doubt the
truth of the rumor, for nothing that is told of that brother
indicates that he would commit such an act, and in the second
place a man who will eat shrimps in mid-summer, that have
been brought thirty miles from the sea without ice might
expect to die.   Of course all the Soron officials were willing
to believe the heir did it and one of them advised that a silver
knife be stuck into the king's dead body, for it is popularly
believed that poison in the system will tarnish silver; but it
was not done.   There was no way to prevent the hated heir
assuming his royal prerogative, which he did the same year, 1724.

The new king, known by his posthumous title of Yŭng-
jong Tä-wang, now entered upon the longest and one of the
most brilliant reigns in the annals of the present dynasty; a
reign which proves, so far as circumstantial evidence can prove,
that he was not guilty of the murder of his brother.   As may
be surmised, his deadly enemies, the Sorons, were driven from
office and the Norons reinstated.   It is probable that the king
found it impossible to restrain the Norons from taking revenge upon their enemies and we are told that a thousand
men were killed each year for some years.   That this was done
in spite of the king, rather than by him, will be seen from the
strenuous efforts which he made to destroy the lines of party
demarcation.

He began his reign with a statement of his inability to rule the people rightly, and blaming himself for the sufferings of the people from famine and plague. He immediately proclaimed his son crown prince, so that from the very first there might be no question as to the succession. He had to give way to the importunities of his councillors and decapitate Kim Il-gyŭng who had charged him with the murder of his brother.

On the very first day of the new year he proclaimed that all party strife must cease ; that men must think and plan for the good of the whole country rather than for a particular party. As he was returning one day from a royal tomb a man beside the road shouted "There goes the man who poisoned his predecessor with shrimps." Recognizing in this nothing but an attempt to keep open the old party sore, the king handled the man severely together with certain others of the Soron party who had instigated him to the outrage.

From that day to this the Noron party has been uniformly in power. Party strife practically ceased, not by the dissolution of the other parties but because one party obtained such an overwhelming ascendency that the others died of starvation. Several things led to this result. A series of unsuccessful conspiracies on the part of the Soron party, each of which weakened it to the point of exhaustion ; and secondly the extreme length of the reign, during which, with one short interval, the king held firmly to the Noron party. The closing act of his first year was a reform which he forced in the government dispensary. It had long been a rich morsel for conscienceless officials to fatten upon, but now the whole personnel of the institution was changed and it again performed its normal function of dispensing medicines for the public health. The king's forbearance is seen in the fact that when a thief was caught, bearing upon his person a letter from two of the palace women asking him to procure for them a deadly poison, the king executed the thief but refused to proceed against the women, on the ground that they had no possible cause for wishing his death.

We here meet the curious statement, not mentioned heretofore, that from the earliest times the Lords of Tsushima received seals from the king of Korea. At this time the daimyo

of that island sent and asked the king to renew the custom,
which had probably been discontinued for a short space of
time. The king complied with the request and had the
seal cut and sent. It is not possible to conclude from this
that the daimyo of Tsu hima considered himself a vassal of
Korea, for it is not mentioned elsewhere in the Korean annals. We can form but one theory that will account for it.
This seal may have been only for the purpose of identification
to vouch for the authenticity of letters that might pass between Korea and Tsushima. The time may come when, in
the light of facts not yet discovered, this incident may throw
light on the early relations between Korea and Japan.

A striking feature of this king's reign was the promulgation and enforcement of the principle of the prohibition of the
manufacture and use of spirituous liquors. We venture to
affirm that this king was the first in history, if not the only
one, to boldly assert and rigidly enforce the principle of total
abstinence from the use of wines and liquors. His three
commands were (1) Party strife must cease. (2) Luxury
must be curtailed. (3) The making, selling or drinking of
fermented wines or distilled liquors is a capital offense.

But this and other reforms were about to be eclipsed by
the great upheaval of 1727, after the relation of which we
will return to them. The Norons made such desperate attempts to induce the king to continue the persecution of the
Soron party that he underwent a revulsion of feeling and for
a short time punished the Norons by calling back into power
many of the opposition. It may be that this short respite
awoke the slumbering ambition of the Soron party so that
when they found it was but partial and temporary their
chagrin drove them into sedition. There appeared at Nam-
wŭn in Chŭl-la Province an insulting circular asserting that
the king had killed his brother and that the whole Noron
party were traitors. It called upon all good men to oppose
the government in every way possible. The governor sent a
copy to the king who simply said "Burn it up." But he
greatly miscaculated the amount of sentiment that lay behind
that circular, and his enemies took advantage of his unsus-
piciousness to work up a wide-spread and powerful conspiracy
against the government. It was headed by Kim Yŭng-hŭ,

This conspiracy was headed by the son of the executed Kim Il-gyŭng, by Mok Si-ryŭng the brother of Mok Ho-ryŭng and by the sons and other near relatives of the killed and banished leaders of the Soron party.   A large force was collected in Kyŭng-sang Province and Yi In-jwa and Chŏng Heui-ryang were put in command.   The conspiracy honeycombed the whole country, for we are told that in P'yŭng-an Province Yi Sa-sŭng took charge of an insurrectionary force, while at the capital Kim Chung-geui and Nam T'ä-jung worked in its interests.   It was agreed that on the twentieth of the third moon Seoul should be entered and that Prince Mil-wha be put on the throne.   But there was a weak point in this as in all such ventures.   One of the leaders in the south, An Pak, had a friend living at Yong-ju, in the direct line of the approach to Seoul and he warned him to move, as something was about to happen.   The friend coaxed him into telling him the whole affair, and then brought the story straight to Seoul.   This informer was Choé Kyo-sŭ.   Immediately the king sent out a heavy guard to the river and also manned the wall of the capital.   Troops were thrown into Yang-sŭng, Chin-wi, Su-wŭn, Yong-in, Chuk-san and Ch'un-ch'ŭn, and were told to seize anyone who made the least disturbance.   The brother of An Pak being caught, he gave the details of the position of the rebel troops and other important particulars.   The king appointed O Myŭng-hang of the Soron party as general-in-chief of an expedition against the seditious people of the south. He took with him 2,000 soldiers, but gathered more as he proceeded south.   Strong bodies of troops were also sent north along the Peking road and to Puk-pawi outside the East Gate, to guard the appoaches to the city.   In the south loyal troops were in force at Mun-gyŭng Fortress near Cho-ryŭng Pass and the governor of Whang-hä Province also took soldiers and stationed himself at Whang-ju, near P'yŭug-yang.   Others were stationed in the defiles of the mountains just beyond Song-do. It is quite evident from these extensive precautions that the plot was a wide-spread and dangerous one and that it had powerful leaders, not only in the country but at the capital itself.

In the south, the great rebel leader, Yi In-jwa, with banners flying, led his powerful army northward to the town of

Chüng-ju. Here was stored a large amount of government provisions and arms. It was taken not by storm but by strategem. Arms were sent into the city on litters covered with vegetables and other things and soldiers went in, disguised as coolies. Once inside, they soon put the small garrison out of the way and killed the commandant. Yi then resumed the march on Seoul, appointing prefects in the dis tricts through which he passed and assuming the title "Great General-in-Chief." The claim was that the uprising was in behalf of the dead king. All the soldiers were in mourning for him and they carried in their ranks a shrine to his memory, before which they offered sacrifices.

The road from the south coming up to Seoul divides at Mok-ch'ün, one branch proceeding by way of Chik-san and the other by An-süng, but they unite again at Su-wün. The rebels arrived at Mok-ch'ün just as the royal troops arrived at Su-wün. It was of prime importance to the rebels to know by which road the royal army, under O Myüng hang, were coming. Whichever way they came the rebels must take the other road and so evade an action. Gen. O was astute enough to surmise this but he did not propose to let the rebels steal a march on him in this way; so he sent forward a small part of his force toward Chik-san, but with the main body of his troops he took the road by way of An-sung. His calculations were correct, and when he neared An-süng he found that the enemy were encamped there in fancied security. Taking a picked band of 700 men Gen. O made a detour and came around the hill on whose slope the rebels were encamped. In the night he made a wild charge down from its summit into the camp. The effect was instantaneous. A moment later the whole rebel force was in full flight, racing for their lives, while the pursuers cut them down at pleasure. Yi In-jwa was captured and brought to Seoul. Meanwhile Pak P'il-pön the prefect of Sön-san opposed the remaining rebels in Kyüng-sang Province, capturing and killing a great number of them, especially the 'leaders Ung Po and Heui Ryang, whose heads he sent to Seoul in a box.

When Gen O Myüng-hang returned in triumph to Seoul the king went out to meet him, and after the traitors' heads had been impaled on high, they all adjourned to the palace where a great feast was spread, at which the king gave Gen. O a sounding title and to Ch'oĕ Kyo-sŭ, who betrayed the plot he gave the house near the present English Church, which has in connection with it a memorial shrine. The king had a book printed giving in details the evil deeds of the Soron party. Since that time there have been no great party struggles. Sacrifices were offered for all who had been killed by the rebels. The king showed his clemency by liberating the five-year-old son of one of the traitors. He had been imprisoned according to the law of the country, to be kept until his fifteenth year, and then he would be led out to execution.

Hand in hand with the king's prejudice against the use of wine went a similar prejudice against mining, so that not only did he peremptorily forbid the mining of silver at An-byŭn but hearing that copper was being mined near the same place he sent and put a stop to it.

In 1727 the heir apparent died and was given the posthumous title of Hyo-jang Se-ja. Two years later another incipient rebellion broke out in the south having as its object the placing of Ha Keui, a relative of the king, on the throne. It is said that with him died several hundred more of the doomed Soron party.

The next thirty-two years were crowded full of reforms and their mere enumeration throws much light on the social and economic conditions of the time.

A map was made of the northern boundary and a fortress was built at Un-du; the law was promulgated that the grandson of a slave woman should be free; on account of drought the king ordered the making of numerous reservoirs in which to store water for irrigation, and a commission was appointed with headquarters at Seoul, under whose supervision these reservoirs were built; the king had a new model of the solar system made, to replace the one destroyed by the Japanese during the invasion; at last China amended that clause in her history which stated that Kwang-hă was a good man and that In-jong Tă-wang had usurped the throne, and the king presented one of the corrected copies at the ancestral temple; the cruel form of torture, which consisted in tying the ankles together and then twisting a stout stick between the bones, was done away; a granary was built on the eastern

coast, to be stocked with grain each year by the people of
Kyŭng-sang Province, for use in case of famine in the northern province of Ham-gyŭng; the king claimed that the scarcity of rice was due to the fact that so much of it was used in
the making of wine and again threatened to kill anyone who
should make, sell or use that beverage; in fact he placed
detectives all about Seoul, along the main roads, whose
business it was to smell of the breath of everyone whose face
or gait indicated indulgence in the flowing bowl!

A boatload of men belonging to the overthrown Ming
dynasty appeared on the southern coast and asked aid in an
attempt to wrest again the scepter from the Manchus, but
they were politely refused; the king abolished that form of
punishment which consisted in applying red hot irons to the
limbs; he built the Chung-sŭng, or inner wall at P'yŭng-yang
in order to cut off the view of a *kyu-bong* or "spying peak,"
which in Korea is supposed to bring bad luck. Any place
from which may be seen the top of a mountain peak just
peeping above the summit of a nearer mountain is considered
unfit for a burial or building site.

About the year 1733 famines were so frequent that the
king appointed a bureau of agriculture and appointed inspectors for each of the provinces to help in securing good irrigation; a man named Yi Keui-ha invented a war chariot with
swords or spears extending out from the hubs of the wheels
on either side. He was rewarded with a generalship. The
king established a special detective force differing from the
ordinary detective force in being more secret in its operations
and in holding greater powers. The rules for its guidance
were as follows, and they throw light upon existing conditions.

(1) After careful investigation they may close up any
prefectural office and send the prefect to Seoul for trial.

(2) This does not apply to prefectures where animals are
being reared for use in ancestral sacrifices.

(3) In order to maintain their incognito they shall not
demand food for nothing at the country inns but shall pay
the regular prices.

(4) For the same reason they shall not stop long in the
same place.

(5) They must look sharply after the district constables

and thief-catchers and see that they are diligent and effective.

(6) They must put a stop to the pernicious custom of prefects' servants taking money in advance from farmers as a bribe to remit in part future government dues.

(7) They shall prevent the sending in of incorrect estimates of the area of taxable land.

(8) They shall see to it that prefects do not receive extra interest on government seed loaned to the people and payable in the autumn after the crop is harvested.

(9) They shall prevent prefects appropriating ginseng which they confiscate from illegal sellers.

(10) They shall prevent the king's relatives and friends seizing people's land.

(11) They shall stop the evil custom of prefects withholding the certificate of release from pardoned exiles until they have paid a certain sum of money.

(12) They shall prevent the enlistment of too many men, who thereby claim their living from the govenment granaries.

(13) They shall see to it that the prefects do not keep the good cloth paid by the people for soldiers' clothes, and hand over to the soldiers a poorer quality.

(14) They shall prevent creditors compounding interest if a debtor fails to pay on time.

(15) They shall stop the making of poor gun-powder and of muskets with too small a bore.

(16) They shall enforce the law that the grandson of a slave is free.

(17) They shall see to it that the prefects in P'yŭng-an Province do not receive revenue above the legal amount.

Each of these specifications might be made the heading of a long chapter in Korean history. We have here in epitome the causes of Korea's condition to-day.

The governor of Kang-wŭn Province stated that on account of the frequent famines he could not send three men annually as heretofore to the island of Ul-leung (Dagelet), but the king replied that as the Japanese had asked for that island, it would be necessary to make the annual inspection as heretofore.

In the year 1734 the king made his second son heir to the throne; he did away with the punishment of men who sold

goods in competition with the guilds or monopolies established at Chong-no, the center of the capital.   There had been so
many royal deaths that the people had become accustomed to
the use of white clothes, and had forgotten all other custom.
But the king now declared that white was the worst of colors
because it soiled so easily, and he ordered the use of blue,
red or black, but giving the preference to the first as being
the color that corresponds with east.   In the early years of
the dynasty King Se-jong had made a gauge of the size of
whipping rods.   It was shaped like a gun barrel, and no one
was to be whipped with a rod that could not be put into this
gauge like a ramrod.   The king revived this law and had
many gauges made and sent all about the country to the different prefectures.   He also forbade anyone but a properly
authorised official to administer a whipping, and he abrogated
the law by which thieves were branded by being struck in the
forehead and on each cheek with a great bunch of needles after which ink was rubbed into the wounds.   He next did
away with the clumsy three-decked war-vessels which were
slow and unseaworthy and in place of them substituted what
he called the "Sea Falcon Boat" which had sails extending
from the sides like wings and which combined both speed and
safety.   These he stationed all along the coast.

While on a trip to Song-do the king paid a compliment to
the people of Pu-jo-ga, the ward in that city where dwell the
descendants of the men of the former dynasty, who do not
acknowledge the present dynasty, and thus show their loyalty
to their ancient master.   At the same time he, for the first
time, inclosed in a fence the celebrated Sön-juk Bridge, where
still shows the blood of the murdered statesman Chöng Mong-
ju.

Since the days of King Se-jong, who determined the length
of the Korean yard-stick, that useful instrument had shrunk-
en in some measure and its length differed in different localities.   So now again the king gave strict orders about it and
required all yard-sticks to be made to conform to a pattern
which he gave.   Previous to the days of King Myŭng-jong
men of the literary degrees dressed in red, but white had
gradually taken its place; and now the king ordered them to
go back to the good old custom.   The official grade called

Halyim became such an object of strife among the officials that
the king was constrained to abolish it, though it has since
been revived. Two of the emperors of the Sung dynasty in
China have their graves on Korean soil in the vicinity of Kap-
san. The duty of keeping these graves in order was now
placed in the hands of the governor of Ham-gyŭng Province.
The king anticipated the death of all party strife by setting up
a monument at the Song-gyun-gwan in memory thereof and he
ordered the people of different parties to intermarry and become good friends. During the Manchu and Japanese invasions all the musical instruments had been either destroyed
or stolen, and as yet they had not been wholly replaced, but
now there were found in a well at the palace a set of twenty-
four metal pendants which, when struck with a hammer, gave
four various musical notes. The inscriptions on them indicated that they had come down from the time of King Se-jong.
This aroused the king's interest and he set skillful men at
work making various instruments, notably a small chime of
bells to be used at the royal ancestral worship.

CHAPTER XII.

Gates roofed   superstition   sorcery interdicted....a plebiscite....
wine-bibber executed   a female Buddha ....growth of Roman
Catholicism....sanitation .. a senile king:....suspicions against the
Crown Prince... plot against him .. an ambitious woman....the
prince's trial ... a painful scene .. the prince killed....law against
wine relaxed....sacrifice... census ..various changes ... party
schism . emancipation proclamation.....a dangerous uncle....a
new king .. literary works .. justice .. study of Christianity....
various innovations .. rumors of war...."birthplace" of Roman
Catholicism in Korea . opposition . terrible scourge of cholera
....conspiracy....women's coiffure ... Roman Catholic persecution
....Roman Catholic books declared seditious .. prosperity and
adversity... a Chinese priest enters Korea ...types made....liter-
ary works . suggestion as to coinage . Chinese priest asks that a
Portugese embassy be sent to Korea ..the king not violently opposed to Christianity.

In the year 1743 the king put roofs upon the West and
North-east Gates. Before that time they had been simply

arches. He set on foot an agitation against the use of silk, and
ordered that no more banners be made of that material. He
utterly did away with the last remnant of the Soron party by
an edict in which he stated that all who would go by that
name were traitors. There was a popular superstition that
the third and sixth on the list of successful candidates at
the government examinations would soon die; so the examiners were careful to substitute other names, in case a
friend or relative found himself in this awkward predicament.
The king happened to see this done once and upon inquiry
found that the names of two Song-do men were being substituted in place of those of some friends of the examiners.
In anger he ordered the names to be all mixed up again, and
that each man be made to run his chance of sudden death.
One of his most salutary reforms was the doing away with
the *mudang* or sorceress class, who did and still do so
much to corrupt the morals and degrade the manners of the
Korean people. This period beheld the invention of the one-
wheeled chair, but its use was always confined to the third
official grade. A step backward was taken when it was
decreed that no one above the ninth official grade could
be beaten as punishment for crime. It tended to build up
another barrier between the upper and lower classes. And
yet it was not an unmixed evil, for a public beating must inevitably lower the dignity of the office that the culprit holds.
There was such universal complaint against both the land and
the poll taxes that the king put it to vote at a plebiscite called in Seoul in 1750, and the people voted unanimously for a
house tax instead, and the king complied. The next year a
grandson was born to him, who was destined to be his successor. He found it necessary to police the four mountains
about Seoul to prevent the trees all being cut down. He
built for the first time a fortification at the Im-jin River. In
1751 famines in different localities drove crowds of people to
Seoul and the government was obliged to feed them; then the
king's mother died; then the queen died. The king said
there must be some extraordinary cause for all these calamities.
He believed it was because wine was being secretly used in
the palace. It was denied, but he was incredulous and ordered that even in the ancestral sacrifices the use of wine be

dispensed with and that water be used instead. The provincial general of Ham-gyŭng Province was convicted of having used wine and the king went outside the South Gate to see him executed. The culprit's head was set on a pole in view of the populace. Following up the good work of doing away with sorcery, the king banished from Seoul all the blind exorcists.

The year 1753 was marked by two events of importance. A woman created a great disturbance in Whang-hă Province by claiming to be a Buddha and inciting the women everywhere to burn up the ancestral shrines. The trouble ended only when the king sent a special officer to seize and execute her. 6

We are told that by this time the secret study of the tenets of Roman Catholicism had resulted in its wide diffusion in the provinces of Whang-hă and Kang-wŭn. There was uneasiness at court on account of the rumor that the people were throwing away their ancestral tablets, and the king ordered the governors of those provinces to put down the growing sect. This was more easily ordered than done, and as no deaths followed it is probable that the governors did little beside threaten and denounce. Two years later a work of importance was completed. The great sewer of the city was quite inadequate to carry away the sewage of the city and every time a heavy rain fell the sewer overflowed and the street from the great bell to the East Gate became a torrent. The king gave two million cash out of his private purse and the sewer was properly cleaned out. He also appointed a commission on sewerage and ordered that there be a systematic cleaning out every three years.

We have now arrived at the thirty-eighth year of the reign, corresponding to the year 1761 A. D. Up to that time the reign had been a brilliant one, not because of military successes but because of social, economic and other reforms. So far, it stands side by side with the reign of Suk-jong Tă-wang, who with the aid of the illustrious Song Si-ryŭl, effected such far-reaching reforms. We have yet seen but few signs of that growing senility which forms such a marked characteristic of the remainder of this reign. The king was now over seventy years old and he had lost that vigor of mind which characterized the earlier years of his reign. But he still possessed all that imperiousness of will which likewise characterized him. Good judgment and will power should decline together or else the results may be disastrous, as is illustrated in the remaining years of his reign.

We will remember that his first son had died and his second son had been made heir to the throne. He in turn had a son who was now eight years old. The evils which we are about to relate grew out of the fact that the heir was not as strongly attached to the Noron party as its adherents desired and they feared that his accession might result in a resuscitation of the defunct Soron party. The truth is the son carried out in fact what his father commanded, but did not live up to —namely the obliteration of all party lines. The old man, while always preaching the breaking up of party clanishness, remained a good Noron to the end of his days and the Norons had all the good things in his gift. The king perhaps thought that party lines had been lost sight of, but it was only the overwhelming ascendency of the Noron pary, which made comparison absurd. Instead of destroying party lines he did the very opposite in putting all the power into the hands of a single party. This suspicion against the Crown Prince on the part of the party in power was the main cause of the disturbance which followed, but its immediate cause was the ambition of a woman, a not unusual stumbling-block in the path of empire. This woman was the sister of the Crown Prince who desired that her husband be made king. Her name was Princess Wha-whan Ong-ju. One of the palace women also hated the Crown Prince. All these people desired his removal from the field of action and all had different reasons. The Noron rarty wanted to save themselves; the Princess wanted to become queen, and the palace woman wanted revenge ; why, we are not told.

It did not take long to find a way. Hong Kye-heui, Hong Pong-han and Kim Sang-no, three choice spirits came together and began laying plans for the overthrow of the Crown Prince. They first instructed the soldiers about the person of the Prince to steal women or goods and, when questioned about it, claim that it was at the order of the Prince. One day when the king was taking a walk behind the palace he came across a shallow excavation in the earth, covered with thatch. Looking in, he found it filled with mourners' clothes and other objects of mourning. Inquiring what it meant, he was told that the Crown Prince was impatient to have him die and that he had prepared the mourners' garments in advance. This aroused the anger of the king. He never stopped to think that it might be a trick against the Prince. Every thing lent color to the suspicion. Again, one day, the king found the palace woman, above mentioned, weeping bitterly. She said it was because the Crown Prince had offered her indignity. So by degrees plotters, bringing apparent evidence from several sides, which could not but seem conclusive, gradually estranged the king from his son and at last caused the removal of the latter to another palace, the one called the "Old Palace." These things preyed upon the mind of the Crown Prince and made him ill, but to add to this, it is said they administered drugs to him which tended to unbalance his mind and make him violent toward those about him. Then the Princess his sister arranged a trip to P'yŭng-yang for his health. It was intended that while he was there he should be charged with plotting to bring a force to overthrow the king and usurp the government. On his return, as he was approaching the city near night, an official came in to the king and announced that the Crown Prince was outside the gate and intended to come in that night and seize the scepter. This threw the king into a frenzy of rage. He immediately had all the gates put under double guard and sent out demanding the reason of the Prince's treasonable actions. The latter denied all treasonable intentions, but it was too late. The old man was unable to reason calmly about the matter. On the fifteenth day of the fifth moon the king went down to the "Old Palace" to sit in judgment on his son. It was an exceedingly hot day. When the Crown Prince came in and bowed before his father, the latter said "Do you realize how you have sinned?" The Prince replied that he was not conscious of having sinned against his father in any way whatever. As the king had already decided in his mind that the Prince was guilty, this denial made him simply furious. He screamed "If you do not die it will mean the destruction of the dynasty. So die." He then ordered all the assembled

courtiers to bare their swords but they hesitated, for they
knew the Prince was innocent; but when the king leaped up
and drew his sword they had to do likewise.   The Prince
calmly said "I am no criminal, but if I am to die it ought not
to be before the eyes of my father.   Let me return to my
apartments and then do with me as you will."   The king was
too far gone with rage and excitement to care for the dignity
of his high station or to care for appearances.   "No," he
screamed, "It must be here before my eyes."   Thereupon the
Prince undid the girdle about his waist and proceeded to
strangle himself.   The whole court were horrified, excepting
the king, who could no longer be called sane.   They rushed
forward, undid the cord and dashed water in his face to bring
him back to consciousness, in spite of the king's loudly voci-
ferated commands to the contrary.   They joined with one
voice in asking the king's clemency, but they might as well
have asked a maniac.   He threatened to kill them too if they
persisted in thwarting him.   He then ordered a heavy plank
box to be brought in and the Prince was commanded to get
into it.   But at the moment he was trying to beat his brains
out against a stone and did not hear the command.   One of
the officials ran to him and spread out his hands on the stone
and received the blows that were intended to end the life of
the unhappy Prince.   Being dissuaded from this, the Prince
arose and went to his father and said "I am your only son,
father, and though I may have sinned, overlook it and forgive
me.   You are not like my father now.   You will recover from
this passion and lament it."   This enraged the king to such
an extent that he could hardly articulate as he ordered the
Prince to get into the box.   At this moment they brought up
the little grandson to plead for his father's life, but the king
raised his foot and gave the child a kick that sent it reeling
back into the arms of those who had brought it.   It was evident that there was nothing to be done; so the Prince proceeded to climb into the box.   It was now dark and when the
cover was nailed on it was not noticed that there was a large
knot-hole in one side of the box.   One of the officials came
and spoke to the Prince through this hole.   He was overcome by the heat and asked for water and a fan, which were
passed in to him.   One of those who were interested in the

Prince's death told the king what was going on, and he hurried out and ordered a heavy plank nailed over the hole, and banished the man who had helped the Prince. The assembly broke up, but the Prince was left in this narrow prison day after day to starve. Each day one of the palace servants gave the box a heavy blow with a stone. At first it elicited an angry protest from the Prince but the fourth day he only said "I am very dizzy. Please leave me in peace." On the seventh day there was no response, and the servant bored a hole and put in his hand and felt the cold body of the dead Prince. The body was wrapped in grave-clothes and taken away for burial. He received the posthumous name of Sa-do. It is a singular fact that from that day to his end, some fifteen years later, the king never expressed sorrow for this act of cruelty. It is also significant that the Princess never tried to carry out her plan of having her husband become king. The horror of this scene seems to have turned her mind away from its purpose. At any rate she drops from the page of history without being given an opportunity to atone even in part for the terrible crime for which she was largely to blame. The king still looked upon his grandson as the heir to the throne, but he made him disown his dead father and take his uncle as father. He likewise made the boy solemnly promise never to change his mind in this. We see from this that the king continued to the very end to think that the Prince was guilty and his deed justifiable.

The year 1764 found an octogenarian on the throne. From this time on, the king was exceedingly feeble, but he clung to life with a tenacity that was amazing, and was destined to encumber the throne for a full decade still. His increasing weakness made it necessary for his physicians to prescribe a little wine. He acquiesced, and from this time the laws against the use of wine were relaxed somewhat. Its use was soon resumed in connection with the ancestral worship, but only at the importunity of the princess.

These declining years are by no means barren of interesting events. The annual sacrifice in behalf of the country had always been made at Pi-bǎk Mountain in Ham-gyŭng Province, but it was told the king that as Păk tu Mountain stood at the head of the country and dominated the whole, as it

were, the sacrifice should be made on or near that mountain,
So it was decreed that from that time on the sacrifice should
be performed at Un-ch'on Mang-dŭk-p'yŭng, eight *li* beyond
Kap san and in full view of the great Păk-tu-san or "Mountain of the White Head." And it was further decreed that
those who took part in the service should be secluded for four
days before the event, should bathe often and put on clean
clothes and forego all commerce with women.

In 1767 the king ordered a full census of the country. It
was found to contain 1,679,865 houses, containing 7,006,248
people. In other words there had been an increase of over
800,000 since the year 1657. He also ordered the making of
a new rain gauge. The first one is said to have been made by
King Se-jong. He did away with the punishment that consists in beating the tops of the feet until, frequently, the toes
drop off. On account of the danger of ship-wreck in rounding the corner of Whang-hă Province the king ordered the
discontinuance of annual naval tactics at Chang-nyŭn, excepting for the boats regularly stationed there. He built a
palace in Chŭn-ju in Chŭl-la Province and had sacrifices offered there, for although Ham-gyŭng Province is said to be
the birthplace of the line, the family really originated in the
south. The king also revived the ancient custom of having
a bell hang in the palace gateway, to be struck by anyone who
had a grievance to lay before the king.

A split occurred in the Noron party in the year 1771.
The two factions were called respectively the Si and the Pyŭk.
The former held that the father of the Crown Prince was an
innocent man and had been unjustly punished, while the
latter held the reverse. It is evident that those who claimed he
was innocent were making a bid for favor with the prospective
king.

At the time of which we write the great sewer of the city
had a line of ancient willows extending the whole length.
This was found to be a disadvantage and they were hewn
down and the sewer was walled in as we see it today. Two
more factions arose about this time. They were called the
Nak and the Ho. Their differences were caused by conflicting theories as to the interpretation of the Confucian classics.

The greatest act of this king, and the one that casts the greatest luster on his memory, was reserved for the twilight of his reign. What led to it we are not told, but in the eighty-ninth year of his life, by a single stroke of the brush, he emancipated all the serfs in Korea. Up to this time all the common people had been serfs of the *yang-bans* or noble class. In every district and in every ward each man of the common people owed allegiance to some local gentleman. It took the form usually of a tax or tribute in kind and was very loose in its application; but on occasion the master could call upon all these people for service and he could even sell them if he so desired. This is the reason why it is exceedingly rare that a family removes permanently from any locality, at least nominally. A man may go from place to place, or may live permanently at the capital, but when asked where he lives he will invariably name the exact spot where he originated and where the seat of his family is still supposed to be. When the common people were serfs they could not move at will, and the custom became so ingrained in them that to this day its effects are plainly seen. This aged king put forth his hand and decreed that this serfdom should cease once for all. It was different from slavery. That institution still continued and has continued to the present day. This serfdom included all the people who did not belong to the so-called *yang-ban* class. It is quite plain that the line of demarcation between the common people and the nobility was very much more clearly defined than at the present day. We find no indication that the order was resisted in any part of the country. It is probable that the serfdom had gradually become largely nominal and the people only gradually came to realize what the edict really meant. Even to this day the spirit of serfdom is a marked characteristic of the people.

His ninetieth year beheld the complete mental and physical collapse of the king. He could not attend to the ancestral sacrifices; his mind continually wandered from the subject in hand. He would order a meeting of his councillors and then forget that he had ordered it, or forget what he had ordered it for.

Hong In-han hated the young Crown Prince. It had

long been his ambition to see on the throne the son of the princess who had given up the project of becoming queen. He worked with all his might to have the fatal day put off, when the royal seals should be put in the hands of the prince. He was all the more dangerous as he was the prince's uncle, and therefore more difficult to handle.

When the aged king insisted upon giving up, this man said, "Not yet, you have many years more to reign," and he succeeded in delaying the matter, hoping that something might intervene to prevent the consummation that he dreaded. At one time when the king called a clerk to record his decree that the Crown Prince, from that day, should assume the reins of power, Hong violently pushed the clerk away and prevented it. The officials were all in a state of trepidation over these high-handed proceedings, fearing that they might become compromised, but help was at hand. Sŭ Myŭng-sŭn memorialized the king and set forth this Hong in such a light that the king with a last effort asserted himself and the young prince became king. A near friend of Hong was banished as a hint that Hong himself might expect punishment if he persisted in making trouble. Early the next year more of Hong's friends were banished. The aged king took the newly appointed King to the shrine of his foster father and made him swear that he would ever consider himself the son of that man rather than of his real father. The young man asked that the record of his father's death be expunged from the official records and so they were taken outside the Northwest Gate and "washed" in the stream.

In the third moon of 1776 the old man died. The new king is known by his posthumous title of Chöng-jong Tă-wang. He immediately raised his adopted father to the rank of Chin-jong Tă-wang and gave his real father the title Chang-hŏn Se-ja.

The reign just ended had been rich in literary products. The names of same of the books published are : "How to deal with the native fever," "The eveil deeds of the Soron party," "Conduct and Morals," "Fortifications and Military Tactics," "A Catechism of Morals," "A reprint of the Confucian work So-hak-ji," "An Abstract, in 100 volumes, of five important historical and geographical works." This last was called the Mun-hŏn Pi-go.

In spite of the oath that he had taken, the young king built a separate shrine to his father and worshiped at it in the same manner as at the ancestral temple. This was in accord with the letter of the oath, for he religiously refrained from calling his father by that name. He likewise honored the memory of his father by decreeing that if anyone mentioned the fact that he had been enclosed in a box and starved to death it would mean death. He banished the son of the princess who had encompassed his father's death. The highhanded Hong In-han who had worked so hard to prevent his accession was first banished to Yö-san and enclosed in a thorn hedge, and then was poisoned by royal edict.

His first year of rule was marked by an attempt to assassinate him and put his brother on the throne, but the assassin was taken, knife in hand, and upon his confession Hong Sang-bom and his whole family were seized and put to death. At last in sheer self-defense the king was obliged to put his brother to death. At the same time he forbade the presence of sorceresses in the capital and banished many who had been instrumental in his father's death. From this it would appear that there was a powerful clique in Seoul who were trying every means to accomplish his overthrow.

Being without issue, the king, at the instigation of his mother, took a concubine, the sister of one of his favorites, Hong Kuk-yung. This resulted very unfortunately, for when this concubine died her father was drawn into treasonable operations.

Many of the present customs of Korea date from this reign. The king first made the law that after the closing of the gates, they could not be opened except by special permission from himself.

It was in his first year that the scholar Kwŭn Chŭl-sin gathered about him a company of disciples and went to a mountain retreat to study. They possessed one copy of a Christian work. This they diligently studied, and one and all determined to adopt the belief there inculcated. So far as they understood it, they practiced its teachings in secret.

Two years later the king took as a second concubine the daughter of Yun Ch'ang-yun, and Hong the father of the first concubine, because of his opposition to it, was banished.

Up to this time very few officials had been drawn from the northern provinces or from Song-do, but now the king decreed that they were as worthy to receive office as any others and said that they should share in the gifts of the government. He ordered that a record be kept of all the decisions in council and that they be preserved in a book called the Il-deuk-rok. Those were days of severe famine in the land and the king did all in his power to relieve the distress, giving from his private treasure large quantities of silver bullion, black pepper and dyewood, things of great value in Korea.

In the year 1783 strange rumors were afloat. It was said that war had been declared against Korea by some foreign power which was about to throw an immense army into the peninsula. No one knew where it was to come from, but many believed it was Japan. The excitement grew so strong that crowds of people fled to the country, and so great was the influx into the southern provinces that real estate rose rapidly in value. Such was the haste of these deluded people that on the road families became separated and children were lost. Out of pity for the latter the king founded an asylum in Seoul for their maintenance.

Yi Tŭk-cho of Kyöng-ju was one of the men who had accepted the teachings of the Roman Catholic books and in this year he induced a young attaché of the embassy to Peking to look up the missionaries there and get such light as he could on the subject. This young man, Yi Sŭng-hun, met at Peking the Portugese Alexandré de Govea of the Franciscan order. He accepted Christianity and was baptized under the name of Pierre. He brought back with him many books, crosses, images and other religious emblems. Some of these he gave to Yi Tŭk-cho who redoubled his studies and at the same time began to do some proselyting. Two of his most celebrated converts were two brothers Kwŭn Ch'ul-sin and Kwŭn Il-sin of Yang-geun, thirty miles from Seoul. This town is called the birth-place of Roman Catholicism in Korea. Yi Tŭk-cho took the baptismal name of Jean Baptiste and Kwŭn Il-sin that of Francois Xavier. The propagation of the Christian faith soon began in Seoul and from there rapidly spread in the south.

In 1785 the Minister of Justice began active operations

against the new faith and in the third moon of that year a courtier memorialized the king on the subject. This caused the defection of many of the converts.

In 1786 Kim Yi-so informed the king that when envoys came back from China they brought in their train many Catholic books, which caused a "conflagration" in the country, and he denounced it as a bad religion. He said the books were flooding the land and that the only way to stop it was to make Eui-ju, on the border, a customs port and have all baggage strictly examined before being allowed to pass.

Many Chinese had settled on Sin Island off Eui-ju but the Koreans on the adjacent mainland resented it. They collected a considerable band of men and crossed to the island where they burned all the honses of the settlers and destroyed all their property. When the king heard of it he condemned it as a brutal outrage. This year was marked by one of the most destructive scourges that ever visited the country. Cholera swept the land from end to end. It is asserted that 370,979 people perished, among whom was the infant Crown Prince. The government found it necessary to undertake the work of interment. The king gave out from the dispensary 29,000 pills, and in Seoul alone there were 8,149 recoveries. Knowing as we do the frightful ravages of this disease when it takes a virulent turn, the fact that there were over 8,000 recoveries in Seoul indicates that there must have been at least 60,000 deaths. Probably this was more than half the population of the city at that time. It was during this same year that the great mound in Kang-dong, P'yŭng-an Province, was found. It is some 680 feet in circumfeience. It was called, from the first, the grave of the Tan-gun, though there is of course no evidence to show that this is more than the merest fancy.

The king had a half brother named Prince Eun-ön for whom he had a great affection; but Hong Kuk-Yŭng whose daughter had been the king's first concubine and had violently opposed a second union, now conspired with two other choice spirits with a view to putting Prince Eun-ön on the throne. The vigilant Queen Mother discovered the plot and the conspirators were executed. All likewise demanded the death of the young prince but to this the king would not listen. He was forced to banish him to Quelpart, but a short time after had him brought back as far as King-wha, where comfortable quarters were provided for him.

The king interdicted the use of silk excepting by very high officials and by very old people. He set up stones to mark the place where the great-grandfather of T'ä-jo Tä-wang had lived, where his grandfather had fished and where that king himself had once lived, in Ham-gyŭng Province. Some-one found in P'yŭng ch'ang, Ham-gyŭng Province, the grave of T'ä-jo Tä-wang's great-grandmother and the king had it repaired and guarded.

Up to that date the women had been accustomed to wear the hair in a great bunch on top of the head as female profes-sional mourners do to-day in Korea. Large amounts of false hair were used and it was decorated with long pins and with flowers. It is said that a full headdress cost as much as the furnishings of a house. The king ordered a change in this expensive custom, and since that day only mourners and palace women have been allowed to wear them.

The city of Su-wŭn dates its importance from the year 1789, for at that time the king removed his father's grave to that place and went there several times to sacrifice. He secretly called his banished brother from King-wha, but when his mother learned of it she made such an ado about it that he was fain to send him back. At Ham-heung, near the ancestral seat of the dynasty, there was an immense tree, so large that ten men holding each other's hands could but just encircle it. The shadow which it cast was "A hundred furrows wide." So goes the story. The king had it enclosed, in a wall, as being the place where his great ancestor practiced archery.

The year 1791 will always be memorable for the persecu-tion of the Roman Catholics. During the preceding year the Roman Catholic converts had sent a man to Peking to ar-range for the coming of a priest who could administer the sa-craments, for the Koreans had been strictly forbidden by the Catholic authorities in China to administer them among them-selves without the services of a regularly consecrated priest. At the same time certain important questions about ancestor worship were asked. A priest was promised to the Korean church but the answers to the questions about ancestor worship were very unsatisfactory to the Koreans and in consequence there were many defections. It is much to the credit of the Roman propaganda that from the very first it set its face hard against the practice of ancestor worship. In the fifth moon it is said the "flame of Roman Catholicism burned high." In other words it was discovered then what had been going on quietly for many years. Two men of Chin-san in Chŭl-la Province were caught and killed because they had burned their ancestral tablets. It was only after long discussion and with great hesitation that the order was given for their decapitation, and at the very last moment, after the men had already been carried to the place of execution, the king changed his mind and sent a reprieve; but it was too late. The king called the new religion not Ch'ŭn-ju-hak or "Religion of the Lord of Heaven," but Sa-hak or "The Deceiving Religion." The Minister Choă Che-gong advised the king to annihilate all Roman Catholics, but the king answered, "We must do it by elevating Confucianism." He had found the only rational way to deal with religious differences. He said, in substance, let the fittest survive. This is all that Christianity asks in any land, and the opposition of it by force always has been and always will be an acknowledgment of inferiority. The king knew well that China was the source from which the new influences came and he made a very strict law against the bringing across the border of Christian books. An edict was promulgated threatening with punishment all who did not deliver up their Christian books within twenty days, and the prefect of Chin-san, where the two men had been working, was cashiered and forty-five other prefects were degraded one or two degrees, because Christian converts were numerous in their districts. The Roman Catholic writers attribute the numerous defections at this time to the entire lack of pastoral care, the absence of the sacraments and the paucity of Christian literature.

The king did not live up to his advanced ideas about using physical force to combat Christianity, for in the eleventh moon of this year four high officials who had embraced Christianity were seized and put to death, together with a considerable number of the common people.

In 1792 the pope formally put the care of the Korean church in the hands of the Bishop of Peking.

Sacrifices were offered at the tombs of Tan-gun, Ki-ja, Su-ro-wang (the founder of Karak) and of T'ä-jo Tä-wang. Whether this was done to aid in combatting Christianity we are not told but it is not improbable. This was a time of general prosperity among the people and it witnessed a rapid increase in the population of Korea. These things were evidenced by the strong colonizing spirit which sprang up. Thousands flocked northward to the banks of the Yalu and to the islands on the coast, and the area of arable land was largely increased. Two years later this period of prosperity terminated in a terrible famine in all the southern and central provinces, and the government was obliged to dispense 280,000 bags of rice among the sufferers. This same year envoys from the Liu Kiu Islands were well received. The King told them that two hundred years before Liu Kiu officials had been given honorary titles by the king of Korea. In view of the friendly relations that had always existed between Korea and these islands, the envoys were feasted and sent off in grand style. Late in this same year, 1794, the Chinese Roman Catholic priest Tsiou crossed the Yalu and entered Korea. The government was aware of it and his arrest was ordered, but he escaped from Seoul in disguise. Two of his companions were taken, and as they refused to give information as to his whereabouts they were immediately put to death. At the time of his coming the Catholics estimate that there were 400 belivers in Korea, but within a very few years the number increased to 6,000.

The year 1796 was signalised by a most important event in the field of letters. In the beginning of the dynasty a fount of 100,000 pieces of moveable copper types had been cast, and these had been supplemented soon after by 200,000 more. Now the king began to add to them. First he put out 50,000 and a year later he added 150,000 more; then 80,000 more were made, and moveable wooden types were made to the number of 320,000. Already during this reign the following works had appeared. "The Gradation of Penalties," "A Commentary on the Chinese Classics," "The Proper Conduct of the king," "The Record of the Decisions in Council,"

"On Korean Customs," "On Military Tactics," "On Forms of Official Correspondence," "On the Science of Government." These were now followed by several editions of military and Confucian works, one of which was a digest of all the Confucian Classics in ninety-nine volumes. The King was a great lover of books and gathered all the best books that could be procured. One work whose publishing he superintended in person reached the modest number of 191 volumes.

The Minister of Finance advised the minting of five-cash pieces but all the officials united in a protest against it and advised retrenchment as the alternative. In this they were right, for the policy of meeting a deficit by minting money could not but be disastrous.

CHAPTER XIII.

A peculiar plague....a peculiar remedy....a new king ..various reforms....beginning of the policy of Roman Catholic opposition.... Christianity and politics....causes of opposition....prisons full.... Chinese evangelist killed....a traitorous letter intercepted....end of the persecution....conflagration. . eight severe charges....the miners' rebellion....siege of Chöng-ju....the mine explodes.... Catholics send to Peking for a priest... a long list of calamities.... cholera....taxes remitted....Europeans fail to enter Korea....nine years' famine .. terrible suffering... a new king ...reform.... French priests enter Korea ...the persecution of 1839 ...the first French naval expedition against Korea....The Koreans answer the French charges ... a new king ...reforms ....rapid spread of Christianity . consternation upon hearing of the fall of Peking.... a noteworthy memorial ...panic ...a good opportunity lost....a women's riot.

In 1799 a peculiar plague broke out in P'yeng-yang and spread with great rapidity. It began with fever and ague, accompanied by a cough, and death was very sudden. The king decided that if people so afflicted should eat beef they would recover. So he ordered cattle to be killed and the beef to be distributed among the people. The plague suddenly ceased and the people have always believed that it was the

marvelous acumen of the king that enabled him to see the
remedy and stop the ravages of the disease.

Early in 1800 he made his son heir to the throne, and
none too soon, for in the sixth moon he sickened and died.
It is said that his death was caused by his mourning over the
terrible fate of his father, whose cruel and untimely death
preyed upon his mind.   Others say that the cause of his death
was a malignant boil.

The infant king, known by his posthumous title of Sun-
jo Tä-wang, was of too tender an age to undertake the duties
of royalty and so the government was administered during
his minority by his grandmother, the woman who had wielded such a strong influence over his father.   She began by in-
stituting various reforms.   Outside the West Gate, which was
then some distance to the west of the present New Gate,
there was a monastery where sorceresses and fortune-tellers
congregated.   The Queen Mother drove them all out and
razed the monastery to the ground.   The tax by which the
palace body-guard was kept up was very distasteful to the
people and it was now remitted.   Up to this time the
government medical dispensary had been supported by revenue in money or herbs from the country, but this tax was
also remitted.   If we may believe the records when they say
that she freed all the government slaves, we can not but confess that in some directions at least this Queen Regent was
of exceeding liberal mind.

It is from the year 1801 that we may date the determined and systematic opposition on the part of the government
against the Roman Catholic propaganda in the peninsula.
Two other factions had grown up in Seoul, the Si and the
Pyŭk.   The latter were violent opponents of the new religion
but they had been held in check by the neutral attitude of the
late king.   But now he was dead, and the Queen Regent,
being a member of that faction, determined to give full rein
to the anti-Christian prejudices of her partisans.   It must be
remembered that the Koreans were extremely sensitive to
outside influences.   The terrible invasion of the Japanese on
the one hand and of the Manchus on the other had made the
Koreans hate all suggestions of commerce with the outside
world, and they sedulously avoided every possible contact

with foreigners.   This is one of the main causes of the opposition to Christianity.   But besides this, they had been told
that Roman Catholicism struck at the very foundation of the
state and was more than likely to assume a political aspect, a
charge which, from the very claims which it puts forth to
universal temporal as well as spiritual sovereignty, would be
somewhat hard to refute.   We can scarcely wonder then that
there was severe opposition to it.   It was looked upon as a
danger which menaced the state.   It is said that Roman
Catholicism had assumed large proportions in Korea.   Many
were now seized and put to death.   Among them were eleven
high officials.   Release was granted in case the accused would
consent to curse Christ.   The agents of this persecution went
everywhere haling forth believers from city and village.   Soon
the prisons were running over.   Eleven men were executed
in April and fourteen in the following month.   It is said that
two princesses who had adopted the foreign faith were put to
death.   It was at this time that Tsiou, the Chinese evangelist,
whom the Koreans call Chu Mun-mo, was seized and put to
death outside the Little West Gate.   He had at first fled
north to the Yalu and was on the point of crossing, when he
suddenly thought better of it, turned back, gave himself up
and heroically met his death.

A Korean named Whang Sa-yong had been instrumental
in bringing this Chinaman to preach the faith to his fellow-
countrymen.   Now that the evangelist was executed this
Whang sent out a letter to the European residents of China
asking that a military expedition be gotten up to come to the
shores of Korea, overthrow the dynasty and set up another in
sympathy with the Christian faith.   This letter was intercepted, the man seized and cruelly torn to pieces.   As to the
accuracy of these statements it would be rash to vouch.   The
contents of that letter may or may not have been what is
generally believed by the Koreans, but judging from the active
interest which European governments rightly take in missionaries from their shores, it is not unlikely that the letter contained substantially what is here stated.   The persecution
terminated the following year when the government ordered
the execution of those already apprehended but ordered that
no more Christians be proceeded against.   Between three and

four hundred people had perished and the church seemed to have been crushed.

It was in this year 1803 that a terrible conflagration swept P'yŭng-yang, and a thousand houses were destroyed. It was repeated the following year, and it is asserted that almost the entire city was destroyed.

Upon the death of the Queen Regent in 1805 the last remnant of persecution ceased and even the law which prohibited the import of books was allowed to remain a dead letter. Corruption in government circles ran riot. The state of things is well epitomized in a memorial which was sent in at this time. (1) The Ministers spend all their time reading books. (2) Nepotism and bribery are the rule rather than the exception. (3) The judges sit and wait for bribes. (4) The examiners of the candidates' papers receive money in advance, and merit can make no headway against cupidity. (5) The censors have been struck dumb. (6) The prefects do nothing but extort money from the people. (7) Luxury saps the strength and wealth of the land. (8) The whole commonwealth is diseased and rotten to the core.

The year 1811 is marked by an uprising in the north, where Hong Kyŏng nă attempted to set up a kingdom of his own. He was a resident of P'yŭng-an Province and was a man of enormous wealth. He was disaffected against the government because the men of his section were discriminated against in the distribution of offices; so he conferred with the miners who were engaged in digging gold in various places, and he told them an exaggerated story of how ill they were being treated by the government. He ended by proposing that, as he had enough money for them all, they set up a kingdom of their own. The hardy miners, 5,000 in number, accepted the proposal with alacrity and war was on foot. This company of undrilled but hardy miners were formidable and at first carried everything before them. They first took the town of Chŏng-ju, putting to death the prefect and his whole family. When news of this reached Seoul the king appointed Yi Yo-hŏn as general-in-chief against the rebels. Five thousand soldiers were given him with which to do the work. He acted in a characteristic manner, settled himself comfortably at the governor's house outside the New Gate and called it the headquarters. From that point he sent to the front Generals Sü Kum-bo, Kim Kye-on and Pak Keui-p'ung. Meanwhile the rebels were carrying everything before them. Ch'ŭl-san, Ka-san, Song-ch'ŭn, Yong ch'ŭn, Pak-ch'ŭn and Son-ch'ŭn fell in quick succession. All the government provisions and arms fell into their hands. The main camp of the rebels was in the vicinity of An-ju and they wished to take that place. Here they met with strenuous opposition and it was only after a desperate struggle that they ever took the town. It took ten days to reduce the place; but the back bone of the revolt was broken before the government troops from Seoul arrived on the scene. The various captains and local commanders joined their forces, and by the time the government troops had collected in P'yŭng-yang the rebels had been driven into their last remaining fortress, Chŏng-ju, and were being held in siege. During the retreat of the rebels four of Hong's lieutenants were captured and, being sent to Seoul, were there summarily executed. The reduction of Chŏng-ju by siege was a work of some time, and the king becoming impatient, supplanted Gen. Pak Kye-p'ung and put Gen. Yu Hyo-wŭn in his place. The latter immediately decided to attempt to blow up the town of Chŏng-ju. Constructing a fence, or barrier of some kind, a hundred and fifty paces from the wall, he began, under cover of this, to mine the wall, supporting the passage with beams of wood. When he had extended the passage well under the wall he placed a large amount of powder in it and attached a long fuse. After igniting the fuse the soldiers all hastened out of the mine. No explosion followed. No one dared to go in, for fear that the fuse might be burning slowly and that the mine might explode while they were within. After waiting two days, and finding no one who would venture in, Gen. Yu himself entered and found that the fuse had become wet. He remedied the difficulty and soon there was a tremendous explosion that tore down a long stretch of the wall and buried many of the garrison in the debris. The place was soon taken. Hong was caught, "The Man who Would be King," and his head was sent to Seoul.

The Christians had now begun to recover in some measure from the terrible persecution of 1801 and a man was sent to

Peking to urge that a qualified priest be sent to Korea, but the Peking church itself was in great vicissitudes and no help could be promised.

From this time on the reign was one long list of calamities which followed thick and fast upon each other. In 1813 there was a serious rebellion on the island of Quelpart; in 1814 occurred one of those fearful famines that sometimes happen in the southern provinces; this was followed by a flood in Kyŭng-sang Province which wrecked thousands of houses and cost many lives; Seoul was without rice and the government had to open its granaries and sell at starvation rates; 414,000 bags of grain were distributed to the sufferers in the country and 15,000,000 cash, 5,000 pounds of dye-wood and 500 pounds of black pepper were donated toward relief. The next year thousands who had been made destitute by the famine flocked to Seoul and the government had to feed them till the barley crop was harvested; then the native fever, a kind of typhus, broke out and mowed the people down, and the government had to erect pest houses for their accommodation. In 1816 two thousand houses fell in a freshet in Ch'ung-ch'ŭng Province and the government gave timber to help the people rebuild. The year 1821 beheld one of the most terrible scourges of cholera that the country ever experienced. It began in the north, and sweeping southward soon involved the capital. Ten thousand people died in Seoul in ten days. In the south it was equally destructive. The government was obliged to appoint a commission to attend to the interment of the dead bodies along the road. The following year it broke out again with unabated fury. Houses were built at intervals along the roads, by the government, for the sake of those who might be struck down with the plague while traveling and gangs of men were kept busy along the main road burying the dead. It even crossed to the island of Quelpart where two thousand people died. In 1824 the government had to remit 69,300 bags of revenue grain in the north because of the depredations of robber bands.

In 1827 the Crown Prince was appointed deputy king and the same year a son was born to him. But troubles continued. The government was obliged to remit taxes of seaweed, salt, ginseng and fish in Kang-wŭn Province. The fol-

lowing year a terrible freshet swept away whole villages in
Ham-gyŭng Province and the king sent large quantities of
grain to feed the destitute there.

Still troubles multiplied thick and fast. In 1830 the
Crown Prince died. He is the grandfather of the present
Emperor of Korea. The son who had been born to him is
known as the Tä wŭn-gun, who died in the spring of 1898.
The building in which the body of this Crown Prince was
placed burned to the ground and nothing but the charred
bones of the prince were recovered. Two years later, in 1832
an English vessel appeared off Hong-ju and its captain, Basil
Hall, sent the king a letter saying that he had come to trade,
but the king refused permission. As the flag of the ship bore
the device "Religion of Jesus Christ," some Roman Catholic
converts boarded her, but when they found that they were
protestants they beat a hasty retreat. It is said that several
boxes of books were landed and that some of them were sent
to the king, who promptly returned them. The foreigners
who made this attempt to enter Korea were Gutzlaff and
Lindsay.

During this year there were destructive fires and floods,
but the greatest calamity of all was a famine that began at
that time and continued for nine successive years, each year
being accompanied with cholera. It is said that bodies were
piled in heaps inside the South Gate. Many people are still
living who remember that terrible time. The next year, in
addition to famine and plague, the palace burned down. In the
following year there was a devastating epidemic of native
fever in Seoul, and a flood in Eui-ju which wrecked 2,000
houses. That summer, the people driven wild with hunger
mobbed the government granaries but found nothing in them.
They laid the blame on the Prime Minister and threatened
his life. He fled precipitately to the country.

In the last moon of 1834 the king died and his grandson
a boy nine years old came to the throne. He is known as
Hön jong Tä-wang. His grandmother Kim became regent.
She is known as Sun-wŭn Whang-ho. She immediately began
a work of reform. The law that made the relatives of prefects'
clerks liable to punishment for their crimes was abrogated.
Many burdensome taxes were remitted. The government

revenue collectors were kept to a strict account for all the monies passing through their hands. A conspiracy, he·ded by one Nam Ong-jung, was put down with a strong hand. The people were commanded not to slaughter their cattle for food, for the only hope for future crops was the cattle, with-out which the land could not be tilled. All prefects were com-manded to have regular office hours during which they should attend to government business exclusively.

In 1831 Pope Gregory XVI had made Korea a bishopric and appointed M Bruguiere as Bishop. A Chinaman named Yu who was then in Europe was appointed to accompany him to Korea This man Yu went ahead and found means of enter-ing Korea secretly. M. Bruguiere worked three years in the attempt to enter the country by way of the north across the Yalu and at last died on the very border. Yu who had pre-ceeded him desired to hold supreme power in the Korean church, and so put obstacles in the way of the entrance of the Bishop. But in the following year Pierre Philibert Maubant, who had been appointed to Korea, succeeded in entering the country and began work in Seoul at once, but of course in secret. By 1837 two other French priests had arrived, includ-ing Bishop Imbert. It is said that at the time of his arrival there were 9,000 adherents of the Roman Catholic church.

While the king was still but fourteen years old, in 1839, there occurred a cruel persecution of the Catholics. Three foreigners were in Korea, as we have seen, and they were known to the Koreans as Pöm Se-hyŭng, Na-bă Do-ru and Chöng-ă Kak-bak-i.

The persecution began as usual with a change of ministry. Yi Chi-ŏn became Prime Minister. He hated Christianity and averred that the reason why there were so many Christians was that the work of extermination had not been thorougly carried out in 1801. He demanded a house to house inspec-tion. This was done and soon the prisons were full to over-flowing. Hundreds were cruelly beaten, but the yamen-runners were not allowed to loot the houses of the prisoners, which cooled their ardor not a little. Finally the three foreigners were arrested. Being ordered to leave the coun-try they firmly refused. Thereupon they were declared high criminals and were executed on Sept. 21st, 1839. This was followed by still severer presecutions and even the Koreans themselves grew tired of the horrors that were enacted. It is said that seventy were decapitated and that sixty died of beating and strangulation. This is but a fraction however of those who perished in consequence of this persecution.

The last ten years of the reign were marked principally by events connected with the Roman Catholic propaganda. In 1844 two more French priests entered the country by way of Quelpart after a most difficult and hazardous passage from China in a Korean junk. Two years later the French government sent a message to Korea by a gun-boat, complaining of the death of the three Frenchmen and threatening her with punishment if these cruel actions were continued. This only excited the Koreans the more against Christianity, for it seemed to imply that Roman Catholicism had behind it a temporal power, and was therefore of political significance. In consequence of this a new outbreak occurred which cost the lives of several more Koreans, while the two priests were obliged to hide away very closely in the country.

In the summer of 1847 two French boats, the frigate *la Gloire* and the corvette *la Victorieuse* set sail from the Gulf of Pechili to go to Korea and ascertain what had been the result of the former letter. These two boats both struck a mud-bank and when the tide went down they broke in two. The crews to the number of 600 escaped to the neighboring island of Kogeum off the province of Chŭl la, and a pinace was immediately despatched to Shanghai for aid. The Koreans gave every assistance in their power and supplied them with food and other necessaries, and even offered to provide boats to take the men back to China. In fact the action of the Korean government was most creditable throughout. An English ship happened to come by and it carried the survivors all back to China. The Korean government, fearing further visits from the French, decided to answer the letter of the previous year. It was couched in the following terms:

"Last year we received a letter from the foreigners. It was addressed to the ministers of this realm and read as follows: 'Three of our countrymen, Imbert, Chastan and Maubaut, have been put to death by you. We come to demand why you have killed them. You will say perhaps that your law forbids foreigners entering your country, but if Chinese or Manchus should happen to enter your realm you would not kill them, but you would have them carried back to their own country. Why then did you not treat these men the same way? If they had been convicted of murder, sedition or a like crime we would have nothing to say, but they were innocent, and in condemning them unjustly you have committed a grave injury against the French government.' To this letter we beg to reply as follows: In 1839 there were arrested here certain strangers who were brought into the country at a time unknown to us. They wore Korean clothes, they spoke the Korean language, they traveled by night and slept by day; they veiled their faces, concealed their whereabouts and consorted with men whom we consider rebels, godless men and enemies of the government. When brought before the tribunal they claimed that their names were Pierre No and Japanese Cang. Are these the men you refer to? When interrogated, they said nothing about being Frenchmen, and even if they had we could not have sent them back, for we did not know where your country is. What could we do but apply our law, which forbids secret entrance into our kingdom? On the other had, their conduct in changing their names and wearing Korean dress shows that they had ulterior motives, and they cannot be compared to those who have been shipwrecked upon our shores. Such men we save if possible and aid to send back home. Such is our law. Had your fellow-countrymen been shipwrecked upon our coast, they would have received precisely the same treatment as Chinese, Japanese or Manchus under like circumstances. You say that these men were killed without cause and that we have committed a grave offense against the French government. This is most astonishing. We have never had any communication with France. We do not know even how far she is from Korea. What motive could we possibly have for injuring her? How would you act if a foreigner should enter your country secretly and in disguise and do what you consider evil? Would you leave him alone? If a Chinaman or a Manchu should come here and do as your people did they would be treated in the same manner as we did your people. In fact, we did put to death a Chinaman because he came here in disguise and changed his costume ; and the Chinese government never said a word about it, for they knew this to be our law. Even had we known their nationality, their actions were so contrary to our laws that we could hardly have spared them, how much less then when we did know it. This matter hardly needs more explanation. Your letter was sent without the proper formalities and we are not bound to answer it. This is not a matter that a mere provincial governor can handle. As we are China's vassal it is our duty to consult the court at Peking on all foreign matters. Tell this to your chief and do not be surprised that in order to show the true state of the case we have been led to speak thus plainly."

One needs but to read this to see that it is an unanswerable argument. From a merely political and legal point of view the Korean government had all the facts on her side, though from the standpoint of humanity they were wrong. It is strange that they omitted the strongest argument of all namely, that they asked the Frenchmen to leave and they refused. It is evident that by so doing they made themselves amenable to Korean law, and took the consequences, good or bad. One cannot admire enough the heroism which they displayed in staying to suffer with their coreligionists, though the opportunity was given them to save themselves by departure. It cannot be doubted that the rapid spread of Catholicism in Korea is due in large measure to the heroic self-sacrifice of those men and others like them, who literally gave their lives to the work. It would be wrong however to say that the government was wholly without excuse. From time immemorial death had been the penalty for crimes of far less import to the Korean mind than the spreading of heretical beliefs. With the light they had and the provocation under which they labored we should say they needed rather enlightenment than censure.

This answer was not accepted as satisfactory by the French government and a rejoinder was sent saying that thereafter French subjects who should be taken on Korean soil must be sent to Peking, otherwise the Korean government would lay itself open to grave evils. But soon after

this the revolution of 1848 took place in France and these
eastern questions were all forgotten for the time being.

In 1849 the king died without male issue and his grandmother Kim nominated his nephew, the son of a banished
brother. The young man entered upon the duties of his office at the age of nineteen and he is known by his posthumous title of Ch'ül-jong Tä-wang. This reign of fourteen
years beheld some important reforms. The law was reaffirm-
ed that the families of banished men might follow them into
exile. Gambling was severely interdicted. The merchants'
monopolies were broken up. A hard fight was made against
bribery and peculation in high places. Country gentlemen
were forbidden to seize and beat any one belonging to the
lower orders.

This king was the son Prince Chun-gye by a slave woman named Kang. He was the great-grandson of the Crown
Prince, Sado, whom his father nailed up in the box.

His reign was an important one in two respects. First
the very rapid spread of Roman Catholcism and second the
settled policy which was adopted toward all outside influences. When the reign began there were about 11,000 Christians in Korea and when it closed in 1863 there were in
the vicinity of 20,000, or almost double. Everyone knew
that to combat it there would be need of a king of a different
calibre from Ch'ül jong; and so during these years the work
of propagating the new faith went on steadily and without
any considerable drawbacks. The picture of the country as
drawn by the French is indeed a sad one. They say the
king had shown himself quite incapable and had become a
mere debauche. The highest officials were fattening off the
people and the latter were frequently consulting the books of
prophecy which foretold the disolution of the dynasty. And
now foreigners began to enter the country in greater numbers. Maistre, Janson, Berneux followed each other in
quick succession in the early fifties. The latter became
Bishop of Korea.

About the end of 1860 came the news of the fall of Peking
before the combined French and English forces, the flight of
the Emperor and the burning and looting of the Summer
Palace. The news was that thousands of foreigners had come

to overthrow the empire. The utmost consternation prevailed in Seoul. An official memorialised the throne giving three causes for lively concern.

(1) The Emperor, fleeing before his enemies, might wish to find asylum in Korea, or at least might take refuge in some Manchu fortress just beyond the border. Every possible approach ought to be strictly guarded so that the Emperor might not dare to force his way into Korean territory. (This shows the depth of Korea's loyalty to China)

(2) The outlaw bands that infested the neutral strip between Korea and China might attempt an invasion of Korea and forts ought to be built to prevent such an enterprise.

(3) Worst of all, there might be a possible invasion of Korea by the foreigners. Korean cities would be wrecked, the morals of the people would be lowered, a depraved religion would be established. As the foreigners were strong only on the sea or on level ground the mountainous character of Korea would be of material advantage to her. The army should be reorganised, and forts should be built along the principal approaches to Seoul; also at Tong-nă, Nam-yang, Pu-byŭng and In-ju. A fort should be built on high ground commanding the passage of the narrows at Kang-wha. Western boats could not of course ascend the Han River. As the foreign religion spread rapidly in the provinces every precaution should be taken to prevent the foreign priests communicating with their countrymen abroad.

The ministry and the people all applauded this plan and the memorialist was made a judge and given power to carry out his scheme. But news came thick and fast telling of the killing of thousands of Chinese soldiers, and the returning embassy in February 1861, gave definite news of the flight of the Emperor and the treaty wrested from the great Chinese empire. This news electrified the people. All business was suspended. The well-to-do people all fled to mountain retreats the doughty memorialist among the first. The ministers sent away their families and their goods. Many of the high officials asked the protection of the Roman Catholics, and tried to procure Roman Catholic books or badges of any kind, and many wore these at their belts in broad daylight. The yamen-runners were loud in their protestations that they had

had nothing to do with the persecution of the Catholics.   It was believed by the French in Korea at the time that a most favorable treaty could have been concluded just at that time; but no effort in that direction was made by the French.

Gradually the excitement abated and preparations for war were pushed, the wealthy classes supplying the money for the same. Old arms were resurrected, and cannon were cast on the model of one obtained from the French wrecks. At this time there were nine Frenchmen in Korea.

The year 1861 was a hard one for the people They were taxed to the last farthing and local riots were exceedingly common. The French give us an amusing incident, where the widows of a certain prefecture were taxed. They rose up *en masse* and mobbed the prefect's office, caught his mother, tore off all her garments and left her well nigh naked. This of course meant that the prefect was disgraced for life.

Chapter XIV.

Beside the death-bed of King Ch'ŭl-jong....a bold woman....rise of the Tong-hak....its founder killed....the King's father becomes regent ....his two mistakes ...he selects a Queen ...Russian request.... the Regent pushed by the conservative party....death-warrant of ....Bishop Berneux ...French priests executed....priceless manuscript lost .. a French priest escapes to China and tells the news ....China advises Korea to make peace....shipwreck of the "Surprise"....face of the "General Sherman" .. persecution renewed ... French reconnoitering expedition....blockade of the Han announced ...French expedition under Admiral Roze....preparations for defense... correspondence....French defeat....the French retire Koreans exultant .... persecution redoubled .... the Kyŭng-bok Palace rebuilt   American expedition under Admiral Rodgers.... American victory on Kang-wha .. the fleet retires .. monument erected in Seoul.

The events of the present reign, which began in January 1864. are fresh in the memory of many still living, and the account here given is taken largely from statements of eyewitnesses of the scenes therein described. A detailed history of the present reign would fill a volume in itself and of course we can but briefly touch upon the leading events in it.

The circumstances which ushered in the reign are graphically described by Dallet and are substantially as follows. King Ch'ŭl-jong had been suffering for some time with a pulmonary affection, but in January of 1864 he seemed better and he began to walk about a little. On the fifteenth, feeling greater uneasiness than usual, he went into his garden for a walk. There he was suddenly taken with faintness and was just able to drag himself back to his room, where he fell in a dying condition. The Minister Kim Choa-geun, his son Kim Pyŭng-gu and three other relatives were immediately in attendance. As they were deliberating, the nephew of the Dowager Queen Cho, widow of the King Ik-jong, happened to pass, and seeing what was going on, he hastened to his aunt's apartments and exclaimed, "What are you doing here? The king is dead." He advised her to hasten to the king's apartments, gain possession of the royal seals and nominate to the throne some one of her choice, declaring him to be the son and heir of King Ik-jong, her husband. This woman thereupon hastened to the side of the expiring king where she found the attendants, as we have said, and with them the queen, who held the royal seals in a fold of her skirt. The Dowager Queen peremptorily demanded these seals, and when the queen demurred she snatched them violently from her. No one dared oppose the determined woman who thus took fortune by the forelock and in the course of a moment turned the course of empire. She then made proclamation in the name of the king, saying "The king says the royal seals shall be in charge of Queen Cho. The throne shall go to Myŭng-bok, second son of Prince Heung-sŭng (whose name was Yi Ha-eung). Minister Chong shall be executor of the king's will and Minister Kim shall go and find the newly appointed king." The Dowager Queen Cho thus became Regent and the queen's party, the Kim family, had to retire from power.

It was at the very beginning of the reign that the peculiar sect called the Tong-hak arose in the south. Its founder was one Ch'oe Pok-sul of Kyŏng-ju in Kyŭng-sang Province. The great formula of the sect was the mysterious sentence *Ch'ŭn Ju cho a chung yŭng se bul mang man sa eui*, which means "May the Lord of Heaven aid our minds that we may ever

remember, and may He make all things turn out according to
our desire." The adherents of this sect would sit and sing this
formula by the hour. They would also dance, brandishing
swords in a sort of frenzy, and pretend to be rising to heaven.
The name Tong-hak or "Eastern Sect" was given by th·m-
selves to distinguish themselves from the Su-hak or "Western
Sect," namely Roman Catholicism. So at least some affirm.
Its rise was exceedingly rapid and soon it had enrolled an
enormous number of people. The government was at last
obliged to take cognizance of it, and a body of troops was
sent south, who captured and put to death the founder of the
sect. This put an end for the time to its active propagandism
but it was by no means dead, as we shall see.

The Dowager Queen Cho was a violent opponent of Christianity and filled all the offices with enemies of the Roman
Catholics. But she was not to hold the reins of power long.
The king's father in view of his son's elevation to the
throne had received the title Prince Tă-wŭn, or Tă-wŭn-gun
as he is usually called. He was a man of commanding personality and inflexible will and on the whole he was the most
striking character in modern Korean history. He has been
variously estimated. Some have considered him the greatest
statesman in Korea ; others have taken him for a mere dema-
gogue. His main characteristic was an indomitable will
which took the bit in its teeth and swept toward the goal of
its desire irrespective of every obstacle, whether of morals,
economics, politics or consanguinity. He was withal unable
to read the signs of the times. The two great mistakes of his
life were, first in supposing he could eradicate Roman Catholicism by force, and second in supposing that he could prevent
the opening of Korea to treaty relations. The regency naturally passed into his hands and he tacitly agreed to uphold the
principles of the conservative party that had raised him to
power.

His first act was to order a remeasurement of the tilled
land of the country with a view to the increasing of the revenue. The treasury was empty and he had plans in mind
that would require money. One of these plans was the erection of a new palace on the ruins of the Kyong-bok Palace, an
enterprise which the finances of the country by no means war-

ranted. His next act was to betroth his son the king to his wife's niece. His wife had two brothers one of whom was living but the other had died leaving one daughter. It was this daughter of Min Ch'i-rok who became queen. She was the king's senior by four years. As her father was dead she became the 'foster child of her uncle Min Ch'i-gu. In this union, as every one knows, the Regent sought to cement his own power, but, as every one likewise knows, he made a serious mistake.

In January 1866 a Russian gunboat dropped anchor in the harbor of Wŭn-san and a letter was sent to Seoul asking for freedom of trade with Korea. The answer given was that as Korea was the vassal of China the matter must be negotiated at Peking, and an envoy was dispatched for that purpose.

It is said that Roman Catholic adherents made use of the great uneasiness which prevailed in government circles respecting Russia to compose a letter urging that the only way to ward off Russia was by making an alliance with France and England. It is said that the Regent received this communication and gave it special and, as some believe, favorable attention. We are told that the Roman Catholics were all in a most hopeful state of mind, fully believing the hour had come for the awakening of Korea. In the light of subsequent events it is difficult to determine whether the Regent's interest in the plan was real or whether it was a ruse whereby to make the final *coup* all the more effective. All things considered, the latter theory fits the facts more perfectly. The French themselves believed the Regent was pushed on to the great persecution of 1866 by the violent anti Christian party that had put him in power, and that it was simply another case of "If thou do it not thou art not Caesar's friend." They found fault with him for harboring the idea of a combination with this foreign element and demanded the death of the foreign priests and a general persecution. It is said the Regent reminded them of the burning of the Summer Palace at Peking and the taking of that Imperial Capital, but that they answered that they had killed Frenchmen before without harm resulting, and they could do it again.

Whatever may have been the pressure brought to bear on him, he finally signed the death warrant of all the foreign

priests in the land, and on February 23rd Bishop Berneux
was seized and thrown into the common jail, but two days
later he was transferred to the prison where noble prisoners
were confined.　On the 26th he was brought before the tribunal
where he gave his name as Chang.　He said he had come to
save the souls of the Koreans and that he had been in the
country ten years.　He refused to leave except by force.　As
the government had made up its mind as to its course, his
death warrant was then made out, and it ran thus: "The accused, Chang, refuses to obey the king.　He will not aposta-
tize.　He will not give the information demanded.　He refuses
to return to his own country.　Therefore, after the usual
punishments, he will be decapitated."　While he was awaiting his end, Bretenières, Beaulieu, and Dorie were taken, and
after similar trial were condemned to death.　All four of these
heroic men were decapitated at the public execution ground
near the river on the eighth of March and their bodies were
buried together in a trench, from which they were recovered
six months later and given burial by Roman Catholic adherents.　Four days later two more priests, Petitnicolas and
Pourthiè, were executed at the same place.　It was the latter
who lost at this time not only his life but his priceless man-
uscripts, a Korean Grammar and a Latin-Korean-Chinese
Dictionary, on which he had been at work for ten years.
Three more of the priests, Daveluy, Aumaitre and Huin were
seized soon after this and put to death, but not till the latter
had despatched a letter to China, which was destined to turn
up long afterward.　There were three priests left, Calais,
Feron and Ridel.　The last of these was selected to attempt
the journey to China and give information of these terrible
events.　After almost incredible labors he succeeded in getting away from the shore of Whang-hă Province in a junk together with eleven native believers, and made his way to
Chefoo.　From there he hastened to Tientsin and informed
Admiral Roze of the death of his fellow-countrymen.　The
Admiral promised to hasten to the rescue of the remaining two
and the avenging of those who had been slain; but a revolt in
Cochin-China prevented him from redeeming his promise
until the following September.

The Chinese government, through the annual embassy,

informed the king of Korea that the killing of foreigners was
an exceedingly foolish proceeding and that he had better make
peace with France on the best terms possible, for if China
could not withstand her surely Korea could not. The Regent
replied, however, that it was not the first time French blood
had remained unavenged in Korea.

On June 24th an American sailing vessel, the "Surprise,"
was wrecked off the coast of Whang-hä Province. Her captain and crew were hospitably treated and conducted to the
Chinese border with great care by order of the Regent, who
thus illustrated the truth of the assertion that Korea would
do no harm to men who were ship-wrecked on her coast.
Even in the midst of an anti-foreign demonstration of the
most severe type, these men were humanely treated and sent
upon their way.

Early in September the sailing vessel "General Sherman"
entered the mouth of the Ta-dong River. She carried five
white foreigners and nineteen Asiatics. Her ostensible object
was trade. The governor of P'yŭng-an Province sent,
demanding the cause of her coming and the answer was that
they desired to open up trade with Korea. Though told that
this was impossible, the foreign vessel not only did not leave
but, on the contrary, pushed up the river until she reached a
point opposite Yang-jak Island not far from the city of P'yŭng-
yang. It was only the heavy rains in the interior and an exceptionally high tide that allowed her to get across the bar,
and soon she was stuck in the mud, and all hopes of ever
saving her were gone. This rash move astonished the Koreans
above measure. Something desperate must be the intentions
of men who would drive a ship thus to certain destruction.
After a time word came from the Regent to attack her if she
did not leave at once. Then the fight began, but without
effect on either side until the Koreans succeeded in setting
fire to the "General Sherman" with fire-rafts. The officers
and crew then were forced to drop into the water, where
many of them were drowned. Those that reached the shore
were immediately hewn down by the frenzied populace. The
trophies of this fight are shown today in the shape of the
anchor chains of the ill-fated vessel, which hang in one of the
gateways of P'yŭng-yang. No impartial student of both sides

of this question can assert that the Koreans were specially blame-worthy. The ship had been warned off but had rashly ventured where no ship could go without being wrecked even were all other circumstances favorable. The Koreans could not know that this was a mere blunder. They took the vessel, and naturally, to be a hostile one and treated her accordingly.

In September the persecution of Roman Catholic adherents was resumed. This is said to have been caused by a letter from one of the Christians to the Regent urging a treaty of peace with France. But by this time Admiral Roze was ready to redeem his promise, and on the tenth of that month Bishop Ridel boarded his flag-ship at Chefoo. The French authorities had already informed the Chinese at Peking that France did not recognise the suzerainty of China over Korea and asserted that the land about to be conquered would be disposed of as France wished without reference to the Pekin government. It was decided to send the corvette *la Primauguet*, and the aviso, *le Déroulède*, and the gunboat, *Tardif*, to make a preliminary survey of the approaches to Seoul. Bishop Ridel accompanied this expedition in the capacity of interpreter. Arriving off Clifford Islands on the twentieth, the little fleet entered Prince Jerome Gulf, and the following day *le Déroulède* was sent to explore the entrance to the Han River. Finding the channel between Kang-wha and the mainland satisfactory, she returned to the anchorage and together they steamed up the river the only casualty being the loss of the false keel of the Primauguet. These vessels steamed up the river as far as the river towns opposite the capital, silencing a few forts on the way. Bishop Ridel used all his powers of persuasion to induce the commander to leave one of these boats here while the others went to China to report, but without avail. They all steamed away together.

Meanwhile there was panic in Seoul. The end had come, in the estimation of many of the people. A general stampede ensued and nearly a quarter of the citizens of Seoul fled away, leaving their houses and goods. We will remember that when Ridel escaped from Korea he left two companions behind. These made a desperate attempt to communicate with the French boats on the river, but so fierce was the persecution

and so watchful were the authorities that they were quite unable to do so. They finally escaped, however, by means
of junks which carried them out into the Yellow Sea,
where they fell in with Chinese boats that carried them to
China.

Before the surveying expedition sailed back to China
Bishop Ridel was informed by native Christians of the burning of the "General Sherman" and the fate of her crew, the
renewal of the persecution and the order that all Christians
be put to death after only a preliminary trial. He urged the
commandant to stay, but the fleet sailed away and reported in
China, where the real punitive expedition was rapidly preparing. On October eleventh the blockade of the Han River
was announced to the Chinese authorities and to the various
powers through their representatives at Peking, and then the
French fleet sailed away to the conquest of Korea. The
flotilla consisted of the seven boats *Querriere, Laplace, Prim-
anguet, Deroulede, Kienchan, Tardif* and *Lebrethom.*

But while these preparations were going on, other preparations were going on in Korea. The total complement of
troops throughout the peninsula was called into requisition.
Arms were forged and troops drilled. The Japanese government, even, was invited to take a hand in the war that was
impending, but she did not respond. Japan herself was
about to enter upon a great civil war, and had no force to spare
for outside work, even if she had had the desire.

On October thirteenth the French fleet reached Korea
and three days later the attack on Kang-wha commenced. In
an hour's time the town was in the possession of the French
and large amounts of arms, ammunition and provisions were
seized, besides various other valuables such as treasure, works
of art, books and porcelain. This reverse by no means
disheartened the Koreans. Gen. Yi Kyŭng-ha was put in
charge of the forces opposed to the "invaders." This force
was led in person by Gen. Yi Wŭn-heui who found the
French already in possession of the fortress. The Koreans
were in force at Tong-jin just across the estuary from Kang-
wha, and, fearing that the vessels would attempt to ascend
the river, they sank loaded junks in the channel. This
channel must have been much deeper than it is today.

The Regent swore that any man who should suggest peace with the enemy should meet with instant death. A letter was sent to the French saying that the priests had come in disguise and had taken Korean names and had desired to lay their hands on the wealth of the land. It declared that the priests had been well killed. In reply the French said they had come in the name of Napoleon, Sovereign of the Grand French Empire, who desired the safety of his subjects, and that since nine of his subjects had been killed, it must be explained. They also demanded the three ministers who had been foremost in the persecution and in the killing of the priests should be handed over to them and that a plenipotentiary be appointed for the ratifying of a treaty. To this letter no answer was received.

Meanwhile Gen. Yang Hön-su had led 5,000 men to the fortress of Chöng-jok on Kang-wha where a celebrated monastery stands. These men were mostly hardy mountaineers and tiger-hunters from Kang-gye in the far north, the descendants of those same men who in the ancient days of Ko-yuryŭ drove back an army of Chinese 300,000 strong and destroyed all but 700 of them. This fortress is admirably situated for defense, lying as it does in a cup formed by a semi-circle of mountains and approachable from only one direction, where it is guarded by a crenellated wall and a heavy stone gate.

The great mistake of the French was in supposing this place could be stormed by a paltry 160 men. The whole French force could not have done it. No sooner had this little band come well within range of the concealed garrison than it was met by a withering fire which instantly put half of them *hors de combat.* After some attempts to make a stand in the shelter of trees, huts, rocks and other cover, a retreat was called and the French moved slowly back carrying their dead and wounded. They were closely pursued and with difficulty made their way back to the main body. The result would probably have been much more serious had not the retreating party been met by a body of reinforcements from the main body. The next day orders were given to fire the town and re-embark. This caused great surprise and dissatisfaction among the men, but we incline to the belief that it was the only thing to do. The number of men that had been mustered to effect the humiliation of Korea was ridiculously small compared with what was necessary. Six thousand French might have done it, but six hundred—never. We need seek no further than this for the cause of the abandonment of the enterprise. To be sure, it had done infinitely more harm than good, and if it had been possible to succeed even at a heavy cost of life it would have been better to go on; but it was not possible.

The effect of this retreat upon the Regent and the court may be imagined. Peking had fallen before these "barbarians" but the tiger-hunters of the north had driven them away in confusion. If the reader will try to view this event from the ill-informed standpoint of the Korean court, he will see at once that their exultation was quite reasonable and natural. The last argument against a sweeping persecution of Christians was now removed and new and powerful arguments in favor of it were added. The fiat went forth that the plague of the foreign religion should be swept from the land. No quarter was to be given. Neither age nor sex nor quality were to weigh in the balance. From that time till 1870 the persecution was destined to rage with unabated fury and the French estimated the number killed at 8,000. The hardships and sufferings of this time are second to none in the history of religious persecutions. Hundreds fled to the mountains and there starved or froze to death. The tales of that terrible time remind one of the persecutions under the Roman Emperors or the no less terrible scenes of the Spanish Inquisition.

But to return to 1866. There were other events of interest transpiring. The pet scheme of the Regent to build his son a new palace was being worked out. The palace was in process of erection, when suddenly the funds gave out. Here the Regent committed his next great blunder. This time it was in the realm of finance. He entertained the fallacy that he could meet a deficit by coining money. Of course the only way to meet a deficit in this way was to debase the currency. He did it on a grand scale when he once determined upon it, for whereas the people had from time immemorial used a one-cash piece, he began to mint a hundred-cash piece which was actually less than fifty cash in weight. One of these was given as a day's wage to each of the workmen on the palace. This coin bore on its face the legend "The great Finance Hundred Cash Piece," but it proved to be very small finance indeed, for of course its issue was immediately followed by an enormous rise in the price of all commodities, and rice went up two hundred per cent. The government was thus plunged deeper in the mire than ever ; but the Regent had set his will on this thing and was determined to carry it through at any cost. His next move, taken in the following year, was to bring in old, discarded, Chinese cash literally by the cart-load, across the border. This he had bought in China at auction prices and forced on the people as legal tender. At the same time he forced the people to work in gangs of 300 at a time on the palace without pay. In this way the work was finished, but it is safe to say that to this day the country has not recovered from the effects of that mad financiering. Wealthy citizens were called upon to make donations to the building fund, and this gained the soubriquet of "The Free-will Offering."

The year 1868, which meant so much for Japan, was not otherwise signalised in Korea than by a demand on the part of Russia that Korean refugees beyond the border be recalled. It also beheld the publication of the work "The Six Departments and their Duties." In September alone 2,000 Christians were killed, five hundred of them being residents of Seoul. [7]

The United States had not forgotten the fate of the "General Sherman." She had no intention of letting the matter drop. In the early spring of 1871 minister Frederick F. Low, at Peking, received instructions from his government to go in company with Rear-admiral Rodgers to the shores of Korea and attempt to conclude a treaty relative to the treatment of American seamen who might be cast upon the shores of that country. He was also instructed to try to make a trade convention with Korea looking toward the opening of Korea to foreign commerce. The fleet consisted of the war vessels *Colorado, Alaska, Bernicia, Monocacy,* and *Palos.* These vessels rendezvoused at Nagasaki and on May sixteenth they set sail for Korea. Minister Low's correspondence with his

government shows that he had accurately gauged the probabilities of the situation. A long acquaintance with the Korean
could not have rendered his diagnosis of the case more accurate than it was. From the very first he considered it to
be a hopeless case, and he was right. But this in no way lessened the care he exercised in doing every thing in his power
to render the expedition a success. After fourteen days of
struggle against dense fogs, tortuous channels and swift tidal
currents the fleet dropped anchor off the islands known as the
Ferrierre group, not far from Eugénie Island. This was on
May 30th. They had not been there long before they were
boarded by some small officials with whom Minister Low was
of course unable to treat, but through them he sent a friendly
message to Seoul asking that an official of equal rank with the
American envoy be sent to confer with him on important
matters. The Koreans had already received through the
Chinese an intimation of what the Americans desired but they
argued that as their policy of carrying ship-wrecked mariners
safely across the border was well known abroad and as they
did not care to open up relations with other countries, there
was no call to send an envoy to treat with the Americans.
The Regent shrewdly, though mistakenly, suspected that the
"General Sherman" affair was at the bottom of this, as the
death of the French priests had been the cause of the French
expedition and he decided to garrison Kang-wha and deal
with the Americans as he had with the French. Gen. O-
Yo-jŭn was sent with 3,000 troops to Kwang Fort on the island
of Kang-wha. A part of this force was stationed as garrison
at Tok-chin, a little fort at the narrowest part of the estuary
between Kang-wha and the mainland, where the tide runs
through with tremendous force and a dangerous reef adds to
the difficulty of navigation.

Thus it was that when the *Monocacy* and *Palos* steamed
slowly up the channel on a tour of inspection they were fired
upon by the guns of this little fort. No special damage was
done, and as soon as the gunboats could be gotten ready to
reply to this unexpected assault they opened fire upon the little
fort and spedily drove its garrison out. The Koreans supposed
these gunboats were approaching for the purpose of assault.
Indeed, as no intimation had been given the Korean govern-

ment that such a reconnoitering expedition was planned, and as this narrow passage was considered the main gateway of approach to the capital, the Koreans argued strictly from the book and the American contention that the attack was un- provoked was groundless, for to Korean eyes the very ap- proach to this stronghold was abundant provocation.

When the fort had been silenced, the two gunboats steamed back to the main anchorage and reported. It was instantly decided that an apology must be forthcoming from the government, but as none came, retaliation was the only thing left to vindicate the wounded honor of the United States. A strong force was despatched, which, under cover of the ship's guns was landed near the fort, and after a hard hand to hand struggle in which every man of the garrison was killed at his post the place was taken. Thus was the tarnished honor of the Great Republic restored to its former brightness. But mark the sequel. The Admiral plainly was entirely unequal to the task of pushing the matter to the gates of Seoul, and so he withdrew and sailed away to China exactly as the French had done. The great mistake in this lay in ignorance of the Korean character. The government cared little for the loss of a few earth-works on Kang-wha. In fact, even if the Americans had overrun and ravaged half the peninsula and yet had not unseated the king in his capital or endangered his person, their departure would have left the Koreans in the firm belief that the foreigners had been whipped. In the last decade of the twelfth century the Japanese overran the country, forced the King to flee to the very banks of the Yalu, killed hundreds of thousands of the people and for seven years waged equal war in the peninsula, and yet when Hideyoshi died and his troops were recalled Korea claimed that the Japanese had been defeated ; and it was true. The approach of United States gunboats up to the very walls of the "Gibraltar" of Korea was nothing less than a declaration of war, and the paltry loss of the little garrison was a cheap price to pay for their ultimate triumph in seeing the American ships "hull down" in the Yellow sea.

When this glad news was published in Seoul the already plethoric pride of the Regent swelled to bursting. Another briliant victory had been scored.

Another of the great powers of the West had been humbled. Korea could show her great patron China how to handle the barbarians. He immediately ordered the erection in the center of the city of a monument which had been in preparation since 1866. The inscription ran as follows.

"The Western Barbarians have attacked and injured us, with a view either to making war upon us or to forcing treaties upon us. If we consent to the latter it will mean the betrayal of the country. Let our descendants to the ten thousandth generation bear this in mind. Made in the Pyöng-in Year and set up in the Sin-mi Year."

All the court and the nobility vied with each other in congratulating the regent upon the completion of this work and declared that the people were pleased with the prospect of excluding all foreigners and preserving the time-honored seclusion of the land.

Chapter XV.

The "Frontier Guard" .... Japanese attempts at making a treaty .... agent at the palace   the Regent's power on the wane....a "Combination" ...the Regent retires ...a puppet ..."infernal machine" ....reforms .... a dangerous memorial....fight with the Japanese ....two parties in Japan .... Japanese commission....negotiations ....treaty signed....a mysterious conflagration....Japanese minister....French priests released .... a curious book....anti-Christian policy abandoned ...commission to Japan....conspiracy....liberal party....hopeful outlook....the Min policy....split between the Min and liberal factions ...Minister to Japan....military students ....regular troops neglected...emeute of 1882....Japanese legation attacked ...the palace entered....the Queen escapes....the ex-Regent quiets the soldiers....a mock funeral.

In order to understand the interesting train of events that transpired in 1873 it will be necessary to go back and review the relations that existed between Korea and Japan.

At the close of the Japanese invasion an arrangement had been arrived at between Japan and Korea by the terms of which the Japanese placed a number of traders at Fusan. The popular belief of the Koreans that the government ac-

cepted these as hostages in place of an annual tribute of three
undred Japanese female hides is an amusing fiction which ish
intended to offset the ignominy of the ear and nose monument
in Kyoto.

This colony was called the Su-ja-ri or "Frontier Guard."
The Korean government appropriated ten million cash a year
to its support. The Japanese claim that these people were
not hostages but were merchants and were placed there to
form a commercial *point d'appui* between the two countries.
That the money paid for their support was of the nature of a
tribute is neither claimed by the Japanese nor admitted by the
Koreans; in fact the terms always used in describing these
payments implies the coördinate degree of the recipient.

This Japanese colony was continued up to the year 1869
without intermission but it was not destined to remain un-
disturbed. No sooner had the Imperial government become
established in Japan than the Emperor appointed a commission to approach the Korean government through the time-
honored avenue of approach, namely Fusan and the prefect
of Tong-nă, with a view to establishing closer commercial and
diplomatic relations. This commissioner transacted the business through the Daimyo of Tsushima who sent the Imperial
letter to the prefect of Tong-nă and asked that it be transmitted to the capital. After reading it the prefect refused to
send it, on the plea that whereas Japan had always addressed
Korea in terms of respect she now adopted a tone of superiority and called herself an Empire. The envoy urged that
Japan had recently undergone a complete change, that she
had adopted Western ideas and had centralised her government, and urged that the missive must be sent on to Seoul.
The prefect was prevailed upon to copy the letter and send it
on to the Regent but the Reply came back forthwith "We
will not receive the Japanese letter. Drive the envoy away."
The following year the annual grant of rice was suddenly
discontinued without a word of warning and the Japanese in
Fusan were greatly exercised thereby. They made a loud
outcry and their government made repeated attempts to come
to an understanding with the Korean government but without success.

It was in 1870 that the Japanese Hanabusa, called Wha-

bang Eui-jil by the Koreans, came with an urgent request
that a treaty of commerce be signed, but he was likewise unsuccessful. The King, however, was nearing the age when
the Regent must hand over to him the reins of power and the
Queen, a woman of natural ability and of imperious will, was
gathering about her a faction which was wholly inimical to the
plans and the tactics of the Regent. The latter found to his
chagrin that the woman whom he had placed on the throne
with his son with special reference to the cementing of his
own power was likely to become the instrument of his undo-
ing. Sure it is that in spite of the hatred which the Regent
evinced against the Japanese this same Hanabusa came to
Seoul in 1871 or early in 1872, in a quite unofficial manner,
and was given quarters at the palace where he was in constant communication with the Queen and the members of her
faction, and where, by exhibiting curious objects of western
manufacture, such as a toy telephone and the like, he amused
his royal patroness and won his way into the favor of the
party that was shortly to step into the place made vacant by
the retiring Regent.

The queen's faction were diametrically opposed to the
most cherished prejudices of the Regent. They favored, or at
least looked with complacency upon, the growth of Roman
Catholicism, they favored the policy of listening to China's
advice in the matter of foreign relations. They were doubtless urged in this direction partly by pure opposition to the
Regent and partly by the representations of the Japanese who
had gained the ear of royalty. The palace was the scene of
frequent and violent altercations between the heads of these
two factions, but an open rupture did not occur until the year
1873 when an official named Ch'oe Ik-hyŭn memorialised the
throne speaking disparagingly of the presence of the Japanese
in the palace and, toward the end, charging the Regent with
indirection in the use of the public funds. The king had for
some time been growing restive under the control of the Regent, being led to some extent by the new party of which the
queen was the patroness and at whose head stood her brother,
Min Seung-ho. The memorial was received with marks of
approval by the king and he immediately cut off a large part
of the revenues of the Regent. At the same time Min Seung-

ho approached the Regent's son, Yi Chä-myŭn, elder brother to
the king, and suggested that if the Regent could be removed
they two might share the leadership of affairs.   The young
man accepted the offer and ranged himself in line with the
opposition.   The Regent was now in great straits.   The combination against him had proved too strong, and in the last
moon of 1873 he shook off the dust of Seoul from his feet and
retired to Ka-p'yŭng, thirty-five miles to the east of the capital.   After five months of residence there he returned as far
as the village of K-deung, ten miles to the north-east of
Seoul.

Among the people there was still a strong element that
favored the ex-Regent.   They missed a strong personality at
the helm of state, for the Koreans have always preferred a
strong even if tyrannical leadership.   In recognition of this
sentiment it was deemed wise to put the ex-Regent's brother,
whom he had always kept severely in the back-ground, in the
prominent if not necessarily important position of Prime Minister.   He proved as was intended a mere puppet in the hands
of the Min party who by this time had absorbed the whole
power of the government.   He was allowed, in compensation
for this, to control the sale of public offices to his own profit,
but always under the vigilant eye of the dominant faction.

A new era in the metamorphosis of Korea had now begun.
Public affairs in the peninsula took a new direction.   Min
Seung-ho was court favorite and it looked as if matters would
soon settle down to something like their former tranquility.
But the latter days of the year were destined to bring a severe
shock to the leaders of the new party.   One day Min Seung-
ho received a letter purporting to be from a certain party
with whom he was on intimate terms, and with it came a casket
wrapped in silk.   He was requested to open it only in the
presence of his mother and his son.   Late at night in his inner
chamber he opened it in the presence of these members of his
family, but when he lifted the cover the casket exploded with
terrific force killing the three instantly and setting the house on
fire.   As Min Seung-ho had but one enemy bold enough to
perpetrate the deed the popular belief that it was done by his
great rival is practically undisputed, though no direct evidence
perhaps exists.

Min T'ă-ho immediately stepped into the place made vacant by the terrible death of the favorite. Soon after this the government discontinued the use of the 100 cash pieces with which the Regent had diluted the currency of the country. In the second moon of 1874 the crown prince was born. The year was also signalised by the remittance in perpetuity of the tax on real estate in and about the city of Seoul.

In 1875 three of the ex-Regent's friends, led by Cho Ch'ung-sik, memorialised the throne begging that the Prince Tai-wŭn be again reinstated in power. For this rash act they were all condemned to death, and it was only by the personal intercession of the ex-Regent that the sentence was commuted to banishment for life. Even so, Cho Ch'ung-sik was killed at his place of exile.

In September the Japanese man-of-war *Unyo Kwan*, after making a trip to Chefoo, approached the island of Kang-wha to make soundings. Approaching the town of Yŏng-jŭng, they sent a small boat ashore to look for water. As they neared the town they were suddenly fired upon by the Koreans in the little fortress, who evidently took them for Frenchmen or Americans. A moment later the small boat was turned about and was making toward the man-of-war again. The commander gave instant orders for summary punishment to be inflicted for this perfectly unprovoked assault. He opened fire on the town and soon silenced the batteries. A strong body of marines was landed which put the garrison to flight, seized all the arms and provisions and fired the town. The man-of-war then steamed away to Nagasaki to report what had occurred.

At this time there were in Japan two parties who took radically different views of the Korean question. One of these parties, led by Saigo of Satsuma, smarting under the insulting way in which Korea had received the Japanese overtures, would listen to nothing but instant war. The other party, which saw more clearly the vital points in the question at issue, urged peaceful measures. The policy of the latter prevailed and it was decided to send an embassy to attempt the ratification of a treaty, and if that failed war was to be the alternative. This peace policy was so distasteful to the war party that Saigo returned to Satsuma and began to set in motion those agencies which resulted in the sanguinary Satsuma Rebellion.

For many centuries there had been a strip of nautral territory between the Korean border, the Yalu River, and the Chinese border which was marked by a line of stakes. This strip of land naturally became the hiding plece of refugees and criminals from both countries, for here they were free from police supervision whether Korean or Chinese. The statesman Li Hung-chang recognized this to be a menace to the wellfare of both countries and took steps to put an end to it, by sending a strong body of troops who, in conjunction with a gunboat, succeeded in breaking up the nest of desperadoes and rendering the country fit for colonisation. Two years later this strip of land was definitely connected with China and the two countries again faced each other across the waters of the Yalu,

The Korean attack upon the Unyo Kwan off Kang-wha proved the lever which finally roused Japan to active steps in regard to the opening of Korea. The war party regarded it as their golden opportunity, while the peace party believed it would pave the way for a peaceful accomplishment of their purpose. An envoy was despatched to Peking to sound the policy of that government. The Chinese, fearing that they would be held responsible for the misdoings of Korea denied all responsibility and virtually acknowledged the independence of the peninsula At the same time a military and naval expedition under Kiroda Kiyotaku, seconded by Inouye Bunda, sailed for Kang-wha with a fleet of gunboats, containing in all some 800 men. The Chinese had already advised the Korean government to make terms with the Japanese, and this in fact was the wish of the dominant party; so. when the Japanese demand reached Seoul, that commissioners be sent to Kang-wha to treat with the visitors the government quickly complied. Two high officials. Sin Hön and Yun Cha-seung, were despatched to Kang-wha and the first definitive step peace and friendship. The Korean commissioner replied that from the very earliest times Japan had always addressed Korea in respectful language, but that now she had arrogated to herself the title of Great Japan and called her ruler the Great Emperor. This seemed to imply the vassalage of Korea, an entirely new role for her to play. The Japanese replied that the mere assumption of the name of empire on the part of Japan implied nothing as to the status of Korea one way or the other. This seemed to satisfy the Koreans.

The Japanese than asked why they had been fired upon at Yŭng-jŭng. The answer was that the Japanese were dressed in European clothes and were therefore mistaken for Europeans. But when the Japanese asked why the Koreans had not recognized the Japanese flag, especially since the Japanese government had been careful to send copies of their flag to Korea and ask that one be sent to each of the prefectures throughout the land, the Korean commissioners could find nothing to say and had to confess that they had been in error.

All these things were duly reported to the authorities in Seoul where daily councils were being held to discuss the important questions. The ex-Regent sent an urgent appeal to the ministers not to make a treaty, but the tide had turned, and after some sharp discussion as to how the two governments should be designated in the treaty it was finally ratified on Febuary 27th 1876, and Korea was a hermit no longer. Three months later a semi official envoy was sent to Japan in the person of Kim Keui su.

Meanwhile the closing days of 1875 had beheld a curious event in Seoul. In the dead of night the house of Yi Ch'oe-eung, the Prime Minister and the brother of the ex-Regent, was set on fire by an unknown hand and burned to the ground. None of the inmates were injured. The culprit was seized and under torture confessed that one Sin Ch'ŭl-gyun had hired him to do the work. Sin was therefore seized and put to death as a traitor. Whether he was indeed guilty and if so whether he was but an agent in the business are questions that have never been answered.

It was not until the sixth moon of 1879 that, in pursuance of the new treaty, a Japanese Minister, Hanabusa,

was sent to represent his government at Seoul. We will remember that he had already served his government most successfully at the Korean capital in a private capacity. The
new legation was situated at the Ch'ŭn Yŭn-jŭng near the
lotus pond outside the West Gate. At almost the very same
time two French priests arrived in Seoul and took up their
quarters outside this same gate and began to proselyte.
They were forthwith seized by the authorities, and were for
some time in imminent danger. There was however a strong
feeling in the government that this was inconsistent with the
new role that it had elected to play and that it was distinctly
dangerous. A halt was called and the Japanese Minister took
advantage of it to inform the authorities that he had received
a message from the French Minister in Tokyo asking him to
use his good offices in behalf of these endangered men.
The Minister added his own advice that the Korean
government should hand over the imprisoned men at once.
This was done and the Japanese Minister forwarded [them
to Japan.

One year later, in the summer of 1880, Kim Hong-jip,
a man of progressive tendencies, went to Japan. Soon after
arriving there he met a Chinaman who seems to have made
a strong impression on him. This Chinaman had many talks
with him and gave him a long manuscript dealing with the
subject of Korea's foreign relations, which he asked should
be transmitted to the king of Korea. In it he advised the
cementing of friendship with the United States, China and
Japan, but he spoke disparagingly of Russia. It mentioned
Protestant Christianity as being the basis of Western greatness and advised that its propagation be encouraged. It compared the division of Christianity into Roman Catholic and
Protestant to the division of Confucianism into the two sects
Chu-ja and Yuk-sang-san. When Kim Hong-jip brought
this manuscript and placed it in the hands of the king it created a profound sensation, and awakened the bitterest opposi-
tion. Many advised that he be killed as an introducer of
Christianity. The most violent of all were Yi Man-son,
Hong Chă-hak and Păk Nak-kwăn who memorialized the
throne urging the execution of Kim and the overthrow of all
Christian work in the peninsula. This met with the severest

censure from the king, not because it was in itself seditious but because it was an attempt to reinstate the policy of the Regency. Yi Man-son was banished, Hong Chă-hak was executed and Păk Nak-kwan was imprisoned. This put an end to anti-Christian talk for the time being and it was never again seriously raised.

By the fourth moon of 1881 the progressive tendencies of the new regime had made such headway that the king determined to send a commission to Japan to look about and see something of the world, from which Korea had been so carefully secluded. For this purpose His Majesty selected Cho Chun-Yŭng, Pak Chŏng-yang, Sim Sang hak, Cho Pyŭng-jik, Min Chong-muk, O Yun jung, Om Se-yŭng, Kang Mun-hyŭng, Hong Yŭng-sik, Yi Wŭn-whe, and Yi Pong-eui. These men immediately took passage for Japan. At the same time a party of young men was sent to Tientsin under the chaperonage of Kim Yun-sik on a similar errand.

Late in this year, 1881, four of the adherents of the ex-Regent conspired to overthrow the government, dethrone the king and put in his place Yi Chă-sŭn, a son of the ex-Regent by a concubine. The ex-Regent was then to be brought back to power. The last day of the eighth moon was set for the consummation of this plot. But on the day before, Nam-Myŭng sŭn and Yi P'ung-nă divulged the whole scheme to the favorite Min T'ă-ho, and as a result the four arch-conspirators were seized on the morning of the day set for the culmination of the plot and within a few days eleven others were taken. In the eleventh moon they were all beheaded. and at the same time Yi Chă-sŭn was given poison and expired.

By this time a real liberal party had begun to form. Its leading spirits were Kim Ok-kyun, Pak Yŭng-hyo, So Kwang-bom, Hong Yŭng-sik, Yi To-jă, Sin Keui-sŭn and Pak Yŭng-kyo. These were all men of very high family and held important positions under the government. They were in favor of the immediate opening of Korea to intercourse with foreign powers and the establishment of reforms such as had been effected in Japan. The king was largely influenced by the progressive policy mapped out by these men and an era of rapid advancement seemed to be dawning. A special department was established called the Ki-mu or Machinery Bureau which was to take charge of the introduction of foreign machinery and implements of all kinds.

It is important to note the position of the Min faction at this point. It was with the downfall of the Regent that, through the queen's influence, the Min faction sprang to life. With the utmost celerity all government positions were filled with them or their sympathizers and it seemed sure that they would have a long lease of official life. The extreme opposition of the Regent to all reforms and to the opening of the country to foreign intercourse naturally inclined his rivals in that very direction and it was directly through the Min faction that the policy of non-seclusion was inaugurated. The queen likewise was in favor of opening up the country to the civilizing influences of the West. But with the Min faction, as a whole, the question of national policy were entirely secondary to the one main idea of preserving the ascendency which they had gained. Here is the key to all that followed. The Mins were not at that time facing China-ward and they never would have been had it not become necessary in order to preserve the enviable position they occupied. As we have seen, a number of high officials who had imbibed something of the spirit of reform which had permeated Japan were filling the ear of the king and queen with plans for reform. They were meeting with a favorable hearing and in proportion as they succeeded, the power of the Mins must wane; not because the latter disliked the idea of opening up Korea but because it was another faction that had the work in hand, and that faction would naturally attain more and more power at court as success crowned their efforts. It was just here that the difficulty began. If the liberal leaders had been willing to put the working out of the plan into the hands of the Min faction all might have gone along smoothly and Korea might have realized some of the hopes of the would-be reformers. But such self-abnegation could scarcely be expected from men who saw in the carrying out of their brilliant scheme not only rewards for themselves but the advancement of the country. The personal element was present in full force and this was the rock on which the reformation of Korea split. We may believe that it was at this point that the Min faction determined its policy, a policy that led it straight into the arms of

China. From this point it became not the progressive party but the conservative party. Its leading members were Min T'ă-ho, Min Yŭng-muk, Min Tu-ho, Han Kyu-jik and Cho Ryŭng-ha. There was one of the Mins however who held with the liberal party, for a time at least. This was Min Yŭng-ik, nephew to the queen, adopted son of Min Seung-ho who had been killed by the infernal machine in 1874. That this man took his stand at first with the liberals is shown by the fact that in the spring of 1882 he joined Kim Hong-jip, Kim Ok-kyun, Hong Yŭng-sik and other liberal leaders in advising the king to select 200 young men and engage a Japanese instructor to drill them in military tactics. The advice was followed, and Lieutenant Isobayachi was employed for that purpose. Without delay he began work at the Ha-do-gam near the East Gate. At the same time a number of young men were sent to Japan to study military matters. Among these the most prominent was Sŭ Chă-p'il who was intimately connected with the liberal movement, though at that time he was too young to take a prominent part.

The first regularly appointed Minister to the Japanese was Pak Yŭng-hyo the liberal leader. In the early part of 1882 he departed on his mission. It was at Chemulpo on board the little Japanese steamer that the Korean flag was first designed. Pak Yŭng-hyo, Kim Ok-kyun, Sŭ Kwang-bom and Sŭ Chă-p'il were all present when it was hoisted for the first time in honor of the first Minister to Japan.

While the two hunderd men who were being drilled at the Ha-do-gam were being plentifully fed and clothed by the government, the 3,700 troops, called the Hul lyŭn To-gam, the former Royal Guard, were being badly neglected. Their pay was two or three months in arrears and for a similar period they had not received a grain of rice. They were naturally incensed and there were angry mutterings against the two hundred men who were being treated so much better than they. When the king was made aware of this he ordered that a month's allowance of rice be given out to these discontented troops. This work was put into the hands of Min Kyŭm-ho the overseer of the government finances, and he in turn handed the matter over to his major-domo who, it appears, sold the good rice and with the proceeds bought a large quantity of the poorest quality which he mixed with sand and doled out to the hungry troops. The result may be imagined. They congregated in various places and determined that since they must die in any event they would rather die fighting than starving. They strengthened the feeble-hearted among their own number by threats of death in case any proved unfaithful and refused to assist in the work in hand. On the night of the ninth of the sixth moon, in the midst of heavily falling rain, they arose *en masse* and proceeded to their general's house, where they announced that they were going to take revenge on those who had wronged them. That they not only did not attack him but that they even had the courtesy to go and tell him what they were about to do shows clearly that he was in no wise to blame for the ill-treatment they had received. They also sent a messenger to the ex-Regent, but the purport of the message is not known. They then hastened to the residence of Min Kyŭm-ho, but he had heard of the trouble and had fled to the royal presence for protection. The infuriated soldiery vented their rage on the property by tearing down the house and destroying the furniture. They seized the dishonest major-domo and beat him to death upon the spot. The sight of this aroused all their worst instincts and, separating into bands of two or three hundred, they hastened to different parts of the town to complete what had been begun. Some ran to the prisons and liberated the inmates who naturally joined the ranks of the rioters. One of these prisoners was Pǎk Nak-kwan who had memorialized the throne in favor of the ex-Regent. They took him on their shoulders and rushed through the streets shouting "Pǎk Chung-sin" or "Pǎk the patriot." For this, a few months later he was torn to pieces by bullocks outside the West Gate. Part of the mob went to the Ha-do-gam, but on their approach the Japanese military instructor took to his heels and made for the Japanese Legation. But he was overtaken and cut down in the streets. Another detachment hastened to the Japanese Legation itself, but found the gates shut and barred. Within were nine Japanese. In order to make it light enough to carry on their dastardly work the assaulting mob threw firebrands over the wall and thus illuminated the place, for it was night. The little company of Japanese soon became aware that they could not hope to stand a siege and that their only hope lay in a bold dash. Suddenly the gates flew open and the nine determined men rushed out brandishing their swords and firing their revolvers straight into the crowd. The Koreans were taken wholly by surprise and beat a hasty retreat. In their headlong flight many of them fell into the lotus pond adjoining. As the Japanese hurried along to the governor's yamen which was not far away, they cut down a few of the mob. They found that the governor had gone to the palace and so they turned their faces toward Chemulpo and hastened away. Another party of the insurgents went outside the city to various monasteries which they burned to the ground. The most important of these was the Sin-heung Monastery outside the Northeast Gate. This move was dictated by hate of the Min faction whose patroness was known to be very well affected toward Buddhism and to have made friends with the monks.

Other parties scattered over the city carrying the torch to the door of every member of the Min faction. The houses of Min Kyŭm-ho, Min T'ă-ho, Min Yŭng-ik, Min Yŭng-so, Min Yŭng-jun, Min Yŭng-ju Min Ch'ang-sik, Prince Heung-in, Kim Po-hyŭn and Yun Chă-dŭk were torn down by the use of long ropes. The furniture was piled in a great heap in the street and burned. The only member of the Min clan however that was seized that night was Min Ch'ang-sik who lived at Kon-dang-kol. He had the unenviable reputation of having taken large sums of money from the people by indirection. When he was seized he cried "I am not a Min; my name is Păk." They bound him and carried him through the streets shouting "Is this a Min or a Păk?" The populace answered fiercely "He is a Min." So they took him down to the big bell and stabbed him in a hundred places with their swords and cut his mouth from ear to ear.

When the morning of the tenth broke Seoul was in a terrible condition. Bands of frenzied soldiery were ranging through the streets. The people either huddled about their fireplaces with barred doors or else sought safety in flight from the city. At last the mob rendezvoused in front of the palace gate and finding no opposition they boldly entered. Rushing into the inner court of the king's private apartments

they found themselves face to face with His Majesty. About him
stood a few of the officials who had not fled the city.   There
were Min Kyŭm-ho, Kim Po-hyŭn, Cho Ryŭng-ha and Prince
Heung in.   Rushing forward the soldiers struck their swords
against the floor and the door-posts and demanded that these
men be handed over to them.   It was quite evident that there
was no escape and that by refusal they would only endanger
the king's life.   So these men made obeisance to His Majesty
and then stepped down into the hands of the soldiers.   Min
Kyŭm-ho and Kim Po-hyŭn were instantly struck down and
hacked in pieces before the very eyes of the king.   Of Kim
nothing remained but the trunk of his body.   Cho Ryŭng-ha
was spared but Prince Heung-in died the same day for he was
mashed to a jelly by the gun-stocks of the soldiers.

This done, the soldiers demanded the person of the queen.
The king sternly demanded how they dared ask of him the
person of his Queen.   Without answering they rushed away
to her private apartments.   Seizing palace women by the
hair they dragged them about demanding where their mistress
was.   But while this was going on one of the palace guard
named Hong Cha-heui entered the Queen's presence and said
that she was in danger and that her only hope of escape lay
in getting on his back and being carried out.   This she instantly did.   A skirt was hastily thrown over her head and
the heroic man took her straight out through the midst
of the infuriated soldiery.   Some of them seized hold of him
and demanded whom he was carrying.   He replied that it
was one of the palace women, his sister, whom he was conveying to a place of safety.   His heroism was rewarded by
seeing her safely outside the palace and comfortably housed
at the residence of Yun T'ä-jŭn to the west of the palace.
The next day she was taken in a closed chair toward the village of Chang-ho-won in the district of Ch'ung-ju in Ch'ung ch'ŏng

peared on the scene while the sold ers were still raging
through the palace in search of the Queen. He gave the
signal to stop, and instantly the soldiers obeyed and quietly
left the palace. That these soldiers, worked up as they were
to a perfect frenzy, should have obeyed the commands of the
Prince Tai-wŭn so instantly and implicitly would seem to
argue a closer connection with this outbreak than any overt
act on his part would give us warrant to affirm.

The ex-Regent was now in power again. He supposed
that the Queen had been killed, and on the next day he
summoned the officials and said that though the Queen was
dead yet her body had not been found; they must therefore
take some of her clothing and perform the funeral rites with
them instead. The proclamation went forth, and from the
middle of the sixth moon the people went into mourning for
their Queen.

Chapter XVI.

A few days after the flight of the Queen a rumor was
circulated to the effect that a large body of men belonging to

the peddlar's guild had congregated outside the East Gate and were about to enter and loot the city. A panic seized the people, and men, women and children might be seen flying in all directions, some out into the neighboring country and some up the steep sides of the surrounding mountains. The gates being all locked the people forced the South Gate and the two West gates and thus made good their escape. The king himself was affected by the rumor and leaving the palace sought safety at the house of Yi Che-wan. But the panic ceased as quickly as it had begun, and within three hours the people were returning to their homes again. The extreme haste with which the people tried to get away is illustrated in the case of one old man who seized his little grand-son, as he supposed by the hand, and fled up a mountain but found to his dismay that he had taken the boy by the leg rather than by the hand and that the little fellow had succumbed to this harsh treatment.

On the fifth of the seventh moon Count Inouye arrived in Chemulpo as Japanese envoy and immediately sent word to have a high Korean official sent to Chemulpo to discuss the situation. Kim Hong-jip was sent, and as a result the Korean government was asked to pay an indemnity for the lives of the Japanese who had been killed. It appears that besides the Japanese military instructor five or six others had been killed, also a considerable amount of Japanese money had been seized and destroyed at the Japanese headquarters. The indemnity was placed at a million cash apiece for the Japanese who had fallen. This amounted to something like $2,500 each, a ridiculously small sum, but perhaps all the Japanese thought they could get. The ex-Regent replied that if the Japanese demanded this indemnity the Korean government would feel obliged to levy a tax upon all Japanese merchants doing business in Korea. This was practically a refusal to pay the indemnity and the envoy took his departure.

Hardly had he left before a Chinese force 3,000 strong arrived at Nam-yang off the town of Su-wŭn. They were commanded by Generals O Chang-gyŭng, Wang Sŭk-ch'ang, Ma Kŭn-sang and by a lesser officer named Wŭn Se-gă who was destined to play a leading part from this time on. These

troops came, it can hardly be doubted, at the request
of the conservative party and it was from this hour that
that faction turned unreservedly towards China and gave the
latter occasion for beginning a series of encroachments
upon Korea's practical independence which ended in the
China-Japan war.   These troops encamped all about the
capital, some at Pă-o-gă outside the West Gate and some at
the Ha-do-gam just inside the East Gate.

Some of the soldiers who had been most active in creat-
ing the disturbance lived at Wang-sim-yi three miles outside
the East Gate.   The Chinese made it their first work to seize
these men by night.   Ten of them were court-martialed and
were torn to pieces by bullocks.

The Chinese general O Jang-gyŭng was told that the ex-
Regent was at the bottom of the emeute, and he sent a letter
informing the Emperor of this fact.   The latter ordered him
to seize the person of the offending party and bring him to
China.   The Chinese general thereupon visited the palace
where the Prince Tai-wŭn was in full control and invited him
to visit Yong-san on the river, where he said there was something important for him to see.   Having once gotten him on
board a Chinese boat there, under pretext of showing him
over it, the anchor was quickly raised and the baffled Prince
found himself on his way to China.   When he arrived at
Tientsin he was refused audience with Li Hung-chang but
was banished by imperial decree to a place not far from
Tientsin, where he was well cared for until his return to
Korea three years later.

After this *deus ex machina* had spirited the ex-Regent
away, an official, So Sang-jo, memorialized the throne stating
that the Queen was still alive and ought to be brought back
to the capital.   It is said that Yi Yŭng-ik covered the space
between the capital and her place of hiding, sixty-three
miles, in a single day, carrying the message of recall.   A
large retinue of officials and soldiers were sent southward
and brought the Queen back to Seoul where she arrived on
the first day of the eighth moon.   The people immediately
doffed their mourning garb.

Toward the close of 1882 a Foreign Office was established
in the capital and Kim Yun-sik was made Minister of Foreign

Affairs. He invited P. G. von Mollendorf, a member of the customs staff of China, to act as adviser, and the Chinese generals Wang Sŭk-ch'ang and Ma Kŭn-sang were made attachęs of the new department.

The year 1883 witnessed more advance in Korea than any year before or since. In May Gen Foote, the first United States Minister, arrived and on the nineteenth of that month the treaty which had been drawn up at Chemulpo between Commodore Shufeldt and the Korean Commissioners was ratified. After this was done Gen. Foote left Korea to make preparations for the establishment of a legation in Seoul.

Kim Ok-kyun, one of the leading members of the progressive party was made "Whale Catching Commissioner" and departed for Japan to fit out an expedition to carry on this lucrative government monopoly along the Korean coast. He was selected for this work because of his intimate acquaintance with the Japanese. It was a move looking toward the development of Korea's resources and was therefore in direct line with the wishes and plans of the progressionists. At about the same time a powder-mill was built outside the Northwest Gate, and a foreign mint was erected inside the Little West Gate. This was done with the aid of Japanese experts at a great and, as it proved, useless expense to the government. An office was founded for the printing and dissemination of useful literature on the subjects of agriculture, forestry, stock-raising and the like. The ports of Chemulpo and Wŭn-san were opened to foreign trade according to the stipulation of the Japanese and American treaties. In contrast to the progressive moves we find that eight men who were suspected of complicacy with the ex-Regent in the emeute of the preceding year were executed by poison. Of like character was the building of the Kwan-wang temple, devoted to the interests of sorceresses and exorcists who enjoyed the patronage of the Queen.

In the summer of 1883 Min Yŭng-ik was made special envoy to the United States. His second was Hong Yŭng-sik. Among his suite were Sŭ Kwang-bom, Pak Un and others, all of whom were members of the progressive party or at least well affected toward it. This same summer the king founded the American Farm some ten miles east of

Seoul and stocked it with foreign seeds and cattle, with the idea of providing Korean farmers with a sort of object-lesson in farming, and to provide seeds for distribution among the people. The United States Department of Agriculture sent a large stock of seeds by the hand of the special embassy of which Min Yŭng-ik formed the head.

Late in the autumn the German representative arrived and concluded a treaty on behalf of his government. A month later a treaty was ratified with Great Britain and a Consulate General was founded in Seoul.

With the opening of 1884 the state of affairs in the peninsula was something as follows. The progressive and conservative elements in the government were clearly differentiated. The innovations effected by the progressives had raised in them the hope of being able to speedily reorganize the government on a foreign basis, and the degree of their success marked the increasing suspicion and oppositon of the conservative element. The latter were strengthened in their position by the presence and active support of the Chinese generals and troops, and the influence of the foreign adviser von Mollendorf was always on the side of Chinese interests. The ex-Regent was for the time being out of the war and a great stumbling-block to the Min faction was thus removed. The king and queen were both favorably inclined toward a progressive policy but the latter was gradually being drawn back into line with the conservative element of which the Min family was the leading representative. Min Yŭng-ik was still true to his better instincts and was an ardent supporter of the progressionist views but his return from America was the sign for a vigorous attack upon his enlightened views by the members of his family and he was being rapidly alienated from the party whose interests he had tentatively espoused. It was not, however, till later in the year that he broke away entirely from the progressive following.

The spring of 1884 saw the arrival of Ensign Geo. C. Foulk as naval attache of the American Legation. He rapidly became acquainted with the leading officials and it was through his advice and aid that several reformatory measures were promulgated. In the sixth moon the influence of the progressive party secured the position of Mayor of Seoul for Pak Yŭng-hyo, one of the most ardent of the reform party, and he immediately set to work at sanitary reforms and municipal improvements. He began by tearing down houses that had encroached upon the main road between the East and the West Gates. He had not proceeded far in this good work before he was blocked by the influence of the opposing faction. His next move was in the direction of dress reform and he succeed in putting through a law prohibiting the use of the long sleeves, long hat-strings and long girdle strings. In these efforts he was seconded to a certain extent by Min Yŭng-ik, but at this point terminates the latter's active interest in reforms, and from about this time the progressive leaders began to look upon him as a traitor to their cause. Here again personal interest came to injure a cause which, while good in itself, was discredited by the means used to effect its end. One sign of advance was the establishment of a school for the training of interpreters in English, under the charge of a competent foreign instructor.

In the autumn of this year 1884 twelve of the young men who had been sent to Japan to study military tactics returned to Seoul, among them being Sŭ Chă p'il, known in later years as Dr. Philip Jaisohn, who though still a youth of about twenty years began to take an active part in the plans of the liberal or progressive party. By this time Min Yŭng-ik had practically taken his stand with the conservatives, and this tended in no small measure to draw away from the progressives the sympathy and support of the queen. It was becoming evident that the hopes of the liberals were to be dashed to the ground. Yuan, the Chinese commissioner, was staying at the barracks in front of the palace and was active in the interests of his own government, which meant that he urged on the conservative party in their opposition to reforms. It can hardly be wondered at then that the progressives looked more and more to the Japanese from whom they had imbibed their ideas of progress. Japan had recognized the independence of Korea and this naturally carried with it a desire to see Korea progress along the same lines that had raised Japan out of the rut of centuries to the more satisfactory plane of enlightened government.

How to stem the tide that had set so strongly against
them was a difficult problem for the progressionist leaders to
solve. From time immemorial the method of effecting changes
in the Korea government had been to make an uprising,
secure the person of the king and banish or excute the leaders of the opposition. It must be remembered that at that
time, so far as the mass of the people was concerned, the progressive party had little or no backing. On the other hand
the conservatives had the ear of the king and were backed by
a Chinese army. It was evidently necessary to secure military backing, and for this Japan alone was available. But it
was manifestly impossible for Japan to come in and attempt
to effect the change. It must be at the request of the Korean
government, or at least of the king. It seemed that the only
thing to do was to hasten a crisis, obtain possession of the
person of the king and then see to it that Japan be invited to
loan troops to preserve the new status.

Instead of waiting patiently and suffering temporary defeat with the hope of ultimate success, the progressive leaders
determined to have recourse to the old method, and in so doing they made a fatal blunder. Even had they been successful the means they employed would have fatally discredited
them in the eyes of all enlightened people.

It is generally accepted as true that the progressive leaders had a distinct understanding with the Japanese. A Japanese man-of-war was on the way to Chemulpo and was expected to arrive on the fifth or sixth of December and the
uprising was set for the seventh of that month. The leaders
in this movement had not been able to keep it entirely a secret, for some of them talked about it in a very excited manner of the Naval Attache of the American Legation and it
came to the ears of the British Consul-general, who, meeting
Yun T'ā-jun on December fourth, asked him if he had heard
that there was trouble in the air. That gentleman who was
himself a strong convervative and a close friend of Min T'ā-
ho, hastened to the house of the latter and reported what he
had heard. Min advised him to hasten to the house of one of
the relatives of one of the pregressionists and secure information if possible. He did so, and there happened to meet one
of the leaders of the progressive party and intimated to him

that he had heard that trouble was brewing. This man denied all knowledge of any such plan but the minute his caller had gone he hastened to the other progressionist leaders and told them that all was lost unless instant action were taken. News had just arrived that the Japanese gun-boat that was expected at Chemulpo had broken down and could not come. There were only a few hundred Japanese troops in Seoul at the time. But it seemed to these men that it would be better to risk the whole venture on a single cast than to wait passively and see the destruction of all their hopes and plans. The seventh of December was the appointed day but as this was a matter of kill or be killed it was decided to proceed at once to business. Hong Yŭng-sik had been made Post-master General and on this very night he was to give a banquet at the new post-office which was situated in that part of the city called Kyo-dong. It was decided to start the ball rolling at this point. The evening came and the guests assembled to the dinner. They were the Chinese leaders Yuan, Chin and Wang, United States Minister Foote and his secretary Mr. Scudder, the British Consul-general Aston, the Foreign Office Adviser von Mollendorf, the Koreans Hong Yŭng-sik, Kim Ok-kyun, Min Yŭng-ik, Pak Yŭng-ho, Sŭ Kwang-bom, Kim Hŭng-jip, Han Kyu-jik, Pak Chŏng-yang, O Yun-jung and a few others. The Japanese Minister had excused himself on the plea of ill-health. It was noticed that Kim Ok-kyun rose and left the table several times and went out into the court-yard but no special significance was attached to this. The dinner began at an early hour, not far from six o'clock, and about seven o'clock an alarm of fire was sounded. A house immediately in front of the Post Office was in flames. Min Yŭng-ik, being one of the officials whose duty it was to superintend the extinguishing of conflagrations, rose from the table and hastened out, calling to his servants to follow. As he passed out of the inner gate, a man dressed in Japanese clothes leaped out of the shadow of the gate-way and struck at him savagely with a sword, wounding him severely in the head and in other parts of the body. He fell heavily to the ground and in the confusion that ensued the would-be assassin made good his escape. Von Mollendorf was not far behind, and seeing what had happened he hastened forward,

lifted the wounded man in his arms and carried him back
into the dining-room.   The Koreans who were present fled
precipitately making their exit not by the door but by way of
the back wall.

The wounded man was conveyed to the residence of von
Mollendorf which was in the vicinity, where Dr. H. N. Allen
of the American Presbyterian Mission was soon in attendance.

The die had now been cast and there was no retreat.
The leaders of the conspiracy, Kim Ok-kyun, Sŭ Kwang bom,
Pak Yŭng-hyo, Hong Yŭng-sik and Sŭ Chă-p'il, hastened immediately to the palace known to us as "The Old Palace"
where the king had resided since the insurrection of 1882.
Entering the royal presence they announced that the Chinese
were coming to take possession of the king's person and that
he must hasten to a place of safety.   The king did not believe
this report but as they insisted he had no recourse but to sub-
mit.   The little company hastened along under the west wall
of the palace until they came to a small gate leading into
Kyŏng-u Palace which adjoins the "Old Palace" on the west.
As they proceeded Kim Ok-kyun asked the king to send to
the Japanese Minister asking for a body-guard, but he refused.
Thereupon Sŭ Kwang-bom drew out a piece of foreign note-
paper and a pencil and wrote in Chinese the words "Let
the Japanese Minister come and give me his help."   This
was immediately despatched by a servant.   That it was a
mere matter of form was evident when the little company
passed into the Kyŏng-u Palace, for there they found the Japanese Minister and his interpreter already in attendance and
with them some two hundred troops drawn up in line.   When
the king appeared they saluted.   There were present also the
twelve students who had been in Japan. Word was immediately
sent to Sin Ke si sun, Pak Yŭ . . . and O V . . . ng to come
. . .

hastened to the palace but no sooner had they entered the palace gate than they were seized and cut down in cold blood. Then the summos was sent to Han Kyu-jik, Yi Cho-yun and Yun T'ă jŭn. They too were assassinated as soon as they entered the palace. A eunuch named Yu Cha-hyŭn was also put to death. It is useless to ask by whose hand these men fell. Whowever wielded the brutal sword, the leaders of the so-called progressive party were wholly responsible. The twelve young men who had returned from Japan were all fully armed and it is more than probable that they took an active part in the bloody work. Not only was not the king consult-ed in regard to these murders but in the case of the eunuch it was done in spite of his entreaties and remonstrances.

These seven men who thus went to their doom were not entirely unconscious of what awaited them. When Cho Ryŭng-ha received the summons the inmates of his house pleaded with him not to go, but as it was the king's summons he would not disobey even though he knew it meant death.

Just at daylight the king was removed to the house of his cousin Yi Chă-wŭn, escorted by the Japanese soldiers who surrounded him four deep. Kim Ok-kyun gave passes to those who were to be allowed to go in and out and only such had access to the premises. After remaining there some three hours the whole company returned to the "Old Palace." In the reconstructed government Yi Chă wŭn and Hong Yŭng-sik were made Prime Ministers, Pak Yŭng-hyo was made General-in chief. Sŭ Kwang-bom was made Minister of For-eign Affairs, Kim Ok-kyun Minister of Finance and Sŭ Chă-p'il Lieutenant-general. The rest of the young men who had studied in Japan were also given official position.

Before Yun T'ă-jŭn, Yi Cho-yun and Han Kyu-jik went to the palace and met their fate they sent word to Yuan warning him of the state of affairs and asking help, but he made no immediate move. As the morning broke thousands of Koreans came to him and said that the Japauese held the king a prisoner in the palace and begged him to interfere. Yuan re-plied by sending a messenger to the Japanese Minister demand-ing why he had surrounded the king with soldiers and had killed the ministers, and demanding that he immediately evacuate the place. Three hours passed and still no answer came; and at last Yuan and the two other Chinese leaders took a strong body of Chinese troops and several hundred Korean troops and proceeded to the palace. Entering by way of the Sun-in Gate and passing through the Ch'ang-kyŭng Palace they approached the Po-t'ong Gate which gave entrance to the "Old Palace," but they found it strongly guarded by Japanese.   Here a sharp encounter took place which lasted an hour, beginning about three o'clock in the afternoon. About ten each of the Chinese, Japanese and Koreans fell in this assault.   As the darkness came on the Japanese began to fall back and taking the king and the newly appointed ministers they made their way to the extreme northeasterly portion of the palace grounds, not far from the Hong-wha Gate.   The royal party took refuge in a summer house there and the Japanese stationed themselves behind trees and guarded the place, keeping up a lively fusillade with the Chinese who had followed them.   Meanwhile the Crown Prince, the Queen and the king's foster-mother had escaped in small closed chairs out the Sŭn-in Gate and had found refuge in the house of Yi Pom-jin in the village af No-wŭn, twenty li outside the East Gate.

The chances of success for the Japanese were becoming smaller and smaller and the king was anxiously looking for an opportunity of escaping from them and making his way to the Chinese side.   At last, taking advantage of the extreme disorder that prevailed, he made his way to the Puk-chang Gate at the extreme northeastern part of the palace enclosure. Outside there was a crowd of Korean soldiers who wished to gain entrance and rescue the king from his captors.   When the latter made his presence known inside the gate these soldiers effected an entrance and lifting His Majesty on their shoulders carried him in triumph to the North Temple just inside the Northeast Gate. Seeing that all hope of immediate success was gone, Pak Yŭng-hyo, Kim Ok-kyun, Sŭ Kwang-bom Sŭ Chă-p'il and a part of the company of military students accompanied the Japanese troops out the front gate of the palace to the Japanese Legation which was then situated in Kyo-dong.   This was accomplished in the midst of great excitement.

Meanwhile Hong Yŭng-sik, Pak Yŭng-kyo, Sin Keui-sŭn

and seven of the military students had followed the fortunes of
the king. But no sooner did the party arrive at the North
Temple than the people fell upon Hong Yǔng-sik and Pak
Yǔng-kyo and hacked them to pieces before the king's eyes.
Hong Yǔng-sik attempted to hide in a closet behind His
Majesty but the latter indicated by a nod of the head that he
was concealed there and the people dragged him out and dispatched him on the spot.   The seven students tried to effect
their escape but were pursued and killed, one below Chong-no,
and another at Yǔn-mot-kol.

No sooner had the morning dawned than the Japanese Minister formed his little company in a hollow square, placed the
Korean refugees and the Japanese women and children in the
center, fired the legation buildings and marched out through
the city on their way to Chemulpo, shooting at any Koreans
whom they happened to see in their way.   They found the
West Gate locked but they soon forced it and hurried away
to the port. All the Japanese in Seoul did not escape thus,
for there were a few living in Chin-go-gǎ.   That same day
the Koreans mobbed them and killed them all, men women and
children.

A Japanese merchant vessel happened to be lying at
Chemulpo and the Minister with all his company boarded her,
carrying the Koreans with them.   The latter were hidden in
the hold.

That same day, later in the afternoon, the king made his
way to the Ha-do-gam where the Chinese had camped, and
put himself under their protection.   Cho Pyǔng-ho was sent
to Chemulpo to ask the Japanese Minister not to leave, and to
effect the arrest of the fugitives. In neither quest was he
successful.

An anxious month passed by and at last the Japanese,
Count Inouye, came with a guard of 600 troops and took up
his quarters at the governor's place outside the West Gate.
Negotiations were at once begun and as a result the Korean
Government agreed to pay an indemnity of 600,000 yen.   Sǔ
Sang-u and P. G. von Mollendorf were sent as commissioners
to Japan to arrange suitable terms for the renewal of friendly
relations.   To make good their protestations of regret at
the killing of defenseless Japanese in Seoul four men who took

part in that work were arrested and put to death. At the same time Yi Ch'ang-gyu, Sŭ Chā-Ch'ang, Kim Pong-jung and five others who had been charged with complicacy in the plot were seized and executed.

On January ninth 1885 Kim Hong-Jip, Special Korean Commissioner, signed with Count Inouye a convention regarding the trouble of the preceeding month, by the terms of which the government agreed to apologize to the Japanese emperor, to pay an indemnity of 110,000 yen, to execute the murderer of Lieut. Isobayachi, to give a site for a new Legation and 20,000 yen for its construction and to set aside a site for barracks for the Japanese guard. Early in the Spring the Japanese Legation was built, being the first foreign building in Seoul.

The year 1885 beheld many events of importance. The government hospital was founded under royal patronage by Dr. H. N. Allen of the American Presbyterian Mission. It beheld also the arrival of that great vanguard of civilization the Protestant Missionary. Dr. Allen had arrived in the previous year but now the Presbyterian and Methodist Churches of America sent a number of representatives into Seoul to secure property and begin preparations for the founding of regular evangelistic and educational work. In April the Chinese and Japanese signed the celebrated Tientsin Convention by the terms of which they both agreed to evacuate Korea and not to send troops there without previously notifying each other. It was the breaking of this convention by China which was one of the immediate causes of the Japan-China war. At this same time, England, fearing the occupation of Port Hamilton by Russia, sent a fleet of war vessels and occupied the place herself. She was finally induced to leave, but only after China had guaranteed to secure it against occupation by any other power. In October the treaty with Russia was signed and a Legation was established in Seoul. The ex-Regent was still in China, but the Chinese government now deemed it safe to send him back to the peninsula, and Min Chŭng-muk was sent to act as his escort.

Since the day when the Regent threw the finances of the country into confusion by the debasement of the currency and since the officials had learned how much the people would endure of unjust taxation, in the days when every means was adopted to wring from them the funds for the erection of the palace, official indirection had been on the rapid increase. The people were being imposed upon more and more. All the money that dishonest men paid to corrupt officials to purchase office had to be drawn from the people later by dishonest means. The main qualification of a successful prefect was the ability to judge when he had reached the limit of the people's endurance. The year 1885 beheld a serious revolt in Yŏ-ju where the prefect had overstepped the dead-line of the peoples' patience. He was driven out and his *ajun* or clerk, was killed. The prefect of Wŭn-ju also escaped death only by flight, while an *ajun* was killed.

Not the least-important event of 1885 was the completion under Chinese patronage of the Seoul-Peking telegraph line by which Korea was for the first time put into quick communication with the rest of the world. At the dictation of China a commissioner, Yi Chung-ha was sent north to meet a Chinese commissioner and determine the exact boundary between Korean and Chinese territory along the Tu-man River.

A customs service had been begun by von Mollendorf on an independent basis but in July of 1885 he was dismissed from service in the Foreign Office and two months later he was relieved of work in the Customs because of unwarrantable schemes into which he had drawn that department of the government. The whole service was thereupon put under the management of Sir Robert Hart the Inspector General of the Chinese Customs. An entirely new staff of men was sent from China. H. N. Merrill was made Chief Commissioner and Chemulpo, Fusan and Wŭnsan were put in charge of men directly from the Chinese Customs staff. **8** This was a guarantee of excellent management but it proved to be the strongest lever China had in the carrying out her ambitious plans in the peninsula. Before the close of the year Gen. Foote without giving specific reasons retired from the United States Legation and returned to America, Ensign Geo. C. Foulk becoming Charge d'Affaires. **9**

In the early months of 1886 Yi To-jă, Sin Keui-sŭn, Hong Chin-yu, An Chŭng-su and Kyŏ.ıg Kwang-guk were banished to distant islands for complicacy in the plot which led to the emeute of 1884.

In February the king by royal edict abolished the hereditary transmission of slaves and the use of slave labor by the guilds in the work on the palaces. This was a measure of far-reaching import had it been carried out in full; but we find that it had to be re-enacted in 1894.

The government desired to secure the services of a foreign expert as adviser to the Home and Foreign Offices and with the sanction of Li Hung-chang, the Chinese Viceroy, Judge O. N. Denny, ex-Consul-general of U. S. to China, was called and he arrived in the spring of 1886 just in time to be present at the signing of the treaty with France. He had for some years been on rather intimate terms with the Great Viceroy and it is probable that the latter hoped to use the Judge in forwarding Chinese interests in Korea. If so he found himself grievously mistaken for the United States as well as Japan and France, had recognized the independence of Korea, and Judge Denny devoted his energies to the maintenance of that independence. Yuan the Chinese commissior had taken up his residence in Seoul and had dubbed himself "Resident" in opposition to the Korean claim to independence. The Peking government, forgetting or ignoring the fact that whenever Korea had gotten into trouble she (China) had always disavowed responsibility and had practically disclaimed suzerainty, now began to bolster up her claims and to use every means to make good her pretensions. The dominant party which had ridden into power on the shoulders of the Chinese put no obstacles in the way and thus Judge Denny found himself blocked in his efforts to better the condition of the country.

It was generally understood that the right of Japanese and Western foreigners to reside in Seoul was based on the most favored nation clause in the treaties and that if the Chinese removed from Seoul the others could be compelled to do likewise. The Chinese, therefore, hoping, it is said, to secure more exclusive power in the capital by the removal of other foreigners began to agitate the question of removing all their nationals to Yong-san near the river three miles from Seoul. For a time it appeared as if this might be done but the large vested rights of the Japanese in the capital as well as the interests of others caused a counter agitation which frustrated the scheme.

Geo. C Foulk, Ensign in the U. S. Navy, had long been in connection with the Legation in Seoul. Early in 1884 he had suggested to the government the advisability of founding a school for the instruction of young Koreans in Western languages and sciences, and consequently the United States Secretary of State was requested by the Korean government to secure three men as instructors; but the emeute of that year had deferred the matter. In 1886 it was again brought up and in July three men who had been selected by the U. S. Commissioner of Education arrived at the Korean Capital. A terrible epidemic of cholera devastated the city that summer and as many as seven or eight hundred deaths occurred daily. It was in September that the Royal English School was opened.

Chinese claims to suzerainty emboldened the Chinese merchants to attempt to evade the customs regulations and the result was a serious affray in Chemulpo when the Chinese tried to evade the export on ginseng. The Chinese Commissioner tried to uphold them in it but a vigorous protest to Li Hung-chang righted the matter and the offenders were deported and the Customs Service was vindicated.

It was in this year that the trading station Whe-ryŭng on the Tu-man River was established for convenience of trade with Russia but it was not made an open port. About this time the school founded by the American Methodist Mission received royal recognition and the king conferred upon it the name Pai Chai Hak Tang or "Hall for the Rearing of Useful Men."

Contrary to the wishes of the Chinese a Korean Minister to America was appointed in the person of Pak Chöng-yang, but in attempting to start for America he was intercepted by the Chinese just outside the South Gate and compelled to return. Two months later, however, he succeeded in getting away. He was received in Washington with all the punctiliousness due to a Minister from any sovereign power. This helped in a certain way to forward Korea's claim to independence but America's well-known policy of non-interferance in foreign matters largely neutralized its effect.

The year 1888 beheld what is known as the "Baby War."
The report was spread abroad that the Europeans and Americans were stealing children and boiling them in kettles for
food. It was also generally believed that the foreigners
caught women and cut off their breasts in order to extract
from them the condensed milk which was so commonly used
among the foreign residents. The Koreans knew that the
foreigners had no cows and they could explain the use of
milk only on the above theory. The *modus operandi* was said
to be as follows. The foreigners were possessed of a peculiar
drug which became a powerful gas when introduced into the
mouth. Approaching a Korean paper covered lattice door at
the dead of night the operator would make a tiny hole in the
paper and applying his mouth to it would blow the gas into
the room. The effect would be that if there were a woman in
the room she would waken and be seized with an uncontrol-
able desire to go outside. Once without the door, the foreigner would seize her, cut off her breasts and return to his
home. It was believed that they had paid agents among the
people to whom they taught the secret and whom they sent
about the country to secure women's breasts. Two suspicious looking men were set upon in Hong-ch'ön charged with
being breast-hunters. They narrowly escaped with their
lives. For a short time there was imminent danger of an
uprising but a royal proclamation couched in trenchant language did much to calm the excitement and the danger subsided as suddenly as it had arisen. In Eui-ju there was a
most destructive flood in which 300 lives were lost and 1927
houses were swept away.

Chapter XVII.

ese troops arrive .. Japanese movements ...the other powers interfere   Japanese demands .. proposed reforms... the palace taken by the Japanese ...the sinking of the Kowshing....war declared   Korea breaks with China .... Japan promises to leave Shanghai alone   Japanese in Shanghai....battle of Asan....battle of P'yŭng-yang ...battle of the Yalu.

At this time the administration of the government was anything but exemplary. The selling of the same office at such short intervals increased the burden on the people to an almost unbearable point, so that there were frequent uprisings in country districts. In Korea the people form the court of final appeal. If a prefect oversteps the line which marks the limit of the people's endurance and they drive him from the place the government ordinarily accepts it as final.

The following year the government was obliged to take notice of this state of things and the king sent out a proclamation saying that the taking of bribes and the extortion of money in the provinces would be severely punished. He took this opportunity also to speak about robbery and gambling, which had begun to run rife in the land. The people were forbidden to dress in silk, excepting those over fifty years of age.

The year 1890 opened with serious trouble in Ham-gyŭng Province. Cho Pyŭng-sik, a man of indomitable will and one whose unbridled temper had more than once gotten him into serious trouble, was governor in that province. The people had mortgaged their bean crop to the Japanese exporters, of Wŭn-san, and had received some $176,000 therefor. But when the beans had been harvested and were ready for shipment the governor forbade its delivery. He wanted the Japanese to sell it back to the people, as it was a year of scarcity, but this they refused to do; and the beans rotted where they lay. The Japanese promptly took the matter up and demanded an indemnity. The Foreign Office at once recognised the validity of the claim but the king ordered Cho Pyŭng-sik to pay the bill himself, since he had acted throughout without orders from Seoul. The unhappy governor was obliged to part with all his patrimony and several of his relatives had to do likewise. As this was not enough to settle the bill the government paid the balance.

This year saw the first embassy to Europe appointed in the person of Cho Sin-heui but owing to his illness his place was filled by Pak Che-sun who started on his mission but never got further than Hong-kong. It is probable that it was through Chinese influence that he got no further. The fourth moon of the year saw the death of the aged Dowager Queen Cho, through whose influence the present king came to the throne. She was buried with royal honors and the people assumed mourning for one year.

Serious difficulties arose in regard to the fisheries in the south. The Japanese had been accorded the right to fish in Korean waters, but on the island of Quelpart a curious custom prevails. The women do the fishing. They enter the water entirely nude and gather shell-fish. All males are prohibited by law from coming within sight of the fishing-grounds. The Japanese fishing-boats, however, did not hesitate to pass into these prohibited waters and as a result the Koreans were deprived of the means of livelihood. The Korean government took the reasonable ground that the Japanese in coming near the Korean coast should observe the local customs and prejudices, but the Japanese government refused to take any sentimental view of the question and after a long discussion the Koreans failed to carry their point.

The year 1891 beheld the elevation to power of Min Yong-jun a man who championed the most conservative principles of the retrogressive party in power. The king's son by the concubine Lady Kang was made Prince Eui-wha. Corruption in official circles was accentuated by the lessening of the term of office of country prefects thereby entailing fresh burdens on the people, for they had to provide each prefect with money to liquidate the debt he had incurred in purchasing the position. There was an instant and loud outcry from all sides. The powers that be saw that the limit of the peoples endurance had been passed and they hastened to revoke the law. This same year a consulate was founded at Tientsin and Yi Myŭng-sang became the first incumbent.

Another sign of retrogression was the execution of six men charged with being accessory to the insurrection of 1882 although eleven years had passed since that event.

The year 1892 passed without witnessing many events of

special importance, excepting that the state of things kept getting worse and worse. It was a time during which the country was ripening for the great disturbances of the following year. History shows that when the Korean people are treated with anything like a fair degree of justice they are loyal and peaceful. So long as the Korean is called upon to pay not more than three or four times the legal rate of tax he will endure it quietly and there will be no talk of seditious sects arising; but the people are well aware that they themselves form the court of final appeal and when all other means fail they are not slow to adopt any means of righting their wrongs.

In 1893 Korea began to reap what she had sown in 1891 and 1892. Having sown the wind she began to reap the whirlwind. The whole province of P'yŭng-an was in a ferment. Insurrections occurred in Kang-gye, Song-ch'ŭn, Ham-jong and in other parts of the province. But the difficulty was not confined to the North. The sect called the Tong-hak which had arisen in 1864 began to show its head in the south again. Rumors began to multiply in Seoul that they were coming to the capital in great numbers to drive out the Japanese and other foreigners. The government despatched O Yun jung, a civilian, to pacify them and for a time quiet was preserved, but in March threatening plackards were fastened to foreigners' gates in Seoul inveighing against the Christian religion and warning foreigners to leave the country at once. It was the general feeling that although serious trouble was not likely to occur in Seoul it would be well to be in a state of preparedness in case the Tong-hak saw fit to put their words to the test of action.[10]

At this time the Queen was extremely well-disposed toward that class of female spiritual mediums called *mudang*, and one of them was elevated to the rank of Princess. A Korean, An Hyo-je, who memorialized the king against such practices, was overwhelmed with obloquy and was banished to the island of Quelpart. Min Yong-jun had taken advantage of his high position to add private profit to public usefulness and loud complaints were heard on all sides against him and against others of the same name. Insurrections of greater or less degree occurred in different parts of the country and it seemed as if Korea were on the verge of anarchy. It can hardly be gainsaid that this state of affairs was the legitimate outcome of pro-Chinese agitation and was directly in line with immemorial custom in China. Nothing could be truer than that Korea needed reforming. The government found it necessary to deal with great severity in some cases. Four prefects were taken to the center of the city and publicly beaten and then banished. Even Min Yong-jun had to go through the form of punishment in this public way, for the people of the capital were so incensed against him that an insurrection seemed imminent unless they were appeased. The Songdo people revolted against the extortion that was practiced against them but they were overcome and their ginseng was taken away from them by Kim Se-geui, the right hand man of Min Yong-jun.

Late in the year the Tong-hak made a startling proclamation which they secretly nailed to the gate of the governor's yamen in Chŭn-ju. It called upon all right-minded men to join in the march on the capital and the extirpation of the foreigners. This seemed more tangible than the former rumors and foreign men-of-war began to congregate at Chemulpo for the protection of their nationals in Seoul. Hundreds of Japanese left the city and hurried to Chemulpo for safety. A force of Korean infantry marched southward to head off the revolutionists but they were easily defeated and their arms and accoutrements fell into the hands of the enemy.

It was quite evident that the Korean government was without the means or the men to cope with such determined opposition. This deplorable state of things was looked upon by Japan with some uneasiness. Korea seemed to be coming more and more under Chinese influence and in the same proportion her internal management became more corrupt. Japan regarded Korea as an independent power and was determined to see that independence upheld." This feeling on the part of Japan was sharply accentuated when in the spring of 1894 a Korean detective, Hong Chong-u, succeeded in gaining the confidence of Kim Ok-kyun who was living at Tokyo as a political refugee. He was induced to accompany his betrayer to Shanghai where, in a hotel, his betrayer shot him down in cold blood. The Chinese government condoned the dastardly deed and sent the assassin, together with the body of his victim, to Korea in a Chinese gunboat. The body of Kim Ok-kyun was dismembered on April fourteenth in a most brutal manner and the different portions of his body were sent about the country as a warning to traitors. This lapse into the worst excesses of the old regime opened the eyes of Japan to the actual situation and gave her just the impetus she needed to take the strong position which she did later. Soon after this the Tong-hak took the town of Chŭn-ju and defeated all the government troops sent against them. The governor of the province, Kim Mun-hyŭn, made his escape from the place. 12

The government had at last become convinced of its inability to cope with its enemies single-handed and it determined to have recourse to the dangerous policy of asking China to throw troops into the peninsula to aid in putting down the Tong-hak uprising. China immediately complied and on June sixth 1,500 Chinese troops were embarked at Tientsin and were sent to Chemulpo under the escort of three gunboats.

It must be remembered that according to the third article of the Tientsin Convention China and Japan each agreed not to send troops into Korea without first notifying the other. In this case the Chinese failed to notify the Japanese until after the departure of the troops and there can be no doubt that at this point lies the strength of Japan's contention. When, later, the Chinese agreed to leave Korea simultaneously with the Japanese the latter naturally refused. The Chinese broke the convention first ; they must leave first. But there were other important points involved. Korea was rapidly losing all semblance of independence and Japan was being jeopardized. The Chinese abrogation of the treaty gave Japan just the excuse she wanted for throwing troops into Korea and compelling those reforms which she believed could be effected in no other way. No sooner was she informed of China's action than the Japanese Minister Otori, then on leave of absence, was recalled, and sent immediately to Seoul with 400 marines, arriving June ninth.

The Chinese force did not approach the capital but landed at Asan some eighty miles south of Seoul. This force was soon augmented till it amounted to 2,000 men. But Japan was not idle. By the twelfth of June she had approximately 8,000 troops in Korea. Matters stood thus when the news came that the Tong-hak, either frightened by the rumor of the approach of a Chinese army or being pressed by the government troops, had suddenly retired and the south was at peace. This tended to hasten a crisis between the Chinese and Japanese. There was no longer any cause why foreign troops should remain in the peninsula. The Chinese had come to put down the Tong-hak and the Japanese had come ostensibly to protect their nationals. Now that the Tong-haks had retired it did not take long to discover the real reasons underlying the actions of the Japanese. On June 16th she landed 3,000 more troops at Chemulpo and matters began to look so serious in Seoul that all the Chinese residents hastened away from the city and sought safety by embarking for China. About a thousand people thus made a hasty exit from the country.

On June 25th the Russian, British, French and American representatives in Seoul, in the interests of peace, jointly requested the Chinese and Japanese to simultaneously withdraw. But the Chinese refused to go until the Japanese did and the Japanese refused to go until reforms had been introduced which would clear the political atmosphere and give some semblance of truth to the fiction of Korean independence. The Korean government was thrown into consternation when on June 28th the Japanese Minister demanded a formal statement from Korea as to whether she were an independent state or not. She replied that she was an independent power.

Early in July the Japanese Minister handed the government a list of the reforms which it deemed necessary. As they were all incorporated in the reforms inaugurated a little later it is unnecessary to enumerate them here. Fifteen thousand Japanese troops had by this time landed on Korean soil and the capital was thoroughly invested. The prospects of peace seemed to be growing smaller each day. The people of Seoul fled in large numbers leaving their houses and all their effects except such as could be carried on their backs. Such was the terror that the very name of the Japanese inspired.

On July 20th the Japanese Minister sent an ultimatum to

the king complaining of the introduction of Chinese troops whose coming was undeniably to protect a dependent state. He gave the king three days to accept Japanese reforms. If within that time he did not accede to them they would be enforced. On the night of the 22nd the king returned an evasive answer and this decided the immediate policy of the Japanese. On the following morning two battalions of Japanese troops, feigning to start out for Asan, turned suddenly and marched on the palace. They met with a certain weak show of resistance at the gates but easily forced their way in and soon had the king in their care. Every member of the Min faction was forthwith driven out and the Prince Tai-wŭn was called in to assume a leading part in the management of the government.

By this time China and Japan were hurrying troops into the peninsula, the former by way of Asan aad the latter by Fusan and Chemulpo. On July 21st eleven steamers left Taku for Asan and the mouth of the Yalu with 8,000 troops. Those that came to Asan were ostensibly for the purpose of aiding the government in the putting down of the Tong-hak. The Japanese government was immediately apprised of the departure of the transports from the Peiho and on July 25th the Akitsushima, Yoshino and Naniwa, among the best of the Japanese navy, were ordered from Sasebo to Asan. Two days later at six-thirty they encountered the Chinese men-of-war Tsi-yuen and Kwang-ki in the vicinity of P'ung Island off Asan.

The Japanese were not aware of the sudden turn which affairs had taken in Seoul but the Chinese were, and they expected the Japanese to take the offensive. The Japanese became aware of the situation only when they found the Chinese did not salute and that they were cleared for action. The Japanese speedily put themselves in fighting trim. As the channel narrowed and the vessels came within range the Chinese opened fire and were answered with terrible effect by the Japanese. The Kwang-yi was speedily disabled and beached. The Tsi-yuen, her bow-gun being disabled, withdrew toward Wei-hai-wei. It is disputed as to which side began firing first but it is quite immaterial. The fact that the Chinese knew what had occurred at Seoul, that they were cleared for action and that they failed to salute would seem to throw the burden of proof upon them.

While the Yoshino was pursuing the Tsi yuen, two more ships appeared on the horizon. They proved to be the Chinese dispatch boat Tsao-kiang and the British steamer Kowshing carrying about 1,500 Chinese troops. The Akitsushima took the former in charge and the Naniwa took the latter. The Naniwa signalled the transport to follow her, but the Chinese on board of her would not let the English Captain obey. Two parleys were held but the Chinese officers were obdurate and would not listen to reason. When it became apparent that the Chinese were bent upon self-destruction the Naniwa turned her battery upon her and blew her up. More than a thousand of the Chinese troops were drowned. A large number were picked up and held as prisoners of war. The sinking of the Kowshing has been judged as hasty but the situation was a peculiar one. The Chinese would neither surrender nor follow. They were plentifully supplied with small arms and could keep a boarding party at bay effectually. The better judgment of second thought proves that the Japanese were fully justified in their action.

The results of the P'ung incident became apparent at once. It made neutrals more careful, it proved that the sea was dangerous ground for the Chinese, it kept over a thousand men from landing at Asan and it proved beyond the shadow of a doubt that Japan was fully in earnest and would fight to the bitter end. Moreover it changed the whole plan of campaign for China. The Tong-hak were forgotten and the co-operation of the force at the Yalu and that at Asan and a joint attack upon the Japanese was the plan determined upon by the Chinese.

The Japanese forces in and about Seoul were now ready for a land campaign. It was wisely determined to eliminate from the problem all the Chinese forces south of Seoul before advancing against those in the north along the Ta-dong River. The army in the north was being watched by mounted spies. For the time being there was no danger to be apprehended from these troops in the north but the two thousand at Asan, if reinforced, might advance on the capital and make trouble unless they were dispersed once and for all. Accordingly on the twenty-fifth of July Gen. Oshima started for Asan with the greater part of the troops in Seoul. The march was rapid.

On the way the news of the P'ung incident was received and applauded. The vicinity of Asan was reached in three days. As the Japanese approached, the Chinese retreated a short distance to a point which they could easily fortify. On the twenty-eighth the Japanese army arrived within five miles of this position. A night attack was determined upon by Gen. Oshima. It was not explained to the army until midnight when it was aroused and informed of the intended movement. The advance was made in two divisions. The right wing, four companies of infantry and one of engineers under Lieutenant-colonel Tadeka, sought the enemy's left. The left wing under Gen. Oshima, and comprising nine companies of infantry, one battalion of artillery and one company of cavalry, swept forward in the dark to attack the flank and rear of the enemy's right.

It would have been a difficult undertaking even by daylight but in the dark it was fourfold more trying. The Chinese outposts in the neighboring village gave the signal, and, posted among the houses, offered a stubborn resistance. The assaulting column was repulsed and was compelled to lie down to hold the ground already taken. At last however the Chinese had to withdraw. They crowded slowly out into the neighboring rice fields.

This preliminary struggle was followed by a brief breathing space. It had lasted less than an hour but had proved a stiff encounter. At five the Japanese attached the redoubts. The left wing now came into action and under the smoke of the artillery the troops stormed the forts at either extremity. In half an hour the Chinese were dislodged and the rising sun looked down upon its flaming image on Japanese banners flying victoriously from the Chinese ramparts.

The escape of the Chinese general, Yeh Chi-chao has given ground for the alleged Chinese victory at A-san. It often happened during the Japan China war that, unless the Chinese force was almost utterly annihilated, they claimed a victory. It it still a puzzle to many, however, that in the Asan skirmish as well as in the battle of the Yalu the victorious Japanese permitted even a remnant of the enemy to escape. Although thoroughly defeated Gen. Yeh brought a remnant of his force around the city of Seoul and arrived safely at P'yŭng-yang, undoubtedly a difficult and brilliant movement.

This first battle won by Japan in a foreign land, for a period of three centuries, illustrated two points. Not only had the Japanese soldiers learned their lesson from instructors but the officers proved themselves worthy of the steadfastness of the men under them. One man out of every twelve killed was an officer. Nor, when elated by the victory, did the Japanese forget the ends for which they were working. They did not undertake any further subjugation of the south, not even attempting to exterminate the Tong-haks. It was the Chinese in the peninsula with whom they were measuring swords. The forces at A-san being destroyed or dispersed and danger from that quarter was consequently removed, and the banners of rising sun turned northward.

The northern division of the Chinese army, which had been landed on Korean soil near the mouth of the Yalu River and had advanced southward from that point, had now held the city of P'yŭng-yang for upwards of a month. In anticipation of a Japanese advance they had fortified it as best they knew how, but as is usual with Chinese they had forgotten to guard their rear. On three occasions in this war they were attacked in their unprotected rear and utterly routed.

During the second week of August the commander of the Japanese fleet, Admiral Ito, with twenty men-of-war took a cruise into the mouth of the Gulf of Pechili. The feint had its desired effect, though wholly misunderstood by the world at large. It attracted the attention of the Chinese and transport after transport made its way safely across from Japan to Korea with its complement of troops.

On August tenth Major Ichinohe with the vanguard started northward from Seoul. It was the first step toward Peking. Songdo was reached the following day. The next few days were spent in reconnoitering the Ta-dong River, but this part retired eventually to Song-do and there awaited reinforcements.

On the nineteenth Lieutenant-general Nodzu arrived from Japan with the reinforcements for which Gen. Oshima had been growing impatient. The latter immediately forwarded a detachment by another route toward P'yŭng-yang.

This was ordered to occupy an important position known as Sak Pass and was reinforced on September eighth by a battalion of infantry and a company of artillery. This became known as the Sak Division.

On the twenty-third Gen. Oshima set out from Seoul for the north with a Mixed Brigade. This was the name given to the Japanese army which participated in all the operations in the peninsula, so called because it was made up of various portions of the grand army. On the twenty-fifth Oshima joined the forces at Song-do, A few days before this Gen. Tadzumi had landed at Cl emulpo and had been put in command of the Sak Divison. On the twenty-sixth another division under Gen. Sato landed at Wun-san on the east coast nearly opposite P'yŭng-yang, and was immediately put under the command of Gen. Nodzu. This is best known as the Wun-san (Gensan) Division.[3

These three bodies of troops slowly converged upon P'yŭng yang by three routes, and made as if they were about to surround the entire city. But the commanders knew the weak point in Chinese tactics too well to begin trying new methods.

P'yŭng-yang was fortified beyond the expectations of the Japanese and it should have held out indefinitely. The Tadong River flows before its walls giving it defense on the south. On the north stands a high eminence called Peony Mountain. To the west there are no special natural defenses. The plan of attack was to take advantage of the proverbial Chinese weakness, make a feint in the front but send the main body of troops around the city and attack in the rear. The capture of P'yŭng-yang was very much like that of Quebec. The plan of attack was the same in each case. The Japanese made a feint in front of the town as Wolfe did from the shores of Levis, and sent the real attacking party around behind the town. The capture of Peony Mountain like the capture of the Heights of Abraham determined the struggle.

On the morning of the fifteenth the Japanese army was in position. The Sak and Gensan divisions lay before Peony and the other five heights to the north of the city. The Mixed Brigade lay beyond the river along the Seoul road which led by six fortified redoubts to the bridge of boats before the

River Gate of the town. The main body had crossed the river at Iron Island below the city and under cover of the cannonading of the Mixed Brigade had crept nearer and nearer the enemy from the west—the rear.

At half past four on the morning of the fifteenth a terrific cannonading was begun. Under cover of this the Sak Division took the fort nearest the river, on the northeast of the city. At the same time the Gensan Division took by assult the fort at the other end, on the north. From its vantage ground the Gensan Division planted its guns and poured a destructive fire on Peony Mountain. The Chinese commander being killed, the defenders became discouraged and demoralized and this strategic position was carried by the Sak Division by a single assault. The guns of the enemy, being turned upon the city from the summit of this hill, determined the contest. The main body trained its guns on the fifteen redoubts which guarded the western approach and thus cut off all hope of retreat from the city.

While the Japanese were having it all their own way on the north and west the Mixed Brigade across the river was suffering severely. Five Chinese forts guarded this main approach to P'yŭng-yang. The Japanese troops, though ordered to make merely a feint, were carried away by the inspiration of the hour and rashly attempted to capture these forts by assault, but they were greatly outnumbered and were compelled at last to retire having lost heavily. But the fall of Peony Mountain settled the day, and that night the Chinese soldiers, following in the wake of their despicable commanders sought safety in flight toward the Yalu by such avenues as the Japanese left open for them. It is generally believed that the Japanese purposely left open a loophole of escape, not caring to have so many prisoners on their hands.

The feint made by Admiral Ito during the first week in August has been mentioned. During the P'yŭng-yang campaign the Japanese fleet had been patrolling the Yellow Sea about the Korean archipelego. Finally the last company of Japanese troops were landed on Korean soil and the order was given, "On to Peking." Never was an invasion undertaken with such relish since the days when, three centuries before, the hordes of Hideyoshi had landed on the coast of

Korea and raised this same cry. The outcome now was destined to be far different from that of the former invasion.
Marshall Yamagata arriving in Korea on Sept. 12th with
10,000 reinforcements began the new campaign as Commander-in-chief.

During the P'yŭng-yang egagement the Japanese fleet
had been stationed at the mouth of the Ta-dong River, forty
miles from the scene of the battle, ready to be used in any
emergency. On the sixteenth, the campaign in Korea being
settled by the flight of the Chinese army toward the Yalu,
the main and first flying squadrons weighed anchor and departed for the supposed scene of Chinese activity at the mouth
of the Yalu, where it was believed that Chinese troops were
being landed. Two days previous 4,000 Chinese troops had
left Taku to reinforce the new army, being gathered on the
banks of the Yalu for an invasion of Korea. The transports
which contained this detachment were protected by six
cruisers and four torpedo boats and were reinforced at Talien
Bay by the Peiyang squadron. On the sixteenth the transports landed their burden and on the following day departed
again for Taku, attended, as on the trip over, by six cruisers
and the Peiho squadron.

On the same morning the Japanese fleet crossed the path
of the returning transports. At nine oclock the smoke of the
Chinese fleet was first discovered and about twelve the fleet
came into full view. The battle opened with the main and
flying squadrons leading in a single line across the track of
the Chinese fleet, which was advancing at half the pace set by
the enemy. This formation, the ironclads in the center and
the weakest ships on either wing, had been assumed as soon
as it appeared that the Japanese line was coming head on as
if to pierce the Chinese fleet. At a range of 5,200 meters
the battle was opened by the starboard barbette of the iron-
clad Ting-yeun. The whole fleet soon joined in the fight
but the Japanese did not answer for some minutes. As the
Yoshino came on, the course was changed and the enemy
was passed from left to right. The comparatively helpless
ships of the right flank received the severest fire. The two
old cruisers on the extreme right, which were of wood and
very inflamable, at once took fire and were thenceforth use-

less. The Yang-wei took fire at the outset and retired. The Chao-yung was not more fortunate and sank about half past two, the battle having begun at one P.M. Japanese time.

Two of the twelve Chinese ships were thus disposed of at once. Two more, the Tsi-yuen and Kwang-chia, deserted the battle immediately on various excuses and departed for Port Arthur.

When the Japanese line had passed the Chinese fleet the flying squadron had begun to port, when the two Chinese ships, which until then had remained in the mouth of the Yalu, were seen making their way toward the remainder of the fleet. Instantly the flying squadron began to starboard and the oncoming vessels prudently retired. These two ships, the Kwan-ping and Ping yuen, not having come into action, and two, the Yang-wei and Chao-yung, having retired from the battle in flames, and two, the Tsi-yuen and Kwan-chia, having deserted, we find six ships of 23,000 tons bearing the brunt of the battle.

When the flying squadron began to starboard, the main squadron, which was following in fine order, kept to port. The feint against the Kwan-ping and Ping-yuen proving successful, the flying squadron kept to starboard and followed the main squadron. Soon, however, it was seen that the slower vessels of the main squadron were being left exposed and Admiral Ito signalled for the flying squadron to starboard again and intervene between the distressed vessels and the enemy. Thus the main and flying squadrons moved about the Chinese fleet in opposite directions, the former on the inner track.

This second round proved a severe one for the Chinese fleet. The contest now assumed a desperate phase. During the opening of the struggle attention on either side had been paid to the enemy's weaker ships. The two slow and defenseless ships of the Japanese fleet, the Akagi and Saikio, caused the Admiral much trouble, if indeed they did not alter entirely his plan of attack. That he brought them out of the battle at all is a great credit to his ability to manoeuver at short notice and under fire. It is, however, inexplicable that such ships were allowed to follow the main squadron into the engagement.

By two o'clock the ranks of the two struggling fleets were considerably thinned out and the battle became simplified though more desperate than ever, as the main squadron began to close in on the powerful iron-clads and as the flying squadron separated the remainder of the Chinese fleet from their only hope of safety and scattered them broadcast over the sea. The Akagi was now out of the fight and, under the protection of the flying squadron, was making for the Ta-dong River. The Hiyei, also disabled and protected by the main squadron, was making for the same destination. The Saikio having come as it were from the very jaws of death, when attempting to attack the burning Yang-wei, lay between the object of her deadly mission and the fleets, watching how the battle fared.

On the Chinese side there was far more destruction, because of the larger number of slow and inflamable ships. Of the total, two, the Tsi-yuen and Kwan-chia, had long since deserted as we have already said. The Yang-wei and Chao-yung were both desperately burning. The Chih-yuen, having passed from the Admiral's wing to the right wing, had attempted the most ridiculous feat of attacking the flying squadron as the latter come to relieve the Akagi and Saikio. Being severely hit in her foolhardy course, her commander, evidently as revenge for going under, attempted to ram. The guns of the fleet were instantly brought to bear upon the ill-starred ship and, riddled with the fire of the heavy and machine guns alike, she went under, flinging her crew into the air as she listed the last time. A similar fate overtook the Ping-yuen upon whom the flying squadron bore. A terrible fire from the Yoshino riddled her burning hulk and she too, went down like a monstrous bonfire into the tawny waters of Yellow Sea.

Meanwhile the struggle between the two iron-clads and the Japanese main squadron had been raging until both the contestants were nearly exhausted. The former, knowing well that in them rested China's only hope on the sea, and equally desperate because of the cowardliness and incompetency displayed throughout the battle by their own comrades as well as by the determined wrath of their ancient foe, fought to their last charge save three with undaunted heroism. Nothing in the conflict which raged so many hours could have equalled the sight of the crews of the two battered iron-clads, their ammunition far spent, meeting the last onslaught of the main squadron as it bore down upon them for the last time on that memorable afternoon, with perfect calm and a purpose to go down with the ships when the ammunition gave out.

The last onslaught was made and met, but before another could be made night had begun to fall and the Japanese, themselves not far from exhaustion, deemed it wise to withraw. This battle has been called a Japanese victory and probably with reason, though according to the dictum of modern naval warfare a decided Japanese victory could have been achieved only by capturing or disabling the two Chinese iron-clads which were the soul of the Chinese fleet. Technically the failure to do this made it a drawn battle, each side retiring unconquered. But there is every reason to believe that this battle, in reality, decided the Japanese supremacy over the Yellow Sea.

The land battle at P'yŭng-yang and the naval battle off the mouth of the Yalu opened the eyes of the world to the fact that Japan was a power to be reckoned with. The incident at P'ung Island and the battle of Ansan had proved nothing except the fact that Japan was fully prepared to go to extremities and that the war was actually begun. It is probable that a majority of intelligent people thought the Japanese would fall an easy victim to the Chinese forces. On the sea China had several war-vessels that far out-matched anything which Japan possessed and on land she had unlimited population from which to recruit her armies. She had enjoyed the assistance of many foreign military and naval men in getting her army and navy into shape, and in addition to this she had the sympathy of Great Britain in the struggle. It was freely predicted that the superior quickness of the Japanese might bring her certain small victories at first but that as time went on and China really awoke to the seriousness of the situation a Chinese army would be put in the field which would eventually drive the Japanese off the mainland. The Japanese invasion of 1592 was cited to show that though momentarily successful, the Japanese would be ultimately defeated.

The battles of P'yŭng-yang and Yalu changed all this. In the first place it was discovered that the Chinese, with equal or superior numbers, could not hold a strongly defensive position against their assailants. The Chinese had everything in their favor so far as natural surroundings went. They lacked the one essential and it was the demonstration of this lack at P'yŭng-yang that made the world begin to doubt whether the Chinese would really do what was expected of them.

The battle of the Yalu, while technically a drawn battle, proved that the Japnese could stand up against superior ships and hold them down to a tie game. The Chinese ammunition was exhausted and if darkness had not come on the Japanese would have discovered this and the big Chinese vessels would have been captured. From that day the progress of the Japanese was an unbroken series of victories. The myth of China's strength was shattered and the whole history of the Far East, if not of the world, entered upon a new and unexpected phase.

We have already mentioned that 4,000 Chinese troops had been landed at the mouth of the Yalu to reinforce the army that had been gathered there for the invasion of Korea. That invasion was destined not to be carried out, for the routed Chinese army from P'yŭng-yang came streaming north in headlong flight and the Japanese followed them up just fast enough to worry them but without making it necessary to encumber themselves with prisoners. It shows how perfectly the Japanese had gauged the calibre of the Chinese that they should have driven them on in this contemptuous manner. When the Japanese arrived at the Yalu they found that the Chinese had occupied an advantageous position on the further side and would attempt to block the advance but it was too late to stem the tide of Japanese enthusiasm. The passage was made with ease, the Chinese quickly put to flight and the war left Korean territory, not to return.

The subsequent operations of war are of surpassing interest to the general historian but they cannot be called a part of Korean history, so we shall be compelled to leave them and go back to the peninsula, where the results of Japan's victories were to be keenly felt.

Chapter XVIII.

The year 1894 marked the greatest crisis in Korean history since the seventh century, when the kingdom of Silla
gained control of the whole peninsula. Considering the fact
that so many of the old abuses survived after the year 1894,
the above statement may seem extreme but the facts of the
case warrant it. From the early years of the Christian era
Korea had been moulded by Chinese ideas and had been
dominated by her influence. There was no time from the
very first when Korea did not consider China her suzerain.
In a sense this was natural and right. Korea had received
from China an immense number of the products of civilization.
Literature, art, science, government, religion—they had all
been practically borrowed from China. It is a thing to be mar-
velled at that Korea through all these centuries has preserved
any semblance of individualism. She never would have
done so if there had not been a radical and ineffacable difference between the Chinese and the Korean which no amount
of moulding could remove.[4]
Never once during all those centuries did Korea attempt
or desire to throw off the garment of her vassalage. And
even in this crisis of 1894 it was not thrown off through any
wish of the Korean government or people but only through
hard necessity. There had been no radical change in the
mental attitude of the great mass of Koreans which demanded
the severing of the tie which bound them to China and even
at this year of grace 1904, there is every reason to believe
that a great majority of Koreans would elect to go back under
the mild and almost nominal control of China. The change
is not one of attitude on the part of the Korean but it is the
fact that the war proved to the world the supineness of China

and made it forever impossible to revive her claim to suzerainty over Korea or even, it is to be feared, to hold together her own unwieldy bulk. The outward influence of China upon Korea has ceased and other influences have been at work which are slowly drawing her away from her servile obedience to Chinese ideals. This was the first necessary step to the final emancipation of Korea and her national regeneration. It should be carefully noted that from the earliest centuries the Chinese implanted in the Korean no genuine seed of civilization and progress but simply unloaded upon her some finished products of her civilization. These the Koreans swallowed whole without question, unmindful of the fact that by far the greater part of them were wholly unsuited to the Korean temperament. The result was that as time went on these Chinese impositions were overlaid with a pure Korean product just as the little leaden Buddhas that are thrust into the shell of the pearl oyster become coated over with mother-o'pearl. Buddhism came from China but Korea has so mingled with it her native fetichism and animism that it is something radically different from the original stock.

Now this intrinsic freedom of the Korean from Chinese ideals argued strongly in favor of the belief that from the year 1894 Korea would gradually cast off even the mental vassalage and would begin to work along individual lines. This could happen only in case the individualism of the Korean had outlasted the deadening effects of Chinese predominance. There are many evidences that this individualism has survived but it must be confessed that it is in a crippled condition and all but unable to walk alone. It is to the process and method of this great transformation in Korean conditions that we must now turn.

Up to the time when the Japanese began active operations in Seoul by the seizure of the palace, Korea considered herself safe under the aegis of China. Had she not secured the murder of Kim Ok-kyun and the return of his body on a Chinese vessel for the purpose of wreaking upon it the old time vengeance? Had she not invited Chinese troops into the country in direct contravention of the agreement between China and Japan? In every way and by every means Korea had expressed her contempt of Japanese power and of

Japanese interests. Under the hideously corrupt regime of such men as Min Yong-jun the country had been going from bad to worse until the people found it utterly impossible to endure the oppression any longer. The provinces were in a state of anarchy and Yuan Shih-kei, the unscrupulous Chinese 'Resident" in Seoul, stood smilingly by and watched the tragedy without suggesting any remedy for the disease that was destroying the country, but ready to increase the prestige of China in the peninsula by offering troops with which to crush the starving malcontents in the provinces. The condition of things was about as bad as it could be, and it was at this psychological moment that Japan lifted her hand and at a single blow tumbled the Chinese house of cards about their heads.

By the twenty-first of July the situation in Seoul had become unbearable for the Chinese. There was a small Chinese force at Asan but Seoul was occupied by a strong Japanese force and every day the outbreak of hostilities had become more imminent. On the early morning of the 20th Yuan Shih-kei, in a mean little sedan chair, and entirely without escort, made his escape from the city and hastened to Chemulpo, leaving all his nationals to shift for themselves. His flight became known almost immediately and there was a general scramble on the part of the Chinese merchants and other Chinese to escape from the town. When the Chinese Minister left Seoul their interests were put in the hands of the British representative.

On the morning of the 25th the palace was taken and the city walls manned by the Japanese. Min Yong-jun, who was largely responsible for the parlous condition of the government, fled that night to the country, and found refuge in the town of Ch'un-ch'ŭn about sixty miles east of Seoul.

As soon as the Japanese had secured the palace Minister Otori sought the presence of the king and assured him of his personal safety and that of the Royal family. At the desire of His Majesty the ex-Regent, the Tă-wŭn-kun was invited to the palace to participate in the discussion of plans for the future, and to allay by his presence the natural fear of the king. It was understood by common consent

that the former officials had all resigned and it was necessary
to form a new government.   Kim Hong jip was summoned
to act as Prime Minister.   He was a man of strong personality and of progressive tendencies, altogether a valuable man
for the emergency since he had the entire confidence of the
Japanese and was a man of the highest standing in Korea.
Other leading men of progressive tendencies were called in
and a government was formed for temporary purposes
until matters could he put on a firmer footing. Min Yong jun,
Min Eung-sik, Min Hyung sik, Min Ch'i hön, and Kim Se-
geui were declared banished to distant points   No attempt
was made to send and arrest Min Yong-jun but the members
of the "Reighteous Army" in the country seized him and
charged him with being the main author of the disturbances,
and beat him nearly to death.   An enormous amount of
money that he had carried off with him was divided up
and made away with by his followers.   He barely escaped
with his life and fled to China where be gave the Chinese
advice as to the method of reasserting their authority in the
peninsula.

At this same time the government recalled Yi To-jä, Sin
Keui-sŭn, Yun Ung-yŭl and others who had been in banishment for ten years because of their espousal of the liberal
cause in 1884.   The prison doors were opened and innocent
and guilty alike received amnesty.

The government was not yet ready to publish its full
list of reforms, based upon the demands already made by the
Japanese Minister, but the king immediately declared that as it
was necessary to secure good men to administer the Government in Seoul and in the provinces, the demarcation between
the upper and lower classes was a thing of the past and all
men of all grades were eligible to office, and at the same time
he declared the abolition of the great political parties and
forbade the apportionment of government offices along party
lines.   The different leading offices under the government
were put in the hands of the best men that were available
and it is probable that these men formed the best government
that Korea was capable of at the time.   Some of the names
were as follows: Kim Hong-jip, Pak Chöng-yang, Kim Yun-
sik, Kim Chong-han, Cho Heui-yŭn, Yi Yun-yong, Kim Ka-

jin, An Kyŭng-su, Chŏng Kyŏng-wŭn, Pak Chun-yang, Yi Wŭn-gŏng Kim Ha-gu, Kwŭn Yŭng-jin, Yu Kil-jun, Kim Ha-yŭng, Yi Eung-ik, Sŏ Sang jip. Among these names many will be recognized as among the best that Korea has produced in recent times.

On the very next day after the Japanese took the palace and gave a new direction to governmental affairs a special High Commission was called together by the king to consider the matter of reconstructing the government along the new lines. It was composed partly of the members of the Cabinet and partly of other destinguished men. It was well understood that these men were to carry out the ideas of the Japanese authorities. Their deliberations continued for a period of forty-one days during which time they completed a scheme for a new government, along the following lines.

Before this time there had been seven great governmental departments, namely the *Eui-jung-bu* or State Department, *Yi-jo* or Home Department, *Ho-jo* or Finance Department, *Yi-jo* or Ceremonial Department, *Pyŭng-jo* or War Department, *Hyŭng-jo* or Law Department, *Kong-jo* or Department of Public Works. Besides these there were the two *Po-ch'ŭng* or Police offices, the *Eui-gom-bu* or Supreme Court and other lesser offices. In the new regime the seven Departments above named were all retained excepting the Ceremonial Department and in place of this they founded for the first time in Korean history a genuine Educational Department coördinate in dignity with any other of the great Departments. Besides this the Department of Public Works was broadened to include Agriculture and Commerce. A Police Bureau was formed to take the place of the former two Poch'ŭngs.

They also prepared a list of needed reforms in the government.

(1) From this time all Korean documents shall be dated from the year of the present Dynasty. (This was the 503rd year, as the Dynasty was founded in 1392).

(2) Korean treaties with China shall be revised and ministers shall be sent to the various treaty powers.

(3) Class distinctions in Korea shall be wiped out and men shall be judged solely on their merits in the matter of government office.

(4) The distinction between civil and military rank, in favor of the former, shall be done away and they shall stand on an equality.

(5) The family and relatives of a criminal shall not be liable to arrest or punishment for his crime.

(6) The son by a concubine shall be eligible for the succession.

(7) Men shall attain the age of twenty and women the age of sixteen before marriage.

(8) Widows shall be allowed to remarry without loss of social standing.

(9) All slaves are declared free and the sale or purchase of human beings is abolished.

(10) The privilege of memorial is extended to the general public. Anyone shall be at liberty to address the thron through a memorial.

(11) The long sleeves on coats, whether court dress or common are abolished. But officials shall be authorized to wear the sleeveless coat over the ordinary one. Soldiers' uniforms shall continue as at present for a time but may be changed gradually to the foreign style.

(12) The people shall be given one month in which to prepare for these changes.

(13) The Police Bureau shall be an adjunct of the Home Department.

(14) Officials shall not ride on the streets in the high one-wheeled chair nor shall they be accompanied by a large retinue, nor shall the attendants call out for people to clear the way.

(15) No one shall be obliged to dismount when passing an official nor to show any other sign of servility.

(16) The Prime Minister shall have only four attendants, the Vice Prime Minister and all the other ministers of state shall have three, the vice-ministers shall have two and the secretaries one.

(17) Even eunucks, if they are men of ability, shall be eligible for office.

(18) The law that relatives may not sue each other at law shall be abrogated except for very near relatives, and feuds between families shall be given up.

(19) All debts of long standing shall be cancelled (such as debts contracted by a father who is now dead or by relatives).

(20) There shall be but eleven official grades (in place of the eighteen which there had been formerly).

(21) There shall be no longer any outcast class in Korea but butchers, contortionists, acrobats, dancing girls, sorceresses and exorcists shall all be considered equal to others before the law.

(22) Even after holding high office a man may engage in business or other occupation, at his pleasure.

(23) The matter of the national examination shall be reserved for fuller discussion.

It is not necessary to go into an analysis of these proposed reforms. They speak for themselves; some of them were necessary and others were the reverse But they form a striking commentary on the condition of affairs in Korea at the time. Whatever may have been the defects of this plan it was an honest and strenuous attempt on the part of the best statesmen Korea could produce and it promised much. If its terms could have been carried out it would have proved an inestimable blessing to the people of the peninsula, but one can easily see that some of the proposals struck at the very fabric of Korean society. For instance the attempt to make acrobats, dancing-girls and *mudang* the social equals of reputable people was of course absurd. The submerged classes cannot be enfranchised by a stroke of the pen. What Korea needed then and needs still is education. This alone will make fundamental reforms possible.

Early in August the currency of the country received serious attention. Foreign money was in use in the open ports but the general currency of the country consisted of two kinds of perforated "cash," one called *yŭp*, each piece of which was called one cash, and the other called *tang-o* or the "five fitter." These represented five cash each. The *yŭp* was the old, genuine and universally recognized money of the country. It was only in Seoul, the open ports and on the great thoroughfares near Seoul that the *tang-o* circulated. This *tang-o* was a debased coin made in 1883 and several succeeding years. At first each of

the *tang-o* exchanged for five of the *yŭp* but within a few
months the *tang-o* fell to an inevitable discount which increased year by year from 1883 until 1894, when it was
found that they were practically the same.   Successive
issues of the *yŭp* had deteriorated the quality and size of the
coin until it was worth only a fifth of its face value.   For
this reason the Government declared in August that the *yŭp*
and the *tang-o* were on a par and that no distinction should
be made between them.   The fair thing would have been for
the Government to redeem the debased *tang-o* at its face value
but of course no one could expect this under the circumstances.
It had proved an indirect tax upon the people equal to four
fifths its face value.

At the same time the national financiers determined to
place in the hands of the people a foreign style coinage,
and soon a one cent copper piece, a nickel five cent piece
and silver coins of twenty cent and one dollar denominations, which had been in process of manufacture since
1901, were issued.   A few of them had been issued a year
or two before but had not been well received.   Now
they passed current and were used, but it was soon found
that the silver coins were being bought up and hoarded by
wealthy people who placed no faith in banks, and soon not
a single native silver piece could be found anywhere.

It was the intention of the Commission to withdraw from
circulation all the old cash and replace it with the foreign
style money.   How absud this was will be seen at a glance.
There is nothing else that people are so timid about as their
money and the bare idea of making such a sweeping change
was preposterous, but the Japanese were behind all these reforms and, while their intentions were of the best, they made
the serious mistake in this as in other attempted reforms of
hurrying things too fast.

Another important problem attacked by the Reform
Commission was that of the revenue.   It had always been
customary to pay taxes in rice, linen, beans, cotton and a
hundred other commodies, but it was decided now to change
all this and have the revenue turned into cash in the country
and sent up to the capital.   In order to do this it was necessary
to have banking facilities in the provinces and it was planned

to establish a great national bank with branches all over the country.

An attempt was also made to effect an inspection and standardization of all the weights and measures in the country.

It was ordered that every house in the land should have its owner's name and occupation and the number of his family posted in a conspicuous place on his front gate. This was to facilitate the work of postal, police and census officials and agents.

One of the reforms that was carried out was the sending of students abroad to acquire an education.

It was decreed that all land or houses that had been illegally seized by unscrupulous people in power during the past ten years should be restored to their rightful owners. Many officials in Seoul, well known in foreign circles, lost large fractions of their wealth because of this decree.

The policy was adopted of engaging foreign advisers for the various great Departments of State and as a result of this a number of foreigners were employed. Some of them had already been some time in the service of the government.

Chapter XIX.

The Ex-Regent ...The new Cabinet ...the *Tong-hak* pacified... The Tă-wŭn-kun retires .. Japan declares war ...Korea abrogates all treaties with China....Pak Yong-hyo returns....his memorial.... he is pardoned ....Chinese excesses in the north ...new Korean-Japanese treaty....Marquis Saionji visits Seoul ...*Tong-hak* in arms again .. Prince Eui-wha goes to Japan....Count Inouye comes ... amnesty to offenders of 1884 ..Dr. Jaisohn comes ...Army reform ...the privy Council ...the King's Oath.

The Tă-wŭn-kun, the former Regent, was now a prominent factor in the government and the well known strength of his personality did much to give stability to the new regime. The Queen necessarily retired from active participation in politics for the time being and there was apparent promise of better days to come. The new cabinet chosen at this time was a curious mixture of progressive and conservative men. It was composed of Kim Hong-jip, Kim Yun-sik, O Yun-jung, Pak Chöng-yang and An Kyöng-su representing the progressive wing and Min Yong-dal, Sŭ Chŭng-sun, Yi Kyu-wŭn, Yun Yong-gu and Um Se-yŭng representing the conservative wing. Among the secondary officials some were progressive and some conservative. This apparent blending of the various factions was a hopeful sign outwardly but it had no real significance. All were appointed by permission of the Japanese and they worked together only because it was useless to oppose. But the same intrinsic hostility remained and only needed opportunity to manifest itself. It was the calm of repression rather than of genuine reconciliation, and it helped to prove that there is no hope for good government in Korea by Koreans until the country has secured the benefit of genuine education.

These reforms that were proposed had the apparent sanction of His Majesty, as is proved by the fact that after their proposal he called all the high officials to the palace and made them a speech in which he referred to this as a splendid opportunity to make a radical and beneficent change in the government, and laid it as a sacred duty upon the officials to carry out the reforms, and he declared that he, too, would become a new king and do his part in bringing about the desired renovation of the land.

In spite of the previous declaration that the *tong-hak* uprising was at an end there was much unrest especially in the south and the *tong-hak* were really as ready as ever to take the offensive. For this reason the king sent a high official to Kyŭng-sang Province to make an attempt at pacification and told the people that the trouble was because of his own lack of virtue and begged them to be patient a little longer until the reforms could be carried out. The people were pleased, especially with the promise that slavery should be discontinued and that the barriers between the classes should be broken down. The fact that this effort on the part of the king was entirely successful shows that the *tong-hak* were not anarchists or banditti but were merely desperate citizens who required some assurance that certain changes would be made so that life would be bearable.

A word is necessary as to the attitude of the Tă-wŭn-kun toward these reforms. He had been called to the palace and put in a responsible advisory position by the Japanese but he was not the sort of man to hold an empty honor or to pose as a mere figure-head. Several of the proposed reforms were distasteful to him but when he found that his objections carried no weight he retired to his private house in disgust. It took him only a few weeks to discover that his elevation had been merely a formality.

The month of August was an anxious one in Korea. The battle of Asan had been fought on the 28th and 29th of July and it was known that there would be a decisive battle fought at P'yŭng Yang in the near future. Foreign opinion was divided as to the probabilities, some people believing that the Japanese would sweep every thing before them and others being equally sure that the Chinese would win.

But in spite of the state of anxiety and unrest the month of August saw some important results accomplished in civil matters. The Commission on Reforms were at work on their scheme until about the tenth of the month. It was on August 1st that Japan formally declared war on China and a few days later troops began to pour in by way of Chemulpo and join those already here.

It was on August 16 that there occurred the formal act of casting off Chinese suzerainty. On that day the Korean government declared all treaties hitherto signed between itself and China to be abrogated and all political connection between the two countries to be at an end. The Japanese Minister had already on June 28th demanded from the government an expression of its attitude toward China and had received the answer that Korea considered herself an independent power. This was now followed up by a definite diplomatic rupture between the two and, probably forever, the question of Chinese political predominance in the peninsula was disposed of.

It was about the 20th of August that Pak Yong-hyo, the refugee in Japan since his participation in the attempted *coup* of 1884, was brought to Seoul *incognito* by the Japanese. He had long since been declared an arch-traitor by the Korean government, his house had been razed to the ground and his family dispersed. For almost ten years he had enjoyed asylum in Japan and had been treated with great considera- tion by the Japanese who rightly saw in him a man of strong personality, settled convictions and a genuine loyalty to the best interests of his native land. His worst enemies would probably grant that he falls below none in his desire to see Korea prosperous and enlightened. It was the methods adopted that made all the trouble and drove him into exile.

At first he remained in hiding in the Japanese quarter but from that point of vantage he sent a long memorial to the King relating the fact of his high ancestry and the fact that it was purely in the interests of Korea that he participated in the *emeute* of 1884. He had been however, unsuccessful and was branded as a traitor, compelled to fly the country and see his house broken up. Now that the country had fallen upon such critical times and the King had determined to effect a radical change in affairs it was a cause of utmost rejoicing to him and he could not help coming back even though it cost his life. He begged to see the King's face once more, to be allowed to collect and bury the bones of his relatives and be given back his life which had been forfeited. If then the King should wish to use him again he would be at the service of His Majesty.

To this plea the King listened, whether from preference or out of consideration for the Japanese, and replied that the petitioner was forgiven and might resume his former status as a Korean citizen. A number of memorials immediately poured into the palace urging that Pak Yong-hyo be executed as a traitor, but as the decree of pardon had already gone forth these memorials were ignored.

The fall of P'yŭng-yang before the victorious Japanese on September 15-17 and the flight of the Chinese inflicted great sufferings upon the Koreans in the north. The Chinese followed their usual medieval tactics and pillaged right and left. The local magistrates and governors fled to places of safety and the people survived the best they could. The government hastened to send a high official to the north to calm the excitement and counteract the disintegrating effects of the Chinese flight. At the same time the perfect orderli- ness of the Japanese army began to be understood by the

people, and between these two agencies the northern province
speedily settled down to its former status. The city of P'yüng-
yang had been almost deserted by its 60,000 or more of
people and it was many months before the town resumed its
normal status.

As August drew to an end the Japanese deemed the time
ripe for completing the purposed union with Korea and on
the 26th there appeared a provisional treaty between the two
countries, which was not an offensive and defensive alliance
but one in which Japan guaranteed the independence of
Korea and Korea engaged to look to Japan for advice and to
aid her in every possible way. The nature of this agreement was practically the same as that made between the
same countries at the opening of the Japan-Russia War in
1904. In it Japan once more emphasized the independence
of Korea which she had consistently championed ever since
the Japanese-Korean treaty was signed in 1876.

The month of September opened with the arrival of
Marquis Saionji with presents and a friendly message from
the Emperor of-Japan. The visit was merely a complimentary
one and seems to have been devoid of great political significance.

It was evident that Japanese influence was overwhelmingly predominant in Seoul and as the government had committed itself to the policy of selecting advisers for its various
departments there was reason to believe that most of these
places would be filled by Japanese and that they would so
predominate numerically as to seriously impair the autonomy
of the government. As foreign powers had concluded
treaties with Korea on the basis of equality, this possibility
became a matter of concern to them and through their representatives here they protested against the employment of an
undue number of assistants from any one nationality.
Whether there ever was any such danger as was anticipated
we cannot say, but this preventive measure was successful
at any rate and the apparent independence of the government
was never shaken.

The month of October saw the Chinese driven across
the Yalu and order restored in a measure on Korean soil, but
it also saw the resurgence of the *long-hak* in the south.

These malcontents had been temporarily cowed by the coming
of Chinese and Japanese troops but now they seem to have
discovered that the Chinese and Japanese were too busy with
each other to attend to the civil troubles in the interior of
Korea.   So they broke out much worse than ever and the
principal anxiety of the month in Seoul was the putting
down of the serious insurrection.   Sin Chŭng-heui, the
highest Korean general, was sent south to Kong-ju with
three thousand Korean troops to meet a strong body of
tong-hak who were reported to be marching on Seoul.   A
few days later there was a series of fights at various points
throughout the province, notably at Kong-ju, Ung-jin,
U-gum Hill, Yi-in village, Hyo Harbor, Sö-san and Hong-ju.
About two hundred Japanese troops aided the government
forces and at every point the government troops were successful.   Some of the fights were very severe.   It is probable that there were some 20,000 *tong-hak* in all, but they were
a mere rabble compared with the well armed and at least
partially drilled government troops.   A large number of the
tong-hak leaders were captured and brought to Seoul.   Many
were also executed in the country, for the generals were
given the power of life and death for the time being.

Having been thus dispersed the *tong-hak* moved southward and took their stand at various places in Chulla and
southern Ch'ung-ch'ŭng Provinces.   Their main point was the
town of No-sŭng where for eleven days they continued to revile
the government and put up placards defying the government
troops.   The Korean troops moved on them and soon had them
on the retreat again.   Other encounters took place at various
points but by this time the leading spirits in the *tong-hak*
movement had been captured.   Among these were Chŭn
Nok-tu and Kim Kă-nam.   They were brought to Seoul and
the latter was executed and the former is said to have been
taken to Japan, but there is some doubt as to his fate.   Two
tong-hak leaders named Kim Chŏng-hyŭn and An Seung-
gwan were beheaded at Su-wŭn and their heads were raised
high on poles and the people told to take warning from them.
This put an end to the *tong-hak* except for some small
sporadic movements which amounted to nothing.   But the
tong-hak, like the poor, we have ever with us,—*in posse*.

Prince Eui-wha was sent to Tokyo to return the visit of Marquis Saionji and present the compliments of the King to the Emperor of Japan.

The Japanese government evidently realized the necessity of having an exceptionally strong representation in Seoul, for Count Inouye arrived on the 20th of October and assumed the duties of minister. He had more than once helped to straighten out matters in Korea and he had the confidence of the king and of the people as well. No better appointment could have been made under the circumstances.

The end of October was signalized by the murder of Kim Hak-u, the vice-Minister of Law, who was one of the strongest and best men that the reform movement had brought to the front. He was stabbed at night in his house.

The month of November witnessed some progress in the reconstruction of the government. The pardon of Pak Yong-hyo had been the sign for a general amnesty to all those who had forfeited their rights in 1884. Sŭ Chă-p'il, known better as Dr. Philip Jaisohn, who had been many years in America and had become a naturalized citizen of that country, had come back to Korea quietly and was awaiting an opportunity to make himself useful. Sŭ Kwang-böm had also come back from exile in Japan and others who had been kept sedulously in the background because of their liberal tendencies all came forward and received recognition by the king and were put again in line of political preferment. So rapid was the progress of this movement that by the middle of December the king found himself moved to form a new cabinet composed almost entirely of men who had been foremost in the attempt of 1884, as the following list will show. The Ministers were Kim Hong-jip, Yu Kil-jun, Pak Yong-hyo, Sŭ Kwang-böm, Cho Heui-yŭn, Sin Keui-sŭn, Um Se-yŭng, O Yun-jung, Kim Yun-sik, Pak Chong-yang and Yi Cha-myŭn. At the same time Dr. Jaisohn was employed as adviser to the Privy Council for a term of ten years. 15

This era of change also affected the Korean Army. The various regiments in Seoul, numbering five, had heretofore been under wholly independent and separate commands but now they were all placed in the hands of the War Department, their names were changed and many men were dropped because of age and younger men were appointed in their places. The tactics that had been taught were given up and the Japanese tactics were introduced instead.

We have referred to the Privy Council. This was an advisory board or council composed of some forty men whose business it was to take up and discuss all important government matters, and it was supposed to have a sort of veto power. It exercised this power for about three years but lost it when the Independence Club was overthrown. The entire personnel of this Council was progressive and pro-Japanese. There can be no question that the machinery was now all complete whereby Korea could be governed properly. There was no great obstacle in the way. All that was needed was that no serious blunders should be made and that the Japanese should act firmly but wisely. At the same time there was a strong pressure being exerted behind the scenes in the opposite direction and, as we shall see, not without effect. And so the year 1894 came to a close and the new year opened with great promise of better things to come. On the fifth of the new year the king went to the Ancestral Temple and in the most solemn manner took an oath to carry out the reforms already determined upon and partly inaugurated. It is unnecessary to give this oath in full but only to enumerate the principal points. After a long preamble in which the king declares his intention to uphold the government as an independent one he guarantees specifically that—

(1) All thought of dependence on China shall be put away.

(2) The line of succession and rank in the Royal Family shall be clearly marked.

(3) The King shall attend to public business in person and in consultation with his ministers, and the Queen shall not interfere in government matters.

(4) The affairs of the Royal Household shall be kept quite distinct from the general government.

(5) The duties of Ministers and other officials shall be clearly defined.

(6) Taxes shall be regulated by law and additions to them are forbidden.

(7) The assessment, collection and disbursement of the national revenue shall be in the hands of the Finance Department.

(8) The expenses of the Royal Household shall be reduced, that the example may become a law to the other departments.

(9) An annual budget shall be made out so as to regulate the management of the revenue.

(10) The laws governing local officials shall be speedily revised in order that their various functions may be differentiated.

(11) Intelligent young men shall be sent to foreign countries to study.

(12) A method for the instruction of military officers and a mode of enlistment for soldiers shall be determined upon.

(13) Civil and criminal law must be clearly defined and strictly adhered to and imprisonment and fines in excess of the law are prohibited.

(14) Men shall be employed irrespective of their origin. Ability alone shall determine a man's eligibility whether in Seoul or in the country.

CHAPTER XX.

The ex-Regent's influence ... The queen's influence.... continued reforms ... King adopts new title.... cruel punishments abolished .... Arch demolished.... Yun Chi-ho.... Korea astonished at Japanese victory over Chinese.... Buddhist monks allowed in Seoul.... Yi Chun-yong banished.... Independence Day.... Pak Yong-hyo .... again banished .... American Mining concession .... Count Inouye retires ... cholera.... official change.... Educational reform ... arrival of Viscount Miura.... Japanese policy ... Miura directly implicated in murder of queen.... Inouye not concerned ... Japanese Government ignorant of Miura's plot.

The year 1895 was big with history. Its events created a strong and lasting impression upon the whole Korean people and it is in the light of these events that the whole subsequent history of the country must be interpreted. The

year opened in apparent prosperity.   The king had taken
oath to govern according to enlightened principles and had
exhorted his officials to adhere strictly to the reform program, protesting that if he himself failed to do so it would
be an offence against Heaven.   The Tă-wŭn-gun had retired
from public life but as his son, the brother of the king, was
Minister of the Household and his grandson Yi Chun-yong
held a position near the king, there can be no doubt that in
a private way the Tă-wŭn-gun exercised fully as much influence as he had done while in active office.   It is necessary
to bear in mind that the enmity of the queen against the
ex-Regent extended to the sons of the latter and in spite of
the terms of the king's oath constant pressure was brought
to bear upon the king from that direction.   Whatever be
the reason, we find that in January Yi Chun-yong was sent
to Japan as Korean Minister, an act that was really in favor
of the anti-Regent faction since it temporarily removed one
of the chief actors from the immediate stage.

As the king had sworn to pay personal attention to the
details of government it was deemed advisable to remove the
cabinet meeting place to the palace itself.   Whether this
was in accord with the spirit of the reforms may be doubted,
for it worked directly for the complete centralization of
power which later caused a reversal of the whole governmental policy.

The progress of the so-called reforms went on apace.
The outside, the integuments, were changed, whatever may
or may not have happened in the inner mind.   The long
baggy sleeves which had distinguished the true *yang-ban*
were done away and the side-openings of the long coats were
sewed up.   The width of the hat brims was curtailed and
other minor changes were effected.   A salutary change was
made by putting power into the hands of the ministers of
state to carry out the work of their respective offices according to law without referring every thing to the central government, excepting in very important cases where it affected
other departments.   The immemorial customs regarding the
salutations of inferiors to superiors and *vice versa* were
largely done away and more democratic rules formulated.
The Home Minister undertook to correct many abuses in the

country, to ferret out cases where cultivated land returned no revenue, because of the indirection of the *ajŭns*, and by this means the revenue of the government was very largely augmented.

At the advice of the leading members of the Cabinet His Majesty adopted the title of *Ta-gun-ju Pye-ha* (大君主陛下) in place of his former title of *Chon-ha* (殿下). This elevated him to a position somewhat higher than that of *Wang* (王) but still much lower than the title of emperor which he later assumed. All other members of the Royal Family were likewise elevated one degree.

At this time a radical change was made in the manner of punishing criminals. The cruel forms of execution and of torture which had always prevailed were done away and more humane methods instituted. Decapitation was done away and strangulation substituted. This worked no relief for the criminal but the horrible spectacle of public decapitation was relegated to the past.

A large number of men who had been banished or who had fled the country because of connection with the troubles of 1884 and other years, were pardoned and their relatives were again recognized as eligible to office.

On the native New Year which occurred in February the king issued an important edict saying that office should be given not only to men of noble blood but to others of good character and attainments, and he ordered that such men be selected and sent up from the country as candidates for official position. This was very pleasing to the country people and was hailed as a genuine sign of political renovation. At the same time the ancient arch outside the West Gate was demolished. This arch was the only remaining sign of Chinese suzerainty and its demolition broke the last visible thread which bound Korea to her great patron. We say visible advisedly, for there can be no doubt that the intrinsic loyalty of the vast majority of Koreans to China was still practically unimpaired.

On February thirteenth Yun Chi-ho returned from many years' sojourn in America and China where he had gained a genuine insight into truly enlightened government, and his return to Korea would have been a most happy augury had there been enough enlightened sentiment in the country to form a basis for genuine as distinguisbed from superficial reform.

Meanwhile the Japanese were carrying everything before them in Manchuria and the end had now come. The Korean government therefore sent a special envoy to the Japanese headquarters on the field at Hai-cheng, congratulating them upon their brilliant successes. Soon after this the war terminated with the treaty of Shimonoseki by the terms of which China ceded to Japan southern Manchuria, and the island of Formosa, abjured all interest in Korea and paid an enormous indemnity. The result astonished the Koreans but so strong was the feeling in favor of China that very many still clung to the idea that China would pay the money and then go to work preparing for a much greater struggle with the victorious Japanese.

Since the year 1456 Buddhist monks had been forbidden to enter Seoul. This was part of the general policy of this dynasty to give Buddhism no political foothold. Now the Japanese secured from the government a reinstatement of the Buddhists in their original position and for the first time in four centuries and a half the mendicant monk with his wooden gong and rosary begged on the streets of Seoul.

In April a great misfortune overtook the house of the ex-Regent. His grandson, Yi Chun-yong, nephew to the king, was arrested and charged with having connived with *tonghaks* and others to depose the king and assume the reins of power. It was not shown that Yi Chun-yong had been a main mover in the scheme or that he had even favored the idea, but the very fact that his name had been used in such a connection was enough to send him into banishment on the island of Kyo-dong, off Kang wha. Four other men connected with this affair were executed. This was a severe blow to the ex-Regent and did much to bring him to the point which made possible the terrible events of the following October.

The sixth of June witnessed a great celebration in Seoul, which has gone down in history as Independence Day. A fete was held in the "Old Palace" which exceeded in brilliancy any similar demonstration since the opening of Korea to foreign relations.

It was inevitable that, from the moment of his arrival in Korea, Pok Yong-hyo should be at sword's points with the Tä-wŭn-gun, for the returned refugee represented the radical wing of the reform party, which the ex-Regent had always bitterly opposed; and besides the presence of such a strong man would necessarily subtract from the influence of the aged but autocratic prince. It is probable that the Japanese brought Pak Yong-hyo back to Korea under the impression that he would prove a willing instrument in their hands, but they soon discovered that he had ideas and opinions of his own and that he was working rather for Korea than for Japan. He failed to fall in with some of the plans which would help the Japanese but at the expense of Korea and, in fine, be became something of an embarrassment to his former benefactors. Meanwhile the king and queen were both attached to him, and this for several reasons. He was a near relative of the king and would have no cause for desiring a change in the status of the reigning house; in the second place he was a determined enemy of the Tä-wŭn-gun, and in the third place he was sure to work against a too liberal policy toward the Japanese. This attitude of increasing friendliness between him and the Royal family was a further cause of uneasiness to the Japanese, although Count Inouye himself had done much to win the good will of the queen. Finally Pak Yong-hyo had won the lasting gratitude of the king and queen by exposing the machinations of Yi Chun-yong.

The ex-Regent was determined that Pak Yong-hyo should be gotten out of the way. To this end he concocted a scheme which, with the probable sanction of the Japanese, seemed to promise success. He laid before the king certain grave charges of treason against Pak, which, though not believed either by the king or the queen, convinced them that it would be impossible to shield him from probable destruction; for the people still called him a traitor, the ex-Regent would spare no pains to see him put out of the way and it was evident that the Japanese would not take any strong measures to protect him. The queen called him up and

advised him to make good his escape before action could be
taken on the charge of treason.   He complied and forthwith
escaped again to Japan.   He had not as yet broken with
the Japanese and they were doubtless glad to help him away.
It was early in July that he passed off the stage, perhaps for
ever, and thus there were lost to Korea the services of one of
the most genuinely patriotic Koreans of modern times.   If the
Japanese could have determinedly put the ex-Regent in the
background and allowed Pak Yong-hyo to work out his
plans on terms of amity with the Royal family all the evils
which followed might easily have been averted.   It was this
act, as we believe, of allowing the ex-Regent to carry out
his scheme of personal revenge that caused the whole trouble
and there never was a time, before or since, when brighter
hopes for Korea were more ruthlessly sacrificed.

　　But progressive measures kept on apace and during July
the government issued new and important mining, quarantine
and army regulations and organized a domestic postal system.
A valuable mining concession in the district of Un-san in the
north was granted to an American syndicate, a transaction
that has proved the most profitable, at least to the foreigner,
of any attempt to open up the resources of Korea.

　　Near the end of the month Korea suffered the misfortune of seeing Count Inouye retire from the Legation in
Seoul and return to Japan.   Never did the Japanese have
such need of a strong and upright man in Seoul and never
had a Japanese Minister in Seoul opportunity for greater
distinction.   There are those who believe that he despaired
of accomplishing anything so long as the two opposing factions in Seoul were led by personalities so strong and so im-
placable in their mutual hatred as the queen and the ex-
Regent.   It is not unlikely that he felt that until one or
other of these should be permanently removed from the field
of action there could be no real opportunity for the renovation of Korea.   This by no means implies that he desired
such removal to be effected by forcible means but it is not
unnatural to suppose that he must have given expression to
the conviction as to the futility of doing anything under
existing conditions in the peninsula.   There have been some
who have believed that the Japanese authorities in Tokyo

determined upon the removal of the obstacle in Seoul by any means in their power. Subsequent events gave some color to this surmise but we cannot and do not believe that the Japanese government was a party to the plot which ended in the tragedy of the following October but that a fanatical and injudicious Japanese Minister to Korea privately gave his sanction to an act which the Japanese government would have sternly forbidden had they been consulted.

The summer of 1895 witnessed the first serious epidemic of cholera in Korea since the far more destructive one of 1886. Special plague hospitals were erected in Seoul and in spite of their temporary and inadequate nature the foreign protestant missionaries of Seoul, who were in charge, accomplished very much in the way of local relief. It is impossible to say what the total mortality in Seoul was, to say nothing of the country at large, but it is probable that ten or twelve thousand people died in the Capital before the subsidence of the epidemic.

The forces which worked to the expulsion of Pok Yong-hyo also operated to curtail the term of banishment of Yi Chun-yung who was recalled from Kyo dong Island on August 6th, but even the ex-Regent could not secure the residence of his grandson in Seoul, so he sent the young man to Japan, since which time he has been numbered with the political refugees and has never been able to think of returning to his native land. After the departure of Count Inouye, who had enjoyed the partial confidence of the queen, the ex-Regent's prospects improved to such an extent that several of the ministers of state who were well affected toward Her Majesty were removed and others substituted; especially significant was the removal of the king's brother Yi Chä-myŭn from the Ministry of the Household. As he was the son of the ex-Regent, this would seem to be a defeat for that faction but, in fact, his removal from that position was a necessary step to the carrying out of the dangerous plot which was already being formulated in the mind of the queen's determined enemy.

This summer, which witnessed so many curious contradictions, was further distinguished by a determined effort in the line of education. The Educational Department projected a Normal school and a beginning was made. One hundred and seventeen young men were sent to study in Japan and other measures of lesser importance were carried out.

On the first day of September Viscount Miura arrived from Japan to assume the duties of Minister. Over a month had elapsed since the departure of Count Inouye. The Viscount was an entuhsiastic Buddhist and evidently belonged to the old rather than the new Japan. He was, withal, a strenuous man and is said to have considered the settlement of the Korean difficulties merely a matter of prompt and vigorous action. At the time of his arrival the ex-Regent was living at his summer-house near the river and from the very first he was in close relations with the new Japanese Minister. It was quite evident that the latter had espoused the cause of the ex-Regent as against the queen and that instead of trying to close the breach which was constantly widening between these two powerful personages he was preparing to make use of this estrangement to further what he supposed to be the interests of Japan. Min Yong-whan, the most powerful of the queen's friends, was sent to America as Minister; and everything was ready for the *coup* which had undoubtedly been determined upon. From the mass of conflicting evidence, charge and counter charge, it is difficult to escape the following conclusion. There were two different policies held by political parties in Japan as to the best way to handle the Korean question; one was what we may call the radical policy which advocated strong measures and the instant and complete overthrow of all opposition to the will of Japan in the peninsula; the other, or conservative, policy looked to the attainment of the same object by gradual and pacific means. It seems that the failure of Count Inouye to accomplish anything definite in the line of a settlement of internal dissentions at Seoul resulted in the appointment of Viscount Miura as an exponent of the extreme radical policy. He was supposed to do prompt work but what that work would be perhaps neither he nor his constituency saw clearly before his arrival on the sceue. It would be going much too far to say that the assassination of the queen was once thought of, and yet it is more than likely that those

most conversant with conditions in Seoul felt that by some
means or other her enormous influence must be permanently
checked and that affairs must be so managed that she should
have nothing more to do in the handling of questions of
state.   How this was to be accomplished neither Miura nor
any of his advisers knew until he came and looked over the
field.

For this reason it is easy to see how the ex-Regent would
be the first man in Korea with whom the Japanese Minister
would wish to consult, and it is certain that the Tă-wŭn-gun
would have but one word to say as to the solution of the
difficulty.   His experience of twenty years had convinced
him that there was only one way to accomplish the object
which the Minister had in view and while Viscount Miura
naturally shrunk from adopting that course it would seem
he too was at last convinced that it was the only feasible
plan.   That he actually advised it in the first instance we do
not believe, but that he fell in with the plan which others
suggested and which they offered to carry through without
his personal intervention there can be no doubt whatever.
Nor can there be any question as to where the responsibility
for the tragedy rests; not with the Japanese Government,
surely, except in-so-far as its appointment of such a man to
the difficult post of Minister to Seoul may reflect upon its
wisdom.

It has sometimes been hinted that Count Inouye upon
his return to Japan advocated some such policy as that
which was carried out by Marquis Miura but there is nothing
to indicate that this is other than a libel, for the whole
career of that able statesman gives the lie to such suspicions
and his dispatches to his government show the very opposite
spirit from that intimated in these slanderous reports.   For
instance we have the extract from his reports read in the
Japanese Parliament in which he says :

On one occasion the queen observed to me, "It was a
matter of extreme regret to me that the overtures made by
me toward Japan were rejected.   The Tă-wŭn-gun, on the
other hand, who showed his unfriendliness toward Japan,
was assissted by the Japanese Minister to rise in power."
In reply to this I gave as far as I could an explanation of
these things to the queen and after allaying her suspicions I

further explained that it was the true and sincere desire of the emperor and government of Japan to place the independence of Korea on a firm basis and in the meantime to strengthen the Royal House of Korea. In the event of any member of the Royal family, or indeed any Korean, attempting treason against the Royal House, I gave the assurance that the Japanese Government would not fail to protect the Royal House even by force of arms.

This unequivocal promise of protection was made by Count Inouye just before his departure for Japan and we do not and cannot believe that he expressed anything but his honest sentiments and those of the government that was back of him. It has been urged that the action of the Japanese Government in acquitting Viscount Miura in the face of the evidence given proves the complicity of that government in the outrage and its previous knowledge that it was to be perpetrated, but this does not necessarily follow. That government was doubtless unwilling to stultify itself by acknowledging that its accredited minister to Korea was actually guilty of the crime indicated in the charge. This attempt to evade the responsibility was of course futile. There was no escape from the dilemma in which that government was placed but the deduction that it was *particeps criminis* in the events of October 8th is unbelievable. It was the work of Viscount Miura and of his staff and of them alone, as is shown by the following extract from the Decison of the Japanese Court of Preliminary Inquiry, which court sat in Hiroshima in January 1896.

CHAPTER XXI.

We append the decision of the Hiroshima Court in full as it gives the fullest and probably the most nearly correct account of the events which led up to the assassination of the queen. It reads as follows:—

"Okamoto Ryunosuke, Adviser to the Korean Departments of War and the Household, etc.

"Miura Goro, Vicount, Sho Sammi, First class order, Lieutenant General, etc.

"Sugimura Fukashi, Sho Rokui, First Secretary of Legation, and forty-five others.

"Having, in compliance with the request of the Public Procurator conducted preliminary examinations in the case of murder and sedition brought against the above-mentioned Okamoto Ryunosuke and forty-seven others and that of wilful homicide brought against Hirayama Iwawo, we find as follows:—

"The accused, Miura Goro, assumed his official duties as His Imperial Majesty's Envoy Extraordinary and Minister Plenipotentiary at Seoul on Sept. 1st, 1895. According to his observations, things in Korea were tending in the wrong direction. The court was daily growing more and more arbitrary, and attempting wanton interferance with the conduct of state affairs. Disorder and confusion were in this way introduced into the system of administration that had just been reorganized under the guidance and advice of the Imperial government. The court went so far in turning its face upon Japan that a project was mooted for disbanding the *Kunrentai* troops, drilled by Japanese officers, and for punishing their officers. Moreover a report came to the knowledge of the said Miura that the court had under contemplation a scheme for usurping all political power by degrading some and killing others of the Cabinet Ministers suspected of devotion to the cause of progress and independence.

"Under these circumstances he was greatly perturbed inasmuch as he thought that the attitude assumed by the court not only showed remarkable ingratitude toward this country which had spent labor and money for Korea, but was also calculated to thwart the work of internal reform and jeopardize the independence of the kingdom. The policy pursued by the court was consequently considered to be injurious to

Korea, as well as prejudicial in no small degree to the interests of this country.   The accused felt it to be of urgent importance to apply an effective remedy to this state of affairs,
so as on the one hand to secure the independence of the Korean kingdom and on the other to maintain the prestige of
this empire in that country.   While thoughts like these agitated his mind, he was secretly approached by the Tă-wŭn-
gun with a request for assistance, the Prince being indignant at the untoward turn that events were taking and
having determined to undertake the reform of the court and
thus discharge his duty of advising the king.   The accused
then held at the legation a conference with Sugimura Fukashi and Okamoto Ryunosuke on the 3rd of October.   The
decision arrived at was that assistance should be rendered to
the Tă-wŭn-gun's entrance into the palace by making use of
the Japanese drilled Korean soldiers who being hated by the
court felt themselves in danger, and of the young men who
deeply lamented the course of events, and also by causing
the Japanese troops stationed in Seoul to offer their support
to the enterprise.   It was further resolved that this opportunity should be availed of for taking the life of the
queen, who exercised overwhelming influence in the court.
They at the same time thought it necessary to provide against
the possible danger of the Tă-wŭn-gun's interfering with the
conduct of State affairs in future—an interferance that might
prove of a more evil character than that which it was now
sought to overturn.   To this end, a document containing
pledges required of the Ta-wun-gun on four points was
drawn by Sigimura Fukashi.   The document was carried to
the country residence of the Ta-wun-gun on the 15th of
the month by Okamoto Ryunosuke, the latter being on intimate terms with His Highness.[16] After informing the Ta-
wun-gun that the turn of events demanded His Highness' intervention once more, Okomoto presented the document to the
Prince saying that it embodied what Minister Miura expected
from him. The Ta-wun-gun, together with his son and grandson
gladly consented to the conditions proposed and also wrote a letter guaranteeing his good faith.   Miura Goro and others decided
to carry out the concerted plan by the middle of the month.
Fearing lest Okamoto's visit to the Ta-wun-gun's residence

should excite suspicion and lead to the exposure of their plan, it was given out that he had proceeded thither simply for the purpose of taking leave of the Prince before departing for home, and to impart an appearance of probability to this report, it was decided that Okamoto should leave Seoul for Chemulpo and he took his departure from the capital on the sixth. On the following day An Kyung-su, the Minister of War, visited the Japanese Legation by order of the court. Referring to the projected disbanding of the Japanese drilled Korean soldiers, he asked the Japanese Minister's views on the subject. It was now evident that the moment had arrived, and that no more delay should be made. Miura Goro and Sugimura Fukashi consequently determined to carry out the plot on the night of that very day. On the one hand, a telegram was sent to Okamoto requesting him to come back to Seoul at once, and on the other, they delivered to Horiguchi Kumaichi a paper containing a detailed program concerning the entry of the Ta-wun-gun into the palace and caused him to meet Okamoto at Yong-san so that they might proceed to enter the palace. Miura Goro further issued instructions to Umayabara Muhon, commander of the Japanese batallion in Seoul, ordering him to facilitate the Ta-wun-gun's entry into the palace by directing the disposition of the Japanese drilled Korean troops and by calling out the Imperial force for their support. Miura also summoned the accused Adachi Kenszo and Kunitomo Shigeakira, and requested them to collect their friends, meeting Okamoto at Yong-san, and act as the Ta-wun-gun's body-guard on the occasion of His Highness' entrance into the palace. Miura told them that on the success of the enterprise depended the eradication of the evils that had done so much mischief to the kingdom for the past twenty years, and instigated them to dispatch the Queen when they entered the palace. Miura ordered the accused Ogiyara Hidejiro to proceed to Yong-san, at the head of the police force under him, and after consultation with Okamoto to take such steps as might be necessary to expedite the Ta-wun-gun's entry into the palace.

"The accused, Sugimura Fukashi, summoned Suzuki Shigemoto and Asayama Kenzo to the Legation and acquainted them with the projected enterprise, directed the former to

send the accused, Suzuki Junken, to Yong-san to act as interpreter and the latter to carry the news to a Korean named Yi
Chu-whe, who was known to be a warm advocate of the Ta-
wun-gun's return to the palace.   Sugimura further drew up
a manifesto, explaining the reasons of the Ta-wun-gun's
entrance into the palace and charged Ogiwara Hidejiro to
deliver to Horiguchi Kumaichi.

"The accused Horiguchi Kumaichi at once departed for
Yong-san on horse-back.   Ogiwara Hidejiro issued orders to
the policemen that were off duty to put on civilian dress,
provide themselves with swords and proceed to Yong-san.
Ogiwara also himself went to the same place.

"Thither also, repaired by his order the accused Wata-
nabe Takajiro, Oda Yoshimitsu, Nariai Kishiro, Kiwaki Suk-
unori and Sakai Masataro.

"The accused Yokowo Yutaro joined the party at Yong-
san. Asayama Kenzo saw Yi Chu-whe and informed him of the
projected enterprise against the palace that night. Having
ascertained that Yi had then collected a few other Koreans and
proceeded toward the Ta-wun-gun's place Asama at once left
for Yong-san.   Suzuki Shigemoto went to Yong-san in company with Suzuki Junken.   The accused Adachi Kenzo and
Kunitomo Shigeakira, at the instigation of Miura, decided to
murder the Queen and took steps to collect accomplices.
Twenty-four others (names here inserted) responded to the
call, by Miura's order, to act as body-guard to the Ta-wun-gun
on the occasion of his entrance into the palace.   Hirayama
Iwahiko and more than ten others were directed by Adachi
Kenzo and others to do away with the Queen and they decided
to follow the advice. The others who were not admitted into
the secret but who joined the party from mere curiosity also
carried weapons. With the exception of Kunitomo Shigeakira
Tsukinori and two others all the accused went to Yong-san in
company with Adachi Kenzo.

"The accused Okamoto Ryunosuke on receipt of a tele-
gram saying that time was urgent at once left Chemulpo for
Seoul.   Being informed on his way, at about midnight, that
Hoshiguchi Kennaichi was waiting for him at Mapo he
proceeded thither and met the persons assembled there.
There he received from Miura Goro the draft manifesto al-

ready alluded to, and other documents. After he had con-sulted with two or three others about the method of effecting an entrance into the palace the whole party started for the Ta-wun-gun's place with Okamoto as their leader. At about three o'clock A. M. on the eighth of October they left the Prince's place escorting him in his palanquin, with Yi Chu-whe and other Koreans. When on the point of departure, Okamoto assembled the whole party outside the gate of the Prince's residence and declared that on entering the palace the "Fox" should be dealt with according as exigency might require, the obvious purport of this declaration to instigate his followers to murder Her Majesty the Queen. As the result of this declaration, Sakai Marataro and a few others, who had not yet been initiated into the secret, resolved to act in accordance with the suggestion. Then slowly proceed-ing toward Seoul, the party met the Japanese drilled Korean troops outside the West Gate where they waited some time for the arrival of the Japanese troops. With the Korean troops as vanguard the party then proceeded toward the palace at a more rapid rate. On the way they were joined by Kunitomo Shigeakira and four others. The accused Husamoto, Yasumaru and Oura Shigehiko also joined the party having been requested by Umagabara Muhon to accom-pany as interpreters the military officers charged with the supervision of the Korean troops. About dawn the whole party entered the palace through the Kwang-wha Gate and at once proceeded to enter the inner chambers."

At this point the recital of the facts abruptly stops and the court goes on to state that in spite of these proven facts there is not sufficient evidence to prove that any of the Japanese actually committed the crime which had been con-templated, and all the accused are discharged.

It is very much to the credit of the Japanese authorities that they frankly published these incriminating facts and did not attempt to suppress them. Their action discharging the accused was a candid statement that in spite of the actual proof which they adduce it would not be possible to punish the perpetrators of the outrage, for Miura had been sent as the accredited Minister of Japan and his acts, through un-foreseen by his superiors could not but partake of an official character, and therefore the onus of the affair must fall on the Japanese Government. This is the effect that was produced in the public mind, and while the Japanese Government as such must be acquitted of any intention or desire to secure the assassination of the Queen, yet it can scarcely escape the charge of criminal carelessness in according to the Korean Court a representative who would so far forget the dignity of his position as to plan and encourage the perpetration of such a revolting crime.

The description of the scene as given by the Hiroshma court stops abruptly with the entrance into the palace before the actual business of the day began. It is necessary for us to take up the narration from that point. The buildings occupied by the King and Queen were near the back of the palace enclosure almost half a mile from the front gate, so that the Japanese and Korean force accompanied by the ex-Regent had to traverse a long succession of passage-ways through a great mass of buildings before reaching the object of their search. Some of the palace guard were met on the way and easily pushed aside, some of them being killed, among whom was Col. Hong. When the Japanese arrived at the buildings occupied by their Majesties a part of them formed about it in military order guarding all the approaches, but they did not enter the building. A crowd of Japanese civilians commonly believed to be *soshi*, and a considerable number of Koreans, all heavily armed, rushed into the Royal quarters. A part of the crowd went into the presence of the King brandishing their weapons but without directly attacking his person nor that of the Crown Prince who stood beside him. Another part of the crowd ranged through the apartments of the Queen, seizing palace women and demanding information as to the whereabouts of the Queen. They met Yi Kyŭng-jik the Minister of the Household before the Queen's apartments and at once cut him down, but he managed to crawl into the presence of the King, where he was despatched by the Japanese. The Queen was found in one of the rooms which constituted her suite and was ruthlessly cut down. It is impossible to state with absolute certainty whether the blow was struck by a Korean or by a Japanese but the overwhelming probability is that it was done by one of the armed Japanese

The body was wrapped in some sort of blanket, saturated with petroleum and burned at the edge of a pine grove immediately to the east of the pond which lies in front of the royal quarters.

The Royal family had been aware for two days of the danger which threatened. The guards at the palace had been reduced, the arms had been taken away and the movements of Japanese troops were very suspicious. The King advised the Queen to go to a place of safety and she said she would do so if the ·Queen Dowager would also go, but the latter refused. Chong Pyüng-ha who had been raised to high office through the patronage of the Queen but who had struck hands with the Japanese urged with great insistence that there was no danger to Her Majesty's person and it was the confidence expressed by this traitor that did the most to set at rest the apprehension, of the King and the Queen.

During all the time leading up to these events, the palace guard was in charge of Gen. Dye but his efforts to carry out the wishes of His Majesty were continually thwarted and the guard was merely a nominal one.

At about the time when the Queen was being killed the Tä-wŭn-gun came into the presence of the King and took the direction of affairs at the court. As might be supposed, both the King and the Crown Prince were in anything but an enviable frame of mind. They had been pushed about and insulted by low Japanese and felt that their lives were momentarily in danger. Col Yi Kvŭng-jik the Minister of the Household Department had taken his stand at the door of the Queen's apartments and had there been cut down by the Japanese or Koreans but succeeded in making his way, desperately wounded, into the presence of the King. He was there stabbed to death by the Japanese before the eyes of His Majesty. This did not tend to reassure the King and the Crown Prince but the coming of the Tä-wŭn-gun tended to quiet them somewhat. Of course they had no idea as yet that the Queen had been despatched.

Before dawn began to break the King learned that Japanese troops were pouring into the barracks in front of the palace, and as some semblance of order had been restored in the immediate presence of His Majesty, a note was sent in

haste to the Japanese Minister asking what all this meant.
The messenger found Miura and Sugimura already up and
dressed and sedan chairs at the door.   Miura told the messenger that he had heard that troops had been marched to
the barracks but did not know why. The Minister and his
secretary thereupon proceeded rapidly to the palace.   Immediately upon their arrival all the disturbance suddenly
quieted down and the *soshi* dispersed and left the palace
grounds.   The Japanese Minister and secretary immediately
sought an audience with His Majesty, accompained only by
an interpreter and another Japanese who had led the *soshi*.
The Tă-wŭn-gun was also present.

   Three documents we e prepared by those present and
placed before His Majesty for signature, one of them guaranteeing that the Cabinet should thereafter manage the affairs
of the country, the second appointing Yi Chă-myŭn, the
King's brother, as Minister of the Household in place of Yi
Kyŭng-jik who had just been killed, and the third appointing
a vice-Minister of the Household.   These documents the
king perforce signed. Whereupon all Japanese troops were
removed from the palace and only the Japanese-trained
Korean troops were left as a palace-guard.   Later in the day
Ministers of War and Police were appointed in the persons
of Cho Heui-yŭn and Kwŭn Yŭng-jin, both strong partisans
of the Japanese and doubtless privy to the attack upon the
palace and the murder of the Queen.   In other words the
King and court was surrounded by men every one of whom
were in sympathy with the movement which had been planned by Viscount Miura.

   Very early in the morning, while it was still scarcely daylight, Mr. Waeber the Russian *Charge d' Affaires* and Dr.
Allen the American *Charge d' Affaires ad interim* came to the
palace and sought audience with the King but were told that
the King was unwell and could not see them.   They insisted,
however, and succeeded in seeing His Majesty, who told them
that he still had hopes that the Queen had escaped, and besought their friendly offices to prevent further trouble.
Other foreign representatives were received latter in the day.

   It soon became evident that the Japanese authorities
intended to deny any responsibility for the outrages commit-

ted. Miura stated in his dispatches to his government that the origin of the *emeute* was a conflict beween the Japanese-drilled Korean troops, who desired to lay a complaint before His Majesty, and the palace guards who tried to prevent their entrance into the palace. Miura even sought to strengthen his disclaimer by obtaining from the newly appointed Minister of War a definite official statement that the rumors of his (Miura's) complicity in the affair were without foundation. The document that the Minister of War sent in reply proved altogether too much and defeated its own purpose, for it stated baldly that there was not a single Japanese in the palace on the night of the eighth of October, when the Queen was murdered. As this Minister was a creature of the Japanese and as the presence of Japanese in the palace was clearly proved subsequently it is evident that Miura, by this sort of trickery, only succeeded in further implicating himself.

On the ninth, the day after the *emeute*, a full cabinet was appointed composed entirely of Japanese sympathisers, but with one or two exceptions they were not privy to the assassination of the Queen, though they were willing to profit by that crime in accepting office at the hands of the perpetrators. The men appointed were Yi Chă-myŭn, Kim Hong-jip, Kim Yun-sik, Pak Chŏng-yang, Sim Sang-hun, Cho Heui-yŭn, So Kwang-bŏm and Chong Pyung-ha.

One would have supposed that the enemies of the Queen would have been satisfied by her death, but not so. On the eleventh, three days after her assassination, an edict purporting to have originated with His Majesty and signed by the full cabinet appeared in the Court Gazette. In it the Queen is charged with having interfered in public matters, disturbed the government and put the dynasty in peril. It is stated that she has disappeared and that her guilt is excessive; therefore she is deposed from her rank as Queen and reduced to the level of the lowest class.

There can be no doubt that this edict is fraudulent. The King never gave his consent to it and several of the members of the Cabinet knew nothing about it, notably Sim Sang-hun who had already thrown up his position and run away, and Pak Chŏng-yang who denounced the nefarious business and resigned. It was put through by a few of the Cabinet who were thoroughly subservient to the Japanese. The Japanese Minister in reply to the announcement of the Queen's degradation, affected to sympathize with the Korean Government but thought it was done for the good of the State. The United States Representative refused to recognize the decree as coming from His Majesty, and in this he was seconded by all the the other Foreign Representatives except one.

Meanwhile the Japanese government began to learn something of the truth in regard to the Queen's death and felt called upon to defend itself from the charge of complicity in the outrage through its accredited Minister. Consequently it recalled Miura and Sugimura and upon their arrival in Japan they were arrested and charged with complicity in the matter. The fact of their arrest and trial was a distinct disclaimer on the part of the Japanese government that it was accessory to the crime; and in spite of the utter inadequacy of the trial and its almost ludicrous termination we hold to the theory that the Japanese government was not a party to the crime excepting in so far as the appointment of such a man as Miura can be called complicity.

But the vigorous action of Japan in arresting Miura and putting him on trial had a strong influence upon the course of events in Korea. The Korean public and all the Foreign Representatives were demanding that the occurrences of the eighth of October should be investigated and the responsibility for the murder of the Queen placed where it rightly belonged. This itself bore strongly upon the Cabinet, but when in addition to this the Japanese government itself seemed to be weakening and it appeared that Miura's acts would prove to have been unauthorized things began to look rather black for the men who were enjoying office solely through Miura's influence, and although the fiction was still maintained that the Queen was not dead but in hiding somewhere, the situation became more and more strained until at last it became evident even to the Cabinet that something must be done to relieve the situation. Accordingly on the 26th of November the Foreign Representatives and several other foreigners were invited to the palace and it was announced in the presence of His Majesty that Cho Heui-yun the Minister of War and Kwŭn Yŭng-jin the Chief of Police were dismissed, that the edict degrading the Queen was rescinded and that the facts connected with the attack on the palace would be investigated by the Department of Justice and all guilty persons tried and punished. At the same time the death of Her Majesty was formally announced.

The popular feeling against the Japanese-trained troops was so strong that they were dismissed and another guard summoned, but as a matter of fact this new guard was composed almost entirely of the very men who had formerly composed the Japanese-drilled corps.

The position of His Majesty during the months succeeding the attack was anything but comfortable. He had no voice in the direction of affairs, and he considered himself practically a prisoner in the hands of the Cabinet. He even feared for his life, and for weeks ate no food except what was brought to him in a locked box from friends outside the palace. He had requested that two or three foreigners should come to the palace each night and be at hand in case of trouble, feeling that their presence would exert a deterrent influence upon any who might plot injury to his person.

The half-way measures adopted on Nov. 26th by no means satisfied those who wished to see His Majesty freed from practical durance at the hands of men thoroughly obnoxious to him, and a scheme was evolved by a number of Koreans to effect his release by forcible means. The purpose of these men was a laudable one but the execution of it was ill-managed. On the night of the 28th upwards of a thousand Koreans demanded entrance into the palace. They had arranged with one of the members of the palace guard, inside, to open the gate to them, but at the last moment he failed them and they found themselves balked. The palace was in some confusion, the King had called in to his presence the three foreigners who, at his request, were on duty that night, but in spite of their assurances that his person would be protected it was only natural that excitement should run high. The crowd without were shouting wildly and attempting to scale the high wall, and the members of the cabinet, before the King, did not know at what moment the guard might betray them to the assailants, and they knew that once betrayed they would be torn to pieces without mercy. They

tried therefore to induce the King to remove to a distant part
of the palace where he could hide for a long time before he
could be found even though the crowd should effect an
entrance. The night was bitterly cold and the King was
but lightly clad, and as the King's person was safe in any
event, the foreigners who were with him opposed the move
strongly and at last were compelled to use physical force to
prevent the change, which would certainly have endangered
the King's life. The purpose of the cabinet was thus thwarted
but as the hours passed it become evident that the men
outside would not be able to effect an entrance. The shouts
gradually died away and at last the crowd dispersed leaving
in the hands of the palace guard three or four men who had
scaled the wall but had not been followed by their confreres.

In view of the attitude of the Tokyo Government the
Japanese in Seoul were now entirely quescent and the government was standing on its own base. The cabinet held its
own by virtue of the palace guard which was composed of the
soldiers trained by the Japanese. This cabinet and guard
held together from necessity, for both knew that should their
power fail they would be denounced as traitors and under
the circumstances could expect little help from the Japanese.
The cabinet had to make a show of investigating the attack
of Oct. 5th and someone must be killed for having murdered
the queen.[7] At the same time punishment was to be meted out
to the principals in the attempt on the palace on November
28th.

Three men were arrested and charged with being
directly implicated in the crime of regicide. Of these one
was certainly innocent and while the second was probably
privy to the crime, being a lieutenant of the Japanese-trained
troops, there was no evidence adduced to prove his actual
participation in the act of assassination. He had not been
reinstated in his position in the new guard and he knew
altogether too much about the existing cabinet. Their
choice fell upon him as one of the scapegoats. The third
was Yi Chu-hoé formerly Vice Minister of War. There was
no evidence adduced against him at the trial, though from
other considerations he seems to have been implicated in the
outrage. He was chosen as the principal one to bear the

obloquy of the crime, probably because (1) he was a bitter
enemy of the existing cabinet and (2) because it was necessary for the sake of appearances to convict and execute someone of rank and reputation. As a fact the court did not
know and never discovered who the actual perpetrators were.
The three men were executed before the end of the year.

Though only three men were arrested in connection
with the assassination of the queen thirty-three men were
arrested in connection with the comparatively trivial affair
of November 28th. Their trial proceeded simultaneously
with that of the other three. Two of them were condemned
to death, four to exile for life and four to three years imprisonment. To show the kind of evidence on which these convic·
tions were based we will cite the case of Prince Yi Chä-sun
who was proved to have gotten hold of some compromising
documents and to have shown them to the King only, instead
of to *the proper authorities*, namely, of course, the cabinet.
On these grounds he was sentenced to three years imprisonment !

December and January saw matters move to an inevitable climax. The cabinet forced upon the people the edict
ordering the cutting off of the top-knot, the distinctive mark
of Korean citizenship. The whole country was in a ferment
and the people, almost to a man, were gnashing their teeth
at the cabinet. The finding of the Hiroshima court claimed
to have freed Miura and his fellows from blame and it was
rumored that several of them were to return to Korea to take
office under the government. Chöng Pyung-ha, a proved
traitor, had been reinstated in the cabinet as Minister of Agriculture and Cho Heui-yŭn as Minister of War, and it was
reported that Kwŭn Yŭng-jin who had fled to Japan would
be made again Chief of Police. It was perfectly evident,
therefore, that the grip of the Japanese upon the king
through the Goaler Cabinet was tightening and that there
was no escape from it except through heroic measures.
These measures the king was prepared to adopt rather than
longer endure the humiliating position to which he seemed
condemned. At that time the principal men in the cabinet
were Kim Hong-jip, Chöng Pyŭng-ha, O Yun-jung, Yu Kil-
jun. Of these O Yun-jung seems to have been far less cul-

pable than the rest. The king had great confidence in him and had he not met his fate at the hands of the people he would probably have been called back to office.

But now we come to the important step taken by His Majesty to free himself from his unpleasant position. He determined to find asylum in the Russian Legation. C. Waeber was the Russian Minister, a pronounced friend of the dead Queen, and a man of great ability. Just how he was approached and his consent gained to the king's scheme is not generally known but in view of subsequent events and the part that Russia intended to play in Korea it is easy to see how the Russian Representative would welcome an opportunity to do the King such a signal service and one which was of such a personal character as to render it certain that it would never be forgotten.

The plan was carried out successfully in every detail. Women's chairs were caused to be sent in and out the palace gates at frequent intervals by day and night until the guards had become quite accustomed to them. Then on the night of the eleventh of February the King and the Crown Prince without escort slipped by the guards in common women's chairs and were taken directly to the Russian Legation where they were courteously received and given the best portion of the Legation building. This act was of course a grievous lapse from the dignity that befits a king but under the circumstances there is much to say by way of excuse. On the whole it must be considered a mistake so far as the country at large is concerned, for it set in motion a new set of factors which probably did more harm than the temporary enforced seclusion of the King could have done. It acted as a potent factor in embittering the Japanese against Russia and opened the door for Russian intrigue which finally hastened if it did not actually cause the war at present waging. Had Japan been able to preserve the predominance which she held in Korea just after the China-Japan war she might have looked with more or less complaisancy upon the Russian aggression in Manchuria, but when Korea itself became disputed ground the war was inevitable.

At seven o'clock on the morning of February 11th the King and the Crown Prince entered the Russian Legation.

Several hours elapsed before the Cabinet in the palace became aware of the fact. During that interval active operations were going on at the Russian Legation. The organization of a new cabinet was hastened by summoning from various parts of the city such officials as the King could trust. Pak Chŏng-yang was made Prime Minister. No time was lost in putting out a Royal Edict deprecating the necessity of taking refuge in a foreign legation, promising to punish the real authors of the Queen's assassination, rescinding the order for cutting the top-knots. This was posted on the gates of the Legation and at various points throughout the city.

Chapter XXII.

The King at the Russian Legation .... A Royal edict ... Massacre or flight of cabinet ministers .. an excited city.... Japanese consternation ...provincial uprisings ...party reorganization ... The Independence Club ...trial of Queen's murderers.... Apponitment of Dr. Brown as adiviser to Finance Department ...The *Independent* ..The Waeber-Komura Convention .... material reforms .... reaction....The Independence Arch .... Seoul-Chemulpo railway concession ... The new palace planned....retrogressive signs .... postal and other administrative reforms.

When the public awoke to the momentous fact, a thrill of excitement and, generally, of approval went through the whole population of Seoul. The city hummed with excited humanity. The streets swarmed with the crowds bent upon watching the course of such stirring events.

Later in the day the King put forth an edict calling upon the soldiers to rally to his support and urging them to bring the heads of the traitors Cho Heui-yŭn, U Pŏm-sŭn, Yi Tu-whang, Yi Pom-nă, Yi Chin-ho and Kon Yong-jin. But later still this was toned down to read that these individuals should be seized and turned over to the proper authorities for trial.

The reason why the names of Kim Hong-jip, Chŏng Pyŭng-Ha and others of the former cabinet were not included was because they had already met their fate. As soon as it became known in the palace that the King had fled, these men saw that their lives were forfeited. O Yun-jung managed to escape to the country but was set upon and killed by the people, Cho Heui-Yŭu escaped, Yu Kil-jun was spirited away to Japan by the Japanese; but Kim Hong-jip and Chŏng Pyŭng-ha found no way of escape. Being seized by the Korean soldiers, were immediately rushed by the crowd and killed. Their bodies were hauled to Chong-no where they were stamped upon, kicked, bitten and stoned by a half-crazed rabble for hours. A Japanese who happened to be passing was set upon by the crowd and killed and several foreigners drawn to the spot by curiosity were threatened.

The King was shocked when he heard of the summary execution of the two ministers, whom he intended to give a fair trial. Two days later an edict was promulgated by the King deploring the impoverished state of the country and laying the blame upon himself; and concluded by remitting all arrears of taxes due up to July 1894. The new cabinet consisted of the following men Pak Chŏng-yang, Yi Yun-yong, An Kyŭng-su, Ko Yong-heui, Yun Chi-ho, Yun Yong-gu, Yi Wan-yong and Cho Pyŭng-jik.

To say that the Japanese were nonplussed by this *coup* on the part of the King would be to put it very mildly. All their efforts to consolidate their power in Korea and to secure there some fruit of the victory in the war just finished, had been worse than thrown away. The King had thrown himself into the arms of Russia and the whole Korean people were worked up to a white heat against Japan, comparable only with the feelings elicited by the invasion of 1592. It was a very great pity, for Japan was in a position to do for Korea infinitely more than Russia would do. The interests of Korea and Japan were identical or at least complementary and the mistake which Japan made in the latter half of 1895 was one whose effects will require decades to efface.

When the King thus wrenched himself out of Japanese hands the Japanese papers in Seoul bewailed the fact that the country was without a ruler, and almost directly advised the people to put someone else on the throne, and this without censure from the Japanese authorities. And it is well known among Koreans that there was a strong faction among the Koreans who were willing to attempt to put Yi Chun-yong, the grandson of the Tă-wŭn-gun on the throne, had that ambitious young man been possessed of the requisite amount of assurance. Fortunately such was not the case and the country was saved from further upheaval.

But the Japanese authorities though thrown into consternation by this radical movement of His Majesty did not give up hope of mending matters. The Japanese Minister saw the King at the Russian Legation and urged upon him every possible argument for returning to the palace. His Majesty, however, being now wholly relieved from anxiety as to his personal safety, enjoyed the respite too thorougly to cut it short, and so politely refused to change his place of residence. A large number of Japanese in Seoul became convinced that Japan had hopelessly compromised herself, and left the country, but the Japanese Government itself by no act or word granted that her paramount influence in the peninsula was impaired and with admirable *sang froid* took up the new line of work imposed upon her by the King's peculiar action, meanwhile putting down one more score against Russia, to be reckoned with later.

The country was suffering from the excitement caused by the news of the Japanese diplomatic reverses, and the people in many districts rose in revolt and declared that they would drive all the Japanese out of the country. These efforts were however scattered and sporadic in their nature and were successfully quelled by Korean Government troops sent down to the various disaffected districts for this purpose.

Now that it was possible the King hastened to order a new investigation of the circumstances attending the death of the Queen. It was feared that this would result in a very sweeping arrest of Koreans and the punishment of many people on mere suspicion, but these fears were ill-founded. The trials were carried through under the eye of Mr. Greathouse the adviser to the Law Department and a man of great legal ability. Thirteen men were arrested and tried in open court without torture and with every privilege of a fair trial. One man Yi Whi-wha was condemned to death, four banished for life and five for lesser periods. This dispassionate trial was not the least of the signs which pointed toward a new and enlightened era in Korean political history.

Not only in the country but in Seoul as well the prestige of Japan had suffered greatly by the events of the winter of 1895-96.   After the Japan-China war the Koreans were divided into two distinct factions, one holding strongly with the Japanese and the other advocating a more conservative policy, but gradually as the political situation began to crystalize these two split into four, namely the Japanese faction, the King's faction, the Queen's faction, and the Tä-wŭn-gun's faction.   This is merely another way of saying that every strong political possibility will have its own faction in such a land as this, according as each man fancies that his champion will get supreme power and reward those who have followed in his train.   The number of men who follow the standard of this or that party because of any al-truistic or purely patriotic consideration is so small as to be a negligeable quantity.   When, therefore, it appeared that Japan's star was setting in Korea there was a hasty shifting of political platforms and soon it appeared that there were only two, one of which favored Russian influence and the other conservative and very quiet, for the time being, until the extreme pro-Russian enthusiasm should subside somewhat. Of course the Tä-wŭn-gun's had disappeared with the wan-ing fortunes of the Japanese and the Queen's faction had gone over to the Russians.   It was the conservatives alone that held to their former position and desired no foreign inter-ferance whatever.   But many of those who had favored the Jap-anese joined the conservative party but unlike the "moss-back" conservatives wanted to do something actively to coun-teract Russian influence.   They therefore worked to bring English and American influence into greater prominence.   In the heart of this movement was born the "Independence Club." It will be remembered that ever since the previous year Dr. Philip Jaisohn had been acting as adviser to the Privy Council.   This council enjoyed considerable power at first but gradually fell to a secondary place, but now that new conditions had sprung up the element combatting the Rus-sian influence took advantage of the presence of Dr. Jaisohn and other Koreans who had been educated abroad.   The Russians seemed to look with complaisance upon this move-ment and in the Spring of this year seem to have made no

effort to prevent the appointment of J. McLeavy Brown,
L.L.D., as Adviser to the Finance Department, with large
powers; which seemed to bear out the belief that the Russian
Minister was sincere in his statement that Russia wished the
King to be quite untrammelled in the administration of his
government.   It is this generous policy of Mr. Waeber that
is believed to have caused his transfer later to another post,
to be replaced by A. de Speyer who adopted a very different
policy.[18] However this may have been, things began to take
on a very hopeful aspect in Seoul.   Needed reforms were
carried through ; torture was abolished in the Seoul courts,
a concession was given to an American company to construct
a railway between Seoul and Chemulpo, Min Yong-whan
was appointed special envoy to the coronation of the Czar, work
was begun on the American mining concession granted the
year before. various schools were founded, and the outlook
on the whole was very bright indeed.   It looked as if a
solution had been found for the difficulties that afflicted the
state and that an era of comparatively enlightened government was opening.

    For some time there had existed a more or less secret or-
ganization among the Koreans, the single article of whose
political creed was Independence both from China and Japan,
or in other words Korea for Koreans. Now that the King had
been relieved of Chinese suzerainty by the Japanese and of
Japanese restraint by himself, this little society under the
leadership of Dr. Philip Jaisohn blossomed out into what was
called *The Independence Club* The name but partially described the society, for while it advocated the complete independence of Korea it still more insistently advocated a liberal
government, in the shape of a genuine constitutional monar-
chy in which the royal prerogative should be largely curtailed
and the element of paternalism eliminated.   At first the
greater stress was laid upon the general principle of Korean
Indepenence and to this the King in the joy of his newly
found freedom heartily agreed.   The royal sanction was given
to the Independence Club and it was launched upon a voyage
which had no haven, but ended in total shipwreck. This club,
society was composed of young men many of whom were doubtless aroused for the time being to something like patriotic

fervor but who had had no practical experience of the rocky
road of Korean politics or of the obstacles which would be encountered. The cordiàlity of the King's recognition blinded
them to the fact that the real object of their organization, namely the definition of the royal prerogative, was one
that must eventually arouse first the suspicion and then the
open hostility of His Majesty and would become the slogan of
all that army of self-seekers who saw no chance for self-ag-
grandisement except in the immemorial spoils system. These
young men were armed with nothing but a laudable enthusiasm. They could command neither the aid of the Korean
army nor the advocacy of the older statesmen, all of whom
were either directly hostile to the movement or had learned
caution through connection with previous abortive attempts to
stem the tide of official corruption. The purpose of this club, so
far as it knew its own mind, was a laudable one in theory but
the amount of persistency, courage, tact and self-restraint
necessary to carry the plan to a successful issue was so im-
mensely greater than they could possibly guess, that, considering the youth and inexperience of the personnel of the
society, the attempt was doomed to failure. They never clearly formulated a constructive plan by which to buiid upon the
ruins of that system which they were bent upon destroying.
Even had they cleared the way to such construction they
could not have found a statesman in Korea of recognized
standing and prestige, to act as master-builder, whose previous
record would have made him acceptable to themselves or a fit
exponent of their principles.

On April 7th the first foreign newspaper was founded
by Dr. Philip Jaisohn. It was called *The Independent* and was
partly in the native character. From the first it exerted a
powerful influence among the Koreans and was one of the main
factors which led to the formation of the Independence Club.

Both Japan and Russia were desirous of coming to an
understanding as to Korea and on May 14th there was published the Waeber-Komura Agreement which was modified
and ratified later under the name of the Lobanoff-Yamata
Agreement.[19] According to the terms of this convention both
Powers guaranteed to respect the independence of Korea and
not to send soldiers into the country except by common consent.

The summer of 1896 saw great material improvements in Seoul. The work of clearing out and widening the streets was vigorously pushed and although much of the work was done superficially some permanent improvement was effected, and the "squatters" along the main streets were cleaned out, it is hoped for all time. In July the concession for building a railway between Seoul and Wiju was given to a French syndicate. From subsequent events it appears that there was no fixed determination on the part of the French to push this great engineering work to a finish but merely to preempt the ground and prevent others from doing it. Russian influence doubtless accomplished this, and from that time there began to spring up the idea that Korea would be divided into two spheres of influence, the Japanese predominant in the south and the Russians in the north.

In spite of the favorable signs that appeared during the early months of 1896 and the hopes which were entertained that an era of genuine reform had been entered upon, the coming of summer began to reveal the hollowness of such hopes. The King himself was strongly conservative and never looked with favor upon administrative changes which tended to weaken his personal hold upon the finances of the country and he chafed under the new order of things. In this he was encouraged by many of the leading officials, who saw in the establishment of liberal institutions the end of their opportunities for personal power and aggrandisement. The old order of things appealed to them too strongly and it became evident that the government was rapidly lapsing into its former condition of arbitrary and partisan control. Open and violent opposition to such harmless innovations as the wearing of foreign uniforms by the students of Foreign Language Schools indicated too plainly the tendency of the time and the Russian authorities did nothing to influence His Majesty in the right direction. Judging from subsequent events it was not Russia's policy to see an enlightened administration in Seoul. The political plans of that Power could be better advanced by a return to the *status ante quo*. The act of the government in substituting an Independence Arch in place of the former gate, outside the West Gate, which commemorated Chinese suzerainty, was looked upon,.

and rightly, by the more thoughtful as being merely a superficial demonstration which was based upon no deeper desire
than that of being free from all control or restraint except
such as personal inclination should dictate.[20] The current was
setting toward a concentration of power rather than toward
a healthful distribution of it, and thus those who had hailed
the vision of a new and rejuvenated state were compelled to
confess that it was but a mirage.

Pressure was brought to bear upon the court to remove
from the Russian Legation, and it was high time that such a
move be made. As a matter of urgent necessity it was considered a not too great sacrifice of dignity to go to the Legation but to make it a permanent residence was out of the
question. The King was determined however, not to go back
to the palace from which he had fled. It held too many grue-
some memories. It was decided to build the Myŭng-ye
Palace in the midst of the Foreign Quarter with Legations
on three sides of it. The site selected was the same as that
which King Sŭn-jo used in 1593 when he returned from his
flight to the north before the armies of Hideyoshi. He had
lived here for some fourteen years while the Chang-dok
Palace was building. The present King however intended
it as a permanent residence, and building operations were begun on a large scale, but it was not until February of the following year that His Majesty finally removed from the
Russian Legation to his new palace.

All during the latter half of 1896 the gulf between the
Independence party and the conservatives kept widening.
The latter grew more and more confident and the former
more and more determined. Dr. Jaisohn in his capacity of
adviser to the Council of State was blunt and outspoken in
his advice to His Majesty and it was apparent that the latter
listened with growing impatience to suggestions which, however excellent in themselves, found no response in his own
inclinations. The Minister of Education voiced the growing
sentiment of the retrogressive faction in a book called "The
Warp and Woof of Confucianism" in which such extreme
statements were made that several of the Foreign Representatives felt obliged to interfere and call him to account. A
Chief of Police was appointed who was violently anti-reform.

The assassin of Kim Ok-kyun was given an important position under the government. A man who had attempted the
life of Pak Yong-hyo was made Minister of Law, and on all
sides were heard contemptuous comments upon the "reform
nonsense" of the liberal faction. And yet in spite of this the
momentum of the reform movement though somewhat retarded
had by no means been completely stopped. The Summer
and Autumn of this year 1896 saw the promulgation of a
large number of edicts of a salutary nature, relating to the
more systematic collection of the national revenues, the reorganization of gubernatorial and prefectural systems, the
definition of the powers and privileges of provincial officials,
the further regulation of the postal system, the definition of
the powers of the superintendents of trade in the open ports,
the abolition of illegal taxation and the establishment of
courts of law in the various provinces and in the open ports.
As many of these reforms survived the collapse of the liberal
party they must be set down as definite results which justify
the existence of that party and make its overthrow a matter
of keen regret to those who have at heart the best interests
of the country.

All this time Russian interests had been cared for
sedulously. The king remained in close touch with the
Legation and Col. Potiata and three other Russian officers
were put in charge of the Palace Guard, while Kim Hong-
nyuk, the erstwhile water-carrier, continued to absorb the
good things in the gift of His Majesty. And yet the Russians with all their power did not attempt to obstruct the
plans of the subjects of other Powers in Korea. Mr. Stripling,
a British subject, was made adviser to the Police Department, a mining concession was granted to a German syndicate; an American was put in charge of a Normal School,[21]
Dr. Brown continued to direct the work of the Finance Department and the work on the Seoul Chemulpo Railway was
pushed vigorously by an American syndicate. The Russians
held in their hands the power to put a stop to much of this,
but they appeared to be satisfied with holding the power
without exercising it.

Chapter XXIII.

Material reforms.... growth of conservative feeling.... Russian influence.... Mr. de Speyer.... his activity ... attack on Dr. Brown ... England interposes... establishmeut of the Empire.... the Queen's funeral.... opening of 1898 ... Russians over-reach themselves .... the death of Prince Tă-wŭn.... a paradox.... withdrawal of the Russian employees.... Independence Club beyond control.... abdication conspiracy.... Yun Chi-ho before the Emperor.... fall of Kim Hong-nyuk.... attempted regicide.... foreign body-guard ... Independent program.... popular meetings.... peddlars' guild.... Independents ask to be arrested.... more government concessions .... Independents arrested.... final overthrow of the Independence party.

The first half of 1897 was characterized by three special features in Korea. The first was a continuance of so-called reforms, all of which were of a utilitarian character. A gold mine concession was given to a German syndicate, a Chinese Language School and other schools were founded and the difficult work of cleaning out the Peking Pass was completed. It was announced that Chinnampo and Mokpo would be opened to trade in the Autumn. The second feature was the steady growth of the conservative element which was eventually to resume complete control of the government. As early as May of this year the editor of the *Korean Repository* said with truth "The collapse is as complete as it is pathetic. After the King came to the Russian Legation the rush of the reform movement could not be stayed at once nor even deflected. But soon there came the inevitable reaction. Reforms came to be spoken of less and less frequently. There was a decided movement backwards toward the old, well-beaten paths. But it was impossible to reestablish the old order of things entirely. We come then to the period of the revision of laws. Shortly after the King removed to the new palace an edict was put forth ordering the appointment of a Commission for the Revision of the Laws. This was received with satisfaction by the friends of progress. This commission contained the names of many prominent men such as Kim Pyung-si, Pak Chŏng-yang and Yi Wan-yong as well as the names of Dr. Brown, General Greathouse, Mr. Legendre and Dr. Jaisohn.'' But by the

twelfth of April the whole thing was dropped and the strong
hopes of the friends of Korea were again dashed to the
ground. The third feature of this period is the growing
importance of Russian influence in Seoul. The training of
the Korean army had already been taken out of Japanese
hands and given to Russians and in August thirteen more
Russian military instructors were imported. It was plain
that Russia meant to carry out an active policy in Korea.
Russian admirals, including, Admiral Alexeieff, made frequent visits to Seoul, and at last Russia made public avowal
of her purposes, when she removed Mr. Waeber, who had
served her so long and faithfully here and sent Mr. A. de
Speyer to take his place. There was an immediate and
ominous change in the tone which Russia assumed. From
the very first de Speyer showed plainly that he was sent here
to impart a new vigor to Russo-Korean relations; that things
had been going too slow. It is probable that complaints had
been made because in spite of Russia's predominating influence
at the Korean Court concessions were being given to Americans,
Germans and others outside. De Speyer soon showed the
color of his instructions and began a course of brow-beating,
the futility of which must have surprised him. It was on
September 7th that he arrived, and within a month he had
begun operations so actively that he attracted the attention
of the world. In the first place he demanded a coaling
station at Fusan on Deer Island which commands the
entrance to the harbor. This was a blow aimed directly at
Japan and sure to be resented. It came to nothing. Then
Mr. Kir Alexeieff arrived from Russia, an agent of the
Finance Department in St. Petersburg. In the face of the
fact that Dr. Brown was Chief Commissioner of Custom and
Adviser to the Finance Department, Mr. Alexeieff was appointed by the Foreign Office as director of the Finance
Department. But the policy of bluff which de Speyer had
inaugurated was not a success; he carried it so far that he
aroused the strong opposition of other Powers, notably England, and before the end of the year, after only three months
of incumbency, de Speyer was called away from Seoul. As
we shall see, the whole of his work was overthrown in the
following Spring.

But we must retrace our steps a little and record some other interesting events that happened during the closing months of 1897. It was on October 17th that the King went to the Imperial Altar and there was crowned Emperor of Tai-han. This had been some time in contemplation and as Korea was free from foreign suzerainty she hastened, while it was time, to declare herself an empire. This step was recognized by the treaty powers within a short period and so Korea took her place on an equality with China and Japan.

On November 21st the funeral ceremony of the late Queen was held. It was a most imposing pageant. The funeral procession passed at night out of the city to the tomb where elaborate preparations had been made, and a large number of foreigners assembled there to witness the obsequies.

The situation in Korea as the year 1898 opened was something as follows. The conservatives had things well in hand and the Independence Club was passing on to its final effort and its final defeat. The work of such men as Dr. Jaisohn was still tolerated but the King and the most influential officials chafed under the wholesome advice that they received and it was evident that the first pretext would be eagerly seized for terminating a situation that was getting very awkward for both sides. The reaction was illustrated in an attack on the *Independent* by which the Korean postal department refused to carry it in the mails. The Russians had taken the bull by the horns and were finding that they had undertaken more than they could carry through without danger of serious complications. The Russian government saw this and recalled de Speyer in time to preserve much of their influence in Seoul. The Emperor, being now in his own palace but with easy access to the Russian Legation, seems to have lent his voice to the checking of the reform propaganda and in this he was heartily seconded by his leading officials. The most promising aspect of the situation was the determined attitude of the British government relative to the enforced retirement of Dr. Brown. When it became evident that a scarcely concealed plan was on foot to oust British and other foreigners in Korea, Great Britain by a single word and by a concentration of war vessels at Chemulpo changed the whole program of the Russians; but as it appeared later the Russian plans were *only* changed, not abandoned. So the year opened with things political in a very unsettled state. Everything was in transition. The Independents and the Russians had some idea of what they wanted but seemed to be at sea as to the means for accomplishing it. The conservatives alone sat still and held on, sure that in the long run they would triumph even if they could not stop the march of material progress in the cleaning of the streets and the building of railways.

February of 1898 saw the taking off of the most commanding figure in Korean public life during the nineteenth century, in the person of Prince Tä-wŭn the father of the Emperpor, formerly Regent. For almost forty years he had been more or less intimately connected with the stiring events which have marked the present reign. The things which specially marked his career are (1) the Roman Catholic persecution of 1866, (2) the determined oppostion to the opening of the country to foreign intercourse, (3) the building of the Kyŏngbok Palace, (4) the debasing of Korean currency, (5) the feud with the Queen's party, (6) the temporary exile in China, (7) the assassination of the Queen. Whatever may be said for or against the Prince because of his policy he remains in the minds of the people a strong, independent character, and they cannot fail to admire the man even though they have to condemn his policy. His adherents stood by him with splendid loyalty even in the hours of his disgrace, because he was in some sense really great.

This time was characterized by curious inconsistencies. At the same time that an edict was promulgated statirg that no more concessions would be granted to foreigners the Seoul Electric Company was organized to construct a tramway and a lighting plant in Seoul. Material improvements continued parallel with, but in the opposite direction from, the policy of the Government. An agreement was even entered into with an American firm for the construction of a system of water works for Seoul at a cost of some seven million yen.

The failing hopes of the Independence Club drove it to its final place, that of protest. Memorials began to pour in protesting against this and that. In February it complained

of foreign control in Korea, directing the attack apparently
upon the Russian pretentions; but if so it was unnecessary,
for by the first of March the Russians decided that their position was untenable or that a temporary withdrawal of pressure
from Seoul would facilitate operations in other directions, and
so, under cover of a complaint as to the vacillating policy of
the Korean Government they proposed to remove Mr. Alexeieff from his uncomfortable position vis-a-vis Dr. Brown and
also take away all the military instructors. Perhaps they
were under the impression that this startling proposal would
frighten the Government into making protestations that would
increase Russian influence here, but if so they were disappointed for the Government promptly accepted their proposition and dispensed with the services of these men. No
doubt the Government had come to look with some anxiety
upon the growing influence of Russia here and with the same
oscillatory motion as of yore made a strong move in the opposite direction when the opportunity came. The Korean
Government has been nearly as astute as Turkey in playing
off her "friends" against each other.[22]

Just one month later April 12th N. Matunine relieved
Mr. de Speyer, the Russo-Korean bank closed its doors, the Russian military and other officers took their departure and a very
strained situation was relieved for the time being. At about
the same time Dr. Jaisohn was paid off and left the country,
the management of the *Independent* falling into other hands.
This event was important as strowing the hopeless state into
which the Independence Club and all other friends of progress
had fallen. From this time on the tone of the club grew
steadily more petulant. The older men in it who saw that
the time was not ripe for reform withdrew and left the management of the club and the determination of its policy in
the hands of younger men who had not the experience necessary for the handling of such affairs ; and although in Yun-
Chi-ho, the president of the Club, it had a clear-headed and
devoted man he was not able to control the young blood that
had begun to run with something too feverish a course in
the veins of the society. The excited state of the public
mind is proved by the fact that several other daily and weekly
periodicals sprang up, debating societies flourished and people

began to talk about things. The conservations laid all these
things up against the Independence Club and awaited their
time.

The summer of this year furnished Seoul with some excitement in the shape of a discovered conspiracy to force the
King to abdicate, place the Crown Prince on the throne and
institute a new era in Korean history. The plot, if such it
may be called, was badly planned and deservedly fell through.
It was one of the foolish moves called out by the excitement
engendered in the Independence movement. An Kyŭng su,
ex-president of the Independence Club, was the party mainly
implicated and he saved himself only by promptly decamping
and putting himself into the hands of the Japanese.

About the same time the Independence Club came into
direct opposition to the Government in its strong protest against
the appointment of the conservative Cho Pyŭng-sik to the
vice-presidency of the Council of State. The commotion, engendered by this, resulted in Mr. Yun Chi-ho being called before the Emperor, where he made a strong appeal in favor of
the Independence Club and asserted the continued loyalty of
the club toward His Majesty. Unfortunalely he asserted that
the Emperor having sanctioned the founding of the club could
disband it merely by Imperial decree. For the time, this appeal sufficed and the immediate object of the society was secured, but the Emperor did not forget that he had it in his
power to dissolve the club by a single word. As a fact, the
mere sanction of the founding of the Club gave no more power
to dissolve it than the wedding ceremony which a clergyman
performs gives the right in future to dissolve that union.
There can be no doubt that from this time on the Emperor
was determined to eliminate this disturbing element at the
first opportunity. He had no sympathy with its platform,
one plank of which was the curtailment of the Imperial
prerogative.

August saw the fall of Kim Hong-nyuk, the former Russian interpreter, who ruffled it so proudly at Court on account
of his connection with the Russian Legation. For a year he
had a good time of it and amassed great wealth, but when
the Russians withdrew their influence in March of this year
Kim lost all his backing and thenceforward his doom was as

sure as fate itself. The genuine noblemen whose honors he had filched were on his track and in August he was accused, deposed and banished. This did not satisfy his enemies however, but an opportunity came when on September tenth an attempt was made to posion the Emperor and the Crown Prince. The attempt came near succeeding and in the investigation which followed one of the scullions deposed that he had been instructed by a friend of Kim Hong-nyuk to put something into the coffee. How Kim, away in banishment, could have had anything to do with it would be hard to tell. He may have conceived the plan but the verdict of a calm and dispassionate mind must be that he probably knew nothing about it at all. However, in such a case, someone must suffer. The criminal *must* be found; and it is more than probable that those who hated Kim Hong-nyuk thought he would make an excellent scape-goat. He was tried, condemned and executed.

About the same time the Emperor came to the conclusion that he would like to have a foreign body-guard. C. R. Greathouse was sent to Shanghai to find the material for this guard. Thirty men were picked up, of various nationalities, and they arrived in Seoul on September fifteenth. This move caused intense excitement and opposition. The Independence Club was in the fore-front of the protest that was made. A dozen good arguments were adduced showing why this should not be be done, and so unaminous was the sentiment that the Emperor yielded to popular clamor and dismissed the men, but this, again, cannot but have set the Emperor against the Independence Club, inasmuch as they had been principally instrumental in thwarting a pet scheme of his own.

The month of September witnessed better things than these, however. The Japanese obtained their concession for the Seoul-Fusan Railway, an event of great importance every way and one that will mean much to Korea.

In September the Independence Club determined that it would be well to put forward a program of work in place of the merely destructive criticism which had for some time characterized its policy. An appeal was made to the general public to assemble, in order to suggest reforms. Whether this was wise or not is a question. A popular assembly in Korea is hardly capable of coming to wise conclusions or to participate in plans for constructive statesmanship. In addition to this an appeal to the people was inevitably construed by the conservatives as a desperate measure which invited revolution. In a sense they were justfied in so thinking, for the general populace of Korea never has risen in protest unless the evils under which they are suffering have driven them to the last court of appeal, mob law. The move was in the direction of democracy and no one can judge that the people of Korea are ready for any such thing.

However this may be, a mass meeting was held at Chongno, to which representatives of all classes were called. The following articles were formulated and presented to the cabinet for imperial sanction.

(1) Neither officials nor people shall depend upon foreign aid, but shall do their best to strengthen and uphold the Imperial power.

(2) All documents pertaining to foreign loans, the hiring of foreign soldiers, the granting of concessions, &c., in fact every document drawn up between the Korean government and a foreign party or firm, shall be signed and sealed by all the Ministers of State and the President of the Privy Council.

(3) Important offenders shall be punished only after they have been given a public trial and ample opportunity to defend themselves.

(4) To His Majesty shall belong the power to appoint Ministers, but in case a majority of the cabinet disapproves of the Emperor's nominee he shall not be appointed.

(5) All sources of revenue and methods of raising taxes shall be placed under the control of the Finance Department, no other department or officer or corporation being allowed to interfere therewith ; and the annual estimates and balances shall be made public.

(6) The existing laws and regulations shall be enforced without fear or favor.

It will be seen that several of these measures strike directly at powers which have been held for centuries by the King himself and it cannot be supposed that His Majesty would listen willingly to the voice of the common people when they

demanded such far-reaching innovations. The whole thing
was utterly distasteful to him, but the united voice of the people is a serious matter. In such a country as Korea the
clearly announced statement of the common people as to their
wishes carries with it the implication that they have come to
the point where they are ready to make trouble if their demands are not complied with. The intensity of the popular
feeling was shown in the general closing of shops and in the
attendance even of women upon the mass meetings. The reactionists were seriously startled by these demonstrations, and
it became necessary to temporize. These demands were not
such as would involve any immediate changes; they all looked to the future. So it was an easy matter simply to comply
with the demands and wait for the public feeling to subside.
On the last day of September His Majesty ordered the carrying out of these six propositions.

The trouble was that the conservatives felt that they had
not sufficient physical power to oppose a popular uprising.
The temporary concession was made with no idea of real compliance, and was immediately followed by measures for securing a counter demonstration. The instrument selected for
this purpose was the old-time Peddlar's Guild. This was a defunct institution, but the name survived, and the conservatives used it to bring together a large number of men who
were ready for any sort of work that would mean pay. These
were organized into a company whose duty it was to run
counter to all popular demonstrations like those which had just
been made. No sooner was this hireling band organized than
His Majesty, in pursuance of the hint dropped some months
before by the President of the Independence Club, ordered
the disbanding of the Club. From this time on the Independence Club was no longer recognized by the Government
and was an illegal institution, by the very terms of the unfortunate admission of its President that the Emperor could
at any time disband it by Imperial decree. Mr. Yun Chi-ho
had by this time come to see that the Club was running to
dangerous extremes and was likely to cause serious harm ;
and he and others worked with all their power to curb the
excitement and secure rational action on the part of the
members of the Club. But the time when such counsels

could prevail had already passed.   The Club knew that the
principles it advocated were correct and it was angry at the
stubborn opposition that it met.   It was ready to go to any
lengths to secure its ends.   Passion took the place of judgment and the overthrow of the opposition loomed larger in
its view than the accomplishment of its rational ambitions.

Instead of dispersing in compliance with the Imperial
order the assembled Independents went in a body to the
Police Headquarters and asked to be arrested.   This is a
peculiarly Korean mode of procedure, the idea being that if
put on trial they would be able to shame their adversaries ;
and incidentally it embarrassed the adminstration, for the
prisons would not suffice to hold the multitude that clamored
for incarceration.   The crowd was altogether too large and
too determined for the Peddlers to attack and another concession had to be made.   The Independents, for it can no louger
be called the Independent Club, offered to disperse on condition that they be guaranteed freedom of speech.   The
demand was immediately complied with ; anything to disperse
that angry crowd which under proper leadership might at
any moment do more than make verbal demands.   So on the
next day an Imperial decree granted the right of free speech.
This concession, likewise, was followed by a hurried muster of
all the peddlars and their more complete organization.
Backed by official aid and Imperial sanction they were prepared to come to blows with the people who should assemble
for the purpose of making further demands upon the Emperor.

Shortly before this the Emperor had consented to the
proposition that the Independence Club should choose by
ballot from their own number twenty-five men who should
sit in the Privy Council.   This council had for a time exercised some influence during the earlier months of Dr.
Jaisohn's residence in Seoul but it had lost all power and had
become a limbo to which were politely relegated those whom
the government did not care to use and yet was unwilling to
dismiss.   The edict of the Emperor disbanding the Club
would be supposed to countermand this order for election, but
the Independents themselves did not so view it, and the day
set for the election was November 5th.   The conservatives
now deemed themselves strong enough to try conclusions

with the outlawed Club and before daylight of November 5th seventeen of the leading men of the Independence Club were arrested and lodged in jail.   Mr. Yun, the president, narrowly escaped arrest.   It was afterwards ascertained that the plan of the captors was to kill the president of the Club before he could receive aid from the enraged people.

When morning came and the arrest became known the city hummed like a bee-hive.   A surging crowd was massed in front of the Supreme Court demanding loudly the release of the prisoners who had been accused, so the anonymous placards announced, of conspiring to establish a republic! Again the popular feeling was too strong for the courage of the peddlar thugs and they remained in the back-ground. The agitation continued all that day and the next, and the next, until the authorities were either frightened into submission or, deeming that they had shown the Independents a glimpse of what they might expect, released the arrested men.   But the Independents, so far from being cowed, hailed this as a vindication of their policy and attempted to follow up the defeat of the conservatives by demanding the arrest and punishment of the people who had played the trick upon the Club.   As these men were very prominent officials and had the ear of the Emperor it was not possible to obtain the redress demanded.   So the month of November wore away in a ferment of excitement.   Popular meetings were frequent but the crowd had not the determination to come to conclusions with the government.   The conservatives saw this and with utmost nicety gauged the resisting power of the malcontents. The offensive tactics of the latter were confined merely to free speech and the conservatives determined to see what they would do when on the defensive.   Accordingly on the morning of November 21st a band of ruffians, the so-called peddlars, attacked the people who had gathered as usual to discuss the stirring questions of the times.   Weapons were used and a number of people were injured.   The Indepndents had never contemplated the use of force, and this brutal assault aroused the ire of the whole people, most of whom had not as yet taken sides.   Serious hand to hand fights occurred in various parts of the city and the peddlars, conscious that even their most murderous attacks would be condoned in high places, attempted to whip the people into something like quietude.

On the 26th of November in the midst of this chaotic state of things the Emperor granted a great general audience outside the great gate of the palace. The Independence Club was there in force, and foreign representatives and a large number of other foreign residents. It was a little Runnymede but with a different ending. Yun Chi-ho was naturally the spokesman of the Independence party. He made a manly and temperate statement of the position of his constituents. He denounced the armed attacks of the peddlars upon people who intended no violence but only desired the fulfillment of solemnly made pledges. He called to account those who imputed to the Independence Club traitorous designs. He urged that the legal existence of the Club should be again established by Imperial decree and that the six measures so definitely and distinctly promised by His Majesty should be carried out. There was no possible argument to oppose to these requests and the Emperor promised to shape the policy of the government in line with these suggestions. Again it was mere promise, made to tide over an actual and present difficulty. The Independence people should have recognized this. The Emperor was surrounded by men inimical to the reform program, they had the police and the army back of them as well as the peddlars. The Independence party had not a single prominent representative in any really responsible and influential government office. They simply had right and the precarious voice of Korean popular feeling behind them. What was necessary was a campaign of education. The program advocated was one that could be carried out only under a government whose personnel was at least approximately up to the standard of that program. This could be claimed of only two or three members of the Independence Club. Having secured this public promise of His Majesty the club should have waited patiently to see what would happen and if the promises were not kept they should have waited and worked for a time when public sentiment among the leading men would compel reform. But as Mr. Yun himself confesses, "The popular meetings had gone beyond the control of the Indepedence

Club and in the face of strong advice to the contrry they were resumed on December 6th and their language became careless and impudent. On the sixteenth of December the Privy Council recommended the recall of Pak Yong-hyo from Japan. The popular meeting had the imprudence to endorse this action. The more conservative portion of the people revolted against the very mention of the name. Suspicion was excited that the popular agitations had been started in the interests of Pak Yong-hyo and they instantly lost the sympathy of the people." The enemies of the liberal party had probably used this argument to its fullest extent, and when it was seen that the Independence movement had at last been deprived of its strongest support, the popular voice, its enemies came down upon it with cruel force. In spite of voluble promises to the contrary large numbers of the reform party were arrested and thrown into prison; not, to be sure, on the change of being members of this party, but on trumped-up charges of various kinds, especially, that of being accessory to the plan of bringing back Pak Yong-hyo. And thus came to an end a political party whose aims were of the highest character, whose methods were entirely peaceable but whose principles were so far in advance of the times that from the very first there was no human probability of success. But, as Mr. Yun Chi-ho said, though the party dies the principles which it held will live and eventually succeed.

The year 1899 opened with political matters in a more quiet state than for some years past, owing to the violent repression of the Independence Club and the liberal movement. The judgment of the future will be that at this point Japan made a serious mistake of omission. The aims and purposes of the Independence party were directly in line with Japanese interests here and if that powerful government had actively interested itself in the success of the movement and had taken it for granted that the plan was to be definitely carried out the succeeding years would have made very different history than they did.[33] But during all this time Japan seems to have retired into comparative quietude, perhaps because she saw the coming of her inevitable struggle with Russia and was not willing to hasten matters by coming into premature conflict with the northern power in Korea, pending the completion of her preparations for the supreme struggle.

Through all this period Russian influence was quietly at work securing its hold upon the Korean Court and upon such members of the government as it could win over. The general populace was always suspicious of her, however, and always preferred the rougher hand of Japan to the soft but heavy hand of Russia. The progress of the Russian plans was illustrated when in January of 1899 a mission of the Greek Church was established in Seoul. This suggests some remarks upon the general subject of mission work in Korea. The Presbyterian Church of America had established work here in 1884: the Methodist Episcopal Church of America began work in 1885; the Australian Presbyterian Church in 1889; The English Church Mission in 1890; the Southern Presbyterian Church of America in 1892; the Southern Methodist Church of America in 1896; the Canadian Presbyterian Mission in 1898. Besides these there was independent work under some smaller bodies including one Baptist organization and one college mission. When the last year of the 19th century opened these missions had all become firmly established, and important centres of mission work were found all over the country, especially in Seoul, Chemulpo, Pyeng-yang, Fusan, Wonsan, Chǔn-ju, Kunsan, Mokpo, Tä-gu and Song-do. From the very first the Protestant Missions adopted the principle of non-interferance with political affairs and with the ordinary course of justice in Korean courts. [24]It has not always been possible to follow this principle implicitly but the people have come to learn that connection with a Protestant Christian Church will not absolve them from their duties and obligations toward their own government nor shield them from the results of misconduct. It has been found that the Korean temperament makes him easily accessible to the rational idealism of Christianity. From the very first the form of Christianity presented by the Protestant missionaries took hold of the Korears with great power and by the end of the first fifteen years of work the various missions had some twenty thousand adherents. The northern station of the Presbyterian Mission in Korea attained world-wide notice as being, so far as human estimate can go, the most successful mission station in the world ; and this not merely because of the number of people received into Church connection but because of the striking results obtained along the line of self support and independent Christian work. Hospitals were established in Seoul, Fusan, Wonsan, Pyeng-yang, Tä-gu and Chemulpo, and schools of various grades both for boys and girls were established in almost every mission station. 25The work of Bible translation was carried on steadily until by the end of 1899 the whole of the New Testament was put in the hands of the people at least in tentative form. The Korean Religious Tract Society, established early in the last decade of the century, did heroic work in putting forth Christian literature of all kinds. Literary work was represented in various grammars and manuals of Korean, several hymnals, an unabridged dictionary and the publication of a monthly magazine in English called *The Korean Repository*.

Before going forward into the new century we should note some of the more important material advances that Korea had made. Railway concessions for some 600 miles of track had been granted, half to Japanese and half to a French syndicate; several new and important ports had been opened, bringing the total number up to ten, inclusive of Seoul and Pyeng-yang; mining concessions had been given to Americans, English, Germans, French and Japanese, two of which had proved at least reasonably successful; timber and whaling concessions had been given to Russians on the east side of the peninsula and important fishing rights had been given to the Japanese; an attempt at a general system of education had been made throughout the country and the work of publishing text books was being pushed; students were sent abroad to acquire a finished education and legations at all the most important political centers were established; an attempt at a better currency had been made, though it was vitiated by official corruption and the operations of counterfeiters; trade had steadily increased and the imports and exports of Korea passed beyond the negligeable stage; an excellent postal system had been inaugurated under foreign supervision, and Korea had entered the Postal Union.

Thus it will be seen that in spite of all domestic political complications and discouragements the country was making definite advance along some lines. The leaven had begun to work and no conservatism on the part of the public leaders could stop the ferment.

The necrology of the closing year of the century contains the names of Mr. Legender and Mr. Greathouse, the latter of whom, as legal adviser to the government, did excellent work in his department and was recognized by his employers as an able and efficient man in his official capacity.

Chapter XXIV.

The return to Seoul of M. Pavlow on Jan. 15, 1900, marked the definite beginning of that train of events which led up to the declaration of war by the Japanese in 1904. The Russians had been induced, two years previously, to remove the heavy pressure which they had brought to bear upon the government, but it was only a change of method. They were now to adopt a policy of pure intrigue and by holding in power Koreans who were hostile to the Japanese to harrass and injure Japanese interests in every way possible.

At this same time we see a clear indication of the trend of events in the return to Korea of An Kyŭng-su and Kwan Yŭng-jin, two of the best men that late years had developed in Korea. They had been charged with connection with the plot to compass the abdication of His Majesty, and had taken refuge in Japan. Now on the promise of the government that they should have a perfectly fair trial and on the guarantee of protection by the Japanese they returned boldly to Korea and presented themselves for trial. They were strong men and they had to be reckoned with. They strongly favored Japanese influence and the reforms that that influence was supposed to embody. In fact they were thoroughly in sympathy with the best motives of the defunct Independence Club. An Kyŭng-su returned on January fifteenth and was held in detention until May sixteenth when Kwan Yŭng-jin returned. They were to stand a fair trial, but on the night of the twenty-seventh of May they were both strangled secretly in the prison. No more dastardly crime ever stained the annals of this or any other government. Induced to return on the promise of a fair trial they were trapped and murdered. The reactionists looked upon this as a signal victory, and indeed it was such, for it indicated clearly that a man was not safe even when he had the guarantee of the Japanese authorities. Nor would it be difficult to indicate the source from which the government obtained the courage thus to flout the Japanese.

As the summer came on, all interest in things Korean was held in suspension while the great uprising in China swelled to such monstrous proportions and the investment of Peking and the siege of the foreign legations there left the world no time to care for or think of other things. There were fears that the boxer movement would be contagious and that it would spread to Korea. Indeed it was reported in the middle of July that the infection had reached northern Korea; but fortunately this proved false.

In spite of the reactionary policy of the government progress continued to be made on certain lines, just as the momentum of a railway train cannot be checked the moment the brakes are applied. A distinguished French legalist was employed as adviser to the Law Department; mining concessions were granted to British, French and Japanese syndicates; the Government Middle School was established; the Seoul-Chemulpo Railway was formally opened; A French teacher was engaged to open a School of Mines; a representative was sent to the great Paris Exposition.

This year 1900 was the heyday of another *parvenu* in the person of Kim Yŭng-jun. He was a man without any backing except his own colossal effrontery. He had acquired influence by his ability to get together considerable sums of money irrespective of the methods employed. Scores of wealthy men were haled to prison on one pretext or another and were released only upon the payment of a heavy sum. He was a man of considerable force of character but like so many adventurers in Korea he was lured by his successes into a false feeling of security and he forgot that the history of this country is full of just such cases and that they inevitably end in violent death. Even the fate of Kim Hong-nyuk did not deter him, though his case was almost the counterpart of that victim of his own overweening ambitions. Against Kim Yŭng-jun was ranged the whole nobility of the country who waited with what patience they could until his power to extort money began to wane, and then fell upon him like wolves upon a belated traveler at night. But it was not until the opening of the new year 1901 that he was deposed, tried and killed in a most horrible manner. After excruciating tortures he was at last strangled to death.

But even as this act was perpetrated and the fate of all such adventurers was again illustrated, another man of the same ilk was pressing to the fore. This was Yi Yong-ik, who had once been the *major domo* of one of the high officials and in that capacity had learned how to do all sorts of interesting, if unscrupulous, things. He was prominent in a felonious attempt to cheat the ginseng farmers of Song-do out of thousands, back in the eighties. He was an ignorant boor and even when rolling in oppulence failed to make himself presentable in dress or manner. He was praised by some for his scorn of luxury and because he made no attempt to hoard the money that he bled from the veins of the people. The reason he did not hoard it was the same that makes the farmer sow his seed, that he may reap a hundred-fold. Yi Yong-ik sowed his golden seed in fertile soil and it yielded him a thousand fold.

One of his favorite methods of obtaining money for his patron was to cause the arrest of shoals of former prefects who for one cause or another had failed to turn into the public treasury the complete amount nominally levied upon their respective districts. These arrears went back several years and many of them were for cause. Either famine or flood or some other calamity had made it impossible for the people to pay the entire amount of their taxes. There were many cases, without doubt, in which it was right to demand the money from the ex-prefects, for they had "eaten" it themselves; but there were also many cases in which it was a genuine hardship. Literally hundreds of men were haled before a court and made to pay over large sums of money, in default of which their property was seized as well as that of their relatives. In exact proportion as the huge sums thus extorted paved his way to favor in high places, in that same proportion it drove the people to desperation. The taking off of Kim Yŭng-jin, so far from warning this man, only opened a larger door for the exercise of his peculiar abilities, and it may be said that the official career of Yi Yong-ik began with the opening of 1901.

In March a Japanese resident of Chemulpo claimed to have purchased the whole of Roze Island in the harbor of Chemulpo. The matter made a great stir, for it was plain that someone had assumed the responsibility of selling the island to the Japanese. This was the signal for a sweeping investigation which was so manipulated by powerful parties that the real perpetrators of the outrage were desmissed as guiltless, but a side-issue which arose in regard to certain threatening letters that were sent to the foreign legations was made a peg upon which to hang the seizure, trial and execution of Kim Yŭng-jun as before mentioned. Min Yŭng-ju was the man who sold the island to the Japanese and he finally had to put down Y35,000 and buy it back.

Russia made steady advances toward her ultimate goal during the year 1901. In the Spring some buildings in connection with the palace were to be erected and the Chief Commissioner of Customs, J. McLeavy Brown, C. M. G , was ordered to vacate his house on the customs compound at short notice. Soldiers even forced their way into his house. This affront was a serious one and one that the Koreans would never have dared to give had they not felt that they had behind them a power that would see them through.

The British authorities soon convinced the government that such tactics could be easily met and it had to retreat with some loss of dignity.

The Russian Church established itself in Seoul at this time and took active steps to start a propaganda in Korea. Considerable disturbance was caused in the Southern provinces by Koreans who had become Russian subjects pretending to be agents of the Russian church and collecting from the people large sums of money by intimidation. For many months the Russians tried to induce the Koreans to allow the Korean telegraph lines in the North-east to be connected with the Russian line from Vladivostock. Why this should not be done we cannot see but evidently the Koreans considered it a national danger and, try as they might, the Russians never really succeeded in making the connection.

The Russians and French were naturally working together in the peninsula and when Russia adopted the principle of withdrawing her military instructors from Korea she so manipulated the wires that the government threw many positions into the hands of the French. For the next three years the French population of Seoul increased manyfold. Many of the French gentlemen employed by the government were thoroughly competent and rendered good service but their presence tended to add to the tension between Japan and Russia, for it was quite plain that all their influence would be thrown in the scale on Russia's side. The attempt to loan the Korean Government Y5,000,000 was pushed with desperate vigor for many months by the French, but divided counsels prevented the final consummation of the loan and the French thus failed to secure the strong leverage which a heavy loan always gives to the creditor. Yi Yong-ik who had become more or less of a Russian tool was pointedly accused by the Japanese of being in favor of the French loan but he vigorously denied it. It is generally admitted that Yi Yong-ik was something of a mystery even to his most intimate acquaintances and just how far he really favored the Russian side will never be known, but it is certian that he assumed a more and more hostile attitude toward the Japanese as the months went by, an attitude which brought him into violent conflict with them, as we shall see.

Yi Yong-ik posed as a master in finance, whatever else he may or may not have been, and in 1901 he began the minting of the Korean nickel piece. No greater monetary disaster ever overtook this country. Even the desperate measures taken by the Regent thirty years before had not shaken the monetary system as this did. The Regent introduced the wretched five-cash piece which did enormous harm but that five-cash piece was of too small face value to be worth counterfeiting. The nickel was the ideal coin to tempt the counterfeiter, for its intrinsic value was not so great as to require the employment of a large amount of capital and yet its face value was sufficient to pay for the labor and time expended. The effects of this departure will be noted in their place.

In the summer of 1901 Yi Yong-ik performed one act that, in the eyes of the people, covered a multitude of other sins. It was a year of great scarcity. The Korean farmers raised barely enough grain for domestic consumption and in order to prevent this grain from being taken out of the country the government proclaimed an embargo on its export. In spite of the fact that Japan was enjoying an unusually good crop and did not really need the Korean product, the Japanese authorities, in the interest of the Japanese exporters in Korea, brought pressure to bear upon the Korean government to raise the embargo, utterly regardless of the interests of the Korean people. As it turned out however, the enhanced price in Korea due to the famine and the cutting of a full crop in Japan prevented the export of rice. But Yi Yong-ik saw that there would inevitably be a shortage in Seoul and with much forethought he sent and imported a large amount of Annam rice and put it on the market at a price so reasonable that the people were highly gratified. From that time on whenever the mistakes of Yi Yong-ik were cited there was always someone to offer the extenuation of that Annam rice. It was a most clever and successful appeal to popular favor.

All through this year 1901 were heard the distant rumblings of that storm that was to break three years later. Every movement of the Russians by land or sea was watched with a fascinated attention and every proposition of the Japanese was closely scrutinized. As a fact the war was already in

existence, only it had not been declared. Even then Japanese agents were swarming all over Manchuria gaining exact
information of its geography and products and Japan was
hastening the preparation of her navy for the struggle that
she felt to be inevitable.

As the year 1901 came to a close the tension was beginning to be felt. People were asking how much longer Japan
would acquiesce in the insolent encroachments of Russia. But
the time was not yet. As for material advances the year had
seen not a few. Seoul had been supplied with electric light.
The Seoul-Fusan Railway had been begun. Plans for the
Seoul-Wiju Railway had been drawn up. Mokpo had been
supplied with a splendid sea-wall. Building had gone on
apace in the capital and even a scheme for a system of water-
works for the city had been worked out and had received
the sanction of the government. Education had gone from
bad to worse and at one time when retrenchment seemed
necessary it was even suggested to close some of the schools,
but better counsels prevailed and this form of suicide was
rejected.

With the opening of the year 1902 there were several in-
dications that the general *morale* of the government was de-
teriorating   The first was a very determined attempt to revive the Buddhist cult. The Emperor consented to the establishment of a great central monastery for the whole country in the vicinity of Seoul, and in it was installed a Buddhist
High Priest in Chief who was to control the whole Buddhist
Church in the land.   It was a ludicrous attempt, for Buddhism in Korea is dead so far as any genuine influence is concerned.   Mixed with the native spirit-worship it has its millions of devotees, but so far as becoming a fashionable cult is
concerned nothing is more unlikely. But it has been the
case for over a thousand years that when things have gone
badly in the government there has been a harking back to the
old Buddhist mummery, to fortune-tellers, geomancers and the
like, and the only significance of this attempt was to prove
that there was something ''rotten in Denmark.''

Another evidence was the constant and successful attempt to centralize the power of the Government in the hands
of the Emperor.   The overthrow of the Independence Party,

whose main tenet was curtailment of the Imperial prerogative, gave a new impulse to the enlargement of that prerogative
so that in the year 1901 we find almost all the government
business transacted in the Palace itself.   The various ministers of state could do nothing on their own initiative.
Everything was centered in the throne and in two or three
favorites who stood near the throne.   Of these Yi Yong-ik
was the most prominent.

A third evidence of deterioration was the methods adopted to fill the coffers of the Household treasury.   The previous year had been a bad one.   Out of a possible twelve
million dollars of revenue only seven million could be
collected.   There was great distress all over the country and
the pinch was felt in the palace.   Special inspectors and
agents were therefore sent to the country armed with authority from the Emperor to collect money for the Household treasury.   These men adopted any and every means to
accomplish their work and this added very materially to the
discontent of the people.   The prefects were very loath to
forego a fraction of the taxation, because they saw how
previous prefects were being mulcted because of failure to
collect the full amount, and so between the prefect and the
special agents the people seemed to be promised a rather bad
time.   In fact it caused such an outcry on every side that
the government at last reluctantly recalled the special
agents.

Early in the year the fact was made public that Korea
had entered into an agreement with Russia whereby it was
guaranteed that no land at Masanpo or on the island of Kö-je
at its entrance should ever be sold or permanently leased to
any foreign Power.   Russia had already secured a coaling
station there and it was generally understood, the world
over, that Russia had special interest in that remarkably
fine harbor.   Avowedly this was merely for pacific purposes,
but the pains which Russia took to make a secret agreement
with Korea debarring other Powers from privileges similar to
those which she had acquired, naturally aroused the suspicions of the Japanese and of the Koreans themselves, those of
them that had not been in the secret ; and this step, inimical
to Japan as it undoubtedly was, probably helped to hasten the

final catastrophe. Meanwhile Russian subjects were taking advantage of the influential position of their Government in Seoul and through ministeral influence some glass-makers, iron-workers and weavers were employed by the Government without the smallest probability of their ever doing anything in any of these lines. In fact at about this time the Government was induced to take on quite a large number of Russians and Russian sympathisers who never were able to render any service whatever in lieu of their pay. In many cases the most cursory investigation would have shown that such would inevitably be the result. It is difficult to evade the conclusion that the Government was deliberately exploited.

It was in the spring of this year that the project began to be seriously discussed in Japan of colonizing portions of Korea with Japanese. and a society or company was formed in Tokyo with this as its avowed purpose. This naturally evoked a good deal of feeling in Korea where the Japanese were not at the time enjoying any considerable influence at court. The fact then came out for the first time, and has been further emphasized since, that the Korean, whatever he may feel for his Government, is passionately attached to the soil. [26]

But at this time another and a far greater surprise was in store for the world. It was the announcement of a defensive alliance between Japan and Great Britain. By the terms of this agreement Japan and great Britain guaranteed to insure the independence of Korea and the integrity of the Chinese Empire.[27] The tremendous influence of this historic document was felt at once in every capital of Europe and in every capital, port and village of the Far East. It stung the lethargic to life and it caused the rashly enthusiastic to stop and think. There can be no manner of doubt that this alliance was one of the necessary steps in preparing for the war which Japan already foresaw on the horizon. It indicated clearly to Russia that her continued occupation of Manchuria and her continued encroachments upon Korea would be called in question at some not distant day. But she was blind to the warning. This convention bound Great Britain to aid Japan in defensive operations and to work with her to the preservation of

Korean independence and the integrity of China. It will be seen, therefore, that Japan gave up once and for all any thought that she might previously have had of impairing the independence of this country and any move in that direction would absolve Great Britain from all obligations due to the signing of the agreement.

The year had but just begun when the operations of counterfeiters of nickel coins became so flagrant as to demand the attention of all who were interested in trade in the peninsula. Japan had most at stake and Russia had least, and this explains why the Russian authorities applauded the work of Yi Yong-ik and encouraged him to continue and increase the issue of such coinage. In March matters had come to such a pass that the foreign representatives, irrespective of partisan lines, met and discussed ways and means for overcoming the difficulty. After careful deliberation they framed a set of recommendations which were sent to the Government. These urged the discontinuance of this nickel coinage, the withdrawal from circulation of spurious coins and stringent laws against counterfeiting. But this was of little or no avail. The Government was making a five cent coin at a cost of less than two cents and consequently the counterfeiters with good tools could make as good a coin as the Government and still realize enormously on the operation. It was impossible to detect the counterfeited coins, in many cases, and so there was no possibility of withdrawing them from circulation. The heavy drop in exchange was not due so much to the counterfeiting as to the fact that the intrinsic value of the coin was nothing like as much as the face value, and by an immutable law of finance as well as of human nature it fell to a ruinous discount. But even this would not have worked havoc with trade if, having fallen, the discredited coinage would stay fallen, but it had the curious trick of rising and falling with such sudden fluctuations that business became a mere gamble, and the heavy interests of Japanese and Chinese merchants were nearly at a standstill.

Chapter XXV.

Tae Japanese Bank issus notes ...Independence Club scare ...light-
houses.... Opening of work on Seoul-Wiju R.R..... combination
against Yi Yong-ik   be is accused and degraded .. rescued by
Russian guard... protest of the Japanese against his return....Yi
Keun-t'äk   Russian complacency ...Russian policy in the Far
East....contrast between Russia's and Japan's aims.

At this point the First Bank of Japan, called the Dai
Ichi Ginko, brought up a scheme for putting out an issue of
special bank notes that would not circulate outside of Korea.
Korea was importing much more than she exported and the
balance of trade being against her it was impossible to keep
Japanese paper in the country in sufficient quantities to carry
on ordinary local trade.   For this reason the bank received
the sanction of the Korean Government to put out this issue
of bank paper which could not be sent abroad but would be
extremely useful as a local currency.   This was done and it
was found to work admirably.   The Koreans had confidence
in this money and it circulated freely.   It had two advantages
not enjoyed by any form of Korean currency, namely, it was
a stable currency and suffered no fluctuations and it was in
large enough denominations to make it possible to transfer a
thousand dollars from one man's pocket to that of another
without employing a string of pack-ponies to carry the
stuff.

But we must retrace our steps and note some other
events of interest that happened in the spring months.   One
of these was the scare in government circles over the reported revival of the Independence Club under the encouragement of a so-called Korean Party in Tokyo, to which it was
believed some Korean political refugees belonged. A great
stir was made in Seoul and several men were arrested, but
there was no evidence that would pay sifting, and though it
was evident that the government would have been glad to
find a true bill against some of the men who were arrested it
was forced by lack of evidence to let them go.   The incident was of importance only as showing the extreme sen-
sitiveness of the government on the point, and its determi-

nation, now that the Independence Party was down, to keep it down.

The one important material improvement of the year was the adoption of a plan for the building of some thirty light-houses on the coast of Korea. Ever since the opening up of foreign trade the lack of proper lights especially on the western coast had been a matter of growing concern to shipping companies. This concern was warranted by the dangerous nature of the coast where high tides, a perfect network of islands and oft-prevailing fogs made navigation a most difficult and dangerous matter. The fact that light-houses ought to have been built ten years ago does not detract from the merit of those who at last took the matter in hand and pushed it to an issue

The month of May witnessed a spectacular event in the ceremony of the formal opening of work on the Seoul-Wiju Railway. The spirit was willing but the flesh was weak. Neither French nor Russian money was forthcoming to push the work, and so the Korean government was invited to finance the scheme. Yi Yong-ik was made president of the company and if there had been a few thousand more ex-prefects to mulct he might have raised enough money to carry the road a few miles ; but it is much to be feared that his financial ability, so tenderly touched upon by the Japanese Minister in his speech on that "auspicious occasion," was scarcely sufficient for the work, and the plan was not completed. There is much reason to believe that this whole operation was mainly a scheme on the part of the Russians to preempt the ground in order to keep the Japanese out.

As the year wore toward its close the usurpation of numerous offices by Yi Yong-ik and his assumption of complete control in the palace bore its legitimate fruit in the inteuse hatred of four-fifths of the entire official class. He was looked upon as but one more victim destined to the same fate which had overtaken Kim Hong-nyuk and Kim Yŭng-jun. But in his case the difficulties were much greater. Yi Yong-ik had put away in some safe place an enormous amount of Government money and he held it as a hostage for his personal safety. Until that money was safely in the

Imperial treasury even the revenge would not be sweet enough to make it worth the loss. Not only so but the whole finances of the Household were in his hands and his sudden taking off would leave the accounts in such shape that no one could make them out, and enormous sums due the department would be lost. Yi Yong-ik had fixed himself so that his life was better worth than his death however much that might be desired. But the officiary at large cared little for this. There was no doubt that the one person who should accomplish the overthrow of the favorite and thus bring embarrassment to the Imperial purse would suffer for it, but Korean intrigue was quite capable of coping with a little difficulty like this. The result must be brought about by a combination so strong and so unanimous that no one would ever know who the prime mover was. This at least is a plausible theory and the only one that adequately explains how and why the scheme miscarried. The whole course of the intrigue is so characteristically Korean and includes so many elements of guinune humor, in spite of its object, that we will narrate it briefly. It must of course be understood that the officials were keenly on the lookout for an opportunity to get the hated favorite on the hip and in such a manner that even his financial value to the Emperor would not avail him.

One day, while in conversation with Lady Om, the Emperor's favorite concubine who has been mistress of the palace since the death of the Queen, Yi Yong-ik compared her to Yang Kwi-bi a concubine of the last Emperor of the Tang dynasty in China. He intended this as a compliment but as his education is very limited he was not aware that he could have said nothing more insulting; for Kwi-bi by her meretricious arts is believed to have brought about the destruction of the Tang dynasty. At the time Lady Om herself was unaware that anything derogatory had been said and she received the supposed compliment with complacency; but her nephew who was present, not understanding the reference, went and asked someone else about it and learned the truth of the matter. He doubtless knew that Yi Yong-ik was not aware of his *gaucherie* and so held his peace for a time, but in some way the Prime Minister and the Foreign

Minister heard a rumor that something insulting had been said. They called up the nephew of Lady Om and from him learned the damning facts. They also knew well enough that no insult had been intended but here was a "case" to be worked to its fullest capacity. The most sanguine could not hope that the hated favorite would give them a better hold upon him than this; for the position of Lady Om was a very delicate one and there had been a dispute on for years between the Emperor's counsellors as to the advisability of raising her to the position of Empress. A word against her was a most serious matter.

Everything was now ready for the grand *coup* and on the 27th of Novenber fourteen of the highest officials memorialized the throne declaring that Yi Yong ik was a traitor and must be condemned and executed at once. His Majesty suggested a little delay but on the evening of the same day the same men presented a second memorial couched in still stronger language, and they followed if up the next morning with a third. To their urgent advice was added that of Lady Om herself and of many other of the officials. A crowd of offic-ials gathered at the palace gate and on their knees awaited the decision of the Emperor. There was not a single soul of all that crowd but knew that the charge was a mere excuse and yet it was nominally valid. It was the will of that powerful company against the will of the Emperor. The tension was two great and His Majesty at last reluctantly consented, or at least expressed consent; but he first ordered the accused to be stripped of all his honors and to render all his accounts. This was nominally as reasonable as was the charge against the man. It was a case of "diamond cut diamond" in which the astuteness of the Emperor won. The accusers could not object to having the accused disgorge before being executed but it was at this very point that they were foiled Yi Yong-ik's accounts were purposely in such shape that it would have taken a month to examine them, for he alone held the key. Nothing can exceed the desperate coolness of the man under the awful ordeal. At one point, just after the acquiescence of the Emperor, the written sentence of death is said to have gone forth but was recalled just as it was to have gone out of the palace gates, after which there would have been no recall. No man ever escaped by a narrower margin. When Yi Yong-ik presented his accounts the Emperor announced that it would take some days to straighten matters out since the accused was the only man to unravel the skein. Here was probably the crucial point in the intrigue. If the white heat of the day before had been maintained and the officials had demanded instant punishment, accounts or no accounts, the thing would have been done, but as it happened the consciousness of having won relaxed the tension to such a degree that the accused gained time. This time was utilized by calling in a Russian guard and spiriting the accused away to the Russian Legation. This accomplished His Majesty suavely announced that the case would be considered, but that meanwhile the officials must disperse. There were further memorials, resignations *en masse*, passionate recriminations until at last two or three officials who had held their peace saw that the game was up and, in order to curry favor themselves, offered a counter memorial charging Yi Yong-ik's accusers with indirection. This was listened to and the Prime Minister was deprived of his official rank. This made possible a compromise whereby both Yi Yong-ik and the Prime Minister were restored to all their former honors and all went "merry as a marriage bell." But it was thought best to let Yi Yong-ik travel for his own and his country's good, so he was made Commissioner to Buy Annam Rice, which was itself a pretty piece of diplomacy since it recalled prominently to the people the one phase of the injured man's career which they could unhesitatingly applaud. He was taken off in a Russian cruiser to Port Arthur—to buy Annam rice!

When he returned to Seoul a few weeks later the Japanese lodged a strong protest against his return to political power but the Russian authorities made a counter-proposition urging that he was the only man capable of handling the finances of the country. Under existing circumstances the very protest of the Japanese was an argument in his favor and he came back into power on the flood tide, backed, as he had never been before, by the full favor of the Russian party. They naturally expected substantial payment for having saved him, and so far as he was able he liquidated the debt.

Meanwhile another man, Yi Keun-t'ǎk, had risen to
power through servile adherance to Russian interests.   The
somewhat enigmatical character of Yi Yong-ik made him to
a certain extent an unknown quantity.   Not even the Japanese considered him wholly given over to Russia ; but this new
man was definitely committed to Russian interests and with his
rise to important position it became evident for the first time
that the Korean Government had decided to rely upon Russia
and to reject the aid or the advice of Japan.   The end of the
year 1902 may be said to have been the approximate time
when Japan first realized that all hope of a peaceful solution
of the Korean problem was gone.   One naturally asks why
Korea took this step, and, while we are still too near the
event to secure an entirely dispassionate estimate or opinion,
there seems to be little doubt that it was because Russia
made ro pretensions, and expessed no desire, to reform the
administration of the Government.   She was perfectly content
to let things go along in the old way in the peninsula, knowing that this would constantly and increasingly jeopardize the
interests of Japan while she herself had practically no commercial interests to suffer.

The immemorial policy of Russia in Asia sufficiently
accounts for her work in Korea.   Her policy of gradual
absorption of native tribes has never held within its purview
the civilizing or the strengthening of those tribes, until they
have been gathered under her aegis.   On the other hand,
until that has been accomplished she has either waited patiently for the disintegration of the native tribes or has actually
aided in such disintegration.   History shows no case in which
Russia has strengthened the hands of another people for the
sake of profiting by the larger market that would be opened
up; for until very recently the commercial side of the
question has scarcely been considered, and even now the
commercial interests of Russia depend upon an exclusive
market.   So that in any case a dominant political influence
is the very first step in every move of Russia in the East.
Why then should Russia have advised administrative or
monetary or any other reform, since such action would inevitably form a bar to the success of her own ultimate
plans?

The historian of the future, taking his stand above and out of the smoke of battle, will take a dispassionate view of the whole situation. He will mark the antecedents of these two rival Powers, he will compare their domestic and foreign policies, he will weigh the motives that impelled them, he will mark the instruments wielded by each and the men whom they employed as their intermediaries and agents. Then and not till then will it be possible to tell whether the present recorders of events are right in asserting that while the policies of both Powers are essentially selfish the success of Russia's policy involves the disintegration and national ruin of the peoples she comes in contact with while the success of Japan's policy demands the rehabilitation of the Far East.

Much depended upon the attitude which Korea should finally assume toward these two mutually antagonistic policies. If she had sided with Japan and had shown a fixed determination to resist the encroachments of Russia by adopting a policy of internal renovation which would enlist the interest and command the admiration of the world, the present war might have been indefinitely postponed. Whether it could have been finally avoided would depend largely upon the changes that are taking. place in Russia herself where in spite of all repressive agencies education and enlightenment are filtering in and causing a gradual change. Here again the future historian may be able to say with confidence that it was better that the war came when it did in that it confirmed Japan in her course of commercial, industrial and intellectual expansion, guaranteed China against disintegration and opened the eyes of the Russians themselves to their need of radical internal reform. And he may be able to say that the temporary suspension of Korean autonomy was but a small price to pay for these enormous benefits to the Far East and to the world at large. [28]

Chapter XXVI.

Russia....The Russian timber concession....Russia enters Yongampo....Korean prophecies....Japan, England and America urge
the opening of Yongampo....Russia prevents it....Russians exceed limits of concession....Japanese protest ...Port Nicholas....
Japanese suspend business in Seoul....Korean pawn brokers stop
business ...Legation guards ...government protest against them
....fears of popular uprising ...native press incendiary....fears of
trouble in the country.. .Foreigner threatened.

The year 1903 beheld the rapid culmination of the difficulties between Japan and Russia. It had already become
almost sure that war alone would cut the Gordian knot, and
if any more proof was necessary this year supplied it.

Yi Yong-ik in Port Arthur received assurance from the
Emperor that if he returned he would be given a powerful
guard, and in this he was doubtless seconded by the Russians
who could use him to better advantage in Seoul than in Port
Arthur. He telegraphed for 15,000 bags of Annam rice and
arrived in Chemulpo on the very day the rice came. It
formed a sort of peace offering which, in the temporary
scarcity, was very agreeable to the people. His return was
the signal for a vigorous attack upon Japanese interests.
On the eleventh of the preceding September the Acting
Minister of Foreign Affairs had issued an order prohibiting
the use of the Japanese bank notes, alleging that since they
were not government notes they were unsafe. This was a
direct breach of faith. because as we have seen the Japanese
Bank had already obtained the full consent of the government to issue and circulate these notes. It is almost incon-
ceivable that any man of ministerial rank would be so devoid
of ordinary common sense as to attempt such a thing as this.
Of course there was an instant and peremptory protest on the
part of the Japanese authorities and the government had to
stultify itself by taking it all back. The promise was made
that the governors of the provinces would be instructed to remove all objections to the circulation of the notes, but the
promise was never kept. Now on the seventeenth of January Yi Yong-ik, who had but just returned, made a fierce attack upon the Japanese bank and a note was sent from the
Finance Department to that of Foreign Affairs demanding by
what right the latter had ventured to interfere in the finances of

the country. Cho Pyŭng-sik who had reinstated the Japanese notes was dismissed from the Foreign Office and everything fell into the hands of Yi Yong-ik. A few days later the Mayor of Seoul posted a circular forbidding the use of these notes on pain of severe punishment. This went all over the country and there was an immediate run on the bank, which was tided over with the greatest difficulty. Of course the Japanese were in a position to make reprisals, and after a little pointed talk the bluster of the favorite subsided to a weak whisper, and the authorities apologized in the most abject manner. It should be noted that the Russians gave no help to Yi Yong-ik when it came to the point of an actual breach with Japan.

For some time there had been great unrest throughout the province of Whang-hă owing to the lawless acts of the Roman Catholic adherents there. The matter was brought clearly before the notice of the Government through American Protestant missionaries because many of the Protestant native Christians had been involved in those troubles and had been imprisoned, beaten, tortured and robbed by those who were avowedly members of the Roman Church. A number of these lawless acts were committed under the sign and seal of the Church itself. When the matter became too notorious to escape action on the part of the Government a native official named Yi Eung-ik was appointed as a special Commissioner to go to Hă-ju, the capital the province, and investigate the matter thoroughly. Foreign representatives of both the Roman Catholics and of the Protestants were present and the trial was instituted in a perfectly fair and impartial manner. It was clear that the truth, the whole truth and nothing but the truth was to be elicited by this trial and after vain attempts to quash the indictment one of the French Catholic priests left the place accompanied and followed by a considerable number of those against whom there were most serious charges. These people gathered at a certain town and assumed a threatening attitude toward the Korean Government, but though all the foreign Roman Catholic representatives refused to attend the trial of the dozen or more of their adherents who had been arrested, the trial continued and charge after charge of the most grievous nature was proved, one man being convicted of murder.   During the trial various attempts were made to discredit the Commissioner but before the end of the trials his power was greatly increased.   The result was to put an end to the difficulties and though those responsible for the outrages were never adequately punished it is probable that the Korean Government sufficiently demonstrated its purpose to deal with such matters in a strictly impartial manner.

The great preponderance of Russian influence was manifested early in 1903 by the decision on the part of the Government to send a number of young Koreans to Russia to study, but when it came to the point of selecting the men it was found that there was no desire on the part of the students to go.   This was due in part to the feeling that Korean students abroad are not looked after very carefully by the authorities and there are long delays in, if not complete cessation of, transmission of money for their support.

Early in the year it transpired that the Russians had obtained from the Korean Emperor a concession to cut timber along the Yalu River.   The thing was done secretly and irregularly and the government never received a tithe of the value of the concession.   By this act the government dispossessed itself of one of its finest sources of wealth and sacrificed future millions for a few paltry thousand in hand, and a promise to pay a share of the profits, though no provision was made for giving the government an opportunity of watching the work in its own interests.   Soon after the Russians had begun to work the concession they began to make advances for the obtaining of harbor facilities in connection with it. The port of Yongampo was decided upon and the Korean government was asked to allow the Russians the use of it for this purpose.   This created a very profound impression upon Japan and upon the world at large.   It was felt that this was giving Russia a foothold upon the soil of Korea, and Russia's history shows that, once gained, the point would never be given up.   The activity of Russia in the north gave rise to the notion that Japanese influence was predominant in the southern half of the peninsula and Russian in the northern half. This gave birth to all sorts of rumors among the Korean people and the ancient books were ransacked for prophecies that would fit the situation. One of these is worth repeating since it illustrates very perfectly the Korean tendency to consult some oracle in times of national peril. This particular prophecy is supposed to say that "when white pine-trees grow in Korea the northern half of the peninsula will go to the Tartar and the southern half to the Shrimp." Japan, from its shape, is said to resemble a shrimp, while Tartar covers the Muscovite. The people interpreted the "white pines" to refer to the telegraph poles! And thus the prophecy was considered to mean that when Korea is opened to foreign intercourse it will be divided between Russia and Japan. It cannot be said that this caused any considerable stir among the people and its only value lies in the certain indication that it afforded of the general unrest and suspicion among them. As a whole the attitude of the Korean has always been a rational and consistent one as between Russia and Japan. He has a greater personal antipathy for the latter because they have come into closer contact, but there is a mysterious dread in his heart which warns him of the Russian. He will never say which he would rather have in power here, but always says, "I pray to be delivered from them both."

Japan began to urge upon the government the necessity of opening Yongampo to foreign trade, but Russia, of course, opposed this with all her powers of persuasion. Great Britain and the United States joined in urging the opening of the port. The United States had already arranged for the opening of the port of Antung just opposite Yongampo, and for the sake of trade it was highly desirable that a port on the Korean side of the Yalu should be opened. It had no special reference to the Russian occupation of the port, but as pressure was being brought to bear upon the government to throw open the port it was considered an opportune time to join forces in pushing for this desired end. And it was more for the interest of Korea to do this than for any of the powers that were urging it. Such an act would have been a check to Russian aggression and would have rendered nugatory any ulterior plan she might have as regards Korea. But the Russian power in Seoul was too great. It had not upheld the cause of Yi Yong-ik in vain, and the government, while using very specious language, withstood every attempt to secure the opening of the port.   At last the American Government modified its request and asked that Wiju be opened, but to this Russia objected almost as strongly as to the other.   There can be little doubt that this uncompromising attitude of Russia on the Korean border confirmed Japan in the position she had doubtlesss already assumed.   It was quite evident that the force of arms was the only thing that would make Russia retire from Korean soil.

All through the summer complaints came in from the north that the Russians were working their own will along the northern border and taking every advantage of the loose language in which the agreement had been worded.   Again and again information came up to Seoul that the Russian agents were going outside the limits specified in the bond but there was no one to check it.   It was impossible to police the territory encroched upon and there is reason to believe that the Government chafed under the imposition.   At least the telegraph lines which the Russians erected entirely without warrant were repeatedly torn down by emissaries of the Government and apparently without check from the central authorities.

In the Summer when the text of the proposed Agreement between Russia and Korea anent Yongampo became public the Japanese Government made a strong protest.   She probably knew that this was a mere form but she owed it to herself to file a protest against such suicidal action on the part of Korea. The insolence of the Russians swelled to the point of renaming Yongampo Port Nicholas.

In October the Japanese merchants in Seoul and other commercial centers began calling in all outstanding moneys, with the evident expectation of war.   All brokers and loan associations closed their accounts and refused to make further loans.   It is more than probable that they had received the hint that it might be well to suspend operations for the time being.   From this time until war was declared the people of Korea waited in utmost suspense.   They knew war only as a universal desolation.   They had no notion of any of the comparative amenities of modern warfare or the immunities of noncombatants.   War meant to them the breaking up of the

very foundations of society, and many a time the anxious inquiry was put as to whether the war would probably be
fought on Korean soil or in Manchuria. Once more Korea
found herself the "Shrimp between two whales" and doubly
afflicted in that whichever one should win she would in all
probability form part of the booty of the victor.

The year 1904, which will be recorded in history as one of
the most momentous in all the annals of the Far East, opened
upon a very unsatisfactory state of things in Korea. It had
become as certain as any future event can be that Japan and
Russia would soon be at swords points. The negotiations
between these two powers were being carried on in St. Petersburg and, as published later, were of the most unsatisfactory
nature. Japan was completing her arrangements for striking the blow which fell on February the ninth. Of course
these plans were not made public but there was conflict in the
very air and all men were bracing themselves for the shock
that they felt must soon come. The action of Japanese money-
lenders in suspending operations was followed in January by
the Korean pawn brokers and at a season when such action
inflicted the greatest possible harm upon the poor people of
the capital, who find it impossible to live without temporarily
hypothecating a portion of their personal effects. This together with the excessive cold aroused a spirit of unrest
which came near assuming dangerous proportions. Some of
the native papers were so unwise as to fan the embers by dilat-
ing upon the hard conditions under which the Koreans labored. Their sharpest comments were directed at the Government but their tendency was to incite the populace against
foreigners.

All through the month the various foreign legations were
bringing in guards to protect their legations and their respective nationals and this very natural and entirely justifiable
action was resented by the Government. It protested time
and again against the presence of foreign troops, as if their
coming were in some way an insult to Korea. The officials
in charge thereby showed their utter incompetence to diag-
nose the situation correctly. It was well known that the
disaffection among the Korean troops in Seoul was great and
that the dangerous element known as the Peddlars Guild was

capable of any excesses.   The unfriendly attitude of Yi
Yong-ik and Yi Keun-tǎk towards western foreigners, excepting Russians and French, together with their more or less
close connection with the Peddlars was sufficient reason for
the precautionary measures that were adopted.   But the native papers made matters worse by ridiculing both the government and the army.   At one time there was considerable
solicitude on the part of foreigners, not lest the Korean populace itself would break into open revolt but lest some violent faction would be encouraged by the authorities to make
trouble; so little confidence had they in the good sense of the
court favorite.   It was fairly evident that in case of trouble
the Japanese would very soon hold the capital and it was
feared that the violently pro-Russian officials, despairing of
protection at the hands of Russia, would cause a general
insurrection, hoping in the tumult to make good their escape.
It was felt that great precautions should be taken by foreigners not to give any excuse for a popular uprising.   The electric
cars diminished their speed so as to obviate the possibility of
any accident, for even the smallest casualty might form the
match while would set the people on fire.

But popular unrest was not confined to Seoul.   A serious
movement was begun in the two southern provinces where, it
was reported, hundreds of the *ajuns* or prefectural constables
were preparing to lead a formidable insurrection.   The firm
hold that these men have upon the people made it not unlikely that it would prove much more serious than the Tonghak
insurrection of 1894.   From the north, as well, persistent
reports came of the banding together of the disaffected people,
and foreign residents in those parts affirmed that they had
never before seen such a state of affairs.   One of them was
driven from a country village and threatened with death if he
should ever return.   The Korean soldiers who formed the
garrison of Pyeng-yang joined the police in breaking into the
houses of wealthy natives and stealing money and goods.
The authorities remonstrated, but without effect.   By the
twentieth of January the tension became so great in Seoul
that a considerable number of the wealthy natives began
removing there families and there valuables to the country.

About the 20th of January the report circulated that Russia

had proposed that northern Korea be made a neutral zone and that Japan exercise predominant influence in the south. This was only an echo of the negotiations which were nearing the breaking point in St Petersburg. and it confirmed those who knew Japan in their opinion that war alone could settle the matter. On the following day the Korean Government issued its proclamation of neutrality as between Russia and Japan. This curious action, taken before any declaration of war or any act of hostility, was a pretty demonstration of Russian tactics. It was evident that in case of war Japan would be the first in the field and Korea would naturally be the road by which she would attack Russia. Therefore while the two were technically at peace with each other Korea was evidently induced by Russia to put forth a premature declaration of neutrality in order to anticipate any use of Korean territory by Japanese troops. At the time this was done the Foreign Office was shorn of all real power and was only the mouth-piece through which these friends of Russia spoke in order to make their pronouncements official. It was already known that two of the most powerful Koreans at court had strongly urged that Russia be asked to send troops to guard the imperial palace in Seoul and the Japanese were keenly on the lookout for evidences of bad faith in the matter of this declared neutrality. When, therefore, they picked up a boat on the Yellow Sea a few days later and found on it a Korean bearing a letter to Port Arthur asking for troops, and that, while unofficial in form, it came from the very officials who had promulgated the declaration of neutrality, it became abundantly clear that the spirit of neutrality was non-existent. It must be left to the future historian to declare whether the Japanese were justified in impairing a declared neutrality that existed only in name and under cover of which the Korean officials were proved to be acting in a manner distinctly hostile to the interests of Japan.

All through January the Japanese were busy making military stations every fifteen miles between Fusan and Seoul. All along the line small buildings were erected, sufficiently large to house twenty or thirty men. On January 22nd Gen. Ijichi arrived in Seoul as military attaché of the Japanese Legation. The appointment of a man of such

rank as this was most significant and should have aroused
the Russians to a realizing sense of their danger, but it did
not do so.   Four days leter this general made a final appeal
to the Korean Government, asking for some definite statement
as to its attitude toward Russia and Japan.   The Foreign
Office answered that the government was entirely .neutral.
Two days later the Japanese landed a large amount of barley
at the port of Kunsan, a few hours' run south of Chemulpo,
and a light railway of the Decauville type was also landed
at the same place.   On the 29th all Korean students were
recalled from Japan.

On February the first the Russians appeared to be the
only ones who did not realize that trouble was brewing,
otherwise why should they have stored 1,500 tons of coal and
a quantity of barley in their godowns on Roze Island in
Chemulpo Harbor on the second of that month?   On the
seventh the government received a dispatch from Wiju saying that seveal thousand Russian troops were approaching
the border and that the Japanese merchants and others were
preparing to retire from that place.   The same day the Foreign
Office sent to all the open ports ordering that news should
be immediately telegraphed of any important movements.

On the eighth day of February the Japanese posted
notices in Seoul and vicinity that what Japan was about to
do was dictated by motives of right and justice and that the
property and personal rights of Koreans would be respected.
Koreans were urged to report any cases of ill-treatment to
the Japanese authorities and immediate justice was promised.
From this day the port of Chemulpo was practically blockad-
ed by the Japanese and only by their consent could vessels
enter or clear.

Having arrived at the point of actual rupture between
Japan and Russia, it is necessary before entering into any details of the struggle to indicate the precise bearing of it upon
Korea. Japan has always looked upon Korea as a land whose
political status and affinities are of vital interest to herself;
just as England once looked upon the *Cinque* ports, namely
as a possible base of hostile action, and therefore to be carefully watched.   One of two things have therefore been deemed essential, either that Korea should be thoroughly indepen-

dent or that she should be under a Japanese protectorate. These two ideas have animated different parties in Japan, and have led to occasional troubles. There is one radical faction which has consistently and persistently demanded that Japan's suzerainty over Korea should be established and maintained, and it was the unwillingness of the Japanese authorities to adopt strong measures in the Peninsula which led to the Satsuma Rebellion. Another large fraction of the Japanese, of more moderate and rational view, are committed to the policy of simply holding to the independence of Korea, arguing very rightly that if such independence is maintained and the resources of the country are gradually developed Japan will reap all the material advantages of the situation without shouldering the burden of the Korean administration or meeting the violent opposition of the Koreans which such a step would inevitably entail. It is this latter policy which has prevailed and according to which Japan has attempted to work during the past three decades. It is this which actuated her during the period of China's active claim to suzerainty and finally caused the war of 1894 which finally settled the question of Korea's independence. But following upon this came the encroachments of Russia in Manchuria and the adoption of a vigorous policy in Korea. Japan's efforts to preserve the intrinsic autonomy of Korea were rendered abortive partly through mistakes which her own representatives and agents made but still more through the supineness and venality of Korean officials. The subjects of the Czar at the capital of Korea made use of the most corrupt officials at court and through them opposed Japanese interests at every point. Furthermore they made demands for exclusive rights in different Korean ports and succeeded in encroaching upon Korean sovereignty in Yongampo. The evident policy of Russia was to supplant Japan in the peninsula, and no reasonable person can fail to see that it was their ultimate plan to add Korea to the map of Russia. The cause of the war was, therefore, the necessity laid upon Japan of safe-guarding her vital interests, nay her very existence, by checking the encroachments of Russia upon Korean territory.

But before submitting the matter to the arbitrament of the sword Japan exerted every effort to make Russia define her intentions in the Far East. With a patience that elicited the admiration of the world she kept plying Russia with pertinent questions until at last it was revealed that Russia intended to deal with Manchuria as she wished and would concede Japanese interests in Southern Korea, only and even then only as Japan would engage not to act in that sphere as Russia was acting in Manchuria.

All this time the Japanese people were clamoring for war. They wanted to get at the throat of their manifest foe; but their Government, in a masterly way, held them in check, kept its own secrets so inviolable as to astonish the most astute diplomatists of the day, and at last, when the hour struck, she declared for war without having weakened the enthusiasm of her people and without giving occasion to adverse critics to say that she had yielded to popular importunity. When she communicated to Russia her irreducible minimum one would think that even the blind could see that war was certain to follow soon. But even then, if there is any truth in direct evidence, the great majority of the Russians laughed the matter aside as impossible. The moderation and self-control of Japan was counted to her for hesitation, so that when the moment for action came and Japan sprang upon her like a tigress robbed of her whelps, Russia cried aloud that she had been wronged. It was on the morning of the seventh that Baron Rosen's credentials had been handed back to him in Tokyo. The evening before this the Japanese Minister had left St. Petersburg. This in itself was a declaration of war, but forty hours elapsed before Japan struck the first blow. During those hours Russia had ample time in which to withdraw her boats from Chemulpo even though the Japanese refused to transmit telegrams to Seoul. A fast boat from Port Arthur could easily have brought the message.

It was on the sixth and seventh that reports circulated in Seoul that the Japanese were landing large bodies of troops at Kunsan or Asan or both. These rumors turned out to be false, but beneath them was the fact that a fleet was approaching Chemulpo. The question has been insistently asked why the Russian Minister did not inform the commanders of these Russian vessels and see to it that they were clear of the harbor before these rumors were realized. The answer as given is that the Russian Minister had no control over these boats. They had their orders to remain in Chemulpo and they must stay. One would think that there would be at least enough *raport* between the civil and military (or naval) authorities to use the one in forwarding the interests of the other.

Even yet the Russians did not appreciate the seriousness of the situation, but they decided that it was time to send notice to their authorities in Port Arthur of what was rumored at Chemulpo. So the small gunboat *Koryetz* made ready to move out. Her captain, Belaieff, proposed to the Russian Consul that the Russian steamship *Sungari*, which was in port, should go with the *Koryetz* and thus enjoy her protection, but the agent of the company which owned the steamship strongly objected to her leaving the neutral port at such a time. He evidently realized in part the acuteness of the situation. So the *Sungari* remained at her anchorage and the *Koryetz* steamed out of port at two o'clock in the afternoon. Now, the harbor of Chemulpo is a somewhat peculiar one, for in one sense it is land-locked and in another it is not. It is formed by islands between which there are many openings to the open sea, but most of these are so shallow that ships of medium draught do not dare attempt them. There is but one recognized entrance and that is from the southwest, or between that and the south. This entrance is several miles wide and in the center of it lies Round Island. When the *Koryetz* arrived at the exit of the harbor she suddenly found herself surrounded by torpedo-boats. The only witnesses of what occurred at this point are the Japanese and the Russians and we can only give their accounts. The Russians say that the Japanese launched four torpedoes at the *Koryetz* and when within ten feet of her side they sank. Another statement is that a shot was fired on board the *Koryetz* but it was a mere accident! The Japanese claim that the *Koryetz* fired first. If we try to weigh the probabilities it seems impossible that the torpedoes of the Japanese should have missed the *Koryetz* if the torpedo-boats were as near as the Russians claim. On the other hand the admission on the part of a single Russian that the first gun was fired on the *Koryetz*, even though by accident, is rather damaging, for it is more than singular that an accident should have happened at that precise time. It is a tax on the credulity of the public to give this lame excuse.

In any case it makes little difference who began the firing. The Japanese had already seized the Russian steamer *Mukden* in the harbor of Fusan and the war had begun. The Japanese doubtless held with Polonius, that if it is necessary to fight the man who strikes first and hardest will have the advantage.'' The *Koryetz* turned back to her anchorage and the Russians became aware of the extreme precariousness of their position. Whatever attitude one may take toward the general situation it is impossible not to extend a large degree of sympathy to these Russians personally. Through no fault of their own they were trapped in the harbor and found too late that they must engage in a hopeless fight in order to uphold the honor of the Russian flag. But even yet it was not sure that the neutrality of the port would be ignored by the Japanese. Lying at anchor among neutral vessels in a neutral harbor, there was more or less reason to believe that they were safe for the time being.

About four o'clock in the afternoon of February eighth, which fell on Monday, three Japanese transports entered Chemulpo harbor from the south, convoyed by cruisers and torpedo-boats. They seemingly took no notice of the two Russian boats lying at anchor and were evidently sure that the Russians would not fire upon the tansports. It would be interesting to know whether the Japanese were relying upon the declared neutrality of the port in thus venturing or whether they felt sure that their own superior strength would keep the Russians still, or whether, again, they were certain that the Russians had orders not to fire the first gun. But it is bootless to ask questions that can never be answered. Here is where the assailant has the advantage. He can choose the time and method of his attack. We may surmise that had the Russians divined the intentions of the Japanese and had foreseen the outcome they would have acted differently, but divination of Japanese intentions does not seem to be Russia's strong point.

As soon as the Japanese came to anchor preparations were made for the immediate landing of the troops, and the

cruisers and torpedo-boats, that had convoyed them in, left
the port and joined the fleet outside. This fleet consisted of
six cruisers and several torpedo-boats. The *Asama* and the
Chiyoda were the most powerful of the cruisers, the former
being nearly half as large again as the *Variak*.

Night came on, and throughout its long hours the Japanese troops, by the light of huge fires burning on the jetty,
were landed and marched up into the town. When morning
came everyone was in a state of expectancy. If there was a
Japanese fleet outside they doubtless had other work on
hand than simply watching two Russian boats. Nor could
they leave them behind, for one of them was Russia's fastest
cruiser and might steam out of the harbor at any time and
destroy Japanese transports. Knowing, as we do now, that
an immediate attack on Port Arthur had been decided upon
we see it was impossible to leave these Russian boats in the
rear. Japan had never recognized the nuetrality of Korea,
for she knew that the declaration was merely a Russian move
to embarrass her, and she never hesitated a moment to break
the thin shell of pretense.

About ten o'clock a sealed letter was handed to Captain
Rudnieff of the *Variak*. It was from the Japanese Admiral
and had been sent through the Russian Consulate. It was
delivered on board the *Variak* by the hand of Mr. N. Krell, a
Russian resident of the port. This letter informed the Russian commander that unless both Russian boats should leave
the anchorage and steam out of the bay before twelve o'clock
the Japanese would come in at four o'clock and attack them
where they lay. Captain Rudnieff immediately communicated the startling intelligence to Captain Belaieff of the *Koryetz*
and to the commanders of the British, American, French
and Italian war-vessels. We are informed that a conference
of the various commanders took place and that the Russians
were advised to lie where they were. The British commander was deputed to confer with the Japanese. This was
done by signal and it is said a protest was made against the
proposed violation of neutrality of the port, and that the
neutral boats refused to shift their anchorage. But all complications of this nature were avoided by the determination
of the Russians to accept the challenge. This they deemed

to be due their flag. It is not improbable that they now foresaw that the neutrality of the port would not avail them
against the enemy. By remaining at anchor they could
only succeed in involving France, Italy, Great Britain and
the United States, and there would be sure to be those who
would charge the Russians with cowardice. If this was to
begin the war it must at least prove the dauntless courage of
the servants of the Czar. So the commander of the *Variak*
ordered the decks cleared for action. It has been stated that
he would have preferred to have the *Koryetz* stay at her
anchorage, for by a quick dash it was just possible that the
swift *Variak* alone might be able to evade the Japanese
and run the gauntlet successfully. But the commander
of the *Koryetz* refused to listen to any such proposition.
If the only honor to be gotten out of the affair was by a
desperate attack he was not going to forego his share of
it. He would go out and sink with the *Variak*. So the
Koryetz also cleared for action. It was done in such haste
that all moveables that were unnecessary were thrown over-
board, a topmast that would not come down in the usual
manner was hewn down with an axe and by half past eleven
the two vessels were ready to go out to their doom. It was
an almost hopeless task—an entirely hopeless one unless the
Japanese should change their minds or should make some
grave mistake, and neither of these things was at all probable.
The Russians were going to certain destruction. Some call
it rashness, not bravery, but they say not well. The boats
were doomed in any case and it was the duty of their officers
and crews to go forth and in dying inflict what injury they
could upon the enemy. To go into battle with chances equal
is the act of a brave man, but to walk into the jaws of death
with nothing but defeat in prospect is the act of a hero, and
the Japanese would be the last to detract from the noble record that the Russians made. Time has not yet lent its
glamor to this event, we are two near it to see it in proper
proportions, but if the six hundred heroes of Balaclava, veter-
ans of many a fight, gained undying honor for the desperate
charge they made how shall not the future crown these men
who, having never been in action before, made such a gal-
lant dash at the foe?

Chapter XXVII.

The Battle of Chemulpo....Russian survivors on neutral boats....
Blowing up of the Koryetz... sinking of the Variak....Russians
leave Korea....hospital in Chemulpo....skirmish at Pyeng Yang
....Korean Japanese Protocol....end of Peddlar's Guild....Marquis Ito . Yi Yong Ik retires....Japanese conservative policy in
Korea .. skirmish at Chöng-ju....suffering of Koreans in north
....apathy of Korean Government....burning of palace in Seoul
....Korean currency.

It was a cloudless but hazy day and from the anchorage
the Japanese fleet was all but invisible, for it lay at least
eight miles out in the entrance of the harbor and partly
concealed by Round Island which splits the offing into two
channels. The two boats made straight for the more easterly of the channels, their course being a very little west of
south. When they had proceeded about half the distance
from the anchorage to the enemy's fleet the latter threw a
shot across the bows of each of the Russian boats as a command to stop and surrender, but the Russians took no notice
of it. The only chance the Russians had to inflict any
damage was to reduce the firing range as much as possible
for the *Variak's* guns were only six inches and four-tenths
in caliber and at long range they would have been useless. This
was at five minutes before noon. The Japanese fleet was not
deployed in a line facing the approaching boats and it was
apparent that they did not intend to bring their whole force
to bear upon the Russians simultaneously. We are informed that only two of the Japanese vessels, the *Asama* and the
Chiyoda, did the work. It was not long after the warning
shots had been fired that the Japanese let loose and the roar
that went up from those terrible machines of destruction tore
the quiet of the windless bay to tatters and made the houses
of the town tremble where they stood. As the *Variak*
advanced she swerved to the eastward and gave the Japanese
her starboard broadside. All about her the sea was lashed
into foam by striking shot and almost from the beginning of the

fight her steering-gear was shot away so that she had to
depend on her engines alone for steering. It became evident to her commander that the passage was impossible.
He had pushed eastward until there was imminent danger
of running aground. So he turned again toward the west
and came around in a curve which brought the *Variak* much
nearer to the Japanese. It was at this time that the deadly
work was done upon her. Ten of her twelve gun-captains
were shot away. A shell struck her fo'castle, passed between
the arm and body of a gunner who had his hand upon his
hip and, bursting, killed every other man on the fo'castle.
Both bridges were destroyed by bursting shell and the Captain
was seriously wounded in the left arm. The watchers on
shore and on the shipping in the harbor saw flames bursting
out from her quarter-deck and one witness plainly saw shells
drop just beside her and burst beneath the water line. It
was these shots that did the real damage for when, after three
quarters of an hour of steady fighting, she turned her prow
back toward the anchorage it was seen that she had a heavy
list to port which could have been caused only by serious
damage below the water-line. As the two boats came slowly
back to port, the *Variak* so crippled by the destruction of
one of her engines that she could make only ten knots an
hour, the Japanese boats followed, pouring in a galling fire,
until the Russians had almost reached the anchorage. Then
the pursuers drew back and the battle was over. The
Koryetz was intact. The Japanese had reserved all their fire
for the larger vessel. The *Variak* was useless as a fighting
machine, for her heavy list to port would probably have
made it impossible to train the guns on the enemy, but all
knew that the end had not yet come. The Russians had
neither sunk nor surrendered. The threat of the Japanese
to come in at four o'clock was still active. As soon as the
Variak dropped anchor the British sent off four hospital
boats to her with a surgeon and a nurse. Other vessels also
sent offers of aid. But it was found that the Russians had
decided to lie at anchor and fight to the bitter end and at
the last moment blow up their vessels with all on board.
What else was there for them to do? They would not surrender and they could not leave their ships and go ashore

only to be captured by the enemy. They would play out the tragedy to a finish and go down fighting. Upon learning of this determination the commanders of the various neutral vessels held another conference at which it was decided that the Russians had done all that was necessary to vindicate the honor of their flag and that, as it was a neutral port, the survivors should be invited to seek asylum on the neutral vessels. The invitation was accepted and the sixty-four wounded on board the *Variak* were at once transferred to the British cruiser *Talbot* and the French curiser *Pascal*. As the commanders of the neutral vessels knew that the *Variak* and *Koryetz* were to be sunk by the Russians they paid no particular attention to the reiterated statement of the Japanese that they would enter the harbor at four and finish the work already begun. The passengers, crew and mails on board the steamship *Sungari* had already been transferred to the *Pascal* and an attempt had been made to scuttle her but she was filling very slowly indeed. It was about half-past three in the afternoon that the officers and crew of the *Koryetz* went over the side and on board the *Pascal*. A train had been laid by which she would be blown up and it is supposed that she was entirely abandoned, but some spectators assert that they saw several men on the forward deck an instant before the explosion took place.

It was generally known throughout the town that the *Koryetz* would be blown up before four o'clock and everyone sought some point of vantage from which to witness the spectacle. Scores of people went out to the little island on which the light-house stands, for this was nearest to the doomed ship. It was thirty-seven minutes past three when the waiting multitude saw two blinding flashes of light one following the other in quick succession. A terrific report followed which dwarfed the roar of cannon to a whisper and shook every house in the town as if it had been struck by a solid rock. The window-fastenings of one house at least were torn off, so great was the concussion. An enormous cloud of smoke and debris shot toward the sky and at the same time enveloped the spot where the vessel had lain. A moment later there began a veritable shower of splintered wood, torn and twisted railing, books, clothes, rope, utensils and a hundred other belongings of the ship. The cloud of smoke expanded in the upper air and blotted out the sun like an eclipse. The startled gulls flew hither and thither as if dazed by this unheard of phenomenon and men instinctively raised their hands to protect themselves from the falling debris, pieces of which were drifted by the upper currents of air for a distance of three miles landward where they fell by the hundreds in peoples' yards.

When the smoke was dissipated it was discovered that the *Koryetz* had sunk, only her funnel and some torn rigging appearing above the surface, if we except her forward steel deck which the force of the explosion had bent up from the prow so that the point of it, like the share of a huge plow, stood several feet out of water. The surface of the bay all about the spot was covered thickly with smoking debris and several of the ship's boats were floating about intact upon the water.

The *Variak* was left to sink where she lay. The forty-one dead on board were placed together in a cabin and went down with her. She burned on till evening and then inclining more and more to port her funnels finally touched the water and with a surging, choking groan as of some great animal in pain she sank. As the water reached the fires a cloud of steam went up which illuminated by the last flash of the fire formed her signal of farewell.

It was arranged that the British and the French boats should carry the Russians to a neutral port and guarantee their parole until the end of the war.

This wholly unexpected annihilation of the Russian boats naturally caused consternation among the Russians of Chemulpo and Seoul. The Russian Consulate was surrounded by the Japanese troops and the Consul was held practically a prisoner. The Japanese Minister in Seoul suggested to the Russian Minister through the French Legation the advisability of his removing from Seoul with his nationals, and every facility was given him for doing this with expedition and with comfort. A few days later all the Russians were taken by special train to Chemulpo, and there, being joined by the Russian subjects in Chemulpo, they all went on board the *Pascal*. This vessel must have been crowded, for it is said that when she sailed she had on board six hundred Russians, both civilians and military men.

Twenty-four of the most desperately wounded men on board the neutral ships were sent ashore and placed in the Provisional Red Cross Hospital.   For this purpose the English Church Mission kindly put at the disposal of the Japanese their hospital at Chemulpo.   Several of these wounded men were suffering from gangrene when they came off the *Pascal* but with the most sedulous care the Japanese physicians and nurses pulled them through.

After this battle at Chemulpo there was no more question about landing Korean troops further down the coast; in fact as soon as the ice was out of the Tadong River, Chinnampo became the point of disembarkation.   But meanwhile the troops which had landed at Chemulpo were pushing north by land as rapidly as circumstances would permit and within a few weeks of the beginning of the war Pyeng-yang was held by a strong force of Japanese.   At the same time work was pushed rapidly on the Seoul-Fusan Railway and also begun on the projected railway line between Seoul and Wiju. 29

As for the Russians they never seriously invaded Korean territory.   Bands of Cossacks crossed the Yalu and scoured the country right and left but their only serious purpose was to keep in touch with the enemy and report as to their movements.   On February 28 a small band of Cossacks approached the north gate of Pyeng Yang and after exchanging a few shots with the Japanese guard withdrew.   This was the first point at which the two belligerents came in touch with each other.

It was on the night of February 23rd that Korea signed with Japan a protocol by the terms of which Korea practically allied herself with Japan and became, as it were, a silent partner in the war.   Korea granted the Japanese the right to use Korea as a road to Manchuria and engaged to give them every possible facility for prosecuting the war.   On the other hand Japan guaranteed the independence of Korea and the safety of the Imperial Family.   It is needless to discuss the degree of spontaneity with which Korea did this.   It was a case of necessity, but if rightly used it might have proved of immense benefit to Korea, as it surely did to Japan.   It formally did away with the empty husk of neutrality which had been proclaimed, and made every seaport of the peninsula belligerent territory, even as it did the land itself.

March saw the end of the Peddlars Guild. They had been organized in Russian interests but now they had no longer any *raison d'etre*. As a final flurry, one of their number entered the house of the Foreign Minister with the intent to murder him, but did not find his victim. Other similar attempts were made but did not succed.

The Japanese handled the situation in Seoul with great circumspection. The notion that they would attack the pro-Russian officials proved false. Everything was kept quiet and the perturbation into which the court and the government were thrown by these startling events was soon soothed.

Marquis Ito was sent from Japan with a friendly message to the Emperor of Korea and this did much to quiet the unsettled state of things in Korea. At about the same time the northern ports of Wiju and Yongampo were opened to foreign trade. This was a natural result of the withdrawal of Russian influence. It was not long before Yi Yong-ik who had played such a leading rôle in Korea was invited to go to Japan and thus an element of unrest was removed from the field of action. It was believed that the Japanese would immediately introduce much needed reforms, but it seemed to be their policy to go very slowly, so slowly in fact that the better element among the Koreans was disappointed, and got the impression that Japan was not particularly interested in the matter of reform. It is probable that the energies of the Japanese were too much engaged in other directions to divert any to Korea at the time. They had been complaining bitterly about the monetary conditions, but when they suddenly stepped into power in Seoul on February 9th they seemed to forget all about this, for up to the end of 1904 they failed to do anything to correct the vagaries of Korean finance. But instead of this the Japanese merchants in Korea and other Japanese who were here for other reasons than their health immediately began to make requests and demands for all sorts of privileges. The Board of Trade in Fusan asked the Japanese government to secure the Maritime Customs service, permission for extra territorial privileges, the establishment of Japanese agricultural stations and other impossible things. 30

Meanwhile the Japanese were steadily pushing north. At Anju a slight skirmish occurred but there was nothing that could be called a fight until the Japanese reached the town of Chöng-ju where a small body of Russians took a stand on a hill northwest of the town and held it for three hours, but even here the casualties were only about fifteen on either side. The Russians evidently had no notion of making a determined stand this side the Yalu. Already, a week before, the Russian troops had withdrawn from Yong-ampo and had crossed to Antung. This fight at Chöng-ju occurred on March 28th and a week later practically all the Russian forces had crossed the Yalu and Korea ceased to be belligerent territory. It is not the province of this history to follow the Japanese across that historic river and relate the events which occurred at the beginning of May when the first great land battle of the war was fought.

The whole north had been thrown into the greatest confusion by the presence of these two belligerents. Cossack bands had scurried about the country, making demands for food and fodder a part of which they were willing to pay for with Russian currency quite unknown to the Korean. From scores of villages and towns the women had fled to the mountain recesses at a most inclement season, and untold suffering had been entailed. But these are things that always come in the track of war and the Koreans bore them as uncomplainingly as they could. Throughout the whole country the absorption of the attention of the government in the events of the war was taken advantage of by robbers, and their raids were frequent and destructive. As soon as the government found that the Japanese did not intend to rule with a high hand it sank back into the former state of selfcomplacent lethargy, and things went along in the old ruts. It was perfectly plain that Korean officialdom had no enthusiasm for the Japanese cause. It is probable that a large majority of the people preferred to see Japan win rather than the Russians, but it was the fond wish of ninety-nine out of every hundred to see Korea rid of them both. Whichever one held exclusive power here was certain to become an object of hatred to the Korean people. Had the Russians driven out the Japanese the Koreans would have hated them as heartily. Whichever horn of the dilemma Korea became impaled upon she was sure to think the other would have been less sharp. Few Koreans looked at the matter from any large standpoint or tried to get from the situation anything but personal advantage. This is doubtless the reason why it was so difficult to gain an opinion from Korean officials. They did not want to go on record as having any decided sympathies either way. The people of no other land were so nearly neutral as were those of Korea.

The month of April was comparatively quiet. The Japanese were struggling north through frost and mud combined to rendezvous on the banks of the Yalu. On the 14th occurred the great fire in Seoul which in a few hours swept away almost the whole of the Kyŏng-un Palace, the one recently completed and the one occupied by the Emperor at the time. He was forced to vacate it in haste and take up his abode for the time being in the detached Imperial Library building. A strong effort was made by the Japanese to induce him to return to the Chŏng-dŭk Palace, which was his place of residence at the time of the *emeutes* of 1882 and 1884, but this was combatted with all the means available, and the burned palace was rebuilt as quickly as possible.

The temporary effect of the war upon the Korean currency was to enhance its value. Imports suddenly came to a standstill because of the lack of steamships and the possible dangers of navigation. This stopped the demand for yen. The Japanese army had to spend large sums in Korea and this required the purchase of Korean money. The result was that the yen, instead of holding its ratio of something like one to two and a half of the Korean dollar fell to the ratio of one to only one and four tenths. When, however, the sea was cleared of the Russians and import trade was resumed and the bulk of the Japanese crossed the Yalu the Korean dollar fell again to a ratio of about two to one, which it has preserved up to the present time, i.e. December, 1904.

From the time when the Russians retired beyond the Yalu warlike operations between the two belligerents was

confined to northeast Korea though even there very little
was doing. The Vladivostock squadron was still in being and
on April 25 it appeared at the mouth of Wonsan harbor.
Only one small Japanese boat was at anchor there, the
Goyo Maru, and this was destroyed by a torpedo boat which
came in for the express purpose. Of course this created in
tense excitement in the town and there was a hurried exodus
of women and children, but the Russians had no intention
of bombarding the place and soon took their depature.
Only a few hours before. the *Kinshiu,* a Japanese transport
with upwards of 150 troops on board, had sailed for Sŭng-ju
to the north of Wonsan but meeting bad weather in the night
the torpedo-boats that accompanied her were obliged to run
for shelter and the *Kinshiu* turned back for Wonsan. By
so doing she soon ran into the arms of the Russian fleet and
refusing to surrender she was sunk, but forty-five of the
troops on board effected their escape to the mainland.

It was only a few days before this that a force of Cossacks had made a dash down the eastern coast as far as
Ham-heung which they entered after a two hours' skirmish
with Korean troops. They burned about 300 houses in the
suburbs of the town and also fourteen *kan* of the celebrated
"Ten Thousand Year Bridge," the longest in Korea. After
this they retired to the north. But from that time on the
whole northeast has been scoured by parties of Russians and
the Japanese have paid no attention to them except to place
troops at Wonsan and Ham-heung to hold these places.
On August 8th a small Russian force penetrated south to the
very suburbs of Wonsan but were speedily repulsed by the
Japanese who had thrown up intrenchments and were quite
ready to meet any assault. The Russians worked with great
energy in repairing the road from the Tuman River down to
Sung-su, and even south of that place. They even built
good graded roads across two of the high passes south of
Sung-jin until they came in contact with the Japanese outposts twenty miles above Ham-heung. Neither side seemed
to desire to assume the offensive and so matters stood until
the end of the year, and the coming of the northern winter
put a stop to active operations. The only other incident
worthy of mention in this connection was the wanton attack

upon the town of Wonsan by the Russian fleet on the last
day of June. On that morning seven Russian torpedo-boats
entered the harbor and after inquiring where the Japanese
barracks and other public buildings were situated began
shelling the town. In a panic the peaceful denizens of the
place fled to the shelter of the hills. The Russians gave no
warning of the attack even though many foreigners of various
nationalities resided there and might easily have been injured.
After firing over 200 shells without doing any considerable
damage the torpedo boats withdrew.

We must now go back and inquire into important civil
matters. We have seen that no strong attempt was made by
the Japanese to secure reforms in the administration of the
Korean Government and for this reason many of the best
Koreans weae dissatisfied with the way things were going.
Therefore it was doubly unfortunate that on the seventeenth of June the Japanese authorities should make the startling suggestion that all uncultivated land in the Peninsula
as well as other national resources should be thrown open to
the Japanese. This appears to have been a scheme evolved
by one Nagamori and broached by him so speciously to the
powers in Tokyo that they backed him in it; but there can
be no question that it was a grave mistake. There is no
other point on which the Korean is so sensitive as upon that
of his land. He is a son of the soil, and agriculture is the
basis of all his institutions. The mere proposal raised an instant storm of protest from one end of Korea to the other.
The Koreans saw in this move the entering wedge which
would rive the country. It was the beginning of the end.
This excessive show of feeling was not expected by the
Japanese and it is probable that their intentions were by no
means so black as the Koreans pictured them. The very
general terms in which the proposal was worded and the almost entire lack of limiting particulars gave occasion for all
sorts of wild conjectures and, it must be confessed, left the
door open to very wide constructions. The time was unpropitious, the method was unfortunate and the subject-matter
of the proposal itself was questionable. The all-important
matter of water supply and control, the difficulties of jurisdiction on account of the extraterritorial rights implied in the

proposal and other allied questions immediately presented
themselves to the minds of Koreans and they recognized the
fact that the carrying out of this plan would necessarily result in a Japanese protectorate if not absolute absorption into
the Empire of Japan. The Japanese do not seem to have followed the logic of the matter to this point or else had not believed the Koreans capable of doing so. But when the storm
of protest broke it carried everything before it. The Japanese were not prepared to carry the thing to extremes and after
repeated attempts at a compromise the matter was dropped,
though the Japanese neither withdrew their request nor accepted the refusal of the Korean Government. It is a matter
of great regret that the Japanese did not quietly and steadily
press the question of internal reforms, and by so doing hasten
the time when the Korean people as a whole would repose
such confidence in the good intentions of the neighbor country that even such plans as this of the waste lands could be
carried through without serious opposition; for it is quite
sure that there is a large area of fallow land in Korea which
might well be put under the plow.

During the weeks when the Japanese were pressing for
a favorable answer to the waste land proposition the Koreans
adopted a characteristic method of opposition. A society
called the *Po-an-whe* was formed. The name means "Society for the Promotion of Peace and Safety." It had
among its membership some of the leading Korean officials.
It held meetings at the cotton guild in the center of Seoul
and a good deal of excited discussion took place as to ways
and means for defeating the purpose of the Japanese. At
the same time memorials by the some poured in upon the
Emperor, beseeching him not to give way to the demands.
The Japanese determined that these forms of opposition must
be put down, so on July the 16th the meeting of the society
was broken in upon by the Japanese police and some of the
leading members were forcibly carried away to the Japanese
police station. Other raids were made upon the society and
more of its members were arrested and its papers confiscated.
The Japanese warned the government that these attempts
to stir up a riot must be put down with a stern hand and demanded that those who persisted in sending in memorials

against the Japanese be arrested and punished. If the Korean government would not do it the Japanese threatened to take the law into their own hands. The Japanese troops in Seoul were augmented until the number was fully 6,000.

The agitation was not confined to Seoul, for leading Koreans sent out circular letters to all the country districts urging the people to come up to Seoul and make a monster demonstration which should convince the Japanese that they were in dead earnest. Many of these letters were suppressed by the prefects but in spite of this the news spread far and wide and the society enrolled thousands of members in every province.

The effect of this was seen when, early in August, the Japanese military authorities asked for the services of 6,000 Korean coolies in the north at handsome wages. The number was apportioned among different provinces, but the results were meager. Disaffected persons spread the report that these coolies would be put on the fighting line, and it was with the greatest difficulty that two thousand were secured. There were sanguinary fights in many towns where attempts were made to force coolies to go against their will. It was perfecty right for the Japanese to wish to secure such labor, but the tide of public sentiment was flowing strong in the other direction because of the attempt to secure the waste land and because of the suspension of the right of free speech.

The cessation of Japanese efforts to push the waste land measure did not put an end to agitation throughout the country, and the Il-chin society continued to carry on its propaganda until on August 22nd a new society took the field, named the Il-chin society. This was protected by the Japanese police who allowed only properly accredited members to enter its doors. This looked as if it were intended as a counter-move to the Il-chin Society, and as the latter was having very little success a third society took up the gauntlet under the name of the Kuk-min or "National People's" Society. The platforms promulgated by all these societies were quite faultless but the institutions had no power whatever to carry out their laudable plans and so received only the smiles of the public.

During the summer the Japanese suggested that it would be well for Korea to recall her foreign representatives. The idea was to have Korean diplomatic business abroad transacted through Japanese legations. Whether this was a serious attempt or only a feeler put out to get the sense of the Korean government we are unable to say, but up to the end of the year the matter was not pushed, and the nomination by the Japanese of Mr. Stevens, an Amerian subject as adviser to the Foreign Office would seem to indicate that the existing diplomatic arrangements will be continued for the time being.

The various societies which had been formed as protests against existing conditions stated some things that ought to be accomplished but suggested no means by which they could be done. The difficulty which besets the country is the lack of general education, and no genuine improvement can be looked for until the people be educated up to it. For this reason a number of foreigners joined themselves into the Educational Association of Korea, their aim being to provide suitable text books for Korean schools and to help in other ways toward the solution of the great question. About the same time the Minister of Education presented the government with a recommendation that the graduates of the Government schools be given the preference in the distribution of public offices. This had no apparent effect upon the Government at the time, but this is what must come before students will flock to the Government schools with any enthusiasm. Later in the year a large number of Koreans also founded an Educational Society. It made no pretensions to political significance but went quietly to work gathering together those who are convinced that the education of the masses is the one thing needed to put Korea upon her feet, in the best sense.

In September there was celebrated the twentieth anniversary of the founding of Protestant Christian missions in Korea. A great convention had been arranged for and leading men were to attend it but the war interferred with the plan and the convention was postponed till 1909, when the quarter-centennial will be celebrated In spite of this a memorable meeting was held and the results of Christian work in Korea were set forth and discussed. We need say no more here than that this field is rightly considered as being one of the most successful in the world and as giving promise of great things in the future.

In the middle of October the Japanese military authorities sent Marshal Hasegawa to take charge of military affairs in Korea. He arrived on the thirteenth and shortly after went to Wonsan to inspect matters in that vicinity. The news of considerable Russian activity in northeast Korea seemed to need careful watching and the presence of a general competent to do whatever was necessary to keep them in check.

The laying of the last rail of the Seoul Fusan-Railway was an event of great importance to Korea. It adds materially to the wealth of the country both by forming a means of rapid communication and by enhancing the value of all the territory through which it runs. It also gives Japan such a large vested interest here that it becomes, in a sense, her guarantee to prevent the country from falling into the hands of other Powers. But like all good things it has its dangers as well.

Mr. Megata, the new adviser to the Finance Department arrived in the Autumn and began a close study of Korean monetary and financial conditions. This was an augury of good, for Korean finance has always been in a more or less chaotic condition since the time when the late Regent flooded the country with discarded Chinese cash and a spurious Korean coinage whose lack of intrinsic value gave the lie to its face.

Late in the year Mr. Stevens, the newly appointed adviser of the Foreign Department, took up his duties which, though less important than those of Mr. Megata, nevertheless gave assurance that the foreign relations of the government would be carefully handled.

As the year came to a close there were evidences that the Japanese were about to begin what should have been begun before, namely a gradual reform in the administration of the government. Useless offices are to be abolished, the army is to be brought down to its proper proportions, retrenchment is to be effected in various other lines and education is to be encouraged. On the whole the year closed with brighter prospects in Korea than any former portion of the year had shown.

The termination of an historical survey covering four thousand years of time naturally suggests some general remarks upon that history as a whole. And in the first place it is worth noting that the Korean people became a homogeneous nation at a very early date. Before the opening of the tenth century they were so firmly welded together that no sectional difference has ever seriously threatened their disruption.

Since the year 700 A. D. there have been two bloodless changes of dynasty but there has not been a single successful revolution, in the ordinary sense of the word. There have been three great and several small invasions but none of these left any serious marks upon the country either in the line of inter-mixture of blood or of linguistic modification. They served simply to weld the people more closely together and make the commonwealth more homogeneous than ever.

In the second place the power has always been in the hands of the men of greatest average wit, and it has uniformly been used to further personal aims. The idea of any altruistic service has been conspicuously lacking, though there have been brilliant exceptions. The concept of individuality or personality is strangely lacking in all Turanian peoples and this it is which has kept them so far in the rear of the Indo-European peoples in the matter of civilization. The essential feature of true progress, namely the recognition of the present time as on the whole the best time, the present institutions as being the best institution, the present opportunities as being the best opportunities, the present people as being the best people that history has to show—this feature is sadly lacking in the Far East. Japan has grafted this into her life and it already bears fruit, but Korea stands with China as yet.

Individual people cannot be sure of getting their just deserts in this life whether they be good or evil, but this is hardly true of nations. They generally get about what they have deserved. If men lived as long as empires they too might be served the same. It is poor philosophy to mourn the fate of a decadent empire or a moribund civilization. They have served their purposed and are ready to pass away. Upon their ruins there are sure to arise edifices that are worthier of habitation than were those of the past.   In Korea the old is passing away, is crumbling about our ears.   The new wine is bursting the old bottles.   The question for the future to answer is whether the Korean people will allow their ship of state to drift upon the Sarasso Sea until the seaweed "rising strake on strake" shall make her utterly derilict, or whether they will awake from their lethargy, clear away the barnacles and jam the helm down hard a-port until the wind fills the sails and she can forge ahead toward some desired haven.

It is not the province of the historian to play the prophet nor shall we try to forecast what the future may bring forth, but it is permissible to express the hope that Korea will make herself increasingly worthy of a continued and distinguished history.

THE END.

INDEX.

BIOGRAPHICAL INDEX.*

*If the volume is not indicated, Vol. II is understood.

Editor's General Note On Romanization and Transliteration
in the "Chronological Index of the Kings of Korea"

1. *Diacritical Marks.* All diacritical markings were inadvertently omitted in the dynastic tables in the original *History*. To bring the romanization used in the tables into rough agreement with Hulbert's own formula (see Editor's Foreword), the editor has inserted """ and """", wherever that system calls for them, in all of the dynastic lists, including that of "The Kings of Modern Korea" (1392-1910). Professor Hulbert used these marks to produce romanized forms as follows:

"ą" for the Hangŭl ㅓ   (a as in bat) to distinguish it from ㅏ   (a as in father); and

"ŏ" or "ŭ" for ㅓ   (o as in done), to distinguish it from ㅗ   (o as in lone) and ㅜ   (u as in flute).

[The McCune-Reischauer (M-R) reading for ㅓ   is "ae" and for ㅓ   ,
"ŏ".]

2. *Spellings.* The following *corrigenda* are to be understood in the places indicated, which are marked in the left margin of the tables concerned by the symbol+ •

Page	Dynasty	Hangŭl spelling of the Chinese characters	Reading found in tables	Reading consistent with Hulbert system	[M-R Equivalent]
402	"Ancient Chosŭn" [sic]	기 근	Ki-gon	Ki-geum	Kigŭn
403	Silla	탈 해	Tal-hă	T'al-hă	T'alhae
404	"	양 사	Yang-sung	Yang-sang	Yangsang
404	"	수 종	So-jong	Su-jong	Sujong
	"	경 응	Kyŏng-ong	Kyŏng-eung	Kyŏng'ŭng
	"	응 염	Ong-yŭm	Eung-yŭm	Ung'yŏm
	"	위 응	Wi-ong	Wi-eung	Wiŭng
404	Păkche [sic]	근 초 고	Kon-ch'a-go	Keun-ch'o-go	Kŭnch'ogo
405	"	근 구 수	Kon-gu-su	Keun-gu-su	Kŭngusu
405	"	남 무	Nam-mo	Nam-mu	Nammu
406	Koguryŭ [sic]	광 개 토 왕	Kwang-gă-to-wang	Kwang-gă-t'o-wang	Kwang'gae't'o-wang
406	"	나 운	Na-on	Na-un	Naun
	"	평 성	Pyŭng-sŭng	P'yŭng-sŭng	P'yŏngsŏng
407	Koryŭ [sic]	왕 기	Wang-tak	Wang-t'ak	Wangt'ak

[The editor's comments on spellings, as well as on dates and ideographs, referring to Yi Dynasty Chosŏn follow Hulbert's table of "The Kings of Modern Korea."]

This presentation of Tan'gun as a historical figure is misleading. See Section 3 ("Sources and Historicity") of Editor's Introduction and I, 1n. above.

The table of the "Kija Dynasty" as a whole is also unfounded, although the last two kings mentioned (Pu and Chun, shown here as "Ki-bu" and "Ki-jun") are historical. See Section 3 of Editor's Introduction and I, 13n. and 15n. above. —EDITOR.

CHRONOLOGICAL INDEX

OF

THE KINGS OF KOREA.

2332 B.C. Tan-gun 檀君 or Wang-gŏm   王儉

ANCIENT CHOSŬN 上古朝鮮

1122 B.C.	Ki-ja	箕子	Mun-sŏng-wang	文聖王
1082 "	Ki-song	" 松	Chang-hye-wang	莊惠王
1057 "	Ki-sun	" 洵	Kyŏng-hyo-wang	敬孝王
1030 "	Ki-băk	" 伯	Kong-jŭng-wang	恭貞王
1000 "	Ki-ch'un	" 椿	Mun-mu-wang	文武王
972 "	Ki-gong	" 孔	T'ă-wŭn-wang	太原王
968 "	Ki-chang	" 莊	Kyŏng-ch'ang-wang	景昌王
957 "	Ki-ch'ak	" 捉	Heung-p'yŭng-wang	興平王
943 "	Ki-jo	" 調	Ch'ŭl-wi-wang	哲威王
925 "	Ki-săk	" 索	Sŭn-hye-wang	宣惠王
896 "	Ki-sa	" 師	Eui-yang-wang	誼讓王
843 "	Ki-ryŭm	" 炎	Mun-hye-wang	文惠王
793 "	Ki-wŭl	" 越	Sŏng-dŭk-wang	盛德王
778 "	Ki-jik	" 職	To-whe-wang	悼懷王
776 "	Ki-u	" 優	Mun-yŭl-wang	文烈王
761 "	Ki-mok	" 睦	Ch'ang-guk-wang	昌國王
748 "	Ki-p'yŭng	" 平	Mu-sŭng-wang	武成王
722 "	Ki-gwul	" 闕	Chŭng-gyŏng-wang	貞敬王
703 "	Ki-whe	" 懷	Nak-sŭng-wang	樂成王

NOTE. The names in the right hand columns are the posthumous titles of the various sovereigns. In the left hand columns are the ordinary names.

675 B.C.	Ki-jon	箕存	Hyo-jong-wang	孝宗王
658 "	Ki-hyo	" 孝	Ch'ŭl-lo-wang	天老王
634 "	Ki-yang	" 襄	Su-do-wang	修道王
615 "	Ki-i	" 邇	Whi-yang-wang	徽襄王
594 "	Ki-ch'am	" 黍	Pong-il-wang	奉日王
+ 578 "	Ki-gon	" 僅	Tŭk-ch'ang-wang	德昌王
560 "	Ki-sak	" 朔	Su-sŏng-wang	壽聖王
519 "	Ki-yŏ	" 藜	Yŭng-gŭl-wang	英傑王
503 "	Ki-gang	" 岡	Il-sŏng-wang	逸聖王
486 "	Ki-hon	" 混	Che-se-wang	濟世王
465 "	Ki-pyŭk	" 璧	Chŭng-guk-wang	靖國王
432 "	Ki-jeung	" 澄	To-guk-wang	莘國王
413 "	Ki-jil	" 騭	Hyŭk-sŏng-wang	赫聖王
385 "	Ki-seup	" 謵	Wha-ra-wang	和羅王
369 "	Ki-ha	" 賀	Yŭl-mun-wang	說文王
361 "	Ki-wha	" 華	Kyŏng-sun-wang	慶順王
342 "	Ki-ho	" 詡	Ka-dŭk.wang	嘉德王
315 "	Ki-uk	" 煜	Sam-no-wang	三老王
290 "	Ki-sŭk	" 釋	Hyŏn-mun-wang	顯文王
251 "	Ki-yun	" 潤	Chang-p'yŭng-wang	章平王
232 "	Ki-bu	" 否	Chong-t'ong-wang	宗統王
221 "	Ki-jun	" 準	Ă-wang	哀王

Ended in 193 B.C.

KINGDOM OF MAHAN. 馬韓

193 B.C.	Ki-t'ak	箕卓	Mu-gang-wang	武康王
189 "	Ki-kam	" 龕	An-wang	安王
157 "	Ki-sik	" 寔	Hye-wang	惠王
144 "	Ki-mu	" 武	Myŭng-wang	明王
113 "	Ki-hyŭng	" 亨	Hyo-wang	孝王
73 "	Ki-sŭp	" 爕	Yang-wang	襄王
58 "	Ki-hun	" 勳	Wŭn-wang	元王
32 "	Ki-jŭng	" 貞	Kye-wang	稽王
16 "	Ki-hak	" 學	(wanting)	

Ended in 9 B.C.

This table of a revived "Kija Dynasty" in Mahan is unsubstantiated, although it may contain some elements of history. —EDITOR.

KINGDOM OF SILLA. 新羅

57 B.C.	Hyŭk-kŭ-se	赫居世		
4 A.D.	Nam-hă	南解		
25 "	Yu-ri	琉璃		
+ 58 "	Tal-hă	脫解		
81 "	P'a-sa	婆娑		
113 "	Chi-ma	祗摩		
135 "	Il-sŭng	逸聖		
154 "	A-dal-la	阿達羅		
185 "	Pŭl-hyu	伐休		
196 "	Na-hă	奈解		
231 "	Cho-bun	助賁		
248 "	Ch'ŭm-hă	沾解		
262 "	Mi-ch'u	味鄒		
285 "	Yu-rye	儒禮		
299 "	Keui-rim	基臨		
310 "	Heul-hă	訖解		
356 "	Na-mul	奈勿		
402 "	Sil-sŭng	實聖		
417 "	Nul-ji	訥祗		
458 "	Cha-bi	慈悲		
479 "	So-ji	炤智		
500 "	Chi-dă-ro	智大路	Chi-jeung-wang	智證王
514 "	Wŭn-jong	原宗	Pŭp-heung-wang	法興王
541 "	Măk-chong	麥宗	Chin-heung-wang	眞興王
576 "	Keum-yun	金輪	Chin-ji-wang	眞智王
579 "	Păk-chŭng	伯淨	Chin-p'yŭng-wang	眞平王
632 "	Tŏng-man	德曼	Sŏn-dŭk-yŭ-ju	善德女主
647 "	Seung-man	勝曼	Chin-dŭk-yŭ-ju	眞德女主
654 "	Ch'un-ch'u	春秋	Mu-ryŭl-wang	武烈王
661 "	Pŭp-min	法敏	Mun-mu-wang	文武王
681 "	Chŭng-myŭng	政明	Sin-mun-wang	神文王
692 "	Yi-hong	理洪	Hyo-so-wang	孝昭王
702 "	Heung gwang	興光	Sŏng-dŭk-wang	聖武王 *
738 "	Seung-gyŭng	承慶	Hyo-sŭng-wang	孝成王
742 "	Hŏn-yŭng	憲英	Kyŏng-dŭk-wang	景德王

Kingdom of Silla

All except the earlier reigns are clearly historical. Of the 55 dates given here for the accession of Silla kings, 30 agree with those found in O Yun-jŏk's *Tongsa Yŏnp'yo*, re produced in Japanese in Oda and others, *Chōsen Shi Taikei*. In the other 25 cases, Hulbert's date is uniformly one year later than that in the *Taikei*. Also, the *Taikei* shows a total of 56 rather than 55 kings; King Myŭng, or Min'ae Wang (Myŭng or Min-ă-wang by Hulbert's formula), is listed as ac ceding in 838 A.D. and reigning for one year.
—EDITOR.

*Correct characters for "Sŏng-dŭk-wang" (M-R Sŏngdŏk Wang) are : 聖德王 — Ed.

765 A.D.	Kŭn-un	乾運 Hye-gong-wang	惠恭王
+ 780 "	Yang-sung	瓦相 Sŭn-dŭk-wang	宣德王
785 "	Kyŏng-sin	敬信 Wŭn-sŭng-wang	元聖王
799 "	Chun-ong	俊邕 So-sŏng-wang	昭聖王
800 "	Chung-heui	重熙 A-jang-wang	哀莊 "
809 "	Ön-seung	彥昇 Hŏn-dŭk-wang	憲德 "
+ 826 "	So-jong	秀宗 Heung-dŭk-wang	興德 "
836 "	Che-yung	悌隆 Heui-gang-wang	僖康 "
839 "	U-jing	祐徵 Sin-mu-wang	神武 "
+ 840 "	Kyŏng-ong	慶膺 Mun-sŭng-wang	文聖 "
858 "	Eui-jŭng	宜靖 Hŏn-an-wang	憲安 "
+ 862 "	Ong-yŭm	膺廉 Kyŏng-mun-wang	景文 "
876 "	Chŭng	晸 Hŏn-gang-wang	憲康 "
887 "	Whang	晃 Chŏng-gang-wang	定康 "
888 "	Man	曼 Chin-sŏng-yŭ-ju	眞聖女主
898 "	Yo	嶢 Hyo-gong-wang	孝恭王
913 "	Kyŏng whi	景暉 Sin-dŭk-wang	神德 "
918 "	Seung-yŭng	昇英 Kyŏng-myŭng-wang	景明 "
+ 925 "	Wi-ong	魏膺 Kyŏng-ă-wang	景哀 "
928 "	Pu	傅 Kyŏng-sun-wang	敬順 "

Ended in 935 A.D.

THE KINGDOM OF PĂKCHE. 百濟

17 B.C.	On-jo	溫祚
29 A.D.	Ta-ru	多婁
78 "	Keui-ru	己婁
128 "	Kă-ru	蓋婁
168 "	Ch'o-go	肖古
215 "	Ku-su	仇首
235 "	Ko-i	古爾
287 "	Ch'ăk-kye	稽
299 "	Pun-sŭ	份西
305 "	Pi-ryu	比流
344 "	Sŭl	契
+ 347 "	Kon-ch'o-go	近肖古

Păkche (M-R Paekche)

Here again the early reigns are subject to further study by scholars. The traditional date for King Onjo, and the one given by Hulbert himself on I, 40 above, is 18 rather than 17 B.C. In 21 other instances the date in this table is one year later than that in the *Taikei*, and in one case (that of the fifth king, Ch'o-go), two years later. The accepted date for King Kă-ro (M-R Kaero) is not 432 but 455 A.D. In addition to the *Taikei* see Ch'oe Namsŏn, *Kosa T'ong*, Appendix, p. 14, and I, 71 above, where Hulbert refers to the ruler acceding in 455 as

+ 376 A.D. Kon-gu-su 近仇首

"Pă-gyŭng," apparently a variant of "Kyŭng" (M-R Kyŏng), the personal name of King "Kă-ro." Finally, the *Taikei* adds "King P'ung" (661-663) to Hul-bert's list and dates the fall of the dynasty 663 rather than 660. See "The Righteous Army" in Edi-tor's Introduction and I, 106n. above.—EDITOR.

385	"	Ch'im-yu	枕流		
385	"	Chin-sa	辰斯		
392	"	A-sin	阿莘		
406	"	Chön-ji	典支		
421	"	Ku-i-sin	久爾莘		
427	"	Pi-yu	毗有		
432	"	Kă-ro	蓋鹵		
476	"	Mun-ju	文周		
478	"	Sam-geun	三斤		
480	"	Mo-dă	牟大	Tong-sŭng-wang	東城王
501	"	Sa-ma	斯摩	Mu-ryŭng-wang	武寧"
524	"	Myŭng-nong	明穠	Sŏng-wang	聖"
555	"	Ch'ang	昌	Wi-dŭk-wang	威德"
599	"	Kye-myŭng	季明	Hye-wang	惠,,
600	"	Sŭn	宣	Pŭp-wang	法"
601	"	Chang	璋	Mu-wang	武"
642	"	——		Eui-ja-wang	義慈"

Dynasty ended 660 A.D.

KINGDOM OF KOGURYŬ. 高句麗

37	B.C.	Chu-mong	朱蒙	Tong-myŭng-wang	東明王
18	"	Yu-ri	類利	Yu-ri-wang	琉璃"
19	A.D.	Mu-hyŭl	無恤	Tă-mu-sin-wang	太武神"
45	"	Hă-eup-chu	解邑朱	Min-jung-wang	閔中"
49	"	Hă-u	解憂	Mo-bon-wang	慕本"
54	"	Kung	宮	T'ă-jo-wang	太祖"
147	"	Su-sŭng	遂成	C'ha-dă-wang	次大"
166	"	Păk-ko	伯古	Sin-dă-wang	新大"
+180	"	Nam-mo	男武	Ko-guk-ch'ŭn-wang	古國川"
197	"	Yŭn-u	延優	San-sang-wang	山上"
228	"	U-wi-kŭ	優位居	Tong-ch'ŭn-wang	東川"
250	"	Yŭn-bul	然弗	Chung-ch'ŭn-wang	中川"
271	"	Yang-no	藥盧	Sŭ-ch'ŭn-wang	西川"
292	"	Sang-bu	相夫	Pong sang-wang	烽上"

300 A.D.	Eul-bul	乙弗	Mi-ch'ŭn-wang	美川王	
331 "	Soé	釗	Ko-guk-wŭn-wang	古國原 "
372 "	Ku-bu	丘夫	So-su-rim-wang	小獸林 "
384 "	Yi-yŭn	伊連	Ko-guk-yang-wang	古國壤 "
+392 "	Tam-dŭk	談德	Kwang-gă-to-wang	廣開土 "
414 "	Kö-yŭn	巨璉	Chang-su-wang	長壽 "
+491 "	Na-on	羅雲	Mun-ja-wang	文咨 "
520 "	Heung-an	興安	An-jang-wang	安藏 "
532 "	Po-yŭn	寶延	An-wŭn-wang	安原 "
+546 "	Pyŭng-sŭng	平成	Yang-wŭn-wang	陽原 "
560 "	Yang-sŭng	陽成	P'yŭng-wŭn-wang	平原 "
591 "	Wŭn	元	Yŭng-yang-wang	嬰陽 "
619 "	Kŏn-mu	建武	Yŭng-yu-wang	榮留 "
643 "	Chang	藏	Po-jang-wang	寶藏 "

Dynasty ended 668 A D.

Hulbert's date of accession is one year later than that in the *Taikei* in almost all cases.—EDITIOR.

KINGDOM OF KORYŬ. 高麗

918 A.D.	Wang-gön	王建	T'ă-jo	太祖
944 "	Wang mū	" 武	Hye-jong	惠宗
946 "	Wang-yo	" 堯	Chŏng-jong	定宗
950 "	Wang-so	" 昭	Kwang-jong	光宗
976 "	Wang-ju	" 伷	Kyŏng-jong	景宗
982 "	Wang-ch'i	" 治	Sŭng-jong	成宗
998 "	Wang-song	" 誦	Mok-jong	穆宗
1010 "	Wang-sun	" 詢	Hyön-jong	顯宗
1032 "	Wang-heum	" 欽	Tŭk-jong	德宗
1035 "	Wang-hyŭng	" 亨	Chŭng-jong	靖宗
1047 "	Wang-whi	" 徽	Mun-jong	文宗
1083 "	Wang-hun	" 勳	Sun-jong	順宗
1084 "	Wang-un	" 運	Sŭn-jong	宣宗
1095 "	Wang-uk	" 昱	Hŏn-jong	獻宗
1096 "	Wang-ong	" 顒	Suk-jong	蕭宗
1106 "	Wang-o	" 俁	Ye-jong	睿宗
1123 "	Wang-hă	" 楷	In-jong	仁宗
1147 "	Wang-hyön	" 睍	Eui-jong	毅宗

No.		Posthumous title	Name	Style	Acc.	Tomb	Loc.	Queen(s)	Surname	Q. tomb	Q. loc.	Children
								2nd Chang-vul Wang-hu	Jho	Whi	Yang-ju	Son.... Dau....
17.	孝宗	Hyo-jong Sun-mun Ta-wang	Yi Ho	Chong-yun	1650	Yong	Yo-ju	In-sung Wang-hu	Chang	Yong	Yo-ju	Son.... Dau....
18.	顯宗	Hyon-jong So-hyu Ta-wang	Yi Yun	Kyong-jik	1660	Sung	Yang-ju	Mvung-sung Wang-hu	Kim	Sung	Yang-ju	Son. one / Dau. six
19.	肅宗	Suk-jong Hyon-eui Ta-wang	Yi Sun	Myung-bo	1675	Myung	Ko-yang	In-gyong Wang-hu / 2nd In-hyun Wang-hu / 3rd In-wun Wang-hu	Kim / Min / Kim	Ik / Myung / Myung	Ko-yang / Ko-yang / Ko-yang	Dau. three / Son. two
20.	景宗	Kyong-jong Tok-mun Ta-wang	Yi Kyun	Whi-so	1721	Eui	Yang-ju	Tan-eui Wang-hu / 2nd Son-eui Wang-hu	Sim / O	He / Eui	Yang-ju / Ko-yang	Son.... Dau....
21.	英宗	Yung-jong Hyon-hyo Ta-wang	Yi Eum	Kwang-suk	1724	Wun	Yang-ju	Chung-song Wang-hu / and Chung-sun Wang-hu	So / Kim	Hong / Wun	Ko-yang / Yang-ju	Son.... Dau....
+22.	真宗	Chin-jong Hyo-jang Ta-wang	Yi Haing	Song-gyung	....	Yong	Pa-ju	Hyo-sun Wang-hu	Cho	Yong	Pa-ju	Son.... Dau....
*23.	正宗	Chong-jong Chang-hyo Ta-wang	Yi Sun'	Hyang-un	1777	Kon	Su-wun	Hyo-eui Wang-hu	Kim	Kon	Su-wun	Son.... Dau....
24.	純宗	Sun-jo Song-hyo Ta-wang	Yi Kwang	Kong-bo	1801	In	Kwang-ju	Sun-wun Wang-hu	Kim	In	Kwang-ju	Son. one Dau.
+.	翼宗	Ik-jong Hyo-myung Ta-wang	Yi Ta	Tok-in	....	Yu	Yang-ju	Hong-dok Wang-hu	Cho	Yu	Yang-ju	Son. one Dau.
24.	憲宗	Hon-jong Chul-hyo Ta-wang	Yi Whan	Mun-eung	1835	Kyong	Yang-ju	Hyo-hyun Wang-hu / 2nd Chong-mok Ta-bi	Kim / Hong	Yu / Kyong	Yang-ju / Yang-ju	Son. Dau.
25.	哲宗	Chul-jong Yong-hyo Ta-wang	Yi Chung	To-seung	1850	Ye	Ko-yang	Myung-sun Ta-bi	Kim	Ko-yang	Ye	Son. one Dau.
26.	高宗 太皇帝	The Present Emperor	Yi Hyong	Mvung-hu	1864		Hong	Wun-song Wang-hu	Min	Min		Son. one Dau.

26. { Ko-jong   1864   Became Emperor Kwangmu, 1897; abdicated, 1907.

27. 純宗 Sun-jong   1907   Reign name – Yun-heui (M-R Yunhŭi); his puppet regime and the dynasty ended by Japanese annexation, 1910.

The Kings of Modern Korea
[Chosŭn (M-R Chosŏn) of the Yi Dynasty]

1. *General.* Discrepancies in dates are infrequent and slight. Diacritical marks as used by Hulbert have been inserted only in the basic posthumous title ("T'ă-jo," "Chŏng-jong," etc.), for which the characters are given, and in the word Tă-wang (M-R Taewang), or "great king."

2. *The Roster of Rulers.* The twenty-seven kings who actually occupied the throne have been numbered in the left margin as shown in Yi Pyŏng-do (Dean Pyeng Do Yi), *Kuksa Tae'gwan.* To complete the list the editor has extended the table (1) to show that King Kojong (Number 26) and "The Present Emperor" were the same person; and (2) to include both the dynastic name ("Sun-jong") and the imperial reign name ("Yung-heui") of the 27th and last ruler. The four "great kings" who never ruled are identified below.

3. *Cho (jo)* 祖 *and Chong (jong)* 宗 *as the second syllable of the names of Yi kings.* These characters are sometimes used interchangeably. Kings 7 and 23 are unquestionably "Se-jo" and "Sun-jo," respectively, however, and the final character 宗 (chong, or jong) is inconsistent; see footnote. Numbers 21 and 22 are widely used as Hulbert gives them, and romanization and characters are in agreement. At the same time, the *Kuksa Tae'gwan* and the *Taikei* list them as "Yung-jo" (M-R Yungjo) 英祖 and "Chŏng-jo" (Chŏngjo) 莊祖 , respectively.

* Characters for "Se-jo" (No. 7) are 世祖
  Characters for "Sun-jo" (No. 23) are 純祖
† These four "kings" never reigned and are not assigned an ordinal number.
‡ "Yŭn-san-ju (Number 10). Prince "Yŭn-san" (M-R Yŏnsan) may be called by the title "Ju," but the one more commonly used, and the one given here in the Chinese characters, is "Gun" (basically "Kun"). It would be logical also to read "Yŭn-san-gun" for "Yŭn-san-ju" on I, 327 above. Cf. Kwang-hă-gun (Number 15).   —EDITOR.

EDITORIAL NOTES

VOLUME II

Chapter I-A

Note
Number
1.

The Korean sound for the place name 釜山 is 부산 (Pusan), as is well known to the thousands of Americans and Europeans in Korea since 1945. Hulbert, like most Western foreigners in the country before 1945, fell into the habit of using the Japanese sound Fusan (changed to "Husan" by the Japanese during the war years of 1937-1945 at the urging of Tanakadate and other "purists" who attacked the Hepburn system of Japanese romanization as a foreign perversion). "Pusan" is the correct reading here, according to the McCune-Reischauer System. The same correction is to be made on pages 24 (l. 15), 25 (l. 17), 326 (l. 6) and elsewhere. The date to which Hulbert intends to refer here is of course 1595 rather than 1395.

Chapter II

2. In this sentence again "Pusan" is to be read for "Fusan."

3. Pusan.

ED 411

Chapter III

**Note
Number
4.**
This paragraph offers a particularly striking example of Hulbert's imitation of the old Korean scholarly habit of using Korean readings for Chinese and Japanese as well as Korean surnames and personal names. As indicated in part in Notes to Volume I, the account of the "seven years' war" as a whole (from I, 341 to II, 52) is full of these arbitrary Koreanizations of names which are obviously to be rendered, respectively, by the Japanese or Chinese sound of the characters concerned. Here the author refers effectively to Hideyoshi, Katō and Konishi, but when he comes to the most significant name of the four—that of Tokugawa Ieyasu, founder of the Tokugawa Shogunate, 1603-1867—he renders this name according to the Korean sound of the characters 家康 . Few would recognize the most powerful shogan in Japanese history under the name "Gen. Ka Kang." (The port from which Katō and Konishi are here reported as sailing is of course Pusan.)

Chapter XI

5.　The date is 1724 rather than 1624, as is indicated in the final sentence of this paragraph.

Chapter XII

6.　The career of the "female Buddha" is generally agreed to have come to an end in 1758 rather than in 1753.

Chapter XIV

7.　The last sentence of this paragraph, referring to the execution of 2,000 Christians in September, seems to describe events in 1866 rather than in 1868.

Chapter XVI

8.　The M-R readings for "Fusan and Wŭnsan" are Pusan and Wŏnsan, respectively.

Note
Number
9.

Professor Hulbert is suffering from the unavailability of diplomatic correspondence now published when he writes that General Lucius Foote, the first United States minister to Korea, gave up his post in 1885 "without giving specific reasons." Department of State Dispatches and Instructions make it clear that (1) General Foote had long been weary of the Department's lack of interest in Korea and its failure to act promptly on the Korean King's requests for assistance during the golden period of American-Korean relations from May 1883 to November 1884; and (2) the general felt chagrined over the reduction of the rank of the U.S. chief of mission in Seoul from minister plenipotentiary to minister resident in 1885 and refused to accept the demotion. See especially Foote to Bayard, Nos. 32 (Oct. 19, 1883), 105 (Sept. 3, 1884) and 112 (Sept. 17, 1884). These dispatches are reproduced in George M. McCune and John A. Harrison, eds., *Korean-American Relations: Documents Pertaining to the Far Eastern Diplomacy of the United States,* Berkeley and Los Angeles, University of California Press, 1951, Volume I, pp. 37f., 53-55.

Chapter XVII

10.

This and later references to the Tonghak Tang during the Sino-Japanese War seem neither consistent among themselves nor, on the whole, fair to the Tonghak organization and membership. Here, while saying that "threatening plackards [sic] were fastened to foreigners' gates in Seoul," Hulbert omits any mention of the highly respectful and completely peaceable sit-down appeal to the King in front of the palace at this same time—the spring of 1893. In lines 8-11 of page 250 he leaves out the two most significant features of the action at Chŏnju. First, Chŏn Pong-jun, the insurgent Tonghak commander, undertook this military operation against the wishes and without the approval of the head of the society and his chief lieutenants. In the second place, Chŏn faithfully carried out his pledge to the King to withdraw from his almost impregnable position at Chŏnju in June 1894, after the ruler had appealed to the patriotic general to do so and had promised that no more landings of Chinese or Japanese troops on Korean soil would be permitted. The suggestion in lines 2-4 of page 251 that the Tonghak was "either frightened by the rumor of the

Note
Number

approach of a Chinese army or [was] being pressed by the government troops" is thus wide of the mark. The allusion to "starving malcontents" in line 10 of page 265˙ seems to be intended to be sympathetic toward the Tonghak, but it fails to do justice to the social, political and religious ideals of this remarkable movement. The final sentence on page 272 presents the most accurate characterization of the Tonghak Tang to be found in the *History*, but here again its members ought to have been described as more than mere "desperate citizens." The suppression effected in late 1894 and early 1895 by Japanese detachments and Korean Government troops is given a description on pages 275 and 276 which covers the surface facts rather well, although it does not even raise the important question whether the Tonghak organization or individuals in it received aid from Japanese sources before or during the Sino-Japanese War. Finally it may be remarked that on page 276 Hulbert names the independent Tonghak leader who took Chŏnju against the Society's orders in the summer of 1894, but the name used is "Chŭn Nok-tu" rather than the correct one of Chŏn Pong-jun (or Chŭn Pong-jun by Hulbert's formula). "Noktu" was his nickname, by which he was affectionately known to millions of Koreans. The *noktu* is a small bean commonly raised in Korea. Thus in English-language accounts Mr. Chŏn is often called "Little Beans." On all of the Tonghak topics discussed in this note, together with a partial listing of sources in Korean and English, see C. N. Weems, *The Korean Reform and Independence Movement*, cited, especially pages 83-103. A more specialized study of the Tonghak-Ch'ŏndo Kyo movement by Benjamin B. Weems will, when published, deal with all of these matters, including the question of Japanese encouragement of the Tonghak.

11.

It would have been more realistic if the author had said that Japan was determined that Korea's "independence" should not be compromised by any other power, and that reform was desirable from Tokyo's viewpoint only so long as it served to make government in Korea both efficient and compatible with the furthering of Japanese economic and strategic interests. This conditional support on the part of Japan for Korean independence had become clear to the patriotic Pak Yŏng-hyo, who had worked hard for reform coupled with independent Korean strength in 1894-1895 before the murder of the Queen (October 8, 1895). It must have been plain to Hulbert also

Note
Number

after that event and those of the succeeding four months, ending with the King's flight to the Russian legation on February
11, 1896, during which the Japanese minister virtually ran the
Korean government through a puppet cabinet and the ruler
was a terrorized prisoner in his own palace. The same inclination to interpret questionable actions in a manner favorable
to Japan is shown throughout this discussion of the Sino-Japanese War period. See, for example, Hulbert's description of
the first naval engagement, on pages 252-253, and his account,
on pages 253-254, of the initial land fighting, beginning with
the rather subjective statement that "it was wisely determined
to eliminate from the problem all the Chinese forces south of
Seoul. . . ." As a resident of Korea and a journalist, Hulbert
was taking the Japanese side because it was the only one which
seemed to offer any hope for Korea, as is explained by references to his later writings found in the Editor's Profile. It
seems unfortunate, however, that, as a historian, his view
could not have been more detached. At the same time it must
be noted that in lines 35-39 of page 251 he describes factually
the large-scale flight of residents from Seoul and faithfully
reports the traditional fear of Japan in his statement that "such
was the terror that the very name of the Japanese inspired."

12.   This account of the murder of the Korean Reform Party
leader, Kim Ok-kyun, and of the dismemberment of his body
is essentially factual and well presented. There is a difference
among qualified Korean writers, however, on the question
whether he went to China on his own initiative to ask Viceroy
Li Hung-chang for support in his effort to decrease the pre-
vailing influence of the reactionaries in Korea, who were
generally allied with Li's appointee, Yüan Shih-k'ai, the Chinese
"Resident" in Seoul. Hulbert's view is supported in Kim Yŏng-

hi 金永喜 , Chwaong Yun Ch'i-ho Sŏnsaeng Yakch'ŏn
子翁尹致昊先生略傳 , (Concise Biography of
Yun Ch'i-ho), Seoul, Kitokkyo Chosŏn Kamni Hoe Ch'ongni-
wŏn 基督教朝鮮監理會總理院 , 1934,
p. 70f. The opinion that Kim Ok-kyun planned the trip himself is expressed in Ŏm Hang-sŏp 嚴恒爕 , "Hanguk
Tongyip Undong ŭi Yŏksa" 韓國獨立運動
의 歷史 , a manuscript on the Korean independence

Note movement prepared by Mr. Ŏm in Chungking in 1944 at the
Number present editor's request. The best known foreign-language account of the character and skillful maneuverings of Hong
Chong-u is found in Félix Régamy, "Un assassin politique,"
T'oung Pao (Leyden) C (1894), pp. 260-271. See also F. A.
McKenzie, *Korea's Fight for Freedom*, New York, Fleming
H. Revell, 1920, p. 40f. Professor Harrington (*God, Mammon
and the Japanese,* cited, p. 254f.) refers to the strange concern
of Dr. Horace N. Allen in the "ghoulish business" of dis-
tributing the remains of Kim Ok-kyun. For a discussion of this
affair as a whole, see C. N. Weems, *op. cit.,* pp. 77-82.

13. The important east-coast city named here, in line 13 above and
in lines 8 and 10 of page 257 is rendered Wŏnsan by M-R
and would properly be Wŭn-san by Hulbert's own romanization
plan. The standard Japanese form is Genzan rather than
Gensan. It is understandable that Hulbert should use the
Japanese name for the city in referring to a Japanese army
unit, but it would have been helpful if he had indicated his
reason for doing so and had distinguished the Japanese from
the Korean form.

Chapter XVIII

14. In this chapter and in a few of the subsequent ones Hulbert is
at his best as a writer of history because he presents a broad
interpretive background for the individual events of a particular era. Here he makes good use, in general, of this device. If
he is too sweeping in his assertion that "from the early years
of the Christian era Korea has been moulded by Chinese ideas
and dominated by her [China's] influence," he is equally comprehensive in his countervailing statements. Here he refers to
the "radical and ineffacable difference between the Chinese
and the Korean which no amount of moulding could remove";
on page 264 he describes "by far the greater part" of the
finished products of civilization borrowed from China as
"being wholly unsuited to the Korean temperament." The
salient fact which one wishes that he had stressed is the
achievement of control over Korean society by the Neo-Confucian literati only in the fifteenth and sixteen centuries A.D.,
after a millennium of severe competition with social and
political influences associated with Buddhism. The form of

Note
Number

government had often been Confucian but the all-important control over the royal court and over the thought-pattern of the society as a whole had more generally been in the hands of Buddhist monks. Buddhism moved into Korea with its weaknesses as well as its elements of strength, but at least it brought with it no national labels from India or from China. Its priests were often interested in politics as well as in religion, but time and again when the interests of a Korean state were imperilled their loyalty to that state was unmistakeable. The Confucianists, on the other hand, could not import their ethical scheme of social and political control without bringing in their concept of the Chinese "world-state" system and of the Chinese emperor as the supreme earthly figure in the Confucian ethical pyramid. To some extent from 1401, therefore, and almost exclusively from 1544, when the century and one-half of brilliant achievements came to an end, loyalty to China and the assumption that Chinese culture was the supreme way of life acted as a strait jacket on Korean cultural growth. The most serious sufferings of the Korean people came, of course, not from Confucian principles but from their perversion in the hands of the all-powerful Neo-Confucian scholar-officials, who became increasingly factious and corrupt in the sixteenth century and, above all, after the beginning of isolation in 1637. See Sections 3 and 4 (*f* and *g*) of the Editor's Introduction.

Chapter XIX

15.

The "month of November" evidently means November 1894, and everything mentioned in this paragraph is apparently represented as having occurred before the end of that year. If that is what Hulbert intends to say, it is clear that he has Dr. Philip Jaisohn (Sŏ Chae-p'il) arriving back in Seoul more than a year before he actually returned. Dr. Jaisohn received his M.D. degree from George Washington University Medical School and also was married to Miss Muriel Buchanan Armstrong in 1895. In the fall of the same year, after having learned of the death of the conservative Korean Queen, he accepted a long-term contract as advisor to the Korean Government, although he had previously rejected two somewhat similar offers. He left Washington, D.C. early in December 1895 and arrived in Seoul near the end of January 1896, only a few days, indeed,

Note   before the Korean King's sensational flight from the palace to
Number   the Russian legation (February 11, 1896). For a review of
              these and related events, together with the supporting literature,
              see C. N. Weems, *op. cit.,* pp. 150-152.

Chapter XXI

16.   The date of this communication with the Taewŏngun was
              October 5, rather than the 15th, as can be judged from the
              preceding and succeeding events listed in the judgment of the
              Hiroshima Court which Hulbert quotes here.

17.   The assassination occurred on October 8, rather than the 5th.

Chapter XXII

18.   For the fact that de Speyer's replacement of Waeber in Seoul
              was actually delayed from February 1896 to September 1897
              in order that the more experienced Waeber might deal with
              the delicate situation caused by the King's seeking of asylum
              in the Russian legation, see C. N. Weems, *op. cit.,* pp. 145-147.
              In the same study there is (on pp. 277-293) an analysis of the
              international and internal Russian factors which caused Russia
              to use its preponderance of power in Korea sparingly during
              this same period of more than eighteen months. Certainly the
              change of ministers cannot be explained simply on the basis
              of their respective personalities. It may be noted further that
              Waeber, when finally relieved in September 1897, went on to
              the more important post of minister to Mexico, for which he
              had in fact first been designated by the Foreign Office in St.
              Petersburg late in 1895.

19.   The hazy and ineffectual condominium which Russia and
              Japan were to exercise over the peninsula under the Lobanov-
              Yamagata Agreement represented Prince Lobanov's counter-
              suggestion to the proposal made by Marshal Yamagata at
              Moscow, with the full approval of Prince (then Marquis) Itō,
              that Korea be permanently divided at the 38° parallel of north
              latitude, with Russia taking the northern and Japan the southern

half. Enough of this rejected "offer" could easily have leaked through diplomatic circles in Seoul to account for the "idea that Korea would be divided into two spheres of influence . . . ," mentioned on page 309, lines 13-15. Yamagata's proposal to Lobanov in the summer of 1896 is not to be confused with the suggestion made by the Russians in a late stage of the negotiations in 1903 that a "neutral zone" be established in the portion of the peninsula north of the 39° parallel. At that juncture, with the Anglo-Japanese Alliance in effect and the Russians active in Manchuria as well as Korea, Japan rejected this scheme, which it considered insincere.

20.   In justice to Dr. Jaisohn it might have been said here that he promoted the building of the Independence Arch and, at the same time, was teaching the idea of self-control and public responsibility in both domestic and foreign affairs. He was also urging the King to leave the Russian legation long before His Majesty did so, upon the completion of his new palace, in February 1897. It is at the same time not untrue that Jaisohn tended to be "blunt and outspoken" as Hulbert indicates on this same page.

21.   The American was of course Homer Bezaleel Hulbert.

Chapter XXIII

22.   Although Russian policies in and concerning Korea are discussed elsewhere in these Notes, this particular paragraph seems to call for clarification of three points. First, it was not in February 1898 but in the preceding November that the Independence Program (embracing the Independence Club, the *Independent* and other units) made its decisive public break with the Russians and their Korean conservative allies. In the *Independent* of November 18, 1897, the editor, Dr. Philip Jaisohn, finally abandoned his hopeful attitude toward Russian influence and made a scathing attack on the agreement under which Kuril Alexeiev, agent of Russian Finance Minister Witte, had become advisor and virtual dictator of the Korean finance department. Once this open political challenge had been issued, the younger and more positive-minded members of the Independence Program could hardly be held back from the disastrous demonstrations which began in the following February.

Note   [See C. N. Weems, *The Korean Reform and Independence*
Number   *Movement*, especially pp. 360-473.]

         Secondly, the sudden removal of the imperious de Speyer
and the general softening of Russian policy in Korea in March
1898 were evidently caused by the fact that, with Russia's
acquisition of Manchurian warm-water ports through the lease
of Port Arthur and Talien-wan (Russian, Dalny; Japanese,
Dairen) which was obtained in that month, it was St. Petersburg's desire to avoid unnecessary irritation of the British and
the Japanese by any further aggression in Korea at that time.

         Thirdly, Hulbert's frank reference to Korean opportunism
here seems to establish the fact that he was objective in his
estimate of traditional political practices and was not blindly
pro-Korean as he is sometimes described.

23.   It is not certain at what juncture Hulbert penned this paragraph; it may have been written as late as September 1904,
when it appeared in exactly these words in serial form (*The
Korea Review* IV, Sept. 1904, p. 430f.). In any event, a vast
number of Western observers had seen enough of Japanese
actions in Korea by that time to make them reject completely
Hulbert's assumption that "the aims and purposes of the Independence party were directly in line with Japanese interests
here. . . ." Indeed, it was repeated statements of this kind that
caused his critics to brand him as either naïve or subservient to
Japan. Cf. the Editor's Profile.

24.   This is an accurate statement, and this official policy was renewed with respect to the Japanese Government-General in
1910-1941. That fact did not prevent a number of missionaries
from feeling that they could not separate their religious activities from a concern with the social and political troubles of
their parishioners. Nor did it prevent Protestant Korean Christians from being charged with "conspiracies" in 1910 and 1911
or from joining with Ch'ŏndo Kyo members and Buddhists in
leading the great Independence Demonstration of 1919.

25.   For further detail on the country-wide activities of Protestant
churches see the works cited in the Editor's Suggestive Bibliography under "The Christian Movement" in Korea and many of
the articles listed in Elrod's *Index*, which is found under
"Lists and Guides."

Chapter XXIV

Note
Number
26.
This passionate attachment had had a basic part in the countless demonstrations against foreign intrusion throughout history.
Of these, at least six were spearheaded by the Righteous Army,
to which brief reference is made in Section 4d of the Editor's
Introduction. Hulbert mentions at least the first four of the
Ŭibyŏng uprisings, but does not suggest any connection between them and the resentment against the Japanese proposal
regarding Korean lands in 1902.

27.
These guarantees appear in the preamble and in the first
sentence of Article I of the original Anglo-Japanese Alliance,
concluded on January 30, 1902. It would have been more
pertinent to Japan's purpose in obtaining this diplomatic safe-
guard, however, if emphasis had been placed on Britain's
recognition, in Article I, that "Japan, in addition to the interests
which she possesses in China, is interested in a peculiar degree
politically as well as commercially and industrially in Corea
[sic]. . . . ." Gooch and Temperly, editors, *British Documents
on the Origins of the World War, 1898-1914*, London, 1927,
Vol. II, No. 125, p. 114; Vol. IV, No. 118, p. 128.

Chapter XXV

28.
The three paragraphs beginning at the center of page 342
state forcefully the strong criticism of Russian policy and the
admiration of Japan which have been traced in the Editor's
Profile of Professor Hulbert. In this final paragraph he is saying not only that a "temporary suspension of Korean autonomy"
at the hands of the Japanese might prove beneficial, but also
that Korea might have done well to side vigorously with Japan
against Russia, presumably from the beginning of the period
of modern foreign relations. All of this was written a full year
before the author made his sharp turn away from his long-held
line of support for Japan, at about the beginning of October
1905. Indeed, page 342 appeared in the History installment in
The Korea Review for October 1904 and page 343 (with a
minor deletion to accommodate the serial heading) was published at the beginning of the installment for November 1904.

Chapter XXVII

Note
Number
29.

The term "Korean troops" in this paragraph evidently refers to Japanese troops serving in Korea. The railroad running southeastward from Seoul might properly be called the "Seoul-Pusan Railway." In any event it seems unfortunate that Hulbert, following the general Western usage of his day, used a mixture of Korean and Japanese styles. The same combination is found in line 13 of page 372. (A further use of Fusan for Pusan occurs in line 39 of page 364). The McCune-Reishchauer form for "Wiju" is "Uiju."

30.

This paragraph contains a rather sharp criticism of such substantial private Japanese groups in Korea as the "Board of Trade of Fusan" and the plain statement that the failure of official representatives of Japan to propose substantial reforms was a disappointment. It by no means reflects any final conclusion, however, that Japan had been deceitful in its repeated promises of eventual efforts toward genuine reform. Pages 364 and 365 are found in exactly this form (except for pagination) in the final installment, appearing in the *Review* for December 1904.

EDITOR'S SUGGESTIVE BIBLIOGRAPHY

DESIGN AND PURPOSE

These necessarily brief bibliographical suggestions are made in the hope that they will give the reader an adequate key to the Western-language literature on Korea as a whole, from the sixteenth century to today, and will also introduce him to the strikingly extensive and varied writings of Professor Hulbert himself.

Comprehensive listings and commentaries on publications in the Korean field, especially for periods before 1945, are now available. Some of the basic ones, including Miss Soon Hi Lee's valuable study of materials published in the past decade, are named under "Lists and Guides." They offer specialized guidance to the student who wishes to pursue a particular topic beyond the limits of the one hundred sixty titles presented in Part One.

Even with this limitation of the general listings, some selection has been necessary in citing the author's works, in Part Two. It is expected that a more exhaustive presentation can be made in a forthcoming study. Here, so far as available data permit, I have noted all his books and his articles published outside Korea, as well as those appearing in *The Korean Repository* and the *Transactions of the Korea Branch of the Royal Asiatic Society*.

The *Korea Review*, edited and published by Hulbert, poses a vaster problem. Entirely aside from the installments of the *History* appearing in all issues of the magazine during the years 1901-1904 and aside from contributions by other writers, the editorials, articles and stories unquestionably written by him greatly exceed the one hundred forty items listed here. One complicating factor is his practice of discussing several un-

ED 423

related questions in a single "Editorial Comment" without using sub-headings. Another is the fact that much of his best writing which deals with a mixture of history and folklore, usually seasoned liberally with humor, is found in short anecdotes; their complete listing would require a prohibitive allotment of space. In less than four pages (113-117) of the *Review* for March 1901, for example, there appear six of his brief tales—"Prophecy," "Mathematics vs. Chinese," "The Story did it," "Cinderella," "An Engineering feat" and "Brains vs. Muscle"—all under the departmental heading of "Odds and Ends." Useful as abbreviated stories of this nature are in conveying Korean thought and moral values, they are too numerous to be entered individually.

The items listed were chosen with the realization that the Editor of the *Review* was writing primarily about Korean history and culture, on the one hand, and about the often explosive Japanese-Korean question on the other. All of his editorials and captioned articles of a non-fictional nature which concern one or the other of these themes are included, as are also a few of his more appealing adaptations of Korean legends and folk tales.

Any student of the remarkable "early missionary literature" produced in Korea during the half-century beginning with about 1890 would logically welcome a listing of all articles—and not merely those by Homer Hulbert—published in the *Repository,* the RAS *Transactions* and the *Review.* The dilemma facing the editor because of space limitations is resolved by Professor J. McRee Elrod's work, *An Index to English Language Periodical Literature Published in Korea, 1890-1940,* produced on microfilm and also printed electrostatically on paper by Yonsei University in 1960. This classified bibliographical aid, covering ten magazines including the three key ones mentioned, may be obtained in the United States as indicated in the entry under "Lists and Guides" below. One hopes that Professor Elrod will find it possible to add a supplement on two newspapers—the *Independent* (1896-1898), published by the pioneering Philip Jaisohn (Sŏ Chae-p'il) and Yun Ch'i-ho, and the *Korea Daily News,* carried on during the tense years 1904-1908 by the militantly pro-Korean and anti-Japanese British publicist, E. T. Bethell. Even as it stands, however, the *Index* offers valuable guidance to all interested readers. No attempt is therefore made here to duplicate the Elrod listings, although a few indispensable articles by authors other than Hulbert are cited in Part One.

Comparatively few scholars in the East Asian field seem to have made use of various private collections of letters, documents and rare published materials dealing with Korea which are available for use in research. Two of these are the collections of Horace N. Allen and George Clayton

Foulk, held by the Manuscript Division of the New York Public Library.

An exception to the listing of works in Part One by the alphabetical order of their authors' names is found in Section B ("Exploration and Indirect Information on Korea before 1876"), where it seems useful to show the sequence and, in a general way, the frequency, of early Western contacts with the country. Again in Part Two the chronological order of publication is followed, since it appears especially instructive to trace the development of Professor Hulbert's understanding of Korean questions and his points of view through the various stages outlined in the Editor's Profile.

PART ONE: ONE HUNDRED SIXTY BOOKS AND ARTICLES ON KOREA

A. LISTS AND GUIDES

American Universities Field Staff.
A Select Bibliography: Asia, Africa, Eastern Europe, Latin America, New York, 1960, ix, 534 p.

Bibliography of Asian Studies, Feb. 1936-,
[Ann Arbor, Mich., etc.], The association for Asian Studies, 1936-

Title varies: 1936-40 (v. 1-5), Bulletin of Far Eastern Bibliography; 1941-1955, Far Eastern Bibliography.
Published by the Committee on Far Eastern Studies of the American Council of Learned Societies, 1936-40; by the Association for Asian Studies under its early name, Far Eastern Association, 1941-55.
1941-   , issued in and detached from the Journal of Asian Studies.

California. University. Institute of Asiatic Studies.
Korean Studies Guide, compiled for the Institute of East Asiatic Studies, University of California, by B. H. Hazard, Jr. (and others). Edited by Richard Marcus. Berkeley, University of California Press, 1954. xii, 220 p. maps.

California. University. Institute of International Studies. East Asia Studies.
Russian Supplement to the Korean Studies Guide. Compiled by Robert L. Backus. Michael C. Rogers, project director. Berkeley, 1958. xii, 211 p.

Courant, Maurice, *Bibliographie Coréenne: Tableau littéraire de la Corée contenant la nomenclature des ouvrages publiés dans ce pays jusqu'en*

1890, ainsi que la description et l'analyse détaillées des principaux d'entre ces ouvrages, 3 vols., Paris, Ernest Leroux, Editeur Libraire de la Société Asiatique de L'Ecole dēs Langues Orientales Vivantes, 1894-1896, ccxiv, 502; ix, 538; ix, 446, clxxvii p.

————, *Bibliographie Coréene* (Supplement), Paris, 1901, 122 p.

Elrod, Jefferson McRee, *An Index to English Language Periodical Literature Published in Korea, 1890-1940,* Seoul, Yonsei University, 1960, 214 p.
[The magazines indexed are *Korea Bookman, The Korea Field, The Korea Magazine, The Korea Methodist, The Korea Mission Field, The Korea Review, The Korean Repository, Morning Calm, Transactions of the Korea Branch of the Royal Asiatic Society* and *St. Nicholas Chronicle.* A microfilm of these periodicals and of the *Index,* as well as copies of the electrostatically printed *Index,* may be obtained from Professor J. McRee Elrod, Peabody Library School, George Peabody College, Nashville 5, Tennessee.]

Gompertz, E. and G., "Supplement to 'A Partial Bibliography of Occidental Literature on Korea,'" *Transactions of the Korea Branch of the Royal Asiatic Society* (hereinafter cited as TKBRAS) XXIV (1935), 23.

Journal of Asian Studies, annual Bibliography volume.
[See *Bibliography of Asian Studies.*]

Lee, Soon Hi, *Korea: A Selected Bibliography in the Western Languages, 1950-1958,* Washington, Master's thesis, Catholic University of America, May, 1959.
[Miss Lee's thesis can be obtained on microfilm from Rev. James J. Kortendick, Chairman, Library Science Department, Catholic University, Washington, D. C.]

McCune, Shannon B., *Korea's Heritage: Regional & Social Geography,* Rutland, Vermont, Charles E. Tuttle Co., 1956, xiii, 250 p., illus., maps, diagrs., tables.
[See "References and Bibliographical Notes," pp. 195-211.]

Nahm, Andrew C., comp.,
Japanese Penetration of Korea: A Checklist of Japanese Archives in the Hoover Institution, compiled under the direction of Peter A. Berton, [Stanford, Calif.], Stanford University, Hoover Institution on War, Revolution and Peace, 1955 (Hoover Institution Bibliographical Series, 5), v, 103 p.

Underwood, Horace H., "A Partial Bibliography of Occidental Literature on Korea," TKBRAS XX (1931), 17-185.

U.S. Library of Congress. Reference Dept.
Korea: An Annotated Bibliography of Publications in Far Eastern Languages, compiled under the direction of Edwin G. Beal, Jr., with the assistance of Robin Winkler, Washington, 1950, viii, 167 p.

U.S. Library of Congress. Reference Dept.
Korea: An Annotated Bibliography of Publications in the Russian Language, compiled by Albert Parry, John T. Dorosh and Elizabeth Gardner Dorosh, Washington, 1950, xi, 84 p.

U.S. Library of Congress. Reference Dept.
Korea: An Annotated Bibliography of Publications in Western Languages, compiled by Helen Dudenbostel Jones, bibliographer, General Reference and Bibliography Division, and Robin L. Winkler, consultant in Korean bibliography, Washington, 1950, ix, 155 p.

B. EXPLORATION AND INDIRECT INFORMATION ON KOREA BEFORE 1876

(In chronological order of publication)

1597

Lettre annuelle, de Mars 1593, écrite par P. Pierre Gomez a P. Claude Acquavira, général de la Compagnie de Jésus, Milan, 1597.
[Contains references to Korea by Jesuits in Japan; reproduced by the Hakluyt Society.]

1600

"Two Famous Voyages Happily Performed Round About the World by Sir Francis Drake and M. Thomas Cavendish . . . , Whereunto are Appended Certain Rare Observations Touching the Present State of China and the Kingdome of Coray, Lately Invaded by Quabacondono [Hideyoshi], the Last Monarch of the 66 Princedomes of Japan," (1600), in *Works of the Hakluyt Society,* London, No. 4, 1849.
[See also *Hakluyt Principal Navigations,* London, Hakluyt Society, 1600, Vol. III.]

1668

Hamel van Gorcum, Hendrik, *Journael van de ongelukige Voyagie von t'Jacht de Sperwer gedestineert na Tayovan in t'iaar 1653, hoc t' selve Jacht op t' Quilpaarts Eyland is gestrant; als made een perinente beschryvinger der Landen, Provintien, Staten ende Forten leggende in t' Coningryk Coree,* Rotterdam, 1668.

[An English version of Hamel's story, taken from an intervening French translation, is published in TKBRAS IX (1918), 91.]

1797

Mireau, M. L. A. Milel, ed., *Voyage de la Perouse autour du monde, publié conformient au décret du 22 avril 1791 et rédigé par M. L. A. Milel Mireau*, Paris, 1797.

1804

Broughton, William Robert, *A Voyage of Discovery to the N. Pacific Ocean in which the Coast of Asia from the lat. of 35 degrees N. to the 52 degree N; the island Ensu (commonly known under the name of the land of Yeso), the north, south, east coasts of Japan, the Lieuchieux and the adjacent isles, as well as the coast of Corea have been examined and surveyed. Performed in H. M.'s sloop "Providence," and his tender, in the years 1795, 6, 7, 8, by W. Rob. Broughton*, London, T. Cadell and W. Davies, 1804.
[Contains a Korean vocabulary.]

1818

Hall, Captain Basil, *Account of a Voyage of Discovery to the West Coast of Corea and the Great Loo-choo Island*, London, John Murray, 1818, xv, 222, cxxx, 72 p., plates (part col.), maps, diag.
[Compare the work of John McLeod, surgeon of Captain Hall's ship, the *Alceste*.]

McLeod, John [Surgeon of the *Alceste*], *Voyage of His Majesty's Ship Alceste, Along the Coast of Corea, to the Island of Lewchew; With an Account of Her Subsequent Shipwreck*, second edition, London, John Murray, 1818, 323 p.
[Compare the work of Captain Basil Hall, master of the *Alceste*].

Gutzlaff, Charles,   ### 1834
Journal of Three Voyages along the Coast of China in 1831, 1832 and 1833, London, T. Ward & Company, 1834.
[The first Protestant missionary to visit Korea.]

Belcher, Captain Sir E.,   ### 1848
Narrative of the Voyage of H. M. S. "Samarang" during the years 1843-46, London, Reeve, Benham, and Reeve 1848, 2 vols., 359 and 574 p.
[Vol. I, pp. 324-358 and Vol. II, pp. 444-466 contain interesting discussions on Korea; a vocabulary is included.]

C. GENERAL DESCRIPTION: LAND, PEOPLE
AND ECONOMY

Brunner, Edmund de Schweinitz, "Rural Korea: A Preliminary Survey of Economic, Social and Religious Conditions," *The Jerusalem Meeting of the International Missionary Council, March 24-April 8, 1928,* New York, International Missionary Council, Vol. VI, pp. 84-172.

Chung, Kyung Cho, *Korea Tomorrow: Land of the Morning Calm,* New York, Macmillan, 1956, xxv, 384 p.

Gilmore, Rev. George W., A. M., *Korea from Its Capital: With a Chapter on Missions,* Philadelphia, Presbyterian Board of Publication and Sabbath-School Work, 1892, 328 p.

Grajdanzev, Andrew J., *Modern Korea,* New York, The John Day Company, 1944, X, 330. p.

Griffis, William E., *Corea, The Hermit Nation,* New York, C. Scribner's Sons, enlarged edition, 1904, 502 pp., illus., fold. map., bibliog.

Ireland, Alleyne, *The New Korea,* New York, E. P. Dutton and Company, 1926, xii, 352 p.
[Written from the Japanese viewpoint.]

Jones, George Heber, *Korea, the Land, People and Customs,* Cincinnati, Jennings and Graham; New York, Eaton and Mains, 1907, 110 p.

Keith, Elizabeth and Elspeth Keith Robinson, *Old Korea: The Land of Morning Calm,* London, Hutchinson & Co., 1942, 77 p., 16 color prints, 24 water colors.

Kim, Changsoon, ed., *The Culture of Korea: Racial Background, Sketch of Geography, History of Korea, Religion, Literature, Art, Science, Music, Economic Background, and History of Revolutionary Movement,* [Honolulu], The Korean American Cultural Association, Inc., [1945], 334 p.

Korea: Its Land, People and Culture of All Ages, Seoul, Hakwon-sa, 1960. Text, 29 and 718 p.; black and white illus. (no pagination), 460 p.; color illus. (no pagination), 32 p., map.

Lautensach, Hermann, *Korea: Land, Volk, Schicksal,* Stuttgart, K. F. Koehler, 1950, 135 p.

Lee, Hoon Koo, *Land Utilization and Rural Economy in Korea,* Chicago, University of Chicago Press, 1932, 289 p.

Lowell, Percival, *Choson, The Land of the Morning Calm: A Sketch of Korea, illustrated from photographs by the Author,* second edition, Boston, Ticknor and Company, 1886, x, 412 p.

Moose, J. Robert, *Village Life in Korea,* Nashville, Tennessee, Publishing

House of the M. E. Church, South, Smith and Lamar, Agents, 1911, 242 p.

McCune, Shannon B., *Climate of Korea*, Korean Research Associates, Research monographs on Korea, Series B., No. 3-4, [1941], 2 v., illus., maps.

Nelson, M. Frederick, *Korea and the Old Orders in Eastern Asia*, Baton Rouge, Louisiana State University Press, 1945, XVI, 326 p., bibl.

Oppert, Ernest, *A Forbidden Land: Voyages to the Corea, with an account of Its Geography, History, Productions, and Commercial Capabilities*, etc., etc., London, Sampson Low, Marston, Searle, and Rivington, 1880, xix, 349 p.

Pogio, M. A., *Korea, (aus dem Russischen übersetzt von St. Ritter von Ursyn-Pruszynski)*, Wien und Leipzig, Wilhelm Braumuller, 1895, 248 p.

Ross, Rev. John, *History of Corea Ancient and Modern with Description of Manners and Customs, Language and Geography*, London, Elliot Stock, 1891, xii, 404 p.
[A pioneer among books devoted entirely to the Korean land and people.]

Taeuber, Irene B., "The Population Potential of Postwar Korea," *Far Eastern Quarterly*, V: 3, May, 1946.

Trautz, Friedrich Max, *Japan, Korea and Formosa: the Landscape, Architecture, Life of the People*, New York, Westerman, [1931], xxix p., 256 plates.

Underwood, Horace Grant, *The Call of Korea: Political, Social, Religious*, New York, Fleming H. Revell, 1908, 204 p.

UNESCO Korean Survey, compiled by the Korean National Commission for UNESCO, Seoul, Dong-a Publishing Company, 1960.

U.S. Army Map Service.
Gazetteer to Maps of Korea, AMS 2, Washington, 1950.

Wagner, Ellasue, *Korea: The Old and the New*, New York, Fleming H. Revell, 1931, 160 p.

White, Trumbull, *Glimpses of the Orient, or The Manners, Customs, Life and History of the People of China, Japan and Corea*, Philadelphia and Chicago, P. W. Ziegler and Co., 1897, 400 p.
[The discussion of Korea—especially pages 331-338—contains an unusually good summary of the Yi dynasty system of isolation.]

Zaichkov, V. T., *Georgraphy of Korea*, tr. by Albert Parry, N. Y., International Secretariat, Institute of Pacific Relations, 1952, vii, 141 p.

D. HISTORY, POLITICS AND INTERNATIONAL RELATIONS

Allen, Richard C. [pseudonym], *Korea's Syngman Rhee: An Unauthorized Portrait*, Rutland and Tokyo, Charles E. Tuttle, 1960, 259 p., Illus., notes, bibliog., index.
[See the editor's review of this work in a recent issue of the *Journal of Asian Studies*. Allen's viewpoint differs sharply from that of Dr. Robert T. Oliver in his biography.]

Asakawa, Kanichi, *The Russo-Japanese Conflict: Its Causes and Issues*, Boston, Houghton Mifflin, 1904, 383 p.
[A relatively mild and sympathetic view of the Korean people, less colored by Japanese nationalism than the accounts of Hishida and Kawakami.]

The Bethell Trial, official report of proceedings from *Japan Chronicle*, Kobe, 1908, 56 p.

Bishop, Isabella L. (Bird), *Korea and Her Neighbors*, New York, Fleming H. Revell, 1898, 480 p., front., illus., plates.

Brandt, Maximilian von, *Drei Jahre Ostasiatischer Politik (1894-1897): Beitrage zur Geschichte des chinesich-japanischen Krieges und seiner Folgen*, Stuttgart, Stretcker & Moser, 1897, 263 p.
[Chapter V, "Japan und Russland in Korea, Juni 1894 bis Februar 1897," gives a fairly good sketch of diplomatic pressures in Korea during these years.]

Brown, Arthur Judson, *The Mastery of the Far East: The Story of Korea's Transformation and Japan's Rise to Supremacy in the Orient*, New York, Charles Scribner's Sons, 1919, ix, 2, 9-671 p., front. (6 port.), plates, port. group, fold. map.

Cable E. M., *United States-Korean Relations, 1866-1871*, Seoul, English Publication Number 4, Literary Department of Chosen Christian College, 1939 (Reprint from the *Transactions of the Korea Branch of the Royal Asiatic Society*, Vol. 26.)

Chavannes, E., "Les monuments de l'ancien royaume coréen de Kao-keou-li," *T'oung Pao* (Leyden) IX (1908), lième serie, pp. 236-265.

Chung, Henry, A. M., Ph.D., *The Case of Korea: A Collection of Evidence on the Japanese Domination of Korea, and on the Development of the Korean Independence Movement*, New York, Fleming H. Revell, 1921, 365 p.

Croly, Herbert, *Willard Straight*, New York, Macmillan, 1924, 569 p.
[Refreshingly honest evaluation of the Korean scene in 1904-1905

by Willard Straight, Secretary to the U. S. Minister. See especially pages 132-194.]

Cynn, Hugh Hung-Wo, *The Rebirth of Korea,* New York, The Abingdon Press, 1920, 272 p.

Dennett, Tyler, *Americans in Eastern Asia: A Critical Study of the Policy of the United States with reference to China, Japan and Korea in the 19th Century,* New York, Macmillan, 1922, 725 p.

Un établissement Japonais en Corée: Pusan depuis le XVième siècle, Paris, Bibliothèque de la France coloniale moderne, 1904, 24 p.

Fisher, J. Earnest, *Democracy and Mission Education in Korea,* New York, Bureau of Publications, Teachers College, Columbia University, 1928, xiii, 187 p.

Gale, James Scarth, *A History of the Korean People,* Seoul, The Christian Literature Society of Korea, [1927], no consecutive pagination. Published serially in *The Korea Mission Field,* July 1924 to September 1927; bound in one volume, 1927.
[This work is remarkable because of the insight and Chinese-character knowledge of the scholarly Dr. Gale, but it is rather unsystematic in presentation and lacks continuity and balance among periods and topics.]

Gale, James Scarth, *Korea in Transition,* New York, Young People's Missionary Movement of the United States and Canada, 1901, xi, 270 p.

Goldie, F., "Modern History of Corea," *Monthly* (London), 1875, 15:281.

Harrington, Fred Harvey, *God, Mammon and the Japanese: Dr. Horace N. Allen and Korean-American Relations, 1884-1905,* Madison, The University of Wisconsin Press, 1944, 362 p.

Henderson, Gregory, "Korea through the Fall of the Lolang [sic] Colony," *Koreana Quarterly* I:1, Summer 1959, pp. 147-168.
[The *Quarterly* is published by The International Research Centre, 282 Nagwon Dong, Chongno Ku, Seoul Korea.]

Hishida, Seiji, G., *The International Position of Japan as a Great Power,* New York, The Columbia University Press, 1905, 289 p.

Hsü, Shushi, *China and Her Political Entity: A Study of China's Foreign Relations with Reference to Korea, Manchuria and Mongolia,* New York, Oxford University Press, 1926, 438 p.

The Independence Movement in Korea, reprints from *Japan Chronicle,* Kobe, 1919, 72 p.

Kawakami, Kiyoshi Karl, *Japan in World Politics,* New York, The Macmillan Company, 1917, xix, 300 p.

Kendall, Carlton Waldo, *The Truth About Korea*, San Francisco, The Korean National Association, 1919, 104 p.

Korea: Treaties and Agreements, Washington, Carnegie Endowment for International Peace, Pamphlet No. 43, vi, 68 p., 1921.

The Korean Conspiracy Case, [Official report of proceedings in appeal], *Japan Chronicle*, Kobe, 1913, 309 p.

Korean Liberty Conference, Mirrow Room, Lafayette Hotel, Washington, D. C., February 27, 1942, February 28, 1942, March 1, 1942, The United Korean Committee in America, Los Angeles and Honolulu, [1942], 103 p.
[Speakers at this meeting, held on the twenty-third anniversary of the Samil uprising of March 1, 1919, included Professor Homer B. Hulbert, Dr. Philip Jaisohn and Dr. Syngman Rhee.]

The Korean Situation: Authentic Accounts of Recent Events, New York, Commission on Relations with the Orient of the Federal Council of Churches of Christ in America, 1919, 125 p.
[A report of the same title with "Number 2" added was published by the Commission in 1920.]

Ladd, George Trumbull, LL.D., *In Korea with Marquis Ito: Part I, A Narrative of Personal Experiences; Part II, A Critical and Historical Inquiry*, New York, Charles Scribner's Sons, 1908, x, 477 p.
[Professor Ladd approaches the Korean people from the standpoint of Japanese concepts and prejudices; idealizes Prince (then Marquis) Itō; and has harsh words for Hulbert, Bethell and others who regarded the "Protectorate Treaty" of November 1905 as fraudulent and fought for Korean freedom.]

Liem, Channing, *America's Finest Gift to Korea: The Life of Philip Jaisohn*, New York, William-Frederick Press, 1952, 89 p.

Macdonald, Donald S., "The American Role in the Opening of Korea to the West," TKBRAS XXXV (1959), 51-66.

Moellendorff, Rosa von, *P. G. von Moellendorff: Ein Lebensbild*, Leipzig, O. Harrassowitz, 1930, viii, 166p. facsims, front., plates, ports., 8vo, bibliog., p. [121-] 124. [Includes extracts from his diaries and letters.]

McCune, Evelyn Becker, *History of Lo-lang, with Special Attention to the Ways in Which Chinese Institutions Were Adopted by Surrounding Korean Tribes*, M. A. thesis, University of California at Berkeley, 1950.
[Available on microfilm through University of California Libraries.]

McCune, George M., *Korean-American Relations*, Berkeley, University of California Press, 1951, 163 p.

McCune, George M., *Notes on the History of Korea: Early Korea*, 29 p., Research Monographs on Korea, Series 1, No. 1, Korean Research Associates, 1952.

McKenzie, Frederick Arthur, *Korea's Fight for Freedom*, New York, Fleming H. Revell, 1920, 320 p.

McKenzie, Frederick Arthur, *The Tragedy of Korea*, London, Hodder and Stoughton, 1908, 312 p.

Oliver, Robert Tarbell, *Syngman Rhee: The Man Behind the Myth*, New York, Dodd, Mead, 1954, 380 p.
[This biography is highly favorable to Dr. Rhee. Contrast it with Richard C. Allen, *Korea's Syngman Rhee*, cited.]

Reischauer, E. O. and J. K. Fairbank, *History of East Asian Civilization*, Vol. I, *East Asia: The Great Tradition*, Boston, Houghton Mifflin, 1960.
[For chapter on Korea see pp. 394-449.]

Report of U.S. Secretary of the Navy to Congress, 1872, pp. 275-313.
[Official account of the "Little War of 1871" with Korea.]

Rosny, Léon de, *Les Coréens: Aperçu ethnographique et historique*, Paris, Maisoneuve Frères et Ch. Leclerc, Editeurs, Libraires de la Société d'Ethnographie, 1886, 91 p.

Sansom, Sir George B., "An Outline of Recent Japanese Archeological [*sic*] Research in Korea and its Bearing upon Early Japanese History," *Transactions of the Asiatic Society of Japan*, Vol. VI, Series 2, December 1929, pp. 5-12.

Slawik, Alexander, "The Chinese Prefecture in Korea During the Han, Wei and Chin Dynasties," *Wiener Beitrage zur Kunstgeschichte Asiens* (Vienna) VII, 1932.

Stead, Alfred, ed., *Japan by the Japanese: A Survey by its Highest Authorities*, New York, Dodd, Mead and Company; London, William Heinemann, 1904, 697 p.
[Ariga, in his chapter on "Diplomacy" (pp. 142-218), gives the standard Japanese view on pivotal factors in the Korean question, as well as valuable references to other Japanese sources.]

Story, Douglas, *To-Morrow in the East*, London, Chapman & Hall Ltd., 1907, ix, 267 p.
[The principal actor in the drama of the Korean Emperor's first effort to place his protest against the "protectorate treaty" before the world, while Hulbert was on his Washington mission, is writing here. For Mr. Story's principal references to the Korean issue as a whole see especially pages 97-142.]

Suematsu, Yasukazu, *The Rise and Fall of Mimana: Japanese-Korean Relations before A.D. 646*, Tokyo, Yoshikawa Kobunkan, 1956, 27 and 219 p. (in Japanese); 9 p. (English summary).

Tewksbury, Donald, ed., *Source Materials on Korean Politics and Ideologies*, New York, Institute of Pacific Relations, 1950.
[A valuable collection, despite some important omissions and some minor errors.]

Underwood, Horace Horton, *Korean Boats and ships*, TKBRAS XXIII, Pt. 1, 1934, 99 p., port., plates.

"Vladimir" [pseudonym for Z. Volpicelli], *Russia on the Pacific and the Siberian Railroad*, London, S. Low Marston, 1899, 373 p.
[Valuable source on Russian purposes and actions regarding Korea in 1860-1876.]

Wagner, Edward W., *The Korean Minority in Japan, 1904-1950*, New York, Institute of Pacific Relations, 1951, 108 p.

————, *The Recommendation Examination of 1519: Its Place in Early Yi Dynasty History* (*Chōsen Gakuhō* XV), Tenri, 1960, 80 p.

Weems, Benjamin B., "Ch'ŏndokyo: A Religio-Nationalist Movement in Korea," M.A. thesis, Georgetown University, 1955.
[Available in bound typescript form through the Library of Georgetown University.]

Weems, Clarence N., *The Korean Reform and Independence Movement (1881-1898)* (Ph.D. dissertation, Columbia University, 1954), Ann Arbor, Michigan, University Microfilms, 1954, 546 p.

E. PATTERNS OF CULTURE: BELIEFS, CUSTOMS, ART, LITERATURE AND EDUCATION

Allen, Horace N., *Korea, Fact and Fancy, being a republication of two books entitled "Korean Tales" and "A Chronological Index,"* Seoul, Methodist Publishing House, 1904, 285 p.

Carpenter, Frances, *Tales of a Korean Grandmother*, Garden City, Doubleday, 1947, 287 p.

Clark, Charles Allen, *Religions of Old Korea*, New York, Fleming H. Revell, 1932, 295 p.

"Choi Chiwon [Ch'oe Ch'i-wŏn]: Selections," *Korea Magazine* I (1917); 13.

Culin, Stewart, *Korean Games*, Philadelphia, University of Pennsylvania, 1895, xxxvi, 177 p.

Eckardt, Andreas, *A History of Korean Art,* translated by J. M. Kindersley, London, Edward Golston; Leipzig, Earl W. Hiersemann, 1929. 225 p., plates CLXVIII.

Eckardt, Andreas, *Koreanische Maerchen und Erzälungen,* St. Ottilien, Bavaria, Oberbayern Missionverlag, 1928, 135 p.

Gale, James Scarth, trans. and ed., *Korean Folk Tales: Imps, Ghosts and Fairies, Translated from the Korean of Im Bang and Yi Ryuk,* London, J. M. Dent & Sons, Ltd.; New York, E. P. Dutton Co., 1913, 233 p.

Gompertz, G. St. G. M., "The Development of Koryo Wares," *Transactions of the Oriental Ceramic Society,* July 26, 1951, pp. 11-26, 4 plates.

———— ,"The 'Kingfisher Celadon' of Koryo," *Artibus Asiae* (Ascona, Switzerland) XVI, 1953, pp. 5-24, 3 drawings, 13 plates.

————, "Koryo Inlaid Celadon Ware," *Transactions of the Oriental Ceramic Society,* October 28, 1954, pp. 37-50, 8 plates.

Henderson, Gregory, "Chŏng Ta-san: A Study in Korea's Intellectual History," *Journal of Asian Studies* XVI: 3 (May 1957), 377-386.

Honey, W. B., *Corean Pottery,* London, Faber & Faber, 1947; New York, Van Nostrand, 1948, XV, 19 p., 100 plates.

Hong-Tjong-Ou [Hong Chong-u], *Le Bois Sec Refleuri,* Paris, E. Leroux, 1895, 192 p.
[Hong Chong-u was the Korean detective who killed Kim Ok-kyun in Shanghai in 1894.]

Kang, Younghill, *The Grass Roof,* New York, C. Scribner's Sons, 1931, 367 p.

Karl, Hongkee, *A Critical Evaluation of Modern Social Trends in Korea,* Chicago, private edition distributed by the University of Chicago Libraries, 1938.

Kim, Doo Hun, "The Rise of Neo-Confucianism against Buddhism in Late Koryo," *Bulletin of the Korean Research Center: A Journal of Social Sciences and Humanities,* Number 12, May 1960, pp. 11-29.
[The Korean Research Center is located at 90-1, 1-Ka, Chungjong Ro, Sŏdaemun Ku, Seoul, Korea.]

Kim, Won-Yong, *Early Movable Type in Korea,* Publication of the National Museum of Korea, Series A, Vol. I, Seoul, Eul-Yu Publishing Co., 1954, 36 p. Korean text; 15 p. abridged English translation, 52 plates with bilingual captions.

Lee, Peter H., "Epigrams from the Korean," *The Hudson Review* VIII:4 (1956), 487-498.

————, *Kranich am Meer: koreanische Dichtung*, München, 1958, 163 p.

————, *Studies in the Saenaenorae: Old Korean Poetry*, Serie Orientale Roma XXII, Rome, 1959, 212 p.

Li, Mirok, *The Yalu Flows: A Korean Childhood*, tr. by H. A. Hammelmann, London, Harvill Press [1954], 185 p. 19 c.m.

McCune, Evelyn Becker, *Korean Art*, Rutland and Tokyo, Charles E. Tuttle, 1961.

Osgood, Cornelius, *The Koreans and their Culture*, New York, Ronald Press Company, 1951, xvi, 387 p.

Paik, Nak Choon (Dr. L. George Paik), "Tripitaka Koreana: Library of Woodblocks of Buddhist Classics at Haein Sa, Korea," TKBRAS XXXII (1951), 62-82.

Pyun, Yung Tai, *Tales from Korea*, Seoul, International Cultural Association of Korea, 1946, 148 p.

Satow, E., "The Korean Potters in Satsuma," *Transactions of the Asiatic Society of Japan*, 1878, VI, Part 2.

Starr, Frederick, *Korean Buddhism, History—Condition—Art*, Boston, Marshall Jones Company, 1918, xix, 104 p.

Underwood, Horace Horton, *Modern Education in Korea*, New York, International Press, 1926, 336 p.

Yang, Key P. and Gregory Henderson, "An Outline History of Korean Confucianism," *Journal of Asian Studies* XVIII:1, Nov. 1958, pp. 81-101; XVIII:2, Feb. 1959, pp. 259-276.

Youn Eul Sou, M. L'Abbé Laurent, *Le Confucianisme en Corée*, Paris, Librairie Pierre Téqui, 1939, 198 p.

Zŏng In-Sŏb [Chŏng In-sŏp], trans. and comp., *Folk Tales from Korea Collected and Translated with an Introduction by Zŏng In-sŏb*, London, Routledge & Kegan Paul Ltd., 1952, xxviii, 257 p.

F.   THE CHRISTIAN MOVEMENT
1. Roman Catholic

The Catholic Church in Korea, Hongkong, Imprimerie de la Société des Mission-Etrangères, 1924, 108 p.
[This English version of the original French work, *Le Catholicisme en Corée*, was translated by the late Bishop Patrick Byrne, M. M., who was killed by Communists in Korea.]

Dallet, Ch., *Histoire de l'Eglise de Corée, précédée d'une introduction sur l'histoire, les institutions, la langue, les moeurs et coutumes*

coréennes, Paris, Librairie Victor Palme, 1874, 2 vols. cxcii, 383 and 595 p., map, 8vo.
[Almost all of Dallet's valuable introduction was reprinted in Adrien Launay, *La Corée et les missionaires français,* Tours, Alfred Mame et Fils, 1895, 368 p. The entire introduction is republished in English in Charles Dallet, *Traditional Korea,* New Haven, Human Relations Area Files, 1954.]

Gilmore, Florence, *For the Faith: Life of Just de Bretenières (Adapted from the French of C. Appert),* Maryknoll, Ossining, New York, Catholic Foreign Mission Society, 1918, 179 p.

Launay, Adrien, ed., *Ma captivité dans les prisons de Séoul, par Mgr. Ridel avec une biographie de l'auteur,* Paris, Desclee de Brouwer, 1901, 189 p.

Launay, Adrien, *Martyrs, français et coréens (1838-46), beatifiés en 1925,* Paris, P. Téqui, 1925, 272 p., 8vo.

2. Protestant

Brown, George Thompson, *Missions and Unity—A Study of the Relationship between the Missionary Enterprise and the Ecumenical Movement* (T. H. D. thesis, Union Seminary, Richmond, Virginia, 1958), Nashville, Tennessee, Board of World Missions, Presbyterian Church in the United States, 1958, mimeographed, 100 p., bibliog. [Mr. Brown presents an interpretation of the historic development of the Korea Mission of the Presbyterian Church in the United States.]

Clark, Charles Allen, *The Korean Church and the Nevius Method,* New York, Fleming H. Revell, 1930, 278 p.

Fifty Years of Light, prepared by Missionaries of the Woman's Foreign Missionary Society of the Methodist Episcopal Church in Commemoration of Fifty Years of Work in Korea, Seoul (printed by the Y. M. C. A. Press), 1938.

McCully, (Miss) E. A., *The Corn of Wheat,* Toronto, The Westminster Company, 1903, 290 p.
[This book is essentially a biography of Rev. W. J. McKenzie, pioneer Canadian Presbyterian missionary to Korea, but it deals with the early work of the Canadian Presbyterian Church (later a component of the United Church of Canada) as a whole, as well as with general conditions in Korea in 1893-1895 and the Tonghak movement.]

Paik, L. George, *The History of Protestant Missions in Korea,* 1832-1910, Pyeng Yang [P'yŏng'yang], Korea, Union Christian College Press, 1929, ix, 438, XIII p.

Rhodes, Harry A., ed., *History of the Korea Mission, Presbyterian Church U.S.A., 1884-1934,* Seoul, Chosen Mission, Presbyterian Church (printed by the Y. M. C. A. Press), 1934, xii, 672, x p.

Ryang, J. S., editor, *Southern Methodism in Korea—Thirtieth Anniversary,* Seoul, Board of Missions, Korea Annual Conference, Methodist Episcopal Church, South [1929], English text 186, LXVIII p.; Korean mixed script text 299 p.

Sauer, Charles A., ed., *Within the Gate, Comprising the Addresses Delivered at the Fiftieth Anniversary of Korean Methodism, First Church, Seoul, Korea, June 19-20, 1934, and An Historical Play, "At the Hermit's Gate," by Ellasue Wagner,* Seoul, Methodist News Service, 1934.

Wasson, Alfred W., *Church Growth in Korea* (Studies in the World Mission of Christianity, Occasional Papers, No. 1), New York, International Missionary Council, 1934, xii, 175 p.

G. LANGUAGE: DICTIONARIES AND TEXTS

Chang, Sung-Un and Robert P. Miller, *Intermediate Korean,* New Haven, Institute of Far Eastern Languages, Yale University, 1959, 472 p.

Clark, Elinor McCullough, *Introduction to Spoken Korean,* by Elinor M. Clark with the collaboration of San Soon Yun, New Haven, Institute of Far Eastern Languages, Yale University, 1948-49. 2 v.

Gale, James Scarth, *The Unabridged Korean-English Dictionary,* third edition, edited by Alexander A. Pieters, Seoul, The Christian Literature Society of Korea, 1931, xvii, 1781 p.
[First published in 1897 under the title "A Korean-English Dictionary."]

Lee, Chang-Hei, *Practical Korean Grammar,* Seattle, University of Washington Press, 1955, 225 p.

Lew, Hyungki [Yu Hyŏng-gi] *Sinsaeng Han-Young Sajon (New Life Korean-English, English-Korean Dictionary in Korean),* Seoul, Sinsaeng-sa (New Life Press), 1945, 2 vols., 866 and 1143 p.
[Reproduced photolithographically by Educational Services, Washington, D. C.]

Lukoff, Fred, *Spoken Korean,* Holt Spoken Language Series (Identical with the edition prepared for the United States Armed Forces Institute), New York, Henry Holt, [1945-1947?], 2 v.

Martin, Samuel E., *Korean in a Hurry,* Rutland, Charles E. Tuttle, 1954, 137 p.

Pae, Eui Whan, *Conversational Korean,* Washington, D. C., Korean Affairs Institute, Inc., 1944, xiv, 171 p.

Ross, Rev. John, *Corean Primer, Being Lessons in Corean on all Subjects, Transliterated on the Principles of the "Mandarin Primer," by the Same Author,* Shanghai, American Presbyterian Mission Press, 1877, 89 p.

Sunoo, Hak-won, *A Standard Colloquial Korean Text Book for University Students,* Seattle, University of Washington Bookstore, Vol. I, 1944.

Underwood, Horace Grant, *An Introduction to the Korean Spoken Language,* second edition, revised and enlarged with the assistance of Horace Horton Underwood, New York, Macmillan, 1914, XV, 475 p.

Underwood, H. G. and H. H., *An English-Korean Dictionary,* Seoul, Y. M. C. A. Press, 1925, 741 p.

Underwood, Joan V., *Concise English-Korean Dictionary,* Rutland, Vermont, Charles E. Tuttle, 1954, xvii, 320 p.

H. MATERIALS ON THE POST-1945 PERIOD

Berger, Carl, *The Korea Knot: A Military-Political History,* Philadelphia, University of Pennsylvania Press, 1957.

Deane, Philip, *I Was a Captive in Korea,* New York, W. W. Norton and Co., 1953, 253 p.

Kahn, Ely Jacques, Jr., *The Peculiar War: Impressions of a Reporter in Korea,* New York, Random House, 1952, ix, 211 p.

Higgins, Marguerite, *War in Korea:* the *Report of a Woman Combat Correspondent,* Garden City, N. Y., Doubleday, 1951, 223 p.

Lauterbach, Richard E., *Danger from the East,* New York and London, Harper and Brothers, 1947, 430 p.

Meade, Edward Grant, *American Military Government in Korea,* New York, King's Crown Press, 1951, xii, 281 p.

McCune, George M., *Korea Today,* Cambridge, Harvard University Press, for the Institute of Pacific Relations, 1950, 372 p., bibl., map on end papers.

Riley, John W., Jr. and Wilbur Schramm, (narratives translated by Hugh Heung-wu Cynn), *The Reds Take a City: The Communist Occupation of Seoul with Eyewitness Accounts,* New Brunswick, New Jersey, Rutgers University Press, 1951, xiv, 210 p.

United Nations Command. Office of the Economic Coordinator for Korea. *Digest of Korean Civil and Criminal Law,* prepared by Public Administration Division, 1956, 63, 17 p. (Includes Constitution of the Republic of Korea.)

U.S. Congress. Senate. Committee on Foreign Relations.
The United States and the Korean Problem; Documents, 1943-1953, Washington, U.S. Govt. Print. Off., 1953, vii, 168 p., map. (83rd Cong., 1st Session. Senate. Document No. 74.)

U.S. Information Agency.
Korea: In the Public Interest, Washington, Distributed by U.S. Information Service, 1955, 69 p., illus., ports.

Weems, Clarence N., *Korea: Dilemma of Underdeveloped Country,* Headline Series Number 144, New York, Foreign Policy Association—World Affairs Center, November-December, 1960.

PART TWO: ONE HUNDRED NINETY OF HOMER B. HULBERT'S PUBLISHED WRITINGS
(in chronological order of publication)

A. *Books*

1. Works Concerning Korea

A Concise Dictionary of the Korean Language, in two parts, Korean-English and English-Korean, by Horace Grant Underwood, assisted by Homer B. Hulbert and James S. Gale, Yokohama, Kelly and Walsh; New York, A. D. F. Randolph, 1890 (two parts in one volume).

The History of Korea, 2 vols., Seoul, Methodist Publishing House, 1905.

A Comparative Grammar of the Korean Language and the Dravidian Languages of India, Seoul, The Methodist Publishing House, 1905, 152 p.

The Passing of Korea, New York, Doubleday, Page, 1906, 473 p.

The Japanese in Korea, Seoul, 1907, 82 p. (extracts, with some editing, from *The Korea Review*).

Omjee the Wizard: Korean Folk Tales, Springfield, Massachusetts, Milton Bradley, 1925, 156 p.

2. Miscellaneous Works

In Search of a Siberian Klondike, as Narrated by Washington B. Vanderlip, the Chief Actor, and Herein Set Forth by Homer B. Hulbert, New York, The Century, 1903, 315 p.

The Face in the Mist, Springfield, Massachusetts, Milton Bradley, 1926, 245 p.

The Mummy Bride: A Farce Comedy in Three Acts, Minneapolis, Northwestern College of Speech Arts, 1928, 109 p.

"Play Ball," A Comedy in One Act, Minneapolis, The Northwestern College of Speech Arts, 1929, 13 p.

The Antidote: A Farce Comedy in One Act, Minneapolis, The Northwestern Press, 1930, 12 p.

Exhibit "A": A Comedy in Three Acts, Minneapolis, The Northwestern Press, 1931, 86 p.

PARTIAL LIST OF HOMER B. HULBERT'S PUBLISHED
WRITINGS (Continued)

B. *Periodicals*

1. *Articles Published in the United States and Elsewhere Outside Korea*

1898   "The Enfranchisement of Korea," *North American Review* 166 (1898): 780.

1899   "Korea," *Independent* (New York) 51 (1899): 1220.
"Korea and Its People," *Forum* 27 (1899): 217.
"Korean Inventions," *Harper's Magazine* 99 (1899): 102.

1903   "The Korean Language," *Smithsonian Report,* 1903: 808-810.

1904   "Korea, The Bone of Contention," *Century Magazine* 68 (May 1904), 151-154. (Also in *Current Literature* 36 (1904): 158-163.
"Korea's Opening by Rail," *World's Work* 11 (1904): 6849.
"Russo-Japanese War and Christian Missions in the East," *Missionary Review* (New York) 27 (June 1904): 408-413.

1908   "Japanese and Missionaries in Korea," *Missionary Review* (New York) 31 (March 1908): 205-209.
"Japan's Object Lesson in Korea," *Pacific Monthly* (Portland, Oregon) 20 (Aug. 1908): 167-175.

1916   "Japan and Isothermal Empire," *Journal of Race Development* VI (1916): 4.

1919 "What About Korea?" *Korea Review* (Philadelphia) I:7 (Sept. 1919), 1-4.

"Korea's Part in the War," *Korea Review* (Philadelphia) I:8 (Oct. 1919), 1f.

1920 "Japan in Korea," *Journal of International Relations* (Worcester, Massachusetts) 10 (Jan. 1920): 270-277.

1921 "Chautauqua and Korea," *Korea Review* (Philadelphia) III:8 (Oct. 1921), 1-3.

1955 "Korean Contributions to Civilization," *Far Eastern Economic Review* (Hongkong) 19 (Aug. 25, 1955), 225f. [Described by the editor of the *Economic Review* as "a posthumous article by the greatest student of Korean history."]

PARTIAL LIST OF HOMER B. HULBERT'S PUBLISHED WRITINGS (Continued)

2. Articles in *The Korean Repository*

Vol.	*Year*	*Title, Month and Page*
I	1892	"The Korean Alphabet," January, 1-9; March, 69-74.
II	1895	"Korean Reforms," January, 1-9. "The Origin of the Korean People," June, 219-229; July, 255-264. "Romanization Again," August, 299-306. "Rise of the Yangban," December, 471-474.
III	1896	"Korean Vocal Music," February, 45-53. "Korean Poetry," May, 203-207. "The Korean Alphabet," June, 233-237. "The Ham Heung Messenger Again [letter to the editor]," September, 375. "The Geomancer," October, 387-391. Uncaptioned letter to the editor, dealing with the Korean Alphabet, October, 418f.
IV	1897	"Korean Art," April, 145-149. "Korean Proverbs," August, 284-290; October, 369-373; December, 452-455. "An Ancient Gazetteer of Korea," November, 407-416. [The *Yŏji Sŭngnam*]

Vol.	*Year*	*Title, Month and Page*
V	1898	"The Itu," February, 47-54.
		"The Mongols in Korea," April, 133-143; May, 171-179; June, 201-206.

3. Articles in the *Transactions of the Korea Branch of the Royal Asiatic Society*

Vol.	*Year*	*Title and Page*
I	1900	"Korean Survivals," 25.
II, Pt. 2,	1902	"Korean Folk-tales," 45.
XIV	1923	"National Examination in Korea," 9.

PARTIAL LIST OF HOMER B. HULBERT'S PUBLISHED WRITINGS (Continued)

4. Selected Editorials and Articles in *The Korea Review*
(Exclusive of the installments of the *History,* published monthly, 1901-1904)

Vol.	*Year*	*Title, Month and Page*
I	1901	"The Spirit of the Bell: A Korean Legend [poem]," Jan., 1-2.
		"The New Century," Jan., 3-11.
		Editorial Comment [on purposes of the *Review*], Jan., 22-24.
		"Korean Proverbs," Feb., 50-53: Sept., 392-396.
		"Xylographic Art in Korea," March, 97-101.
		"A Vagary of Fortune," April, 145-155; May, 193-202.
		[This "Korean Romance" was signed "Narro" but is recognized to have been written by Hulbert. It appeared in substantially the same form in G. Lynch, "Viyun's Vow," *Cassel's Magazine,* October 1904.]
		"Baron von Mollendorff [a sketch of his work in Korea]," June, 245-252.
		"Korean Etymology," June, 254-257.
		Editorial Comment [on Christian missions in Korea and East Asia], June, 261-263.

Vol.	Year	Title, Month and Page

"Korean and Efate," July, 297-301; Aug., 341-344.

"The Korea Branch of the Royal Asiatic Society," Aug. 337-340.

"George C. Foulk," Aug., 344-349.

[This essay on conditions in Korea during Ensign Foulk's service there (1883-1887) is notable for its unusually sympathetic view of the Min family and their purposes.]

"A Notable Book on China [by E. H. Parker]," Oct. 433-440.

"Rear Admiral Schley in Korea," Oct., 440-445.

"The Price of Happiness," Oct., 445-454.

[This story, like the "Vagary of Fortune," is fictional but is based on one or more Korean tales and demonstrates Professor Hulbert's ability to write gripping fiction at the same time that he is actually describing Korean mores and folkways.]

"The Founding of the Korea [*sic*] Dynasty," Nov., 481-486.

Editorial Comment [an unusually sharp criticism, for this early period of the *Review*'s life, of Japanese actions toward the Korean Government and toward individual Koreans], Nov., 497-499.

"The Status of Woman in Korea," Dec., 529-534.

"The Marble Pagoda," Dec., 534-538.

II   1902   "The Status of Woman in Korea (Second Paper)," Jan., 1-8; Third Paper, Feb., 53-59; Fourth Paper, March, 97-101; Fifth Paper, April, 155-159.

"Notes on Southern Korea," Jan., 13-17.

"The Products of Korea," Feb., 49-53; March, 108-112; May, 203-206; July, 300-304; Aug., 341-345; Sept., 393-396.

Editorial Comment, Feb., 69-71.

[A somewhat naïve and idealistic discussion of the significance of the Anglo-Japanese Alliance of January 30, 1902.]

"A Celebrated Monument, Marking the Fall of Pakje [*sic*]," March, 102-107.

"Slavery in Korea," April, 149-155.

Vol.	*Year*	*Title, Month and Page*

III   1903   "The Test of Friendship," March, 97-100.

"The Bridges and Wells of Seoul," March, 104-110.

"The Korean Mudang and P'ansu," April, 145-149; May, 203-208; June, 257-260; July, 301-305; Aug., 342-346; Sept., 385-389.

"The Hun-min Chong-eum," April, 154-159; May, 208-213.

"The Privileges of the Capital," May, 193-203.

"Across Siberia by Rail," May, 218-222; June, 253-256; July, 305-309; Aug., 349-355.

"Note on Ch'oe Ch'i-wun [*sic*]," June, 241-247.

"Korean and Formosan," July, 289-294.

"Korean Relations with Japan: The *Cheung-jung Kyo-rin-ji* (增訂交隣誌)," July, 294-300; Aug., 347-349; Sept., 394-398; Oct., 438-443; Nov., 492-497; Dec., 537-544.

Editorial Comment on Western European incidents of the 1903 journey, July, 311-313.

"The Peddlars' Guild," Aug., 337-342.

Editorial Comment on the decreasing interest in education in Korea, Sept., 408f.

Editorial Comment asserting the belief that Japan will honor Korean independence, Oct., 453f.

"Banishment," Nov., 481-487; Dec., 532-537.

IV   1904   "Korean Relations with Japan (continued)," Jan., 9-13.

"Retrospect of 1903," Jan., 13-20.

[Pages 16-20 are devoted largely to Hulbert's argument that a Japanese, rather than a Russian, predominance in Korea would be advantageous to the other foreign powers as well as to the Koreans themselves.]

"The Ajun [Ajŏn]," Feb., 63-70; June, 249-255.

"The Russo-Japanese War," Feb., 49-63; March, 97-103; April, 145-155; May, 193-207; June, 241-249; July, 302-305.

Editorial Comment, Feb., 70-77.

[The first of Hulbert's editorials on the Russo-Japanese War period, this discussion generally justi-

Vol.	*Year*	*Title, Month and Page*
IV	1904	

fies Japanese actions but also calls on the Korean people to use the international crisis as an occasion for strengthening their body politic to the point of genuine independence.]

"A New Book on Korea," March, 109-118.

[An elaborate criticism—employing considerable sarcasm—of Angus Hamilton, *Korea,* London, William Heinemann, 1904.]

"The Burning of the Palace," April, 155-163.

"The Internal Condition of Affairs in Korea," April, 163-168.

"The Oldest Relic in Korea," June, 255-259.

"Japanese Industrial Projects in Korea," July, 289-297.

Editorial Comment [a discussion of the Nagamori Scheme for settling Japanese farmers on all "waste lands" in Korea, written in a manner primarily unfavorable to Japan] July, 306-312.

"The Fusion of Korean Society," Aug., 337-344.

"The Fallow Lands," Aug., 344-350.

[Here Hulbert lists six factors which he believes to have contributed to a shrinkage of land in cultivation in Korea since 1864.]

What Korea Owes to Japan [a generally objective appraisal of Korean-Japanese relations, 1876-1904], Aug., 350-356.

Editorial Comment [another unfavorable criticism of the Nagamori Scheme, together with a discussion of the Koreans' resistance to serving in Manchuria as coolies for the Japanese army and a description of the attitude of the Protestant missionaries toward the political and personal problems of their Korean converts], Aug., 360-362.

"Spelling Reform [in the Korean *Ŏnmun,* or *Hangŭl*]," Sept., 385-393.

Editorial Comment, Sept., 402-407.

[A rather strained apology for Hulbert's position that predominant Japanese influence is good for the Korean people.]

"Koreans in Manchuria," Oct., 433-437.

Vol.	*Year*	*Title, Month and Page*
IV	1904	"Russians in Northeast Korea," Oct., 438-440.

"The Educational Needs of Korea," Oct., 443-453; Nov., 481-486; Dec., 533-539.

Editorial Comment, Oct., 456-461.

[A further statement of Hulbert's preference for Japanese over Russian influence in Korea, this time coupled with a sharp criticism of both Mr. Bethell's *Korea Daily News* and the *New York Herald*.]

"Mr. Kennan on Seoul," Nov., 505-507.

"Retrospect of 1904," Dec., 529-533.

[The theme that Japan's interests are compatible with the independence and strength of Korea is repeated here; the incompatibility of Russian autocracy with the well-being of Korea is again emphasized.]

| V | 1905 | "Korea and Formosa," Jan., 1-8. |

[Here Hulbert returns to his thesis that southern Korea was populated by people from southern Asia.]

"The Russo-Japanese Conflict: A Review [of Professor K. Asakawa's book of that title]," Jan., 12-16.

[Hulbert's comment in the review itself is generally favorable, but on pages 20-21 and 26-29 he points out unfavorable aspects of Japan's action in Korea and expresses the wish that Asakawa could come and see for himself.]

"The Seoul-Fusan [Pusan] Railway," Jan., 16-21; May, 183-187.

"The Stone-fight," Feb., 49-53. [See also page 72.]

Editorial Comment, February, 63-68.

[The Editor on balance favors the large proposed Japanese loan to the Korean Government for the stabilization of Korean currency, although many Western residents thought it dangerous from the Korean standpoint.]

"A Korean Mint," March, 87-97.

"Admiral Schley on the Little War of 1871," March, 97-106.

| *Vol.* | *Year* | *Title, Month and Page* |

V   1905   Editorial Comment, March, 110.

[Praise of American Minister Horace N. Allen, (whose replacement in Seoul by H. V. Morgan had just been announced in Washington), despite the personal tensions existing at various times between Allen and Hulbert.]

"Korea and Japan," May, 161-172.

[Generally a well-balanced analysis of Korean-Japanese relations since 1876 and a clear challenge to Japan to show its good faith.]

Editorial Comment, May, 187-189.

[Hulbert points to Admiral Togo's victory of May 28, 1905 off Tsushima as the effective end of the war with Russia and an assurance of Japanese predominance in Korea; again he expresses the belief that Japan's influence will on the whole be helpful to the Korean people.]

"Dr. Morrison on Korea," June, 201-205.

[Hulbert sharply questions many favorable statements regarding Japan's actions in Korea made by Dr. Morrison, correspondent of the London *Times*.]

"A Possible Protectorate," June, 205-212.

[Here the Editor declares that a protectorate over Korea is not necessary to Japanese interests and would be a serious misfortune to the Koreans.]

"Korean Business Life," June, 219-223.

Editorial Comment, June, 228-230.

[Confidence in the sincerity of the Japanese Government, as distinct from the mass of Japanese adventurers in Korea, is expressed again; the idea of a Japanese offer to "protect" the country temporarily, under a positive guarantee to restore Korean independence when the "genuine waking up of Korea" had taken place, is advanced by Hulbert.]

"A Notable Movement in Korea," July, 249-254.

[Strong support for the proposal of united Protestant missionary activity in Korea, with Hulbert's emphasis being placed on opportunities for more effective work in the field of education.]

Vol.	*Year*	*Title, Month and Page*
V	1905	"Japanese Plans for Korea," July, 254-260.

[Hulbert says Tokyo finally understands the vicious character of the conduct of many Japanese and will control these injustices as well as those practiced by corrupt Korean officials, by establishing impartial courts of appeal at many places in Korea.]

Editorial Comment, July, 266-270.

[The *Review* editor here returns to an emphasis on the ruthlessness of Japanese actions, including wholesale confiscations of private property, but he calls attention again to his confidence that Japan is "hastening plans" for setting up equitable courts.]

"A Protest," Aug., 281-287.

[There is no apology for Japan here, but rather a carefully supported charge that confiscations of Koreans' lands are going forward ruthlessly and are threatening Japan's ability to command the respect of the Korean people.]

"A Visit to Pyeng Yang [P'yŏng'yang]," Aug., 287-292.

[Sharp criticism of Japanese injustices to Koreans in the P'yŏng'yang area, interspersed with interesting information on the new Seoul-Uiju railway.]

"Japanese Finance in Korea," Aug., 298-304.

[More critical of the Korean officials and people than of Mr. Megata, the Japanese finance "adviser."]

Editorial Comment, Aug., 305-310.

[This editorial, a part of which was actually written after Sept. 5, 1905, when the Russo-Japanese peace treaty was signed at Portsmouth, refers again in strong terms to the vicious treatment of Koreans by Japanese, but also contains a reassertion of the belief that the government of Japan would bring justice to the peninsula with the end of the war.

"The Visit of Miss Roosevelt," Sept., 332-334.

[Here, writing very nearly a month after the Portsmouth Treaty, Hulbert returns once more to the

Vol.	*Year*	*Title, Month and Page*
V	1905	

argument that, after all, a temporary "tutelage" of Korea by Japan may be desirable.]

"The Sources of Korean History," Sept., 336-339.

"A Striking Corroboration," Sept., 339-342.

["We affirm that scores of Koreans have brought the deeds of their property to the office of the REVIEW and have begged us to buy it at any price in order to save it from seizure by the Japanese."]

"Missionary Union in Korea," Sept., 342-346.

"Korean Forced Labor," Sept., 346-348.

Editorial Comment, Sept., 348-350.

[In the portion of this editorial beginning on page 349, Hulbert makes his first unequivocal attack on the policy of the Government of Japan itself, by referring to the proposed protectorate as a "death blow to Korean independence." He evidently wrote these lines late in September or during the first few days of October. By about October 20 he had left Seoul with the Emperor's appeal to President Roosevelt.]

"Japan as a Colonizer," Oct., 361-367.

[An all-out attack on Baron Kaneko's proposals for Japanese colonization.]

"The Korean Customs Service," Oct., 367-380.

[A eulogy of the able Commissioner of Customs, the British subject, Dr. J. McLeavy Brown, who had been just informed that he would be relieved, at the request of the Japanese, at an early date.]

"How Yi Outwitted the Church: A Legend of Medieval Korea," Oct., 380-384.

"Places of Interest in Korea," Oct., 385-393.

"Korean Domestic Trade," Nov., 403-411.

"The Koreans in Hawaii," Nov., 411-413.

[Based on Professor Hulbert's brief stopover in Hawaii, where he arrived on November 7, en route to Washington on the Emperor's errand. The ms. was evidently mailed from Hawaii to the *Review* office in Seoul.]

Editorial Comment, Nov., 430.

[Presumably written by Hulbert himself, this edi-

Vol.	*Year*	*Title, Month and Page*
V	1905	

torial praises his old rival, former American Minister Horace N. Allen. It was evidently written *en voyage* and mailed back to Seoul to the interim editors.]

"Korean Sociology," Nov., 432-436.

[The December 1905 issue, published early in January 1906, while Hulbert was in the United States, consists entirely of articles contributed by outside volunteer writers and of notes on current events.]

VI	1906	

[Issues for January through April appear to contain nothing from the pen of the absent Hulbert.]

Editorial Comment, May, 190-194.

[This editorial presents arguments to disprove the statements made in the *Outlook* by Mr. George Kennan, Sr. regarding the supineness of the Koreans and the general correctness of Japanese actions. Professor Hulbert, who had talked at length with Mr. Kennan in the United States and who returned to Seoul early in June, personally wrote this statement.]

"Kennan and Korea," June, 203-217.

[Further condemnation of Mr. Kennan's conclusions, as having been made on extremely limited and one-sided observation.]

"A Korean Cyclopaedia [the *Munhŏn Pigo*]," June, 217-223; July, 244-248.

"Korean and Ainu," June, 223-228.

Editorial Comment, June, 228-235.

[A comprehensive adverse criticism of Japanese action, especially in the fields of finance and education, carefully based on fact but giving no quarter.]

"The Korean Mining Laws," July, 241-244.

"Opium in Korea," July, 248-251.

"The Korean Emigrant Protection Law," 256-258.

[A telling indictment of Japanese avarice.]

"The Pyeng-yang [P'yŏng'yang] Land Case, July, 261-266. [A full-scale and well documented exposé of arbitrary confiscations by Japanese.]

Vol.   *Year*   *Title, Month and Page*

VI   1906   Editorial Comment, July, 266-271.

[The desperate plight of the ordinary Korean, fleeced on the one hand by his own magistrates and on the other by Japanese adventurers who cannot be controlled by the Residency-General.]

"Ul-leung Do (Dagelet Island)," Aug., 281-285.

"The Prophets of Seoul," Aug., 294-300.

"Korea's Internal Affairs," August, 300-303.

[The thesis in this essay by Hulbert is that, since the Japanese are in complete control, it is their duty to clean up the administration and to give the people a chance for a decent existence and thus remove the cause of the serious wave of crime.]

Editorial Coment: The Torture of Koreans, Aug., 303-313.

[Two matters are discussed here: First, the *Review's* earlier charge that a Korean eunuch had been severely beaten by Japanese police and exchanges of correspondence with the Residency-General on this matter; and secondly, an answer to the *Japan Mail's* criticisms of Hulbert's charges of Japanese failure to reform the Korean administration.]

"Korean Finances," Sept., 325-333.

"Prince Eui-wha [Ŭihwa]; An Appeal," Sept., 333-338.

[The appeal is to the Prince—son of the Emperor by a concubine—to use his experience in the United States and his friendship with influential Japanese to help his countrymen obtain justice and a better life.]

"Japan in North-east Korea," Sept., 338-341.

[Discussion of insults and violations of property rights perpetrated on Canadian and United States citizens by Japanese soldiers.]

"Japanese Immigration," Sept., 341-346.

[The predatory nature of Japanese agricultural expansion into Korea.]

Editorial Comment, Sept., 346-352.

[A castigation of the bestial conduct of Japanese in

Vol.	*Year*	*Title, Month and Page*
VI	1906	Korea, including reference to assaults on Western women, the officially condoned sale of narcotics and the widespread introduction of Japanese prostitutes.]

"Missionary Work in Korea," Oct., 361-366.

[Hulbert's comment on the manner in which the Korea Mission of the Presbyterian Church in the U.S.A. gave expression to its policy of non-interference in political matters.]

"Tax Collection in Korea," Oct., 366-376.

[Serious questions are raised regarding the new system of taxation to be supervised by the Japanese.]

"Koreans in America," Oct., 376-378.

"Swift Retribution," Oct., 383-386.

[The killing by a group of Koreans of a Japanese who had killed a neighbor for refusing to give the Japanese his house.]

Editorial Comment: Douglas Story on Korea, Oct., 389-393.

"Min Yong-whan," Nov., 406-412.

"The Religion of the Heavenly Way," Nov., 418-424; Dec., 460-465.

[This account of the Tonghak-Ch'ŏndo Kyo movement contains some errors in fact; more important, it reflects the unfavorable predisposition toward this remarkable reform effort which most Westerners shared.]

"Gambling in Korea," Nov., 425-428.

Editorial Comment, Nov., 428-435.

[A rejoinder to the Japanese-financed *Seoul Press's* bitter attack on all publications by Westerners in Korea, and new instances of greedy exploitation of the country by Japanese operating under official Residency-General approval.]

"A 'Skeleton in the Closet' " [a Korean folktale], Dec., 452-457.

An Eminent Opinion, Dec., 457-459.

[Hulbert quotes from an article by Bishop Warren A. Candler of the Methodist Episcopal Church,

ED 456   BIBLIOGRAPHIES (*Korea Review*)

Vol.	*Year*	*Title, Month and Page*
VI	1906	South, who had just traveled widely in Korea. The bishop found the Koreans "utterly discouraged" and their country ruthlessly overrun by "Japanese scalawags."]
		Editorial Comment on Japan's responsibility for bringing genuine improvement to Korea, Dec., 465-470.